LANGUAGES, COMPILERS AND RUN-TIME ENVIRONMENTS FOR DISTRIBUTED MEMORY MACHINES

ADVANCES IN PARALLEL COMPUTING

VOLUME 3

NORTH-HOLLAND
AMSTERDAM • LONDON • NEW YORK • TOKYO

LANGUAGES, COMPILERS AND RUN-TIME ENVIRONMENTS FOR DISTRIBUTED MEMORY MACHINES

Edited by

Joel Saltz
and
Piyush Mehrotra
Institute for Computer Applications
in Science and Engineering
NASA Langley Research Center
Hampton, VA, U.S.A.

1992

NORTH-HOLLAND
AMSTERDAM • LONDON • NEW YORK • TOKYO

ELSEVIER SCIENCE PUBLISHERS B.V.
Sara Burgerhartstraat 25
P.O. Box 211, 1000 AE Amsterdam, The Netherlands

Distributors for the United States and Canada:

ELSEVIER SCIENCE PUBLISHING COMPANY INC.
655 Avenue of the Americas
New York, NY 10010, U.S.A.

Library of Congress Cataloging-in-Publication Data

Languages, compilers and run-time environments for distributed memory
machines / edited by Joel Saltz and Piyush Mehrotra.
p. cm. -- (Advances in parallel computing ; v. 3)
Includes bibliographical references.
ISBN 0-444-88712-1
1. Electronic data processing--Distributed processing.
2. Programming languages (Electronic computers) 3. Compilers
(Computer programs) I. Saltz, Joel. II. Mehrotra, Piyush.
III. Series.
QA76.9.D5L36 1992
004'.36--dc20 91-39628
CIP

ISBN: 0 444 88712 1

Printed in The Netherlands

PREFACE

Distributed memory architectures have the potential to supply the very high levels of performance required to support future computing needs. However, programming such machines has proved to be awkward. The problem is that the current languages available on distributed memory machines tend to directly reflect the underlying message passing hardware. Thus, the user is forced to provide a myriad of low level details leading to code which is difficult to design, debug and maintain. The major issue is to design methods which enable compilers to generate efficient distributed memory programs from relatively machine independent program specifications. An emerging approach is to allow the user to explicitly distribute the data structures while using global references in the code. The major challenge for compilers of such languages is to generate the communication required to satisfy non-local references.

Recent years has seen a number of research efforts attempting to tackle some of these problems. Several of these groups were invited to present their work at the Workshop on Languages, Compilers and Run-Time Environments for Distributed Memory Machines held in May 1990 under the auspices of the Institute for Computer Applications in Science and Engineering (ICASE) at NASA Langley Research Center, Hampton, VA. This book is a compilation of the papers describing the research efforts of these groups.

The papers cover a wide range of topics related to programming distributed memory machines. The approaches taken by the authors are quite eclectic; in presenting these papers we chose not to impose an arbitrary classification scheme on this research. Consequently, we have chosen to list the papers in the order in which the corresponding talks were presented at the workshop.

- The paper by Gerndt & Zima describes their experiences with SUPERB, a semi-automatic parallelization tool for distributed memory machines.

- Rosing et al. survey the issues and challenges facing the developers of languages for programming distributed memory systems. They also provide a description of their own effort in this direction, the programming language DINO.

- Chapman et al. present the language extensions, Vienna Fortran, which allow the user to program in a shared memory environment while explicitly controlling the distribution of data to the underlying processors and memories.

- Pingali & Rogers discuss the techniques for generating optimal message passing code from the functional language, ID Noveau, extended with data distributions. Most of these techniques are applicable to general imperative languages as well.

- Snyder discusses the idea of phase abstractions to support portable and scalable parallel programming.

- The paper by Malki & Snir presents Nicke, a language which supports both message passing and shared memory programming.

- Balasundaram et al. describe a system to predict the performance of Fortran D programs.
- The paper by Hiranandani et al. describes the principals behind the Fortran D compiler being constructed at Rice. Fortran D is a dialect of Fortran which includes language extensions to specify data distribution.
- The Pandore system, as described by André et al., extends C with data distribution statements. The compiler then translates this into code suitable for distributed execution.
- Das et al. discuss techniques for generating efficient code for irregular computations and for implementing directives that make it possible to integrate dynamic workload and data partitioners into compilers. The work of Das et. al. is presented in the context of Fortran D.
- Sinharoy et al. describe the equational language EPL, and discuss the issues involved in analyzing loops for aligning data and scheduling wavefronts.
- The paper by Chen et al. describes the CRYSTAL compiler which attempts to reduce communication overhead by recognizing reference patterns and using a set of collective communication routines which can be implemented efficiently.
- The papers by Ramanujam & Sadayappan, and Wolfe describe aspects of analyzing loops for optimal scheduling and distribution across a set of processors.
- Hamel et al. and Reeves & Chase present data distribution extensions to SIMD languages and discuss the issues involved in translating such programs for execution on distributed memory MIMD machines.

This book presents a set of papers describing a wide range of research efforts aimed at easing the task of programming distributed memory architectures. We very much enjoyed hosting this workshop and discussing technical issues with the authors of these papers; we hope that the reader will find these proceedings to be a valuable addition to the literature.

We would like to thank Dr. R. Voigt, Ms. Emily Todd and Ms. Barbara Stewart for all their help in organizing this workshop and the resulting book.

CONTENTS

Languages, Compilers and Run-Time Environments
for Distributed Memory Machines
J. Saltz and P. Mehrotra (Editors)

SUPERB: Experiences and Future Research

Michael Gerndt
Hans P. Zima
University of Vienna
Institute for Statistics and Computer Science
Rathausstr. 19/II/3
A-1010 Vienna, Austria
EMAIL: A4424DAN@AWIUNI11.bitnet

Abstract

In this paper, we report on experiences with the automatic parallelization system SUPERB. After analyzing the strengths and limitations of the approach, we outline the salient features of a successor system that is currently being developed at the University of Vienna and describe the direction of future research in the field of automatic parallelization.

Keywords: multiprocessors, analysis of algorithms, program transformations

1 Introduction

SUPERB (SUprenum ParallelizER Bonn) is a semi-automatic parallelization tool for the SUPRENUM supercomputer [Giloi 88, Trott 86]. The SUPRENUM machine is a distributed-memory multiprocessing system (**DMMP**) with a kernel system containing up to 256 nodes, a host computer, and a hierarchical interconnection scheme. Each node consists of an off-the-shelf microprocessor, local memory, a pipelined vector unit, and a communication unit. No shared memory exists in the system; processors communicate via explicit, asynchronous message passing.

The **programming model** for SUPRENUM can be characterized as a **Single-Program-Multiple-Data** model: a parallel program consists of a **host program** and a **node program**. The host program executes all input/output statements and performs global management functions; it runs on the host processor. The node program performs the actual computational task; it is activated as a separate **process** for each individual node.

The idea underlying this model is that the node processes execute essentially the same operations on different parts of the data domain in a **loosely synchronous** manner.

SUPERB is a source-to-source transformation system which generates parallel programs in SUPRENUM Fortran, a Fortran dialect for the SUPRENUM machine which supports the programming model outlined above and provides array operations in the style of Fortran 90 as well as message-passing primitives SEND and RECEIVE for inter-process communication. SUPERB combines coarse-grain parallelization with vectorization and thus exploits both the multiprocessing structure of the machine as well as the vector units in its individual nodes. The parallelization strategy is based on the **Data Decomposition Technique** [Fox 88] which is used for the manual parallelization of scientific codes. Starting with user-defined distributions of the program's arrays, SUPERB automatically transforms the code to exploit as much parallelism as possible. The reasoning behind this approach can be outlined as follows: While the decomposition and distribution of data is currently too hard a problem to be solved automatically (see, however, 8.4), the parallel program determined by a given data partition can be automatically generated by a restructuring system. This relieves the user from a significant amount of highly error-prone routine work.

SUPERB is the first implemented tool that performs automatic parallelization for a distributed-memory machine, based on data parallelism. It has been implemented in C in a UNIX environment and currently contains 110.000 lines of code. An obvious **success** of the project is the mere fact that the tool exists and can be actually applied to real programs. We took particular care to ensure that virtually the complete ANSI standard Fortran 77 language is accepted as the source language, which (among other things) made it necessary to hand-code the scanner and handle COMMON and EQUIVALENCE as well as data and entry statements. As a result, we have an operational tool which can be used to gain experience with parallelization and serve as a starting point for new research.

Furthermore, the theory of the compilation approach has been completely developed in Gerndt's Ph.D thesis [Gerndt 89b].

There are some obvious **shortcomings**: SUPERB is a prototype and as such still contains programming errors of different degrees of severity. Since the real SUPRENUM machine was not operational until recently, our tests so far were restricted to running parallel programs on a simulator. Moreover, the size of programs that can be handled is currently restricted to about 5000 lines of code.

The rest of the paper consists of two parts. In the first part, we will discuss the experiences with the system in more detail. Parallelization can be described as a process consisting of the following steps:

1. Program splitting
2. Data partitioning
3. Interprocedural partitioning analysis
4. Initial adaptation: Masking and insertion of communication
5. Optimization

In the five sections below we will discuss each of these steps individually. The second part of the paper outlines current and future research, which extends SUPERB in various new directions (Section 8). A short summary is given in the conclusion (Section 9).

In this paper, we will not elaborate the compilation strategy of SUPERB in full detail: this material is contained in a number of published papers and theses [ZBGH 86, GerZi 87, KBGZ 88, ZBG 88, Gerndt 89a, Gerndt 89b, Gerndt 90]. The evaluation is based upon the work of people (mainly from SUPRENUM GmbH and Rice University) who have actually used the system for the parallelization of programs. In addition, we compared our strategy with the techniques of other groups working in the field of parallelizing compilers for DMMPs [KoMeRo 88, CalKen 88, RogPin 89].

2 Program Splitting

Program splitting transforms the input program into a host and a node program according to the programming model of the SUPRENUM system (Section 1). All I/O statements are collected in the host program, and communication statements for the corresponding value transfers are inserted into both programs.

In the resulting code, the host process is loosely synchronized with the node processes. Thus, the host process may read input values before they are actually needed in node processes. The output generated by the parallelized program is in exactly the same format as that of the sequential program.

In a simpler and intuitively more appealing approach described in the literature [Fox 88], I/O statements are directly inserted into the (hand-coded) node program for a Cosmic Cube and specially handled in the CUBIX operating system. The disadvantage of their approach is that additional communication has to be inserted to synchronize the node processes, if for example the values of the elements of a distributed array should be output in the original order.

Program splitting is performed automatically in the front end of SUPERB. In the current version of the system, individual I/O statements are mapped to single messages. Optimization of the message communication between host and node processes, in particular vectorization and fusion of messages along the lines of the techniques described in Section 6, will be included in a later version.

3 Data Partitioning

The major part of the node program's data domain consists of arrays. The selection of a **data partition**, by which we mean here a set of specifications for array distributions, is the starting point for coarse-grain parallelization. It will determine the degree of parallelism, load balancing and the communication/computation ratio of the resulting parallel program.

The main restrictions on data partitioning are that the number of processes and the parameters of the distributions are compile-time constants. Furthermore, no facility for dynamic redistribution exists.

Our tool allows the specification of a number of distribution strategies. A distribution is determined by the **decomposition** of an array into rectangular **segments** and the segment-process mapping. This mapping permits the replication of segments across a range of node processes.

Decompositions are specified for each dimension of an array individually. The strategies provided by SUPERB range from stipulating the number of sections in a dimension to a precise definition of the index ranges. A specification may use variables whose values are determined by solving a system of linear equations at compile time.

Besides a canonical mapping scheme the segment-process mapping can be explicitly given using a notation which resembles that for implied do-loops in Fortran 77.

Thus SUPERB provides powerful language constructs for specifying array distributions. Experience so far indicates that real programs do not require such flexibility. The most commonly used features include the standard sectioning of an array dimension into equal-length parts and the replication of segments across several processes. A more elaborate specification may be necessary if the work load is to be optimally balanced to get very efficient programs.

The capacities for specifying array distributions in a very flexible manner considerably increase the overhead involved in the adaptation of the code according to a given partition. Further experience with SUPERB will tell us just which distribution strategies are really required in practice.

A special feature of the data partitioning language is the **workspace concept**. Applications written in Fortran 77 frequently define large arrays (workspace arrays) to circumvent the lack of dynamic storage allocation. These workspace arrays are typically accessed in a regular manner via run time dependent virtual arrays. SUPERB supports this programming method by providing a special notation for the declaration of virtual arrays, which can be distributed in the usual way. This technique has been used to parallelize multigrid programs and will be described in a forthcoming paper.

4 Interprocedural Partitioning Analysis

As discussed in the previous section, the user specifies distributions for non-formal arrays. Dummy arrays inherit their distribution at run time when the subroutine is called. Since the in-line expansion of all subroutines is practically impossible, a parallelization tool must be able to handle subroutines in an adequate manner. SUPERB performs an interprocedural partitioning analysis to determine which dummy arrays are distributed and which distributions may occur at run-time. The resulting information is stored in a set of **partition vectors** which describe the actual distributions of arrays for every incarnation of a subroutine.

In order to be able to generate efficient code, incarnations where a dummy array is distributed are separated from those where the same array is non-distributed. This separation is implemented by cloning the subroutine and redirecting its calls appropriately. Thus, different code can be generated for these two cases.

The disadvantage of this strategy is the high memory overhead which in the worst case may grow exponentially depending on the number of calls and dummy arrays. Fortunately, this effect has not been observed for real programs, partly due to the fact that large programs generally use common blocks as their main data structures.

5 Automatic Insertion of Masking and Communication

The core of the parallelization process consists of two phases, the first of which performs an initial **adaptation** of the input program according to the given data partition. In the second phase, the adapted code is subjected to a set of optimizing transformations. In order to facilitate the implementation of the optimization, the adaptation is performed by manipulating special internal data structures without modifying the program code. The actual generation of parallel Fortran code is referred to the back end (see Section 7). We believe that this implementation strategy is more flexible than the approach described in [CalKen 88].

In this section we discuss the initial adaptation, while Section 6 deals with the optimization phase. The initial adaptation distributes the entire work assigned to the node program across the set of all node processes according to the given array distributions, and resolves accesses to non-local data via communication. The basic rule governing the assignment of work to the node processes is that a node process is responsible for executing all the assignments to its local data that occur in the original sequential program.

The distribution of work is internally expressed by **masking**: A mask is a boolean guard that is attached to each statement. A statement is executed if and only if its mask evaluates to *true*. Masks clearly separate the distribution of work from the control flow and thus can be handled efficiently.

After masking has been performed, the node program may contain references to non-local objects. The remaining task of initial adaptation is to allocate a local copy for each non-local object accessed in a process, and to insert code so that these copies are updated by communication. SUPERB uses a technique called **overlap communication** to compute the communication overhead at compile time and to organize communication at run-time in an efficient way.

The overlap concept is especially tailored to efficiently handle programs with local computations adhering to a regular pattern. For such programs, the set of non-local variables of a process can be described by an **overlap area** around its local segment.

Overlap descriptors are also computed for each reference to a distributed array. They provide important information for the user since they determine the run-time communication overhead and thus display inefficiencies resulting from an ill-chosen data partition, non-local computations or imprecise analysis information. Overlap areas may be inspected at different levels, including program, subroutine and statement level. This feature of SUPERB is especially important when handling large programs, as it facilitates the identification of those parts of the source code which must be interactively transformed to obtain efficient code.

In summary, **the overlap concept is valuable** because it allows us to

- statically allocate copies of non-local variables in the local address space of a process
- handle identically those iterations of a loop which access local data only and those which handle non-local data
- generate a single vector statement for a loop.

On the other hand, the overlap concept cannot adequately handle computations with irregular accesses as they arise in sparse-matrix problems, for example, since it requires the allocation of memory for any potentially non-local variable and an additional overhead for the resulting communication which may be superfluous.

6 Optimization

The code resulting from the initial adaptation is usually not efficient, since the updating is performed via single-element messages and work distribution is enforced on the statement level. In the optimization phase, special transformations are applied to generate more efficient code.

First, communication is extracted from surrounding do-loops [Gerndt 90] resulting in the **fusion of messages** and secondly, loop iterations which do not perform any computation for local variables are suppressed in the node processes. This transformation is called **mask optimization** and will be described in a forthcoming paper. Additional transformations are applied to eliminate redundant communication and computation.

SUPERB determines **standard reductions** and treats them in an efficient way. This transformation is a good example to demonstrate the advantages of the two-level approach. For example, let the reduction, e.g. a dot product of two distributed arrays, be implemented via an assignment statement to a scalar variable in a loop. This reduction is computed entirely in each node process since scalar variables are replicated.

```
S=0
Update local copies of entire arrays in each process
EXSR (A(*),...)
EXSR (B(*),...)
DO I=2,100
S: ALWAYS→S=S+A(I)*B(I)
ENDDO
```

The optimizing transformation first generates a new mask from one of the arrays accessed on the right side. This mask enforces that each node process computes the dot product only for its local values. Then a call to a subroutine is inserted behind the reduction code, to combine the local values to the global dot product and to communicate this value to all node processes.

```
S=0
no communication since all references are local
DO I=2,200
S: owned(A(I))→S=S+A(I)*B(I)
ENDDO
CALL COMBINE(S,"+")
S now contains the global dot product
```

If the access patterns of both arrays are different it may be necessary to insert communication to perform the local part of the dot product. In the two-level approach the communication is automatically inserted since the analysis algorithm depends on the mask of the statement and the reference to the distributed array. For the same reason the code is correctly transformed even if one of the arrays on the right side is non-distributed.

```
S=0
Updating of the copy for the accessed non-local variable
EXSR (B(*),...)
DO I=2,200
S: owned(A(I))→S=S+A(I)*B(I-1)
ENDDO
CALL COMBINE(S,"+")
```

Another important optimization is **Mask Propagation**. This transformation eliminates redundant computation in the node processes. Scalar variables are used frequently inside loops to store intermediate results. Since scalar variables are replicated, all intermediate results are computed in each node process, although an individual node process does not need all of them.

```
Update local copies of the entire array A in each process
EXSR (A(*),...)
DO I=2,48
S: ALWAYS→S=...A(2*I)...
S1:owned(B(2*I))→B(2*I)=0.5*(S+A(2*I+3))
ENDDO
```

When propagating the mask *owned(B(2*I))* to S, the redundant computations in the node processes as well as the accesses to non-local array elements have been eliminated.

```
DO I=2,48
If A and B have the same distribution, a node process only accesses local elements
S: owned(B(2*I))→S=...A(2*I)...
S1:owned(B(2*I))→B(2*I)=0.5*(S+A(2*I+3))
ENDDO
```

The implemented transformations are very useful, but have to be extended in several directions. For example, the pattern matching algorithm for detecting reductions is only able to detect these reductions if they are implemented via scalar variables. Mask propagation which eliminates redundant computation in the case of scalar temporaries in loops, works only inside a single loop and cannot detect the same situation for temporary arrays.

One important optimization area has not been dealt with up to now. All optimizing transformations are local transformations, i.e. they are applied to a single loop nest. There are no global transformations in the sense that entire procedure calls are masked or communication is propagated in the flow graph or extracted from subroutines.

7 System Structure

The structure of SUPERB is shown in Figure 1. The system is made up of six main components: the kernel, the frontend components, the backend and the reconstructor, which utilize the program database. The different components perform the following tasks:

Frontend 1:	scanning, parsing and normalization of individual program units
Frontend 2:	program splitting, collection of global information, e.g. call graph
Frontend 3:	execution of a predefined transformation sequence on each program unit
Backend:	machine dependent transformations
Reconstructor:	reconstructor of the final code from the syntax tree
Kernel:	system organization, execution of analysis services and transformations

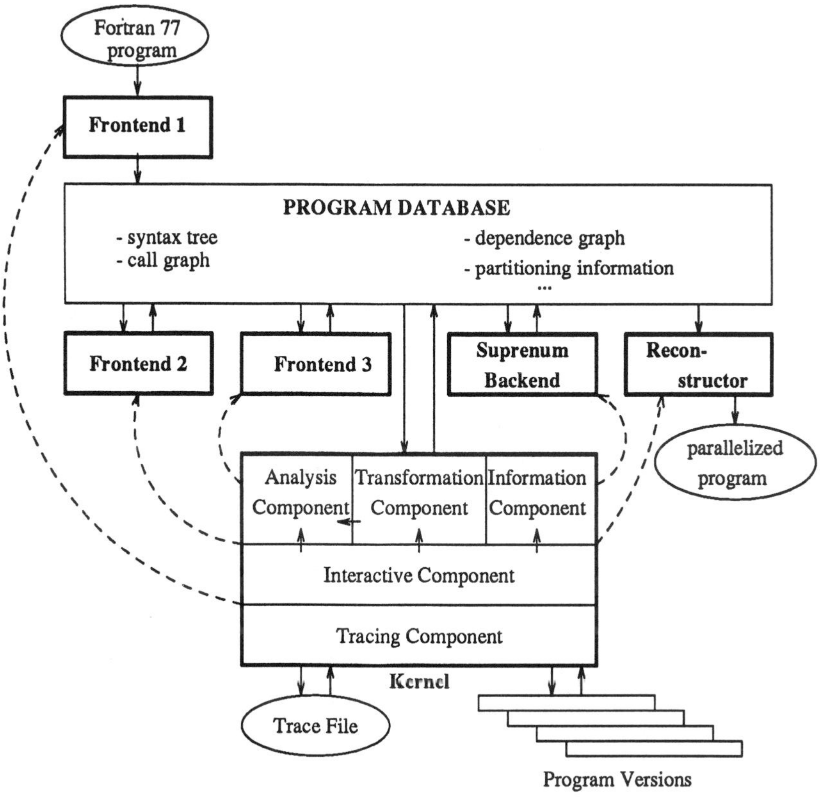

Figure 1: System Structure

The system components are implemented via individual programs, except for Frontend 3 which is integrated in the kernel system. This structure facilitates future extensions for other target machines and other input languages.

The kernel implements the user interface. The user may activate other system parts and select analysis services and transformations. He is able to inspect the internal information via the services of the information component. Since the program database contains only the actual version of the program, SUPERB provides the additional service to save program versions. The user may thus return to an earlier state of the parallelization process if the performed transformations were not successful.

SUPERB is inherently interactive because of the specification of the data partition and the various points during the transformation process where the user has to supply special information to the system, e.g. if the workspace concept is applied or worst-case assumptions would make an effective parallelization impossible. This interactivity has advantages and drawbacks.

The ability of an interactive system to provide information about the program on a selected level is useful during the parallelization process as well as for the development of new transformations. For example, it is easy to find inefficiencies via the inspection of the computed overlap information, or to identify vectorization inhibiting factors by analyzing data dependences. Since dependences guide the process of communication optimization, the interactive dependence analysis is also useful in this context.

A disadvantage is that the tool cannot be used as an automatic compiler. It provides some assistance in the automatic recompilation of the same source code via the tracing of the actions performed during an interactive session. The trace files can be automatically executed as long as changes in the source code do not effect positioning commands which are necessary to identify source code regions on which special transformations have been executed. Another component which supports the automation of the parallelization process is Frontend 3. This part of the frontend consists of a predefined transformation sequence, including for example deadcode elimination followed by loop distribution, which is executed on each node program unit. This sequence can be redefined in a user profile and thus be adapted to the special needs of an individual user.

Furthermore, the effect of each transformation is visible to the user, so that it is not always easy to work with the transformed program versions.

Another problem with the flexibility of SUPERB is that information supplied by the user, e.g. interactive modification of the computed overlap information, may be ignored if the initial adaptation has to be redone due to a change of the specified data partition. A modification of the data partition may affect the communication between different node processes, so that the information has to be generally recomputed.

SUPERB transforms standard Fortran 77 programs into parallel SUPRENUM Fortran programs. To perform the analysis services and transformations, SUPERB must be supplied with the entire source code of the input program. It is currently not possible to handle libraries or to work with worst case assumptions, if a subroutine is not available.

8 Current and Future Research

8.1 Overview

In this section, we give an overview of the research conducted by our group at the University of Vienna in the field of automatic and semi-automatic tools for the parallelization of sequential programs.

An important part of this work deals with the design and development of a successor system, SUPERB-2 (Subsection 8.2), and with retargeting SUPERB to SIMD architectures and shared-memory multiprocessor systems (8.3). In a new project, we examine methods for the automatic determination of data decomposition and distribution (8.4). More detailed accounts of this research will be published in separate papers.

8.2 SUPERB-2

SUPERB-2 is currently being developed as a successor to the SUPERB system which has been described in the first part of this paper. The discussion in the previous sections already indicated some of the areas in which we intend to improve the actual system and eliminate some of its weaknesses. We do not intend to consider these aspects further, but rather concentrate on new research that will significantly broaden the scope and capabilities of the system as it currently exists.

We discuss three topics:

- Inclusion of new source languages
- Inclusion of new distributed-memory target architectures
- Construction of an interprocedural data base

The input language of SUPERB is Fortran 77, extended by a notation for the specification of data partitioning and distribution (see Section 3). SUPERB-2 will be able to handle **additional source languages**, including C and the new Fortran standard Fortran 90. We place special emphasis on developing methods for the effective parallelization of programs written in Fortran 90. This poses a number of interesting problems, including the necessity to generalize conventional dependence analysis algorithms and to deal with recursive procedures as well as pointers. At least partial solutions to these problems already exist and have been reported in the literature. A more interesting question relates to data decomposition and distribution. Fortran 90 statements operate on multi-dimensional arrays in a way that can be characterized by a fetch-before-store semantics, and thus explicitly specify a fine-grain parallelism which can be exploited by vector computers and SIMD machines in an obvious fashion. It is much less clear whether programs written in this style can be effectively analyzed with respect to coarse-grain parallelism and, if so, how a trade-off between different grains of parallelism can be achieved.

We now turn to **target architectures**. SUPERB is a source-to-source transformation system which generates parallel programs in SUPRENUM Fortran, a Fortran dialect for the SUPRENUM machine which provides (among other features) message-passing primitives SEND and RECEIVE for inter-process communication. In effect, SUPERB produces code for an abstract distributed-memory architecture, consisting of a fixed set of abstract processors with local memories and an abstract interconnection scheme which can be considered a complete graph. Thus, idiosyncrasies of the real SUPRENUM machine such as the hierarchical interconnection mechanism are not taken into account at this level (machine-specific optimization is performed on top of this structure, and is not further discussed here). As a consequence of this organization, we are able to retarget the parallelizer rather easily for different distributed-memory machines. Our current plans include code generation for transputer arrays as well as the Intel iPSC/860.

SUPERB-2 will be built around an **interprocedural data base**. The data base will support the effective development and parallelization of modular programs by providing a knowledge base containing information about application programs and their (independently compiled) units and modules. Information about objects may include control flow graphs, results of data flow analysis, the call graph, dependence graphs, and performance information. Furthermore, the data base defines a common interface for a dynamically changing set of tools developed in the system. Our design will be based on experiences with well-known Fortran-based programming environments such as $\mathbf{R}^n$ [CoKeT 86] and FAUST[GGJMG 89] as well as on new research in this field, as illustrated by the environment for the high-level language PCN.

8.3 Retargeting SUPERB to Other Architectures

One of the topics discussed in the previous subsection was the retargeting of SUPERB to distributed-memory architectures other than SUPRENUM. For reasons outlined above this can be done in a rather straightforward way.

A more difficult problem arises when code generation for an SIMD machine such as the MasPar or the Connection Machine is considered. We plan to address this topic in future research in which we will examine the relationship between the "loosely synchronous" problems which constitute essentially the domain of SUPERB and the synchronous programming paradigm related to SIMD architectures.

In another project, we will study the application of SUPERB to shared-memory multiprocessing systems with a hierarchical memory structure. Consider, for example, the IBM RP3 system in which the access times for cache, local and global memory are related by 1:10:16. While being much smaller than the typical ratio between local and remote memory accesses for a distributed-memory machine, this ratio shows that the machine can be slowed down by more than one order of magnitude if memory is accessed in an unstructured way. We believe that the SUPERB paradigm of parallelization on the basis of data parallelism provides an efficient way to the solution of this problem. Data partitioning can be used to exploit the locality of computations on shared-memory machines and, in combination with conventional restructuring techniques for these architectures, to optimize the traffic between different levels of the memory hierarchy. Our work will examine code generation for the IBM ACE multiprocessor workstation and the SEQUENT architecture.

8.4 Automatic Support For Data Partitioning

We stated above that SUPERB requires the programmer to explicitly specify the decomposition of the sequential program's data domain and the mapping of the resulting segments to processes. The choice of the partitioning strategy determines the important parameters of the execution behavior of the generated program, in particular with respect to its degree of parallelism, load balancing and the communication/computation ratio.

This places a heavy burden on the user who must have a profound understanding of the program in order to be able to make the right decisions. Currently, the support of the system for making this decision is essentially limited to the computation of overlap descriptions, which for example may indicate the necessity to distribute an array or change a decomposition in order to obtain better alignment. Beyond that, the only way to (indirectly) obtain relevant information is by examining the program generated by the parallelizer, analyze its dynamic behavior, and, if necessary, actually compile and run the program on the simulator or the real machine.

We pursue research with the objective of providing an interactive programming environment that **automatically supplies the user with information about how to partition a sequential Fortran program.**

Our approach will be guided by the following observations:

- We consider data locality to be a **global issue**, that is, the data partitioning strategy must depend on the global behavior of the program **and** on the reference patterns in individual loops.
- In order to select a data partitioning and alignment strategy in an intelligent way, the system will need more analysis information than currently provided by SUPERB. In particular, we require an **analysis of the global data flow** of the program on an interprocedural basis.
- A tool must be developed that, given a sequential Fortran program, a data partitioning specification, and a specification of input data, can **predict the performance of the corresponding parallel program.** The performance analysis tool must possess knowledge of the restructuring strategy and incorporate this knowledge into its estimation of the required run time.
- The success of any strategy developed in our automatic system will depend on how close we can come to the efficiency obtained by hand coding the data partitioning (although, as has been mentioned above, this may not always be practical). In view of the enormous complexity of the general problem and the large number of special cases that have to be taken into account, we plan the use of **knowledge-based techniques** for the implementation of the system. This approach will also provide a reasonably efficient way to deal with the necessity of constantly updating the knowledge base and the set of transformation heuristics in the system.

This is a new problem, which has not yet been solved in any existing system. Related work is being performed by Marina Chen's group at Yale University in the context of a parallelizer for the functional language Crystal [ChChLi 89], at COMPASS in the framework of a parallelizing Fortran compiler for the Connection Machine [KnLuSt 90], and by Ken Kennedy's group at Rice University.

9 Conclusion

SUPERB has been operational since mid 1989, and has been analyzed and evaluated by a number of different people. The first part of this paper has been based on the experiences gained in this phase. We have identified limitations and weaknesses as well as the successes of our current system. Furthermore, in the second part we have outlined the major directions of research that are currently being pursued by our group in Vienna. This work – which is conducted in parallel to similar efforts in a number of other groups – will provide the system designer with more practical and intelligent tools for automatic parallelization than the ones in existence today.

Acknowledgment We want to thank Barbara M. Chapman for her valuable corrections to an earlier version of this paper.

References

[CalKen 88] David Callahan, Ken Kennedy, Compiling programs for distributed-memory multiprocessors, J.Supercomputing, 2(2), 151-169,(Oct.1988)

[ChChLi 89] Marina Chen, Young-il Choo, Jingke Li, Theory and Pragmatics of Compiling Efficient Parallel Code, Yale University, Technical Report YALEU/DCS/TR-760, December 15, 1989

[CoKeT 86] Keith D. Cooper, Ken Kennedy, Linda Torczon, The impact of Interprocedural Analysis and Optimization in the Rn Programming Environment, ACM Transactions on Programming Languages and Systems, Vol.8, No.4, Oct.86, 491-523

[Fox 88] Geoffrey C. Fox et al., Solving Problems on Concurrent Processors, Prentice Hall,Englewood Cliffs, 1988

[Gerndt 89a] H.M.Gerndt, Array Distribution in SUPERB, Proceedings of the 3rd International Conference on Supercomputing 1989, 164-174, ACM,(1989)

[Gerndt 89b] H.M.Gerndt, Automatic Parallelization for Distributed-Memory Multiprocessing Systems, Ph.D. Dissertation, University of Bonn, Informatik Berichte 75, (1989)

[Gerndt 90] H.M.Gerndt, Updating Distributed Variables in SUPERB, to appear in: Concurrency: Practice and Experience, Vol.2, Sept. 1990

[GerZi 87] H.M.Gerndt, H.P.Zima, MIMD parallelization for SUPRENUM, In: E.N. Houstis, T.S. Papatheodorou, C.D. Polychronopoulos (Eds.), Proc. 1st International Conference on Supercomputing, Athens, Greece (June 1987), LNCS 297, 278-293

[Giloi 88] W.K.Giloi, SUPRENUM: A trendsetter in modern supercomputer development, Parallel Computing 7 (1988), 283-296

[GGJMG 89] V.A.Guarna Jr., D.Gannon, D.Jablonoswski, A.D.Malony, Y.Gaur, Faust: an Integrated Environment for the Development of Parallel Programs,IEEE Software, July 1989

[KoMeRo 88] C.Koelbel, P.Mehrotra, J.Van Rosendale, Semi-Automatic Process Partitioning for Parallel Computation, International Journal of Parallel Programming, Vol.16, No.5, 1987, 365-382

[KBGZ 88] U.Kremer, H.-J. Bast, H.M.Gerndt, H.P.Zima, Advanced tools and Techniques for Automatic Parallelization, Parallel Computing 7, 1988, 387-393

[KnLuSt 90] Kathleen Knobe, Joan D. Lukas, Guy L. Steele, Data Optimization: Allocation of Arrays to Reduce Communication on SIMD-Machines, Journal of Parallel and Distributed Computing 8, 102-118, 1990

[RogPin 89] A.Rogers, K.Pingali, Compiling Programs for Distributed Memory Architectures, Proceedings of the 4th Hypercube Concurrent Computers and Applications Conference, March 1989, Monterey

[Trott 86] U.Trottenberg: SUPRENUM - an MIMD Multiprocessor System for Multi-Level Scientific Computing, In: W.Händler et al., eds.: CONPAR86, Conference on Algorithms and Hardware for Parallel Processing, LNCS 237, Springer, Berlin, 48-52

[ZBGH 86] H.P.Zima, H.-J. Bast, H.M.Gerndt,P.J.Hoppen, SUPERB: The SUPRENUM Parallelizer Bonn, Research Report SUPRENUM 861203, Bonn University,Dec. 1986

[ZBG 88] H.P.Zima, H.-J. Bast, H.M.Gerndt, SUPERB: A tool for semi-automatic MIMD/SIMD parallelization, Parallel Computing 6, 1988, 1-18

Languages, Compilers and Run-Time Environments
for Distributed Memory Machines
J. Saltz and P. Mehrotra (Editors)

Scientific Programming Languages for Distributed Memory Multiprocessors : Paradigms and Research Issues

Matthew Rosing, Robert B. Schnabel, and Robert P. Weaver

Department of Computer Science, University of Colorado, Boulder, Colorado 80309

Abstract

This paper attempts to identify some of the central concepts, issues, and challenges that are emerging in the development of imperative, data parallel programming languages for distributed memory multiprocessors. It first describes a common paradigm for such languages that appears to be emerging. The key elements of this paradigm are the specification of distributed data structures, the specification of a virtual parallel computer, and the use of some model of parallel computation and communication. The paper illustrates these concepts briefly with the DINO programming language. Then it discusses some key research issues associated with each element of the paradigm. The most interesting aspect is the model of parallel computation and communication, where there is a considerable diversity of approaches. The paper proposes a new categorization for these approaches, and discusses the relative advantages or disadvantages of the different models.

1. Introduction

This paper attempts to identify some of the central concepts, issues, and challenges that are emerging in the development of parallel programming languages for distributed memory multiprocessors. It describes a common paradigm for such languages that appears to be emerging, discusses some key differences between current approaches that highlight interesting research issues, and mentions some important needs that are only beginning to be, or are not yet being, addressed.

Our orientation is to languages that are being developed to utilize scalable distributed memory multiprocessors, such as hypercubes, for scientific computation. This orientation implies that the algorithms one wishes to express in the parallel programming languages are predominantly data parallel ones. By this we mean algorithms where at each stage, parallelism is achieved by dividing some data structure(s) into pieces, and performing similar or identical computations on each piece concurrently. The parallel language concepts and issues discussed in this paper are tied closely to this parallel algorithmic paradigm.

We also confine our attention to languages where the programmer takes some explicit actions to indicate the parallelism in the algorithm, as opposed to languages where the programmer specifies a purely sequential algorithm. In conjunction, we restrict our attention to imperative languages. Some examples of alternative approaches include Crystal [7,20], SISAL [22], and [27]. Finally, we are mainly oriented towards languages for MIMD distributed memory computation, but also refer to common issues in language support for SIMD distributed memory computers.

Recently, a number of parallel language research projects have been undertaken that share much or all of the orientation described in the previous two paragraphs. These include AL [36], Arf [37], C* [28], DINO [8,30], FortranD [9,15], Kali [18,23], Linda [6], Onyx [21], Pandore [2], Paragon [26], ParallelDistributedC [14,25], PC [3], Spot [35], Superb [12,38], Suspense [33]. Only some of these have so far led to completed and distributable languages and compilers.

In our view, the general goals of all these research projects are to make it easy to express data parallel algorithms for distributed memory multiprocessors, without causing significant degradation in the efficiency of the resultant code. They all seem to be motivated by three important points. First, the vendors selling such machines have generally provided only low level interprocess communication and process management primitives to support parallel computation, and these make the development of parallel programs far too difficult and error-prone. Second, the provision of compilers that automatically convert purely sequential programs into efficient parallel programs on distributed memory machines seems unattainable, at least in the near future. These two points make the higher-level, explicitly parallel languages that are the topic of all these projects a natural research target. The third point is that scientific users of these machines will probably only tolerate reasonably small degradations in efficiency, say 10-40%, if they are to use higher level approaches as opposed to the cumbersome low level primitives. This means that efficiency needs to be carefully considered from the outset in such research.

This remainder of this paper discusses some important general issues connected with this area of research. In Section 2 we briefly describe a common paradigm for distributed parallel languages that we believe is starting to emerge from these research projects. The key elements of this paradigm are mechanisms for specifying a virtual parallel machine and the distribution of data structures onto this machine, and the provision of some model of parallel computation and communication. Section 3 attempts to make these abstract concepts more concrete through one example, our own research on the DINO parallel programming language. This example also enables us to motivate many interesting research issues and challenges that we return to later. The remaining sections consider some key research issues and unanswered questions related to each element of the general paradigm. Sections 4 and 5 briefly consider distributed data structures and virtual parallel machines, respectively; on these topics the agreement between current approaches is fairly high. Section 6 discusses the model of parallel computation and communication, which appears to us to be the most interesting topic, for there are several significantly different approaches under consideration. These are described and contrasted in some detail in this section. Some additional communication issues are briefly discussed in Section 7. Finally, in Section 8 we discuss an important research issue that is only barely being addressed by current research, namely high level language support for complex programs that may have multiple phases and/or multiple levels.

2. An Emerging Paradigm for Distributed Parallel Languages

Most current research in languages for distributed, data parallel computation appears to be aimed primarily at the level of a single algorithmic kernel. By this we mean a basic mathematical computation such as the multiplication or factorization of dense or sparse matrices, or a multi-color method for solving differential equations. At this level, the key features for support of parallel computation in most of these languages appear to be some forms of the following :

- Distributed Data Structures
- A Virtual Parallel Computer

- A Model of Parallel Computation with Associated Communication Model
- Additional Communication Features

The remainder of this section briefly defines and discusses each of these features, at an abstract level. The following section gives some concrete examples, in the context of the DINO language. Sections 4-7 then discuss research issues related to each of these language features.

Distributed data structures, meaning the ability to somehow indicate how data structures can be divided into parts that can be acted upon concurrently, are the key to data parallel computation. They are found not only in distributed parallel languages such explicit parallelism such as Kali [23] and DINO [30], but also in systems for annotating sequential programs to indicate potential parallelism to the compiler, such as FortranD [9]. The fundamental capability, found in almost all these systems, is the ability to partition single and multiple dimensional arrays along one or more of their axes, with some languages allowing overlaps as well.

By a *virtual parallel computer* we mean some conceptual organization of processors, such as a single or multiple dimensional array, that may or may not correspond to the underlying target parallel machine. Almost any system that includes distributed data structures will require such a virtual computer, to serve as the target set of the mapping that defines the distributed data structure(s). The virtual parallel machine may be explicitly designated, or it may arise implicitly via the data distribution declarations. Languages that include explicit virtual parallel computers include DistributedParallelC [14] and DINO. The virtual parallel computer may also play a role in the model of parallel computation.

The *model of parallel computation* means the programming mechanism by which the programmer indicates operations that can be performed concurrently. Along with the associated model of communication, this appears to us to be the most interesting of the key constructs. This is because, while the capabilities of distributed data structures and virtual parallel machines in most proposed languages for distributed data parallel computation appear reasonably similar, a number of substantially different models of parallel computation and communication are being employed in these research projects. One key distinction between them is the view that is taken of the computation. One possibility is a "complete program view", where code similar to sequential code is written, describing the entire computation, and parallelism is designated via some annotations of the data declarations and possibly of the executable statements of the program. For example, the code may be purely sequential code with distributed data annotations, with the compiler attempting to infer parallelism from data dependency analysis combined with these annotations, or it may also use statements such as *forall* loops that indicate parallel execution. A second possibility is a "concurrent process view", where code is written that will be executed concurrently by each virtual processor. This may use a "per data element" view, where the programmer writes code that designates the operations to be performed upon each member of some distributed data structure(s), or a "per task" view, where the programmer aggregates data element operations into the code to be performed by an actual or virtual processor.

Associated with the *model of parallel computation* is a model of communication, the method for designating the transfer of data between virtual processors. The three models that appear to be commonly used are SIMD (Single Instruction, Multiple Data), Block SIMD (also called "copy-in/copy-out"), and SPMD (Single Program, Multiple Data) with sends and receives explicitly designated in some manner. In the Block SIMD model, there are designated blocks of concurrent code, for instance the bodies of forall loops, with global synchronization implicitly enforced at the boundaries of each block, and all necessary communication of non-local values occurring at these boundaries.

The communication can either be explicitly designated or, more commonly, determined implicitly by the compiler from an analysis involving the code and the distributed data declarations. The SIMD model can be viewed as the block SIMD model where the blocksize is one operation. Again, communication usually is determined implicitly. In the SPMD send/receive model, the programmer does not designate global synchronization/communication points. Instead, the programmer generally may explicitly or implicitly designate communication between two or more processors at any point in the program.

In practice, these models of parallel computation and communication have been combined in most but not all ways. These included the complete program view with forall loops and block SIMD communication model, or the concurrent process view with with any of the three communication models. Clearly, each of these models has advantages and disadvantages in comparison to the others. These will be discussed in some detail in Section 6.

Additional communication features may include mechanisms that are important to parallel computation but are not captured naturally by these basic models. Common examples are reduction operators, operators for taking global sums, products, or extrema of distributed data structures.

Finally, we reiterate that this paradigm is most appropriate for a single algorithmic kernel, where in particular a single mapping of each data structure, and a single virtual computer, is likely to suffice. Complete computations may consist of sequences and/or nestings of such kernels, and thus may involve different distributions of given data structures, different virtual machines, and maybe even different models of parallelism at different stages. Additional language mechanisms may be required to accommodate this added complexity, but very few current research projects address this issue. Thus we consider this largely an issue for future research, and discuss it briefly in Section 8.

3. An Example of the Paradigm : The DINO Language

DINO (DIstributed Numerically Oriented language) is a language for distributed, data parallel computation developed at the University of Colorado [8,30]. It fits the paradigm presented in Section 2 and provides specific instances of each of its major features. In this section we use two sample DINO programs to illustrate these general features. We also use these examples to motivate some research issues concerning these general features. Where it is helpful, this discussion includes a critique of the relevant DINO constructs.

DINO consists of standard C, augmented by constructs for describing parallelism. The primary constructs are *structures of environments*, for describing virtual parallel computers; declarations of *distributed data structures* including facilities for describing the mapping of data structures onto virtual parallel computers; *composite procedures* for expressing SPMD parallel computations; and a combination of explicit and implicit means for specifying interprocessor communication.

Example 3.1 is a DINO program for multiplying an $N \times N$ matrix A by a N-vector x, using P processors. (It is complete except for the routines *init* and *display* for reading the data and displaying the results, respectively.) The algorithm it employs is to have each processor concurrently multiply a block of N/P contiguous rows of A by x, providing N/P elements of the result vector b. The statement "environment row [P: id]" declares a virtual parallel machine of P processors, named row_0, $\cdots$, row_{P-1}, and the statement "environment host" declares a master processor named *host*. The three statements starting with the words "float distributed" declare the distributed data structures. They partition A and b into blocks of N/P contiguous rows and elements, respectively, mapping the ith block onto the ith virtual processor, and map all of x onto each virtual processor. The words *blockrow*, *block*, and *all* are predefined mappings provided by the language. The statement "composite matvec (in A, in x, out b)" declares a process called *matvec* that resides on each virtual processor row_i. When it is called by the statement "matvec (At[][], xt[], bt[])#" in *host*, the body of the composite procedure, i.e. the doubly nested for-loop, is executed on each virtual processor row_i using its portion of the distributed data. This provides an SPMD form of parallel computation.

The execution of this (and any) DINO program begins in the process *main* in the host processor. When *matvec* is called by *host*, the input parameters *At* are *xt* are distributed to the processors row_i according to the distributed data declarations of the formal parameters A and x, respectively. When all the processors row_i have concluded the execution of *matvec*, the output parameter b is collected into the variable *bt* of *host*. These are the only interprocessor communications required by this algorithm, and are accomplished without any explicit designation by the programmer.

Example 3.2 is an artificial smoothing program that is provided here to illustrate the one key feature of DINO that is not illustrated by Example 3.1, communication between concurrently executing processes in the SPMD model. This is accomplished in DINO using explicitly designated send and receive operations, which are specified by a reference to an element or subarray of a distributed data structure, followed by a # sign. In Example 3.2 the virtual parallel computer is the $N \times N$ array of processors *grid*. The distributed data structures are U and *maxderiv*. The mapping *FivePoint* maps element $U[i][j]$ to virtual processors $grid[i][j]$, $grid[i+1][j]$, $grid[i-1][j]$, $grid[i][j+1]$, and $grid[i][j-1]$. The composite procedure *smooth* defines the process that is executed by each virtual processor concurrently when it is called from *host*. The first if statement in *smooth* calculates a new

Example 3.1 -- Matrix-Vector Multiplication in DINO

```
#define N 512
environment node [N:id]  {     /* defines array of N virtual processors  */
  composite MatVec (in M, in v, out a)     /* Row-wise Parallel Algorithm to Calculate  a <-- M*v  : */
    float distributed M[N][N] map BlockRow;       /* maps row id of M to node[id] */
    float distributed v[N] map all;      /* maps v to each environment  */
    float distributed a[N] map Block;       /* maps a[id] to node[id] */
    {
    int j;
    a[id] = 0;
    for (j=0; j<N; j++)       /*  a[id]  <--  dot product of (row id of M) and v  */
      a[id] += M[id][j] * v[j];
  } }
environment host   {   /* master process */
  main ()   {
    float Min[N][N];       /*  Matrix Multiplicand  */
    float vin[N];          /*  Vector Multiplicand  */
    float aout[N];         /*  Vector Answer  */

    InputData (Min);         /*  omitted for brevity  */
    MatVec (Min[][], vin[], aout[])# ;       /*  Call the Composite Procedure  */
    PrintResults (aout);         /*  omitted for brevity  */
  } }
```

value of each $U[xid][yid]$, by averaging it with the four neighboring values of U. By using the reference $U[xid][yid]\#$, it also sends this new value to each other processor to which $U[xid][yid]$ is mapped, namely $grid[xid+1][yid]$, $grid[xid-1][yid]$, $grid[xid][yid+1]$, and $grid[xid][yid-1]$. (The default paradigm used in DINO is that only the home processor, in this case $grid[xid][yid]$ for $U[xid][yid]$, sends out new values of this variable, while the others processors to which the distributed variable is mapped receive its new values.) The next two if statements calculate numerical approximations to the second derivative of U in the x and y directions, respectively. The references $U[xid+1][yid]\#$, $U[xid-1][yid]\#$, $U[xid][yid+1]\#$, and $U[xid][yid-1]\#$ on the right side of the assignment statements receive the new values of these variables that were sent out in the aforementioned send statement. These receives block until the new value of this variable is received from its home processor. This enforces local, produce-consume synchronization between the processors but no global synchronization. Finally, the operator *gmax* in the statement "maxderiv[] = gmax(myderiv[])#" is an instance of a reduction operator. This statement takes the maximum of each *myderiv* $[i]$ over all the virtual processors *grid* $[i][j]$, and assigns this value to *maxderiv* $[i]$.

Example 3.2 -- Two Dimensional Smoothing Illustrating DINO Communication Features

```
#define N 128
environment grid [N:xid] [N:yid]  {     /* defines N x N grid of virtual processors */
   composite Smooth (in U, out maxderiv)      /* parallel process executed on each environment */
      float distributed U[N][N] map FivePoint;      /* maps U[x][y] to grid[x][y] and four neighbors */
      float distributed deriv_max[2] map all;      /* mapped to all environments */
      {
      float myderiv[2];
      if ((xid != 0) && (yid != 0) && (xid != N-1) && (yid != N-1))    /* if not a border point */
         U[xid][yid]# = (U[xid][yid] + U[xid-1][yid] + U[xid+1][yid] +  U[xid][yid-1] + U[xid][yid+1]) / 5;
         else U[xid][yid]# = BorderSmooth (U, xid, yid);    /* omitted for brevity */
      if ((xid != 0) && (xid != N-1))    /* approximate second derivative in x direction */
         myderiv[1] = U[xid][yid] - (U[xid-1][yid]# + U[xid+1][yid]#)/2 ;
         else myderiv[1] = 0;
      if ((yid != 0) && (yid != N-1))    /* approximate second derivative in y direction */
         myderiv[2] = U[xid][yid] - (U[xid][yid-1]# + U[xid][yid+1]#)/2 ;
         else myderiv[2] = 0;
      maxderiv[] = gmax(myderiv[])#;     /* reduction operator on myderiv[1] and myderiv[2] */;
   } }
environment host   {   /* master process */
   main ()   {
   float U [N][N];
   float maxderiv [2];

      InputData (U);     /* omitted for brevity */
      smooth (U[][], maxderiv[])# ;        /*  Call the Composite Procedure  */
      printf(" Maximum Second Derivative of Smoothed Data in x Direction is %.3f", maxderiv[1]);
      printf(" Maximum Second Derivative of Smoothed Data in y Direction is %.3f", maxderiv[2]);
   } }
```

Now we comment briefly on some interesting issues raised by these two examples. With regard to virtual parallel computers, note that in Example 3.1, the virtual parallel machine *row* has the dimension P that presumably would correspond to the underlying physical parallel machine, as opposed to the size N that would match the maximum parallelism of the algorithm. In contrast, in Example 3.2 the dimensions of the virtual parallel machine *grid* match the full data parallelism of the algorithm, in this case $N \times N$. We have purposely used these two different styles in the two examples, to raise the general issue of whether the programmer needs to cater the degree of parallelism of the parallel program to the parallel computer, or just to the parallel algorithm. In DINO one can do either but programs that have more virtual than actual processors usually will be inefficient. In general this issue is closely tied to the model of parallel computation that is used, and thus will be discussed in Sections 4 and 6.

One noteworthy feature of distributed data structures in DINO is that they are referred to using global rather than local names. A second is that the mappings of these data structures onto virtual parallel machines allow replication, i.e. the mapping of a particular data element to multiple processors, as illustrated by Example 3.2. This has possible implications for interprocessor communication and storage management. A third issue is the variety of mappings that are provided; DINO provides a fairly rich general mechanism for describing mappings that is not illustrated by these examples [ref]. These are among the issues that will be discussed in Section 5.

Parallelism execution in DINO arises from calls to composite procedures, which provide a concurrent process model of computation. The programmer writes code for one process, using either a per task or per data element view of the computation in the terminology of Section 2. An alternative approaches that we are currently pursuing is discussed in Section 6.

The examples illustrate that there are two main interprocessor communication mechanisms in DINO. The first is that communication arises implicitly when distributed data structures are used as input, output, or input/output parameters to composite procedures. This communication is implicit and follows a block SIMD model, with the data structures being distributed or collected automatically at the composite procedure invocation or termination, respectively. The second mechanism is the explicit designation of communication between processes through the use of # signs following references to distributed variables. The new value of the distributed variable is either sent to all the processors it is mapped to (as defined by the distributed data declaration), or received from its "home" processor, using a produce-consume paradigm. While the syntax of these statements is much simpler than the low level interprocessor communication statements provided by vendors, they still require the programmer to explicitly specify communication. A key issue that will be addressed in Section 6 will be the connection between the model of parallelism used, the need for explicit specification of communication, and the expressiveness and parallel efficiency of the language.

Finally, the reduction statement (*gmax*) in Example 3.2 illustrates two additional communication features in DINO. One is reduction operators, and the second is the addition of array operations that allow communication primitives to be applied to arrays or sub-arrays. These and other specific communication issues are addressed in Section 7.

Many features of DINO are not illustrated in this section. Some important ones include the ability to specify multiple virtual parallel machines, to support non-blocking as well as blocking receives, and to support functional parallelism. Complete descriptions are available in [8,30,32]. The DINO compiler is freely available from the authors.

4. Research Issues Regarding Virtual Parallel Computers

It appears likely that most languages for distributed, data parallel computation will include an explicit or implicit designation of virtual parallel computers. This seems to be an integral part of the definition of distributed data structures, which is at the heart of these languages, and may be used in the model of parallel execution as well. This section discusses some important issues regarding language constructs for virtual parallel computers that have been raised by current research, and then mentions some future opportunities regarding this language construct.

A key issue illustrated by the examples in Section 3 is whether the virtual parallel computer should correspond to the underlying target parallel machine, or only to the parallel algorithm. We have purposely used Example 3.1 to illustrate the former approach, which uses a P processor virtual computer and a "per task" algorithm, and Example 3.2 to illustrate the latter approach, using an $N \times N$ processor virtual machine and a "per data element" algorithm. In DINO, either approach is possible, but currently an algorithm that has more virtual than actual processors will be implemented by multiprogramming the processors, which is likely to be inefficient.

In our view, it is highly desirable to allow the virtual parallel machine to correspond to the parallel algorithm and be independent of the target parallel machine. In order for this approach to result in efficient code, however, it almost certainly is necessary to be able to *contract* the many virtual processes. By this we mean that the compiler must efficiently be able to produce an equivalent, efficient parallel program whose number of processes equals the number of processors of the target machine. Whether this is possible is strongly dependent on the communication model that is used in the language. In languages using SIMD and block SIMD models, which provide a global view of all synchronization and communication, contraction is relatively straightforward. In languages where synchronization and communication can be designated between arbitrary pairs of processors at arbitrary points, such as DINO or any language employing a full SPMD send/receive model, automatic contraction seems more difficult and sometimes may be infeasible. On the other hand, there are limitations to the expressiveness of languages that only support SIMD or block SIMD communication. This general issue is discussed in detail in Section 6.

A more minor, related issue is whether the number of processors in the target parallel machine needs to be known at compile time or only at run time. For example, in Example 4.1 the question becomes whether the program needs to be recompiled each time the define statement for P changes. (In current DINO, the answer is yes.) In a fully data parallel program, the program is independent of the target machine, but the question becomes whether the compiler needs to know the target number of processors to produce an efficient, *contracted* program. From our experience in writing compilers for parallel machines, we suspect that it will be very difficult to produce efficient parallel programs from high level language descriptions without recompiling for each different number of processors. To our knowledge, all existing compilers do require the number of processors to be known at compile time.

A final issue regarding the facilities of current languages for virtual parallel machines is the mapping of the processors of the virtual machine to the processors of the target parallel computer. In almost all current languages, including DINO, the virtual machines must be single or multiple dimensional arrays of processors. In this case, the obvious strategy is to maps contiguous virtual processors (whose indices differ by one in exactly one index) onto contiguous actual processors. This is fairly straightforward to accomplish, see e.g. [16]. As long as most communications occur between pairs of contiguous virtual processors, as is generally the case, this simple strategy also is efficient. If communication patterns are more random, however, then determining an efficient mapping of virtual to actual processors may be very difficult and may even require programmer guidance. Implicit in this discussion is that it is preferable for communication to occur between contiguous actual processors. The importance of this has varied among recent distributed architectures, but we assume that in a congested situation where many pairs of processors are communicating simultaneously, almost any architecture will perform more efficiently when utilizing contiguous rather than noncontiguous communications.

An important challenge that we see regarding language constructs for virtual parallel computers is the provision of more general virtual parallel machines than single and multiple dimensional arrays. This could include virtual parallel machines that are defined statically but use more general data structures, for example fixed undirected graphs, as well as virtual parallel computers that are defined dynamically as the computation proceeded, such as dynamically generated trees. While such features are not required for many scientific computations, such as those based on dense, regular grids or dense matrices, they may be useful for less regular computations, such as adaptive grid methods or particle physics algorithms. Key questions regarding such constructs include : What language constructs are most natural for expressing such virtual parallel computers? How do such constructs, especially dynamic virtual machines, interact with distributed data declarations and models of parallel execution? How are such virtual machines mapped to the actual parallel computers? How efficient will the resultant code be? These are all difficult questions. In particular, whether it will be possible to produce *efficient* parallel programs from descriptions that use dynamic virtual parallel machines is an open and challenging research issue.

5. Research Issues Regarding Distributed Data Structures

As discussed earlier, the provision and use of distributed data structures appears to be the key and fundamental element of parallel programming languages for distributed, data parallel computation. So far, most distributed language research projects have taken reasonably similar approaches to distributed data structures. These are predominantly based on making fixed mappings of regular arrays of data onto regular arrays of virtual processors. In this section we briefly discuss issues relating to this current research, and then discuss future challenges. These are mainly related to accommodating less regular data structures, and allowing mappings to change as the algorithm proceeds.

Many languages support, in some form, the mappings of single or multiple dimensional arrays of data onto virtual parallel machines that are also single or multiple dimensional arrays. Generally they allow each axis of the data structure to be partitioned onto a given axis of the virtual parallel machine, and in most cases, support *block*, *wrap*, and sometimes *block-wrap* partitionings. Most systems also allow certain data structures to be replicated among all the virtual processors.

One distinction between current languages is whether they allow "overlaps", i.e. the mapping of elements of the data structure onto multiple virtual processors, or just partitions of the data structures. Languages that support overlap include Superb [38], FortranD [9], and DINO (see Example 3.2). Where overlap mappings are provided, they are generally used to provide information concerning communication and storage to the compiler. For example, they may tell the compiler that processors $i-1$, i, and $i+1$ all store the value of x_i, and that when a new value of x_i is generated it must be sent to each of these processors. This type of sharing of data is fairly common in scientific computation. Languages that do not use overlap mappings rely instead on the compiler to determine the communication and storage requirements from the code. It will be interesting to see which approach is preferred by users and by language and compiler developers.

An interesting distinction between current approaches is whether they use a global or local name space to refer to elements of distributed data structures. For example, if a program partitions a data structure y with n elements onto a array of n processors, does the program for processor i refer to its element as y_i, or y_0, or just plain y? Most languages have used the former, global, approach, and we find this to be more natural in most cases, for it usually causes the program to correspond more closely to the sequential code that the programmer is used to.

In our opinion, two key future challenges concerning distributed data structures are remapping distributed data structures as the computation proceeds, and handling irregular data structures. Both have only had preliminary consideration in work that has been done so far.

In the context of making regular mappings of arrays data structures onto arrays of virtual processors, it is fairly straightforward to provide language features for remapping the data by somehow changing the distributed data declaration. Several recent proposals [9,29,31] incorporate this feature in some form. It will be interesting to see how efficiently these remappings can be implemented and how general they can be in practice. In the context of irregular data structures, remapping is just part of the larger challenge that we discuss next.

Mapping and accessing irregular distributed data structures is a difficult but important challenge. It is important because irregular data structures are necessary to efficiently model many scientific phenomena, such as the behavior of shock waves in fluids. The approach that is taken to incorporating irregular data structures into parallel languages is likely to be related to the underlying language. In Fortran, irregular data structures are represented by indirectly indexed arrays, and some recent research projects are considering incorporating these data structures into languages for distributed memory multiprocessors [kali, arf, fortrand]. Some of the key issues that need to be addressed in this context are how the array is mapped to the virtual parallel machine, and how efficiently indirect accesses to the array can be resolved, including generating communications as required that we will mention briefly in Section 6. A series of papers from ICASE [17,24,34] has begun to address many of these issues.

In many other languages, irregular data structures are represented by pointer-based data structures. To our knowledge, work aimed at using pointer-based structures as distributed data structures in languages for distributed memory MIMD computation is just beginning. An interesting distinction between the two approaches is that pointer-based structures naturally impose a local view of the data, whereas indirectly accessed arrays utilize an underlying global name space. This is likely to have implications upon the programming model. Another interesting issue in using distributed pointer-based data structures is whether the associated virtual parallel machine is an array, or an undirected graph tied to the data structure. If the virtual parallel machine is an array, then a key question appears to be how one maps the pointer-based data structure onto this virtual machine. If the virtual parallel machine corresponds to the data structure, then the problem is the mapping of the virtual machine onto the physical machine in a way that gives good load balancing. The latter approach may be necessary if one is to naturally express parallel algorithms involving complex data structures that change dynamically as the algorithm proceeds. Some of our current research is addressing these issues in the context of the DINO language.

6. Research Issues Regarding Models of Parallel Computation

Inherent in any parallel language is a model of parallel computation and an associated model of communication. By "model of parallel computation" we mean the view that the programmer takes of the concurrent execution of the code. By "model of communication" we mean the view that the programmer takes of the transfer of data between virtual processors. Whereas most languages for data parallel scientific computation so far have taken similar approaches to the other key aspects of the parallel language, distributed data structures and virtual parallel machines, they have taken several rather different approaches to models of parallel computation. This section describes and contrasts these approaches. Then it very briefly mentions a new approach that we are taking in our research.

The main models of parallel computation that are being used in imperative languages for data parallel computation on distributed memory multiprocessors appear to be :

Annotated Complete Program -- The programmer writes standard serial code with one of the following two levels of annotation. In both cases, the programmer writes the instructions of the entire algorithm.

Data Distribution Annotations -- The programmer gives indications to the compiler of how data structures should be partitioned among actual or virtual processors. The compiler then determines how to parallelize the program.

Data Distribution and Parallel Execution Statements -- In addition, the programmer indicates how the program can be parallelized, generally by indicating loops that can be performed in parallel. The compiler may or may not attempt to find additional parallelism beyond that indicated by the programmer.

Concurrent Process -- The programmer writes code that will be executed in parallel by each (virtual) processor. Thus the programmer only writes the instructions for a typical portion of the algorithm. (The indices of the virtual processor may be used in the code.) There appear to be two main ways in which this may be done :

Per Data Element -- The programmer writes code at the full level of data parallelism for the particular algorithm. That is, the number of virtual processes equals the amount of data parallelism.

Per Task -- The programmer writes the code that aggregates a number of data parallel operations into a task. This occurs most commonly in models where the programmer writes the code for one actual processor.

If the programming model is complete program with only distributed data annotations, then the programmer is not concerned with any communication model. In all other cases, some communication model must be used along with the model of parallel computation. Three communication models appear to be in common use in imperative languages for data parallel computation on distributed memory multiprocessors :

SIMD (Single Instruction Multiple Data) -- The communications are the same as if the code were executed in lock step using standard SIMD semantics.

Block SIMD -- For some designated block of parallel code, all off-virtual-processor values required within the block are obtained immediately preceding the beginning of the block, and all off-processor values generated within the block are communicated immediately following the end of the block. (This model is sometimes called "Copy-In/Copy-Out".) If the size of the block is a single operator, then this is the SIMD model.

SPMD (Single Program Multiple Data) with Sends/Receives -- Sends and receives between virtual processors may be designated at any point in the code. Typically they obey produce/consume semantics.

The SIMD and Block-SIMD models can use either explicit (programmer designated) or implicit (compiler determined) communication. Typically, they use implicit communication because it appears to take some of the work away from the programmer. As we discuss below, the SPMD send/receive model must use explicit communication.

In theory the choice of a communication model is orthogonal to the choice of a computation model. In this section, we only discuss those combinations we have seen. They are the annotated complete program computation model with block SIMD communications, and the concurrent process computation model with any of the three communication models.

We note that the above categorization of models of parallel computation and communication is new, and that we have selected the names for the categories. Quite possibly, these names could be improved. The terms "annotated complete program" and "concurrent process" are new in this context and alternatives clearly exist. The acronyms SIMD and SPMD are well established but generally connote models of computations as well as communication. Here we are using just the communication part of their meaning. An alternative set of terms of the three communication models could be "operation synchronous", "block synchronous", and "asynchronous produce/consume".

THE ANNOTATED COMPLETE PROGRAM MODEL

The idea of deriving a parallel program for distributed memory machines from a serial code annotated solely by distributed data declarations was discussed by Callahan and Kennedy [5] and is the basis of the Superb [38] and Pandore [2] languages. It also is at the heart of the recent FortranD proposal [9] although this proposal also allows for parallel execution annotations in the form of forall loops. Presumably, serial programs annotated solely with data distribution declarations are easier to write than explicitly parallel programs, and clearly any algorithm can be expressed in this paradigm. The view the programmer takes is of the entire problem, as in any sequential language. The compiler has the entire job of detecting potential sources of parallelism, and the associated required communications, by using data dependency analysis, and of using this information to generate a parallel program that is equivalent to the serial one. The data distribution annotations may help the compiler to identify parallelism, and also aid it in distributing the problem to the processors once parallelism is identified. The key question regarding this model is how well a sophisticated compiler will be able to identify parallelism, and generate efficient communication, and how efficient the resultant parallel program will be in comparison to explicitly parallel programs for the same algorithms. Currently this is an open research issue.

In the other variant of the annotated complete program model, the programmer also provides parallel execution annotations. Typically this means that particular loops are flagged for parallel execution, for example by using a "forall" or "*DO" statement in place of a standard "do" or "for" loop. The implication of this annotation is that the compiler may assume that there are no inter-iteration dependencies, and thus that it may execute all the iterations of the loop in parallel. If there are inter-iteration dependencies, then the result of the parallel execution may be different than if the code were executed serially. Thus the programmer must understand the implication of the parallel loop annotation. Languages that use this model include AL [36], Arf [37], Kali[23], and FortranD [9]. In contrast to FortranD, most of these do not attempt to have the compiler detect additional parallelism beyond that specified by the programmer.

Since the semantics of parallel loops in the annotated complete program model assumes that there are no inter-iteration dependencies, the natural communication model is the Block SIMD model, where the block is the body of the parallel loop. Many of the languages mentioned above use this communication model. It is the compiler's job to assure that the block SIMD semantics are followed, meaning that if a virtual processor refers to a variable residing on another virtual processor, the value that is obtained is the one that variable had just before the start of the parallel loop. Similarly, if any virtual processor assigns a new value to a variable residing on another virtual processor, the compiler must send that value to that variable immediately after the conclusion of the forall loop. Implementing these rules in a way that efficiently aggregates communication and minimizes processor idle time awaiting communications is a challenging research issue, but one that has already been extensively investigated by some researchers (see e.g. [17,21,24,34]). This research has included the difficult case of irregular data structures that are specified through the use of indirect index arrays in Fortran.

While there is limited experience in using the annotated complete program model, it appears to be fairly easy to use for many regular applications. No communication is specified by the programmer, and the Block SIMD semantics make it fairly easy for the compiler to determine where communications are required. The model also fits the loosely synchronous model of parallel computation, which has been said to apply to a good portion of parallel scientific algorithms [10, pp. 43-44]. On the other hand, the Block SIMD semantics may be confusing to the programmer, and may force the programmer to break parallel loops in unnatural places to force communications. An example of this is given below. Finally, there are certainly problems to which the block SIMD communications model does not apply, and for which it is difficult or impossible to obtain an efficient parallel algorithm from an annotated serial program.

THE CONCURRENT PROCESS MODEL

The concurrent process computation model has been used by a number of research projects into data parallel languages for distributed memory machines, in conjunction with all three communication models. In each case, the programmer writes code for one typical virtual process that will be executed concurrently by each virtual processor.

An example of a language that uses a concurrent process computation model together with a SIMD communication model is DataParallelC [14]. The SIMD communication model has its origins in languages developed for SIMD machines, such as C* [28] for the Connection Machine. In SIMD languages, one generally writes code for one generic virtual process that is then executed concurrently, in lock step, by each virtual process. Thus the programmer's view of the problem is per virtual process, which is often the same as per data element. Typically, no communication is specified by the programmer. Due to the lock step semantics, it is fairly easy for the compiler to analyze where communications must occur. The experience in using languages such as C* seems to be that such programs are easy to write.

When SIMD languages are used on MIMD machines, they do not need to synchronize at each operation, rather just at the communication points that are inferred from the SIMD semantics. Thus they can lead to efficiently executing programs even on machines where communication is expensive relative to computation. In order to do this, there must be enough computation available to hide the latency of the required inter-processor communications. Various optimizations also may be used to reduce the communication overhead. One optimization is to utilize the high degree of virtual parallelism to perform the computation for those virtual processors that do not require any off-processor communications while waiting for the required communications. Another optimization is to use extensive dependency analysis to to eliminate unnecessary communication points, pre-send data, and aggregate sends.

The big disadvantage of the SIMD form of the concurrent process model is its limited expressiveness. Only a subset of data parallel algorithms are naturally expressed as SIMD algorithms.

Some other algorithms may be coerced to fit this model by specifying that certain processors do nothing at certain steps ("masking"), but this reduces the efficiency of the parallel algorithm in a way that may be totally unnecessary for an MIMD machine. Examples of algorithms which do and don't fit the SIMD model are given below.

As discussed in Section 3, the DINO language uses a concurrent process model with both block SIMD and send/receive forms of communication. The communications that results from using distributed data as parameters to composite procedures follow a block SIMD communication model, where the block is the composite procedure. The communication semantics are the same as those discussed above for forall loops. The main distinction is that in DINO, the programmer specifies which data may need to be communicated, by including them as parameters. Thus the compiler needs to do less work to determine communications than for forall loops, but the possible communication patterns are restricted to distributed data mappings whereas in forall loops there is no restriction. Another language that uses the concurrent process model with (only) block SIMD communication is Spot [35]. In this language an iteration is a basic programming construct and blocks correspond to single iterations.

Communications between concurrently executing processes in DINO uses the SPMD send/receive communications model. This is also the model used in low-level programming systems supplied by vendors of distributed memory MIMD machines, and in a variety of portable systems that have been produced including PICL [11] and PVM [4]. In the concurrent process model with send/receive communications, the programmer writes code that will be executed by each virtual or actual processor on its part of the data structure concurrently. In contrast to the SIMD model above, the instructions of each process are not assumed to execute in lock step. Rather, communications generally are specified explicitly, such as with the # operator in DINO. Synchronizations between processors, if any, are determined by the requirements imposed by these communications. Because the communication patterns may be completely arbitrary (as opposed to the SIMD or Block SIMD communications models), it appears infeasible to have the programmer omit the specification of communications and have the compiler determine where they are needed. For related reasons, it may be difficult to efficiently contract programs written in this model if the parallelism in the program is greater than the actual parallelism.

Because the programmer needs to explicitly specify communications, the concurrent process model with general send/receive communications may be more difficult to program in than the other models. On the other hand, this model is more expressive than the other parallel models discussed (except serial programs with just data annotations) and may be more likely to lead to efficient parallel code for difficult or irregular parallel algorithms. An example of this is given later in this section.

DISCUSSION

The annotated complete program model, especially with only data distribution annotations, is particularly attractive because it lends itself to reuse of existing code and because a programmer used to an existing serial language has fewer new things to learn to do parallel programming. It should be realized, however, that the programmer will sometimes still have to understand the parallel aspects of the program if it is to run efficiently. Not all algorithms parallelize easily. The programmer may have to understand what the compiler is doing to a particular annotated serial program to be able to determine which annotations will allow the compiler to produce an efficient parallel program. In addition, it is still an open research question how well a parallelizing compiler can be made to perform on distributed memory machines using just information provided by data distribution annotations.

The concurrent process model has exactly the opposite problems. It does not lend itself as well to reuse of serial code, and it requires the programmer to learn more new concepts. Additionally, many current languages using this model may require the programmer to specify things that a compiler could figure out. The long term result may be research focusing on ways to combine these two models.

An example of something that the compiler often can determine is communications. It is a widely held opinion, and probably the correct one, that all other things being equal it is better to relieve the programmer of the chore of designating communications. The gain from doing this, however, may not as large as one might think at first glance. The problem is that to understand and improve the performance of any modestly complex program, the programmer still has to understand where communications and synchronizations are occurring. Thus the programmer may only be relieved of the chore of designating the communications, not of understanding where they occur. To complicate this trade-off, with the current state of the art in compilers, having the compiler determine the communications may result in loss of efficiency.

A more subtle difference between the annotated complete program model and the concurrent process model is the relationship between the mapping of virtual processes and distributed data to the virtual parallel machine. In the concurrent process model, both processes and data are mapped together to the same virtual machine. In the annotated complete program model, data is mapped to a virtual machine, and concurrent processes may be specified in forall loops, but they are not mapped to the same virtual machine. Instead the compiler has the job of aligning the data and processes. This means that the programmer has to specify less, and has less control. Experience will show which approach is advantageous.

The discussions of these models illustrates what we believe is the key dilemma in choosing the model of parallel computation and communication to use in a parallel programming language : the tradeoffs between ease of use (and re-use), expressiveness, and parallel efficiency. Ideally, one would like the model to be easy to use while still leading to efficiently executing parallel programs for a wide variety of data parallel algorithms. Unfortunately, among the parallel models we have discussed, there appears to be an inverse relationship between ease of use and the breadth of efficient parallel algorithms that they can naturally express. The next section illustrates the expressiveness of the various models with three examples. Then we will conclude this section with a brief discussion of one possible, hybrid, approach to combining expressiveness, ease of use, and parallel efficiency in a concurrent process model.

EXAMPLES

As the first example, consider an LU decomposition algorithm for solving dense systems of linear equations. Assume that the matrix is distributed among the (virtual) processors by columns, which is the arrangement most conducive to parallel efficiency. Then the desired parallel algorithm is:

For j = 1 to n-1

Processor with column j determines pivot row and multipliers and broadcasts this information

All processors pivot their columns and perform elimination on columns > j

A language using the concurrent process model with SIMD communications can express this algorithm easily, using a mask for the pivot step. A language using the concurrent process model with send/receive communications also has no problem expressing the algorithm, but the programmer must explicitly designate the communications which seems unnecessary for this algorithm. A compiler for a serial language using data distribution annotations will almost certainly produce an efficient parallel algorithm for this example. If the annotated complete program model with forall loops and block SIMD communications is used, however, an interesting and subtle issue arises. The programmer might place the forall loop around the entire iteration (pivot/multiplier plus elimination), with a statement like "if mycolumn = j then do pivot/multiplier calculation" for the first segment of the iteration. This program would not work correctly, however, since communication would be required in the middle of the iteration and this would not occur using the block SIMD model. Instead, one would need to write the pivot/multiplier segment as a sequential block of code and place just the elimination segment in a forall loop. While there are more convincing examples, this illustrates the need to accommodate the block SIMD communications semantics when placing forall loops in annotated complete program model.

As a second example, consider a simplified view of an algorithm for solving a system of n nonlinear equations in n unknowns, using finite difference Jacobian matrices. There are two basic and potentially expensive steps at each iteration : calculating the finite difference Jacobian matrix by performing n evaluations of the user-provided system of nonlinear equations (which are independent of one another and thus can be performed concurrently), and performing an LU decomposition of this matrix as discussed in the first example. A serial program annotated only with data distributions is unlikely to be able to successfully parallelize the finite difference Jacobian evaluation in many applications, since each function evaluation may be a call to a subroutine that contains thousands of lines of code, and it may be impossible to determine that these function evaluations are independent. Adding a forall annotation to the loop for these n function evaluations would, however, permit them to be performed in parallel. It may still be difficult for the compiler to determine what communications is required when in fact, very little is. A concurrent process model with SIMD communications will not be able to express this algorithm unless the nonlinear function can be executed concurrently in lock-step, which is rarely the case in practice. (For example the function is commonly a differential equations solver that uses variable time steps.) A concurrent process model with send/receive communications will have no problem expressing the finite difference Jacobian evaluation, although again it will require some explicit communication designations that other models do not. We note that the new model we discuss at the end of this section is very well suited to this example.

As a final example, consider a distributed triangular solve (forward or back solve) using a matrix that is distributed by columns. This situation arises commonly in practice, for example in parallel algorithms for solving systems of nonlinear equations. The standard sequential triangular solve algorithm does not parallelize effectively, but researchers have constructed pipelined algorithms that are equivalent to the standard algorithm on serial processors but obtain more parallelism on distributed memory machines [19]. These algorithms are not described in any natural way by annotating a complete program with forall loops, or by using the concurrent process model with SIMD communication. They certainly would not be derived by any compiler from a serial algorithm with just data distribution annotations. It appears that, among the models we have considered, only a concurrent process model with explicit sends and receives permits a reasonable representation of this algorithm.

Hopefully, these examples illustrate that no parallel language model is optimal with respect to both ease of use and expressiveness. They also indicate that in any model, the programmer may often have to think about parallelism and communication. Finally, it is reasonable to expect that many complex numerical algorithms will have aspects of all three of these examples. This makes it clear that providing a language that easily leads to efficient parallel programs for complex applications is a very challenging problem.

A NEW HYBRID COMMUNICATIONS MODEL FOR EXPLICITLY PARALLEL LANGUAGES

As part of our current research, we are attempting to develop a language incorporating the concurrent process model of parallel computation that combines ease of use, expressiveness, and parallel efficiency to a greater extent than those described above. Its basic new component is a "pseudo-SIMD" communications model. This model differs from the standard SIMD model in that it allows the programmer to include arbitrary, standard function calls as statements, with the semantics that these calls are executed concurrently and independently, that is without SIMD semantics. Communications may be required to obtain the values parameters to the function before it is called, but otherwise each virtual process performs its function call independently. With this small extension to the SIMD model, many data parallel algorithms can be written easily and with no explicit designation of communication. For instance, the first two examples above are handled easily and naturally using this model. To be very broadly expressive, however, we feel it is also necessary to provide the possibility of explicitly designated sends and receives. In our current research we allow each concurrent process segment (composite procedure in DINO) to use either pseudo-SIMD or SPMD semantics, but not both, and we allow the parallel program to be composed of arbitrary combinations of these two types of composite procedures. This allows the send/receive model to be used only where necessary and in an encapsulated manner. This new model is described in [29]. It will be interesting to see whether future research can come up with a cleaner model that provides for ease of use, expressiveness, and parallel efficiency.

7. Additional Research Issues Regarding Communication Features

In all of the language approaches discussed in this paper, the programmer has to think to some extent about communication. The most important ways this is done is via the models of communication discussed in Section 6, and when making the distributed data declarations discussed in Section 5. There are some additional issues of general interest in designing languages, compilers, and run-time support systems for data parallel languages for distributed memory multiprocessors. This section very briefly mentions some of these.

Several communication features that are useful in data parallel computation are supported by the hardware or low-level software of most distributed memory machines. These include reduction operators (global sums, products, maximums, and minimums), and non-blocking receives such as are used in "chaotic" parallel algorithms. An interesting issue is whether, and how, parallel languages provide access to these features. Reduction operators appear crucial to data parallel computation. They are easy to provide in any language that uses an concurrent process model, and almost all do so. It may prove useful to provide them explicitly in annotated serial languages as well, and FortranD, for example, does so. It is not as clear how important it is to provide access to non-blocking receives, and this probably only is easy in languages with some form of explicit sends and receives.

There are several issues that a compiler and run-time system for a production quality distributed data parallel language needs to consider. These are all influenced by the fact that communication latency on distributed memory machines is relatively high, and can reasonably be expected to remain so. One issue is pre-sending communications, in order to eliminate the potential idle time that can result if a processor must wait for a message. In any language that does not explicitly designate sends, pre-sending communications requires analysis by either the compiler or the run-time system. A second issue is aggregating communications to reduce the total communications latency. In the annotated complete program model or the concurrent process model with SIMD or block SIMD communications, most aggregations appear to require similar analysis to that used to vectorize arithmetic computations. Thus this process should be quite feasible. A final, more subtle issue is that many distributed memory machines turn out to have various low-level communication methods that have different latency costs, for reasons such as differing usages of low-level buffering, or different utilizations of special hardware features. Language and compiler designers will ultimately need to consider how they can cause their communications to utilize the most efficient low-level communications methods in most cases. They will also need to interact with multiprocessor vendors to encourage them to provide hardware and low-level software features that are consistent with the needs of parallel languages.

8. Research Issues Regarding Support for Complex Parallel Programs

The preceding discussion, and almost all research so far in language support for distributed, data parallel computation, is primarily oriented at supporting single algorithmic kernels, such as a matrix factorization algorithm or a conjugate gradient solver. As even the simple examples in Section 6 illustrate, real applications generally are composed of many such kernel algorithms. These algorithms may follow one another serially in the computation, or may be nested within one another, or both. A number of additional issues arise when considering language support for such complex computations. This section very briefly mentions some of these. Among the research projects currently considering these issues are the Orca project at the University of Washington [1,13] and the DINO project [29, 31].

A complex parallel algorithm may have serially executed phases, concurrently executed phases, and/or nested phases. Different phases may be expressed naturally using different virtual parallel machines. Thus one issue that arises immediately is whether and how to support serially changing, multiple, or nested virtual parallel machines. The latter two cases raise challenging problems with regard to contraction and load balancing.

A related issue is that different phases of a complex algorithm may most naturally desire different mappings of the same data structure. One question this raises is how the language will support remapping of distributed data structures. This question is addressed in the recent FortranD proposal [9,15] and to a more limited extent in [29]. A second question is how efficiently the compiler will be able to perform remappings. This may require a library of common remapping operations that are optimized with regard to communication costs.

Finally, almost all research so far into distributed data parallel languages has been oriented towards algorithms that use static process structures and, for the most part, static data structures. Dynamic parallel algorithms, such as those used in adaptive grid methods for partial differential equations, pose many additional challenges that have been discussed somewhat in Sections 4 and 5. It remains to be seen whether these will be effectively addressed using the frameworks discussed in this paper.

9. References

[1] Alverson, G.A., Griswold, W.G., Notkin, D., and Snyder, L. A flexible communication abstraction for nonshared memory parallel computing. *Proc. of Supercomputing 90,* 1990, 584-593.

[2] Andre, F., Pazat, J., and Thomas, H. Pandore: a system to manage data distribution. In *Proc. of the 1990 International Conference on Supercomputing,* ACM, Jun. 1990.

[3] Bagheri, B., Raghavachari, B., Scott, L.R. PC-a parallel extension of C. Technical Report, Computer Science Department, Pennsylvania State University, Nov. 1990.

[4] Beguelin, A., Dongarra, J., Geist, A., Manchek, B., and Sunderam, V. A user's guide to PVM, parallel virtual machine. Technical Report ORNL/TM-11826, Oak Ridge National Laboratory, Apr. 1991.

[5] Callahan, D. and Kennedy, K. Compiling programs for distributed-memory multiprocessors. *Journal of Supercomputing* 2, 1988, 151-169.

[6] Carriero, N. and Gelernter, D. Linda in context. *Communications of the ACM,* 32(4), Apr. 1989, 444-458.

[7] Chen, M., Choo, Y., and Li, J. Crystal: from functional description to efficient parallel code. *Proc. from The Third Conference on Hypercube Concurrent Computers and Applications,* 1988, 417-33.

[8] Derby, T., Eskow, E., Neves, R., Rosing, M., Schnabel, R., and Weaver, R. The DINO User's Manual. Department of Computer Science Technical Report CU-CS-501-90, University of Colorado at Boulder, Nov. 1990.

[9] Fox, G., Hiranandani, S., Kennedy, K., Koelbel, C., Kremer, U., Tseng, C., and Wu, M. Fortran D language specification. Center for Research on Parallel Computation Technical Report CRPC-TR90079, Dec. 1990.

[10] Fox, G., Johnson, M., Lyzenga, G., Otto, S., Salmon, J., and Walker, D. *Solving Problems on Concurrent Computers,* Prentice-Hall, Englewood Cliffs, NJ, 1988.

[11] Geist, G.A., Heath, M.T., Peyton, B.W., and Worley, P.H. PICL: a portable instrumented communication library, C reference manual. Technical Report ORNL/TM-11130, Oak Ridge National Laboratory, Oak Ridge, TN, Jul. 1990.

[12] Gerndt, M. Updating distributed variables in local computations. *Concurrency: Practice & Experience,* 1990.

[13] Griswold, W.G., Harrison, G.A., Notkin, D., and Snyder, L. Scalable abstractions for parallel programming. *Proc. of the Fifth Distributed Memory Computing Conference,* IEEE Press, 1990, 1008-1016.

[14] Hatcher, P., Quinn, M., Lapadula, A., Seevers, B., Anderson, R., Jones, R. Data-parallel programming on MIMD computers. To appear in *IEEE Trans. on Parallel and Distributed Systems,* Jul. 1991.

[15] Hiranandani, S., Kennedy, K., Koelbel, C., Kremer, U., Tseng, C. An overview of the Fortran D programming system. Center for Research on Parallel Computation Technical Report CRPC-TR91121, Mar. 1991.

[16] Intel iPSC Programmer's Reference Guide, Number 310612-002, Mar. 1987.

[17] Koelbel, C., Mehrotra, P., Saltz, J., and Berryman, S. Parallel loops on distributed machines. In *Proc. of the 5th Distributed Memory Computing Conference,* IEEE Press, 1990.

[18] Koelbel, C., Mehrotra, P., and Van Rosendale, J. Supporting shared data structures on distributed memory architectures. *Proc. of 2nd SIGPLAN Symposium on Principles and Practice of Parallel Processing.* ACM, 1990, 177-186.

[19] Li, G. and Coleman, T. A parallel triangular solver for a hypercube multiprocessor. *Hypercube Multiprocessors 1987,* SIAM, 1987, 539-551.

[20] Li, J. and Chen, M. Generating explicit communication from shared-memory program references. In *Proc. of Supercomputing '90,* 1990.

[21] Littlefield, R. Efficient iteration in data-parallel programs with irregular and dynamically distributed data structures. Technical Report 90-02-06, Department of Computer Science and Engineering, University of Washington, Feb. 1990.

[22] McGraw, J., Allan, S., Glauert, J., and Dobes, I. SISAL: streams and iteration in a single assignment language. Language Reference Manual. Technical Report M-146. Lawrence Livermore National Laboratory, 1983.

[23] Mehrotra, P. and Van Rosendale, J. Programming distributed memory architectures using Kali. ICASE Report 90-69, Institute for Computer Application in Science and Engineering, Hampton, VA, Oct. 1990.

[24] Mirchandaney, S., Saltz, J., Mehrotra, P., and Berryman, H. A scheme for supporting automatic data migration on multicomputers. In *Proc. of the 5th Distributed Memory Computing Conference,* IEEE Press, 1990.

[25] Quinn, M. and Hatcher, P. Data-parallel programming on multicomputers. *IEEE Software,* Sep. 1990, 69-76.

[26] Reeves, A. The Paragon programming paradigm and distributed memory compilers. Technical Report EE-CEG-90-7, Cornell University Computer Engineering Group, Ithaca, NY, Jun. 1990.

[27] Rogers, A. and Pingali, K. Process decomposition through locality of reference. In *Proc. of the ACM SIGPLAN '89 Conference on Program Language Design and Implementation,* Jun. 1989.

[28] Rose, J., and Steele, G. C*: an extended C language for data parallel programming. Technical Report Pl85-7, Thinking Machines Corp., 1987.

[29] Rosing, M. Efficient language features for complex data parallelism on distributed memory multiprocessors. Ph.D. Thesis, Department of Computer Science, University of Colorado at Boulder, Aug. 1991.

[30] Rosing, M., Schnabel, R., and Weaver, R. The DINO parallel programming language. To appear in *The Journal of Parallel and Distributed Computing,* 1991.

[31] Rosing, M., Schnabel, R., and Weaver, R. Massive parallelism and process contraction in DINO. In Dongarra, J., Messina, P., Sorensen, D.C., and Voigt, R.G. (Eds.), *Parallel Processing for Scientific Computation,* SIAM, 1990, 364-369.

[32] Rosing, M., and Weaver, R. Mapping data to processors in distributed memory computers. *Proc. of Fifth Distributed Memory Computing Conference,* IEEE Press, 1990, 884-893.

[33] Ruppelt, T., and Wirtz, G. From mathematical specifications to parallel programs on a message based system. *Proc. 1988 International Conference on Supercomputing,* ACM, 1988, 108-118.

[34] Saltz, J., Berryman, H., and Wu, J. Multiprocessors and runtime compilation. ICASE Report 90-59, Institute for Computer Application in Science and Engineering, Hampton, VA, Sep. 1990.

[35] Socha, D.G. Spot: a data parallel language for iterative algorithms. Department of Computer Science Technical Report TR 90-03-01, University of Washington, 1990.

[36] Tseng, P.S. A parallelizing compiler for distributed memory parallel computers. In *Proc. of the ACM SIGPLAN '90 Conference on Program Language Design and Implementation,* Jun. 1990.

[37] Wu, J., Saltz, J., Berryman, H., and Hiranandani, S. Distributed memory compiler design for sparse problems. ICASE Report 91-13, Institute for Computer Application in Science and Engineering, Hampton, VA, Jan. 1991.

[38] Zima, H., Bast, H.-J., and Gerndt, M. SUPERB: A tool for semi-automatic MIMD/SIMD parallelization. *Parallel Computing, 6, 1986, 1-18.*

Languages, Compilers and Run-Time Environments
for Distributed Memory Machines
J. Saltz and P. Mehrotra (Editors)

VIENNA FORTRAN – A FORTRAN LANGUAGE EXTENSION FOR DISTRIBUTED MEMORY MULTIPROCESSORS*

Barbara M. Chapman[a], Piyush Mehrotra[b] and Hans P. Zima[a]

[a]Department of Statistics and Computer Science, University of Vienna, Rathausstrasse 19/II/3, A1010 Vienna AUSTRIA

[b]ICASE, MS 132C, NASA Langley Research Center, Hampton VA. 23666 USA

Abstract

Exploiting the full performance potential of distributed memory machines requires a careful distribution of data across the processors. Vienna Fortran is a language extension of Fortran which provides the user with a wide range of facilities for such mapping of data structures. However, programs in Vienna Fortran are written using global data references. Thus, the user has the advantages of a shared memory programming paradigm while explicitly controlling the placement of data. In this paper, we present the basic features of Vienna Fortran along with a set of examples illustrating the use of these features.

1 Introduction

In recent years, a number of distributed memory multiprocessing computers have been introduced into the market (e.g. Intel's iPSC series, NCUBE, and several transputer based systems). In contrast to shared memory machines, these architectures are less expensive to build and are potentially scalable to a large number of processors. However, the associated programming paradigm requires the user to specify complete details of the synchronization and the communication of data between processors as dictated by

*The work described in this paper is being carried out as part of the research project "Virtual Shared Memory for Multiprocessor Systems with Distributed Memory" funded by the Austrian Research Foundation (FWF) under the grant number P7576-TEC and the ESPRIT project "An Automatic Parallelization System for Genesis" funded by the Austrian Ministry for Science and Research (BMWF). This research was also supported by the National Aeronautics and Space Administration under NASA contract NAS1-18605 while the authors were in residence at ICASE, Mail Stop 132C, NASA Langley Research Center, Hampton, VA 23666. The authors assume all responsibility for the contents of the paper.

the algorithm. Experience has shown that forcing the user to provide such low level details not only makes distributed memory programming tedious and error prone but also inhibits experimentation.

The apparent advantages of using a shared memory programming paradigm have led to a number of attempts at simulating shared memory on such machines. These efforts range from providing a suitable combination of hardware mechanisms and operating system support (e.g. automatic paging and conflict resolution), to automatic parallelization.

Research in the last of these areas has resulted in the development of a number of prototype systems, such as Kali [10], SUPERB [6, 26], and the MIMDizer [16]. These systems allow the code to be written using global data references, as one would do on a shared memory machine, but require the user to specify the distribution of the program's data. This data distribution is then used to guide the process of restructuring the code into an SPMD (Single Program Multiple Data) program for execution on the target distributed memory multiprocessor. The compiler analyzes the source code, translating global data references into local and non-local references based on the distributions specified by the user. The non-local references are satisfied by inserting appropriate message-passing statements in the generated code. Finally, the communication is optimized where possible, in particular by combining statements and by sending data at the earliest possible point in time.

In this paper, we present a machine-independent language extension for FORTRAN 77, called Vienna Fortran, which allows the user to write programs for distributed memory machines using global data references only. Since the distribution of data to the processors is critical for performance, the extensions described here permit the user to explicitly control the mapping of data onto the processors. Vienna Fortran supports a wide range of facilities for specifying data distributions, including distribution by alignment, where one array is mapped so that it has a fixed relationship with another array. It also supports dynamic redistribution of data. Frequently occurring distributions can be specified in a simple manner, whereas the full language permits complex mappings. The overall aim of the language extensions provided by Vienna Fortran is to make the transition from the sequential algorithm to a parallel version as easy as possible, without sacrificing performance.

In this paper, we concentrate on describing the syntax and semantics of the basic language. Future papers will give a full description of both the language features and the compilation model. The next section introduces the Vienna Fortran extensions and supplements their description by several short examples. The use of the language constructs is more fully illustrated in Section 3, where three examples are presented and discussed. This is followed by a discussion of related work. Finally, in the last section we reach some conclusions.

2 The Basic Features of Vienna Fortran

The critical issue in programming distributed memory machines is the distribution of data across the processors of the target machine. An appropriate data distribution is crucial for the performance of the resulting parallel code; factors influencing the choice include the size of an application, the data access patterns, the number of processors available, details of the hardware and the characteristics of the communication mechanisms provided. Vienna Fortran provides an extensive set of language constructs which allow the user complete control over the mapping of the data structures in the program. These language extensions can be divided into a basic set of features which allow the user to handle the most frequently occurring but simple distributions and an extended set which provides more general mechanisms for mapping data structures onto arbitrary subsets of processors. In this section, we describe only the basic set of language constructs; the full language, together with a formal programming model, is specified in [27].

2.1 Processor Structure

The Vienna Fortran programming model requires a set of processors onto which the data can be distributed. Processor arrays can be declared in the program in a manner similar to Fortran arrays as shown here:[†]

PROCESSORS P2D(R, R) **ASSERT** R .GE. 8

The above statement declares a two dimensional processor array, *P2D*, with R^2 processors where the value of R is asserted to be greater than or equal to 8. Here, R is considered to be a constant whose value is determined at load time depending on the total number of processors available in the underlying machine. This allows the code to be parameterized by the number of processors and thus avoids recompilation if the number of processors change. The processor bounds can be compile-time constants if the code has to run on a fixed number of processors.

The R^2 processors introduced in the above declaration can be accessed in the same way as a two-dimensional array by the use of subscripts; for example P2D(3,7) determines a well-defined individual processor. Note, however, that the declaration does not imply a specific topology: in particular, it does **not** specify that the target processors are connected by a two-dimensional mesh.

The **primary processor structure**, as declared above, can be reshaped to lower dimensional **secondary processor structures** as follows:

PROCESSORS P2D(R, R) **ASSERT** R .GE. 8 **RESHAPE** P1D(R*R)

Here, *P1D* is a one-dimensional processor array which provides an alternative view of the two-dimensional array *P2D*. The Fortran column-major ordering is used to establish a relationship between the primary and secondary processor structures.

The primary process structure of a program is implicitly associated with the built-in identifier **$P** while a reference to the parameterless intrinsic function **$NP** yields the total number of processors being used by the program during the current execution. An implicit one-dimensional structure declaration **$PL**(1:**$NP**) is also provided with each program. If there is no explicit processor declaration, then **$P** and **$PL** both are implicitly declared as one-dimensional identical arrays with the subscript range (1:**$NP**).

[†]In this paper, keywords in code segments are emboldened while comments are in italics.

Thus, if the program only requires a one-dimensional array of the maximum number of processors currently available on the target machine, then the processor declaration can be omitted.

2.2 Distribution of Arrays

An array declaration can be annotated to specify the distribution of its elements onto the program's processors. Distributed arrays in Vienna Fortran can be divided into two categories, *static* and *dynamic*. The former category consists of arrays whose distribution is fixed within the scope of the declaration. Arrays whose distribution may be modified during the execution of the program have to be declared **DYNAMIC** as discussed in the next subsection. This strict separation between arrays whose distribution remains static and others whose distribution maybe changed during program execution, facilitates the compiler's task of generating highly efficient code for the target machine.

The semantics of arrays for which no distribution has been specified is the same as that of distributed arrays, i.e., there is conceptually a single copy of the data structure. The compiler may optimize the implementation by replicating the data structure on each of the processors executing the program. It is the compiler's task to maintain consistency among these copies. Note that scalar variables are handled in a similar manner.

Static Distribution of Arrays

The distribution of arrays is specified by associating a *distribution expression* with the declaration of the array. For example,

REAL $ad_1, ad_2, \ldots, ad_r$ **DIST** dex

declares arrays, $ad_i, 1 \leq i \leq r$ and their associated subscript ranges while the distribution expression, dex, specifies how the arrays are distributed. All the arrays specified in one distribution declaration must have the same rank. In the basic language, the distribution expression for a n-dimensional array consists of n distribution functions each of which specifies how the corresponding dimension of the array is to be partitioned into disjoint sections. Intrinsic functions are provided for specifying the commonly occurring distributions such as block, cyclic and block-cyclic. The following declarations show the use of the intrinsic distribution functions for distributing data across a one-dimensional array of processors.

```
REAL  A(100)  DIST ( BLOCK )
REAL  B(100)  DIST ( CYCLIC )
REAL  C(100)  DIST ( CYCLIC (K) )
REAL  D(100, 100)  DIST ( BLOCK, : )
```

Here A is partitioned by blocks such that each processor owns a contiguous block of elements, while the elements of the array B are distributed cyclically, i.e., in a round robin fashion, across the processors. The elements of array C are first partitioned into blocks of size K and then the blocks are cyclically assigned to the processors. The declaration for array D shows the use of the elision function, denoted by :, which "hides" a dimension of the array, i.e. specifies that the corresponding dimension is not to be distributed. Thus, the rows of the array D are partitioned into blocks with a block of rows being assigned to a processor - the columns are left undistributed.

The number of distributed dimensions of a distribution expression is called its *context rank*. In the basic language, the context rank of a distribution expression must match the rank of either the primary processor structure or that of one of the secondary processor structures as shown in the following examples.

```
PROCESSORS P2D(R, R)  ASSERT R  .LE. 8

REAL  A(100, 100)  DIST ( BLOCK, BLOCK )
REAL  B(100)  DIST ( CYCLIC )
REAL  C(100, 100)  DIST ( BLOCK, : )
REAL  D(100, 100, 100)  DIST (:, BLOCK, : )
```

Here, both the rows and the columns of the array A are partitioned by block across the two-dimensional processor array $P2D$, i.e., each processor is assigned a sub-block of the array. The array B is cyclically distributed across the processors of the one-dimensional processor array, **$PL**, implicitly declared for each program. Similarly, the first dimension of the two-dimensional array C and the second dimension of the three-dimensional array D are distributed across the one dimensional array of processors.

The extended language provides more general facilities for distributing data arrays. In all the examples provided above, for instance, the data structures are mapped to the full processor array. The extended language also allows mappings to subsets of processors. Moreover, it removes the restriction on the context rank: the number of array dimensions which are distributed may be smaller than the number of dimensions of the processor array, permitting replication of a data array dimension across a processor array dimension.

Aligning Array Distributions: The Static Case

It is possible to declare the distribution of an array in terms of the distribution of another array, allowing the two arrays to be aligned to each other. The set of basic intrinsic *alignment functions* consists of **DISTRIBUTION**, **PERMUTE**, and **TRANSPOSE**. Intuitively, these functions can be thought of as yielding a distribution when applied to their argument(s).

The expression, **DISTRIBUTION**(A) yields the complete distribution of the array A. This can be syntactically replaced by "= A". The expression, **DISTRIBUTION**(A,d), yields the distribution of the dth dimension of the array A. This can be syntactically replaced by "= ($A.d$)".

The distributions of individual dimensions of an array can be permuted by the expression: **PERMUTE**(A, *perm*), where A is an array of rank n and *perm* is a list $(/i_1, \ldots, i_n/)$ of length n, specifying a permutation of the numbers in the interval $1 : n$. Then the function reference results in the distribution which is obtained when the specified permutation is applied to the distribution expression of A, i.e., $(= (A.i_1), \ldots, = (A.i_n))$. The function, **TRANSPOSE**(A), is a special form of the permuting function applicable only to two dimensional arrays and yields the same effect as **PERMUTE**(A, $(/2,1/)$).

The above alignment functions can be thus be used for distributing arrays as follows:

```
REAL A(100,100) DIST ( BLOCK, CYCLIC )
REAL B(100,100) DIST ( DISTRIBUTION(A) )
REAL C(100,100) DIST ( =A )
REAL D(100) DIST ( DISTRIBUTION(A,1) )
REAL E(100) DIST ( =(A.2) )
REAL F(100,100) DIST ( TRANSPOSE(A) )
```

Here, the arrays B and C are identically aligned with the array A. The distribution of the array D is the same as that of the first dimension of the array A, i.e., **BLOCK**, while E is distributed cyclically based on the distribution of the second dimension of A. The use of the transpose function declares the distribution of F to be (**CYCLIC, BLOCK**).

Note, that the extent of the array being aligned need not be the same as that of the original array as shown below:

```
REAL A(50) DIST ( BLOCK )

REAL B(11:60) DIST ( =A )
REAL C(80) DIST ( =A )
```

The array B is distributed across the processors "in the same way as A"; $B(11)$ will, for example, be placed on the same processor as $A(1)$, and the sizes of blocks of A and B will be the same. In contrast, when C is distributed "in the same way as A", then $A(1)$ and $C(1)$ will be placed on the same processor, but the lengths of the blocks will differ.

Dynamic Arrays

An array whose distribution may be modified during runtime must to be declared as dynamic. Such an array can then be used as the object of a distribute statement, (see subsection below), whenever its distribution needs to be changed. A dynamic array may have an optional initial distribution; if one is not given, the array may not be accessed (read or written) before it is distributed via a distribute statement.

```
REAL A(100, 100) DYNAMIC
REAL B(100) DYNAMIC DIST ( BLOCK )
```

The arrays A and B are declared as dynamic arrays with B having an initial block distribution.

Dynamic arrays may also have an optional *range attribute* which specifies the set of all distributions which can be associated with the arrays during the execution of the program. It consists of the keyword **RANGE**, followed by a parenthesized list of distribution expressions. If a distribute statement associates an array with a distribution not contained in the distribution range attribute, its effect is undefined. For example, in the declaration below,

```
REAL A(100,100) DYNAMIC
&         RANGE( ( BLOCK, BLOCK), ( CYCLIC, CYCLIC) )
```

the dimensions of A can both be partitioned by either block or cyclic distributions only.

Aligning Dynamic Arrays

The alignment functions described earlier can be used to align the initial distribution of a dynamic array with another array. For example, the declaration

```
REAL A(100) DYNAMIC DIST ( =B )
```

declares the initial distribution of the array A to be the same as that of B. However, this relationship is not maintained if either of the arrays is redistributed during the execution of the program. Note that in the above example, B can be either static or dynamic.

In contrast to the above situation, two dynamic arrays can be aligned to each other so that the alignment relationship remains valid throughout the execution of the program. This is done by providing a connect attribute in the declaration: it consists of the keyword **CONNECT** followed by a distribution expression based on the alignment functions as described earlier. For example, consider the following declarations:

```
REAL A(100) DYNAMIC DIST ( BLOCK )
REAL B(100), C(100) DYNAMIC CONNECT ( =A )
```

Here, the arrays B and C are declared to be *connected* to the array A via the identity alignment function. The array A is called the primary array, while B and C are secondary arrays. The connect set of A can be informally described as consisting of the array A together with all the secondary dynamic arrays aligned to it through connect attributes. The alignment relationships between the primary array and the secondary arrays in its connect set are maintained throughout the execution of the programs. A dynamic array can be a member of only one connect set while each connect set has only one primary array. Note that secondary arrays cannot be objects of a distribute statement, i.e., only primary arrays can be redistributed.

Distribute Statement

In contrast to static arrays, dynamic arrays may be the target of one or more distribute statements within the scope of their declaration. A distribute statement may appear at any place where an executable statement is permitted. The most general version of the distribute statement is as follows:

DISTRIBUTE $dg_1, \ldots, dg_s$

Here, $dg_1, \ldots, dg_s$ is a list of one or more *distribution groups*. Each *distribution group* has the form:

$$A_1, \ldots, A_r :: dex\ [notransfer\ attribute]$$

where the $A_i, 1 \le i \le r$, are arrays and *dex* is a distribution expression. In addition to the distribution expressions discussed up to now, *dex* may also use the **INDIRECT** intrinsic distribution function (see below).

Given the statement

DISTRIBUTE A :: *dex* [*notransfer attribute*]

the new distribution of A is determined by evaluating the distribution expression, *dex*, in the context of A. If A is a primary array of a connect set, then the distribute statement results in new distributions for each array in the connect set of A. The new distribution for each of the secondary arrays is determined by the new distribution of the primary array and the alignment relationship.

The *notransfer attribute* (which is optional) takes the form

NOTRANSFER $[(B_1, \ldots, B)]$

where $B_i, 1 \le i \le m$ are elements of connect set of A. If this list is omitted, the attribute applies to all elements of the connect set of A. The effect of this attribute is as follows: the values associated with the arrays B_i before execution of the distribute statement are ignored during execution of the statement, i.e., only the access function associated with the array is updated and no physical transfer of data takes place.

```
REAL A(100, 100) DYNAMIC

REAL B(100, 100) DYNAMIC CONNECT(=A)
REAL C(100, 100) DYNAMIC CONNECT( TRANSPOSE(=A))
   ⋮
DISTRIBUTE A :: ( BLOCK, CYCLIC(M) ) NOTRANSFER(C)
```

Here, A is the primary array while B is a secondary array which is identically aligned with A. The array C is also a secondary array but is aligned with A such that the distribution of the first dimension of A is the distribution of the second dimension of C and vice versa. When the distribute statement is executed, the current value of the variable M determines the size of the blocks of columns which are cyclically distributed across the processors. The same distribution is used for the array B, while a transposed distribution becomes the new distribution of the array C. The notransfer attribute specifies that the old data values of array C are to be ignored, whereas the old values of A and B are moved to their new positions.

INDIRECT Distribution

A special intrinsic distribution function called **INDIRECT** can be used for distributing dynamic arrays. This function allows each element of an array to be individually mapped to a processor. This is done via a **mapping array** as shown below:

```
INTEGER B(M) DIST ( BLOCK )
REAL    A(M) DYNAMIC
   ⋮
DISTRIBUTE A :: INDIRECT(B)
```

Here B, the mapping array, is used to specify the distribution A. That is, the value of $B(i)$ specifies the number of the processor which owns element $A(i)$. Note that B must be completely defined before the distribute statement is executed.

2.3 Subroutines

Distribution annotations can be associated with formal parameter declarations in subroutines to specify how the arrays will be viewed and accessed within the subroutine. In addition, local arrays may either be distributed explicitly or aligned with a formal parameter. While Vienna Fortran usually accesses formal array parameters by the standard Fortran call-by-reference paradigm, there are situations (e.g. when an array slice is transferred and redistributed) in which a copy in/copy out semantics must be adopted. It is also adopted in any situation where there is not enough information to decide whether reference transmission is semantically valid. The user may override this by specifying the *nocopy attribute*, as described below.

If the formal parameter has a static distribution then this distribution is enforced upon subroutine entry, i.e., the array may have to be redistributed to match the specified distribution. If the actual argument is also static, and the corresponding formal parameter has been redistributed at subroutine entry, then the original distribution is restored on subroutine exit. If the actual argument is dynamic, then no such restoration is required. Restoration of the original distribution can always be enforced by using the keyword **RESTORE**, either in the formal parameter annotation or with the argument at the point of the subroutine call.

If the formal parameter is declared dynamic, then no redistribution is required at subroutine entry unless an initial distribution is provided with the declaration. A dynamic formal parameter may be a target of an explicit **DISTRIBUTE** statement within the subroutine. The original distribution is restored if the actual argument is static or if the *restore attribute* has been specified.

For both static and dynamic formal parameters, a **NOTRANSFER** attribute can be specified with the declaration of the parameter. In such a situation, if a redistribution is required at subroutine entry, then only the access function is changed and the elements of the array are not physically moved. This attribute is useful when the values of the formal parameter are first going to be defined in the subroutine before being used. It is also appropriate if a dynamic array has not been distributed before the subroutine call.

A *nocopy attribute* (using the keyword **NOCOPY**) can be specified in the declaration of a formal parameter to suppress the generation of a subroutine-local copy of the formal array. In this case, the parameter transmission is by reference, i.e., the actual argument is directly accessed within the subroutine. For static formal parameters, it is an error if the distribution of the actual argument does not match the specified distribution. For dynamic formal parameters the actual argument may not be static. Note that a *restore attribute* is not permitted with the *nocopy attribute.*

In addition to the explicit distributions described above, a formal parameter may inherit the distribution of the corresponding actual argument. This can be specified using the annotation **DIST(*)** with the declaration. The corresponding actual argument may have different distributions on different call statements and no implicit redistribution takes place on subroutine entry. The set of all possible argument distributions can be specified by an optional *distribution range attribute* as used in the dynamic distribution declaration. A formal parameter which inherits its distribution may not be a target of a distribute statement even if the corresponding actual argument is dynamic.

Thus a number of different situations may arise in conjunction with the transfer of distributed arrays to subroutines. Some of these are exemplified in the following code fragment:

```
PARAMETER (N= 2000)
REAL A(N)  DIST (CYCLIC)
REAL B(N)  DIST (CYCLIC)
REAL C(N)  DYNAMIC
   ⋮
CALL SUB(N,A,B,C)
   ⋮


SUBROUTINE SUB(N,A1,B1,C1)
REAL A1(N)  DIST (*)
REAL B1(N)  DIST (BLOCK)
REAL C1(N)  DIST (BLOCK)  NOTRANSFER

REAL D1(100)  DIST ( =A1)
INTEGER E1(500)  DIST (BLOCK)
```

Here, array $A1$ inherits the distribution of array A; it is not copied. Upon entry to the subroutine, array B must be redistributed: since B is static, the original distribution must be restored when the subroutine is exited. The dynamic array C is the actual argument of the (static) formal parameter $C1$: if C has does not have a block distribution, it is redistributed on entry but no actual values are transferred. There is no redistribution on exit, so C will subsequently have a block distribution. The local parameter $D1$ is distributed in the same way as the formal parameter $A1$, and will thus have a cyclic distribution in this incarnation of the subroutine. Local array $E1$, in contrast, will always have a block distribution.

2.4 Accessing Distributions

The function **DISTRIBUTION**, used for alignment earlier, can also be used to inquire about the distribution of an array during the execution of the program. This may be used, for example, to determine the current distribution of a dynamically distributed array or that of a formal parameter which may inherit several different distributions as described in the last subsection. In general the values of two distributions can be compared, using the new relational operator "==" as shown below:

```
IF DISTRIBUTION(A) == ( BLOCK, CYCLIC(2)) THEN
  ...
ENDIF
```

The operator "==" can also be used for pattern matching as shown here

```
IF DISTRIBUTION(A) == ( BLOCK, *) THEN
  ...
ENDIF
```

where the match is successful *iff* the distribution of A consists of two components and the evaluation of the first component yields block distribution. The * denotes a "don't care" condition, i.e, in the above example, (**BLOCK**, **BLOCK**), (**BLOCK**, :) and (**BLOCK**, **CYCLIC(2)**) would match while (**CYCLIC**, **BLOCK**) and (**BLOCK**, **BLOCK**, **BLOCK**) would not match.

Finally, pattern matching can be combined with a side effect, s shown in the code fragment below:

```
IF DISTRIBUTION(A) == ( BLOCK, CYCLIC(?K)) THEN
  ...
ENDIF
```

Here, the match is successful *iff* the distribution of A yields (**BLOCK**,**CYCLIC**(L)), where L may be any integer number greater than 0. In addition, the value L of the block length is assigned to the variable K.

The language also provides a distribution case statement, the **SELECT DCASE** statement, which can be used to execute different pieces of code based on the distribution of an array variable. The **SELECT DCASE** statement, as shown below, is modeled on the FORTRAN-90 case construct.

```
REAL A(100) DYNAMIC ( BLOCK )
  ...
SELECT DCASE (=A)
   CASE ( BLOCK)
     ...
   CASE ( CYCLIC(?K))
     ...
   CASE ( DEFAULT)
     ...
END SELECT
```

The different code segments can, thus, be written (and optimized) based on the actual distribution of A.

2.5 Advanced Features

In the above subsections, we have provided an overview of the basic features of Vienna Fortran. A large percentage of scientific codes can be expressed using these constructs for efficient mapping onto distributed memory architectures. However, the full language provides more extensive and general mechanisms for situations where the basic features may not be sufficient.

In particular, the extended language, as described in [27], allows a more general mapping of data arrays onto arbitrary subsets of processors. For example, skewed distributions cannot be described based on the above set of features, but may be specified in the full language. It is also possible to mix and match distribution and replication such that a data array may be distributed along one dimension of the processor array while being replicated across another dimension.

In the extended language, the user can specify general alignment functions. This enables the precise specification of a mapping between the index sets of two arrays, so that even complex alignments may be described.

Other features which have not been described here but are part of Vienna Fortran include parallel loops, *on clauses* for mapping of code to processors, and input/output constructs for efficient use of secondary storage.

3 Examples

In this section, we show how the basic features described in the last section can be used to express scientific algorithms. In particular, we present three examples: Gaussian Elimination, ADI iteration, and a sweep over an unstructured mesh. These examples demonstrate the flexibility and versatility of Vienna Fortran.

3.1 Gaussian Elimination

The Gaussian elimination algorithm is a frequently used method to solve a set of linear equations. It has been studied extensively and optimized forms of the algorithm are included in some of the major numerical libraries. Figures 1, 2, and 3, present a version of the algorithm expressed in Vienna Fortran. The code reproduced here has not been written as a library routine, but is a complete program to find the solution to a set of equations. The matrix of coefficients for the set of equations to be solved, is contained in the array A while B is the right hand side. Performance studies of this algorithm on various parallel machines have indicated that a cyclic column distribution for the matrix A frequently leads to a better overall performance than a block or cyclic row distribution, and hence is often the preferred choice for its distribution (although a two-dimensional processor array and a cyclic distribution in both dimensions of A may be superior in some cases (cf. [24])).

Hence, as shown in Figure 1, the second dimension of A is cyclically distributed across the processors available at load time. Note that the processor declaration is, in this case, optional since this is also the default processor structure. The array B is distributed by aligning it with the second dimension of array A; this has the effect of distributing the elements of B in a round-robin fashion to the processors. The other arrays in the program have the same distribution, and hence are aligned with B. We could equally well have aligned them with the second dimension of A or specified a cyclic distribution directly. An advantage of the strategy used here is that, if we want to test the behavior of this algorithm under different distributions, we need to modify at most the distribution annotations for arrays A and B. The alignment of the other arrays with B do not need to be changed.

The program starts by reading in the arrays A and B from a conventional formatted files in the normal manner. All standard FORTRAN 77 file operations are supported by Vienna Fortran. However, the language also supports special concurrent file operations to open close, read, write and manipulate concurrent files. In this program we want to store the results in a concurrent file which must thus be opened by a **COPEN** statement. This statement takes the same arguments as the FORTRAN 77 **OPEN** statement, but it may be used to open existing files only if they were written with the corresponding concurrent write statement **CWRITE**. The concurrent file containing the program's results may be subsequently read in by another program using the **CREAD** statement. The specification **SYSTEM** used here indicates that the array is stored in the file system using a default distribution (which may be different from the one used in the program). Full details of the concurrent file operations can be found in [27].

The first subroutine *FGAUSD*, shown in Figure 2, has the task of decomposing the matrix A. We have chosen to modify the sequential algorithm by expanding the temporary variable used into an array *TEMP*; thus each processor has a local variable for the local columns of A, eliminating unnecessary communication. Some compilers will be able to recognize that this is being used as a local variable and perform this transformation automatically. The DO-loop with loop variable J can be executed in parallel in all iterations.

We do not want to redistribute the arrays in the subroutine, and specify this by using **DIST(*)**. We could have annotated each of the declarations with **DIST(*)** also. However, the alignments given explicitly are equivalent to the distributions in the main program, so no redistribution takes place. If a subroutine is separately compiled, then it is advantageous to explicitly specify any alignments which are to hold, as we have done here, even if the user knows that redistribution will not take place.

The singularity test in the main program uses the function *ANY*, which returns the value **.TRUE.** if any of the elements of its argument are true. We do not reproduce *ANY* here; it is an intrinsic function in Fortran 90. If no singularities are found, execution proceeds with a call to the subroutine *FGAUSS*, shown in Figure 3, where the solution step is performed. Here too, all arrays are used in their original distribution.

Note that only a few changes were made to the sequential program to obtain the above parallel program, the major issue being the specification of data distribution. Thus, it is easy to experiment with different distributions by just changing the declarations and recompiling.

Even though the subroutines inherit the distributions of the arguments, the presumption that the array A is distributed only in the second dimension is built into the code. This assumption may not be appropriate if the algorithm is written as a library routine, rather than a subroutine in a user program. By utilizing the intrinsic distribution query

```
      PROGRAM Gauss

      PARAMETER (N = 4000)
      PROCESSOR (P)

      REAL A(N,N)  DIST ( :,  CYCLIC )
      REAL B(N), TEMP(N)   DIST(=(A.2))
      INTEGER IPIVOT(N)   DIST ( =B)
      LOGICAL SING(N)     DIST (=B)

      COPEN( UNIT = 6, FILE = '/CFS/MM/GAUSS/SOL')
      OPEN( UNIT = 7,  FILE = '/USR/MM/GAUSS/MAT')

C     Read data from conventional files
      READ(7,2100) ( (A(I,J), J = 1,N), I = 1,N))
      READ(7,2100) ( B(I), I = 1,N)

      DO 10 I = 1, N
10       SING(I) =  .FALSE.

C     Perform matrix decomposition
      CALL FGAUSD(N,A,IPIVOT, SING, TEMP)

C     Test for singularity; perform solution step if matrix is not singular
      IF ( ANY(SING) ) THEN
         PRINT 2000
      ELSE
         CALL FGAUSS(N,A,IPIVOT,B, TEMP)
C        Write solution to concurrent file
         CWRITE(6, SYSTEM) B
      ENDIF

2000  FORMAT(22H SINGULARITY IN MATRIX)
2100  FORMAT( F8.3 )
      STOP
      END
```

Figure 1: Program for Gaussian Elimination

```
      SUBROUTINE FGAUSD(N,A,IPIVOT,SING,TEMP)

C     Distributions are inherited from the calling routine
      REAL A(N,N)           DIST(*)
      REAL TEMP(N)          DIST(=(A.2))
      INTEGER IPIVOT(N)     DIST(=(A.2))
      LOGICAL SING(N)       DIST(=(A.2))

      DO 30 K = 1, N-1

C        Find K'th pivot index, store in IPIVOT(K)
         IPIVOT(K) = 0
         DO 40 I = K+1, N
            IF (A(I,K) .GT. A(IPIVOT(K),K)  IPIVOT(K) = I
40       CONTINUE

         TEMP(K) =  A(IPIVOT(K), K)
         IF (TEMP(K) .EQ. 0.0) GOTO 200
         A(IPIVOT(K),K) = A(K,K)
         A(K,K) = TEMP(K)

C        Find scaling factors
         TEMP(K) = -1.0 / A(K,K)
         DO 50 I = K+1, N
50          A(I,K) = TEMP(K) * A(I,K)

         DO 60 J = K+1, N
            TEMP(J) = A(IPIVOT(K),J)
            A(IPIVOT(K),J) = A(K,J)
            A(K,J) = TEMP(J)
            DO 60 I = K+1, N
               A(I,J) = A(I,J) + A(IPIVOT(K), J) * A(I,K)
60       CONTINUE

30    CONTINUE
      GOTO 300
200   SING(K) = .TRUE.
300   IPIVOT(N) = N

      RETURN
      END
```

Figure 2: Subroutine for matrix decomposition

```
      SUBROUTINE FGAUSS(N,A,B,IPIVOT,TEMP)

      REAL A(N,N)         DIST(*)
      REAL B(N)           DIST(=(A.2))
      REAL TEMP(N)        DIST(=(A.2))
      INTEGER IPIVOT(N)   DIST(=(A.2))

      DO 10 K = 1, N-1
         TEMP(K) = B(IPIVOT(K))
         B(IPIVOT(K)) = B(K)
         B(K) = TEMP(K)
         DO 10 I = K+1, N
            B(I) = B(I) + TEMP(K) * A(I,K)
10    CONTINUE

      DO 20 K = N, 1
         B(K) = B(K) / A(K,K)
         DO 20 I = 1, K-1
            B(I) = B(I) - B(K) * A(I,K)
20    CONTINUE

      RETURN
      END
```

Figure 3: Subroutine for the solution step of Gaussian Elimination

functions and the **SELECT DCASE** statement, the routines can be transformed into a version which can accept a wide range of distributions. For example, the distribution of A may determine the most appropriate algorithm for obtaining the pivot element.

3.2 ADI Iteration

ADI (Alternating Direction Implicit) is a well known and effective method for solving partial differential equations in two or more dimensions [14]. It is widely used in computational fluid dynamics, and other areas of computational physics. The name ADI derives from the fact that "implicit" equations, usually tridiagonal systems, are solved in both the x and y directions at each step. In terms of data structure access, one step of the algorithm can be described as follows: an operation (a tridiagonal solve here) is performed independently on each x-line of the array followed by the same operation being performed, again independently, on each y-line of the array.

The code for such a step of the ADI algorithm is shown in Figure 4. Here, the arrays U and F, the current solution and the right hand sides respectively, are distributed such that the columns are blocked over the implicit one-dimensional array of processors, **$PL**.

```
      PARAMETER(NX = 100)
      PARAMETER(NY = 100)

      PROCESSORS (P)

      REAL U(NX, NY)  DIST ( :,  BLOCK)
      REAL F(NX, NY)  DIST ( :,  BLOCK)

      REAL V(NX, NY)  DYNAMIC  RANGE( (:,  BLOCK), ( BLOCK, :))
     &                            DIST (:,  BLOCK)

      CALL RESID( V, U, F, NX, NY)

C     Sweep over x-lines
      DO 10 J = 1, NY
         CALL TRIDIAG( V(:, J), NX)
10    CONTINUE

      DISTRIBUTE V :: ( BLOCK, : )

C     Sweep over y-lines
      DO 20 I = 1, NX
         CALL TRIDIAG( V(I, :), NY)
20    CONTINUE

      DO 30 J = 1, NY
         DO 30 I = 1, NX
            U(I, J) = V(I, J)
30    CONTINUE
```

Figure 4: An ADI iteration

The array V, used as a workarray, is declared to be dynamic with the *range attribute* specifying that the only distributions allowed are blocking by rows or columns. The first loop ranges over the columns (representing the x-lines), calling a subroutine *TRIDIAG* for each column of V while the second loop ranges over the rows (representing the y-lines). Here, the subroutine *TRIDIAG* is given a right hand side and overwrites it with the solution of a constant coefficient tridiagonal system.

In this version of the algorithm, the array V is dynamically redistributed in between the two loops; in the first loop it is blocked by columns while in the second it is blocked by rows. Thus, in each loop, we can employ a sequential tridiagonal since neither x-lines in the first loop nor the y-lines in the second loop cross processor boundaries. Note that the redistribution of the array is a "transpose" of the array with respect to the set of processors and requires each processor to exchange data with each of the other processors. Hence, all the communication in this version of the algorithm is contained in the redistribution while the tridiagonal solves run without interprocessor communication. The final assignment of the array V to the array U also induces communication similar to the "transpose" above since U and V are distributed in different dimensions.

The version of ADI here is only one of a number of ways of encoding the algorithm. For example, one could leave the array V in place and employ a parallel tridiagonal solver in the second loop. This would shift the interprocessor communication in the algorithm from the redistribution (and the final assignment) to the tridiagonal solvers. Similarly, the arrays could be blocked in both the dimensions and a parallel tridiagonal solver used for both the x- and the y-lines.

All versions of this algorithm are equally easy to express in Vienna Fortran. Moreover, it is a trivial matter to change the distributions, or to substitute the calls to the sequential tridiagonal solver used here by calls to a parallel tridiagonal solver. In marked contrast, such changes will typically induce weeks of reprogramming in a message-passing language.

3.3 Sweep over an Unstructured Mesh

Several scientific codes are characterized by the fact that information necessary for effective mapping of the data structures is not available until runtime. Examples of such codes include but are not limited to, particle-in-cell methods, sparse linear algebra, and PDE solvers using unstructured and/or adaptive meshes.

In this section, we consider a "relaxation" operation on an unstructured mesh. As shown in Figure 5, such meshes are generally represented using adjacency lists which denote the neighbors of a particular node of the mesh. Thus, *NNBR(i)* represents the number of neighbors of node i while *NBR(i, j)* represents the jth neighbor of node i. The relaxation operation, as shown here, consists of determining a new value of the array U at each point in the grid, based on some weighted average of its neighbors.

In the code, the primary array *NBR* is explicitly distributed via the **INDIRECT** distribution mechanism. The distribution of *NBR* is determined by the mapping array *MAP*, which is defined in the routine *PARTITION* based on the structure of the mesh. The secondary arrays, *NNBR*, *U*, *UTMP*, and *COEF*, are automatically distributed according on the alignments specified in the respective declarations. The *notransfer attribute* specifies that the values of the array *UTMP* need not be moved when the array is redistributed.

```
      PARAMETER(NNODE = 1000)
      PARAMETER(MAXNBR = 12)

      INTEGER NBR(NNODE, MAXNBR) DYNAMIC  DIST( BLOCK, :)
      INTEGER NNBR(NNODE) DYNAMIC  CONNECT (=(NBR.1))

      REAL U(NNODE)    DYNAMIC  CONNECT (=(NBR.1))
      REAL UTMP(NNODE) DYNAMIC  CONNECT (=(NBR.1))
      REAL COEF(NNODE, MAXNBR) DYNAMIC  CONNECT (NBR)

      INTEGER MAP(NNODE) DIST( BLOCK)

C     Define the array MAP to partition the mesh based on its structure.
      CALL PARTITION( NBR, NNBR, MAP )

C     Redistribute the array NBR based on the array MAP. Arrays NNBR, U, UTMP
C     & COEF are automatically redistributed. The values of UTMP are not transferred.
      DISTRIBUTE NBR :: ( INDIRECT(MAP), :)  NOTRANSFER(UTMP)

      DO 10 ITER = 1, K

C        Copy the values of U into UTMP
         DO 20 I = 1, NNODE
            UTMP(I) = U(I)
20       CONTINUE

C        Sweep over the mesh.
         DO 30 I = 1, NNODE

            T = 0.0
            DO 40 J = 1, NBR(I)
               T  = T + COEF(I, J) * UTMP( NBR(I, J) )
40          CONTINUE
            U(I) = U(I) + T

30       CONTINUE
10    CONTINUE
```

Figure 5: Relaxation sweep over an unstructured mesh

The rest of the code depicts K sweeps over the unstructured mesh. The important point here is that to access the values at neighboring nodes, the elements of the vector *UTMP* are indexed by the array *NBR*. Given that *NBR* is distributed at runtime, the compiler does not have enough information at compile-time to determine which of the references are non-local. In such situations, runtime techniques as developed in [10, 22] are needed to generate and exploit the communication pattern.

4 Related Work

The increasing importance of distributed memory multiprocessing computers and the difficulty of programming them has led to a considerable amount of research in several related areas.

A number of parallel programming languages have been proposed, both for use on specific machines and as general languages supporting some measure of portability (e.g. OCCAM [17]). Languages for coordinating individual threads of a parallel program, such as LINDA [1] and STRAND [4], have been introduced to enable functional parallelism. Most manufacturers have extended sequential languages, such as Fortran and C, with library routines to manage processes and communication.

We discuss below just a few of the developments in language design and compiler technology which are related to Vienna Fortran, in which many of the tasks usually associated with explicit user parallelization of code are expected to be performed by the compiler. Some of the efforts mentioned below are described in articles included in this book.

The concept of processor arrays and distributing data across such arrays was first introduced in the programming language BLAZE [11] in the context of non-uniform access time shared memory machines. The Kali programming language [15], for distributed memory machines, an outgrowth of the BLAZE effort, requires the specification of data distribution in much the same way that Vienna Fortran does. Both standard and user-defined distributions are permitted; a forall statement allow explicit user specification of parallel loops. The design of Kali has greatly influenced the development of Vienna Fortran.

Other languages have taken a similar approach: the language DINO [20, 21], for example, requires the user to specify a distribution of data to an environment, several of which may be mapped to one processor. Again, the programmer does not specify the communication explicitly, but must mark non-local accesses.

The programming language Fortran D [5], under development at Rice University, proposes a Fortran language extension in which the programmer specifies the distribution of data by aligning each array to a virtual array, known as a decomposition, and then specifying a distribution of the decomposition to a virtual machine. While the general use of alignment enables simple specification of some of the relationships between items of program data, we believe that it is often simpler and more natural to specify a direct mapping. We further believe that many problems will require more complete control over the way in which data elements are mapped to processors at run time.

Griswold et al. [7], take a different approach introducing the concept of *ensembles* to partition data, code and communication ports. The data is partitioned into sections, each section being mapped to a processor. This allows the data to scale with the number of processors as is the case with our system. However, the communication graph and the actual movement of data, as well as the code for each processor, has to be explicitly specified by the programmer.

The implementation of Vienna Fortran (and similar languages) requires a particularly sophisticated compilation system, which not only performs standard program analysis but also, in particular, analyzes the program's data dependences [28]. In general, a number of code transformations must be performed if the target code is to be efficient. The compiler must, in particular, insert all messages - optimizing their size and their position wherever possible.

The compilation system SUPERB (University of Vienna) [26] takes, in addition to a sequential Fortran program, a specification of the desired data distribution and converts the code to an equivalent program to run on a distributed memory machine, inserting the communication required and optimizing it where possible. The user is able to specify arbitrary block distributions. It can handle much of the functionality of Vienna Fortran with respect to static arrays.

The Kali compiler [10] was the first system to support both regular and irregular computations, using an inspector/executor strategy to handle indirectly distributed data. It produces code which is independent of the number of processors.

The MIMDizer [16] and ASPAR [9] (within the Express system) are two commercial systems which support the task of generating parallel code. The MIMDizer incorporates a good deal of program analysis, and permits the user to interactively select block and cyclic distributions for array dimensions. ASPAR performs relatively little analysis, and instead employs pattern-matching techniques to detect common stencils in the code, from which communications are generated.

Pandore [2] takes a C program annotated with a user-declared virtual machine and data distributions to produce code containing explicit communication. Compilers for several functional languages annotated with data distributions (Id Nouveau [19], Crystal [13] have also been developed which are targeted to distributed memory machines.

Quinn and Hatcher [8], and Reeves et al. [3, 18] compile languages based on SIMD semantics. These attempt to minimize the interprocessor synchronizations inherent in SIMD execution. The AL compiler [23], targeted to one-dimensional systolic arrays, distributes only one dimension of the arrays. Based on the one dimensional distribution, this compiler allocates the iterations to the cells of the systolic array in a way that minimizes inter-cell communications.

The PARTI primitives, a set of run time library routines to handle irregular computations, have been developed by Saltz and coworkers [22]. These primitives have been integrated into a compiler [25] and are also being implemented in the context of the FORTRAN D Programming environment being developed at Rice University. Similar strategies to preprocess DO loops at runtime to extract the communication pattern have also been developed within the context of the Kali language by Koelbel and Mehrotra [10, 12]. Explicit run-time generation of messages is also considered by [3, 13, 19], however, none of these groups save the extracted communication pattern to avoid recalculation.

5 Conclusions

In view of the increasing investment in distributed memory parallel computing systems, it is vital that the task of writing new programs and converting existing (sequential) code to these machines be greatly simplified. An important approach, which may substantially reduce the cost of developing codes, is to provide a set of language extensions for existing sequential languages (in particular, Fortran and C) that are not bound to any existing system but can be used across a wide range of architectures. These extensions should be as simple as possible, but they should also be broad enough to permit the expression of a wide variety of algorithms in a suitable manner. In particular, since the data distribution has a critical impact on the performance of the program at runtime, tight programmer control of the mapping of data to the system's processors must be possible.

We believe that Vienna Fortran is a significant step on the path towards a standard in this area.

Acknowledgments

The authors would like to thank Peter Brezany, Andreas Schwald, Joel Saltz, John Van Rosendale and the Fortran D group at Rice University for their helpful comments and discussions.

References

[1] S. Ahuja, N. Carriero, and D. Gelernter. Linda and friends. *IEEE Computer*, 19:26–34, August 1986.

[2] F. André, J.-L. Pazat, and H. Thomas. PANDORE: A system to manage data distribution. In *International Conference on Supercomputing*, pages 380–388, June 1990.

[3] A. L. Cheung and A. P. Reeves. The Paragon multicomputer environment: A first implementation. Technical Report EE-CEG-89-9, Cornell University, Ithaca, NY, July 1989.

[4] I. Foster and S. Taylor. *Strand: New Concepts in Parallel Programming.* Prentice-Hall, Englewood Cliffs, NJ, 1990.

[5] G. Fox, S. Hiranandani, K. Kennedy, C. Koelbel, U. Kremer, C. Tseng, and M. Wu. Fortran D language specification. Department of Computer Science Rice COMP TR90079, Rice University, March 1991.

[6] H. M. Gerndt. *Automatic Parallelization for Distributed-Memory Multiprocessing Systems.* PhD thesis, University of Bonn, December 1989.

[7] W. Griswold, G. Harrison, D. Notkin, and L. Snyder. Scalable abstractions for parallel programming. In *Proceedings of the Fifth Distributed Memory Computing Conference*, April 1990.

[8] P. Hatcher, A. Lapadula, R. Jones, M. Quinn, and J. Anderson. A production quality C* compiler for hypercube machines. In *3rd ACM SIGPLAN Symposium on Principles Practice of Parallel Programming*, pages 73–82, April 1991.

[9] K. Ikudome, G. Fox, A. Kolawa, and J. Flower. An automatic and symbolic parallelization system for distributed memory parallel computers. In *Proceedings of the The Fifth Distributed Memory Computing Conference*, pages 1105–1114, Charleston, SC, April 1990.

[10] C. Koelbel and P. Mehrotra. Compiling global name-space parallel loops for distributed execution. *IEEE Transactions on Parallel and Distributed Systems*, 2(4):440–451, October 1991.

[11] C. Koelbel, P. Mehrotra, and J. Van Rosendale. Semi-automatic process partitioning for parallel computation. *International Journal of Parallel Programminging*, 16(5):365–382, 1987.

[12] C. Koelbel, P. Mehrotra, and J. Van Rosendale. Supporting shared data structures on distributed memory architectures. In *2nd ACM SIGPLAN Symposium on Principles Practice of Parallel Programming*, pages 177–186, March 1990.

[13] J. Li and M. Chen. Generating explicit communication from shared-memory program references. In *Proceedings of Supercomputing '90*, pages 865–876, New York, NY, November 1990.

[14] G. I. Marchuk. *Methods of Numerical Mathematics.* Springer-Verlag, 1975.

[15] P. Mehrotra and J. Van Rosendale. Programming distributed memory architectures using Kali. In A. Nicolau, D. Gelernter, T. Gross, and D. Padua, editors, *Advances in Languages and Compilers for Parallel Processing*, pages 364–384. Pitman/MIT-Press, 1991.

[16] *MIMDizer User's Guide, Version 7.02.* Pacific Sierra Research Corporation, Placerville, CA., 1991.

[17] D. Pountain. *A Tutorial Introduction to Occam Programming.* Inmos, Colorado Springs, Co., 1986.

[18] A. P. Reeves. Paragon: a programming paradigm for multicomputer systems. Technical Report EE-CEG-89-3, Cornell University, January 1989.

[19] A. Rogers and K. Pingali. Process decomposition through locality of reference. In *Conference on Programming Language Design and Implementation*, pages 1–999. ACM SIGPLAN, June 1989.

[20] M. Rosing, R. W. Schnabel, and R. P. Weaver. Expressing complex parallel algorithms in DINO. In *Proceedings of the 4th Conference on Hypercubes, Concurrent Computers, and Applications*, pages 553–560, 1989.

[21] M. Rosing, R. W. Schnabel, and R. P. Weaver. The DINO parallel programming language. Technical Report CU-CS-457-90, University of Colorado, Boulder, CO, April 1990.

[22] J. Saltz, H. Berryman, and J. Wu. Runtime compilation for multiprocessors, to appear: Concurrency, Practice and Experience, 1991. Report 90-59, ICASE, 1990.

[23] P. S. Tseng. A systolic array programming language. In *Proceedings of the Fifth Distributed Memory Computing Conference*, pages 1125–1130, April 1990.

[24] E. Van de Velde. Experiments with multicomputer LU-decomposition. Technical Report Series CRPC-89-1, California Institute of Technology, April 1989.

[25] J. Wu, J. Saltz, S. Hiranandani, and H. Berryman. Runtime compilation methods for multicomputers. In *Proceedings of the 1991 International Conference on Parallel Processing*, pages 26–30, 1991.

[26] H. Zima, H. Bast, and M. Gerndt. Superb: A tool for semi-automatic MIMD/SIMD parallelization. *Parallel Computing*, 6:1–18, 1986.

[27] H. Zima, P. Brezany, B. Chapman, P. Mehrotra, and A. Schwald. Vienna Fortran – a language specification. In preparation, Austrian Center for Parallel Computation, University of Vienna, Vienna, Austria, 1991.

[28] H. Zima and B. Chapman. *Supercompilers for Parallel and Vector Computers.* ACM Press Frontier Series, Addison-Wesley, 1990.

Languages, Compilers and Run-Time Environments
for Distributed Memory Machines
J. Saltz and P. Mehrotra (Editors)

Compiler Parallelization of SIMPLE for a Distributed Memory Machine

Keshav Pingali[1] and Anne Rogers[2]

Department of Computer Science, Cornell University, Ithaca, New York

Abstract

In machines like the Intel iPSC/2 and the BBN Butterfly, local memory operations are much faster than inter-processor communication. When writing programs for these machines, programmers must worry about exploiting spatial locality of reference. This is tedious and reduces the level of abstraction at the which the programmer works. We have implemented a parallelizing compiler that shoulders much of that burden. Given a sequential, shared memory program and a specification of how data structures are to be mapped across the processors, our compiler will perform process decomposition to exploit locality of reference. In this paper, we discuss some experiments in parallelizing SIMPLE, a large scientific benchmark from Los Alamos, for the Intel iPSC/2.

1 Introduction

In distributed memory machines like the Intel iPSC/2 or the NCube, each process has its own address space and inter-process communication takes place through sending and receiving messages. Typically, passing messages is about 10 to 100 times slower than reads and writes out of local memory. For example, on the Intel iPSC/2, local memory access takes about a microsecond but passing a message can take 300 microseconds even if there is no congestion in the network. From the perspective of the programmer, this means that a process can access local data items (that is, data items in its own address space) very fast, but access to non-local data items, which must be choreographed through an exchange of messages, can be one or two orders of magnitude slower. Therefore, it is important to exploit locality of reference when programming distributed memory machines.

---

[1]Keshav Pingali was supported by an NSF Presidential Young Investigator award and by grants from the General Electric Corporation, the Digital Equipment Corporation, and the Math Sciences Institute, Cornell.

[2]Anne Rogers was supported by a DARPA Assistantship in Parallel Processing, Grant number 26974C. Her current address is: Department of Computer Science, Princeton University, 35 Olden Street, Princeton, New Jersey 08544-2087.

The solution adopted by manufacturers of distributed memory machines is to provide C or FORTRAN with message-passing extensions. The programmer writes CSP-like programs in which he has control over the distribution of data and code across processes. Unfortunately, this results in a loss of abstraction in programming. For example, consider a matrix X that is distributed across the processes by rows or columns to get effective parallel execution. To access element X[i,j], the programmer cannot just write X[i,j] as he could in C or FORTRAN on a sequential machine – if it is a local data element, he can read it directly, but if it is a non-local data item, he must put in calls for sending and receiving messages. This is a big burden on the programmer.

Can the problem of exploiting locality of reference be tackled by the compiler? Most work to date on compiling for multiprocessors focuses on parallelization of code using techniques like distributing loop iterations among processors. An example of this approach is the Camp system of Peir and Gajski[9]. Parallelization is achieved by distributing loop iterations among processors; synchronization required for loops with loop-carried dependencies is implemented through complex bit-masks at each word of memory. A similar approach is being pursued in the CEDAR system at Illinois. We characterize these approaches as 'code-driven' because they pay little attention to data partitioning – a processor may execute an iteration for which the data is not local.

We have implemented a system in which data partitioning plays a central role because it is used to drive the parallelization of code. The intuitive idea is the following. The programmer writes and debugs his program in a high-level language using standard high-level abstractions such as loops and arrays. Once this is accomplished, he specifies the *domain decomposition* – that is, how data structures are to be distributed across the multiprocessor. Given this data decomposition, the compiler performs process decomposition by analyzing the program and specializing it to the data that resides at each processor. Thus, our approach to process decomposition is 'data-driven' rather than 'program-driven'. It is important to understand that our work is orthogonal to earlier studies on so-called 'assignment problems' that have focused on mapping the topology of the problem onto the interconnection topology of the machine[1,2]. These studies assume a model in which the major factor in the cost of communication is the distance between the source and destination of messages. This model is valid in machines like the Intel iPSC/1 in which a message interrupts every processor on the way from the source to the destination (routing at intermediate nodes was performed by the processor). In more recent machines like the Intel iPSC/2, routing of messages at intermediate nodes is handled by communications co-processors. On the iPSC/2, the cost of start-up and receipt of the message is about 350 microseconds, while the time per hop is only about 10-20 microseconds. As mentioned earlier, the cost of a local access is less than a microsecond. Therefore, for any machine of reasonable size, there is a big difference between the cost of a local access and the cost of sending a message, but once a message has to be sent, the distance it has to travel is relatively unimportant. There are secondary considerations such as bandwidth – if messages have to travel less on an average, the probability of saturating the available network bandwidth when a lot of messages are sent simultaneously is reduced, but all things considered, we decided not to worry about mapping the topology of the problem to the topology of the machine.

In our opinion, the crux of the problem is to achieve locality of reference by matching data distribution to executable code in order to reduce the number of messages sent. However, concerns of locality must be balanced against the overall goal of achieving parallel execution - after all, a simple way to minimize the number of messages sent is to map all the code and data to a single processor! In fact, in some 'particle-pushing' codes, it is difficult to achieve locality of reference and load balancing simultaneously. These codes simulate the motion of charged particles in a grid. Each processor is assigned a region of the grid and it keeps track of physical variables associated with that region. In many of these problems, the particles tend to move together in a bunch. If each processor is assigned the work of pushing particles in its region, the computational load will be unbalanced; if the work of pushing particles is divided equally among all the processors, a processor may have to push a particle in a region residing on some other processor, which leads to loss of locality of reference. The code generation techniques we describe in this paper will work even for such programs but it is unclear to us that the resulting code will have good performance. In fact, some researchers have even questioned the suitability of parallel processing for such codes[13].

In the very large class of 'continuum' problems[6], on the other hand, locality of reference and load balancing are not usually in conflict. SIMPLE is an example of such a problem. In this paper, we discuss experiments in using our compiler to parallelize SIMPLE, a large hydrodynamics application, which is about a thousand lines of FORTRAN[4]. This program incorporates many of the computation and communication paradigms typical of scientific code; therefore, it is a popular benchmark. There is plenty of parallelism in SIMPLE, but it is not an 'embarrassingly parallel' application in the sense that there is a lot of movement of data during the execution of the problems. These aspects of SIMPLE are discussed in Section 2. A simple machine model is presented in Section 3. Section 4 is a discussion of various methods of distributing data across processors. In Section 5, we use parts of SIMPLE to explain our compiling techniques. Some preliminary results were reported in an earlier paper [12]; however, this paper is self-contained. We also report performance results on the Intel iPSC/2 (without vector boards). On a 32 processor Intel iPSC/2, we have obtained about 2MFlops on a 64x64 problem. In Section 6, we present a simple performance model to explain the observed performance. We conclude in Section 7 with a discussion of some extensions to our system.

2 What is SIMPLE?

SIMPLE is a program that simulates the behavior of fluid in a sphere. The fluid is in motion and the physical phenomena being simulated are the propagation of shock waves and conduction of heat through the fluid. By taking advantage of rotational symmetry and transforming co-ordinates appropriately, we can reformulate the problem over a mesh divided into rectangles. The rectangles are called *zones* and the corners are called *nodes*. Physical quantities such as position, velocity, temperature and pressure are associated with nodes and zones. The main computation of SIMPLE is a loop that involves the determination of these quantities over a number of discrete time steps where the size of each step is adjusted each time through the loop to guarantee stability.

For lack of space, we will not describe the details of the various computations in SIMPLE here, and refer the interested reader to an associated technical report [10]. However, it is important to understand the flow of data in the problem – that is, the various patterns of communication and computation that arise during the computation. These patterns and the phases of SIMPLE they arise in are summarized in Figure 1. In Figure 1(a), we see that the velocity associated with a node at any time step is computed using values at the previous time step from neighboring nodes and zones. This computation could be expressed using a DO-ALL style loop[14]. Figure 1(c) is similar, but the computation involves only node quantities. The heat conduction computation shown in Figure 1(d) is a recurrence since node values computed at a time step are used to compute other node values in the same time step. This computation could be expressed using a DO-ACROSS style loop[14]. Finally, Figure 1(b) shows a global accumulation that takes place during the computation of the size of the next time step. In this accumulation, a reduction operation (in this case, addition) is applied to values from all the zones to produce a single value that is used to determine the size of the next time step.

We started with an implementation of SIMPLE written in Id[7] by K. Ekanadham[5]. This program makes heavy use of higher-order functions. Since our compiler does not yet handle such functions, we replaced all higher-order functions by equivalent first-order code. Also, our compiler can handle only flat arrays. Since the coefficient matrices were implemented as matrices of matrices, we replaced them with flattened (two-dimensional) versions.

3 Machine Model

The examples in later sections assume a very simple machine model. There are n processors in the model, each of which executes one process.[3] Each process has its own address space and all communication is done using explicit message passing. Also, each process also has a set of mailboxes for receiving messages. The primitives for message passing are:

- **send**(Bi, Ai, Si, Pi) - The bytes in memory locations Ai to Ai + Si - 1 are sent by the process executing this command to mailbox Bi at process Pi. The sending process does not have to wait for the receiving process to get the message.
- **receive**(Bi, Ai, Si) - The process executing this command waits until it receives a message in box number Bi. The first Si bytes of the message are stored in locations Ai to Ai + Si - 1. While it is waiting, messages it may receive that are destined for other mailboxes are ignored temporarily.

[3]Strictly speaking, the iPSC/2 permits multiple processes to execute on a processor but we can take that into account simply by increasing the number of processors in our model. Hereafter, we use the words process and processor interchangeably.

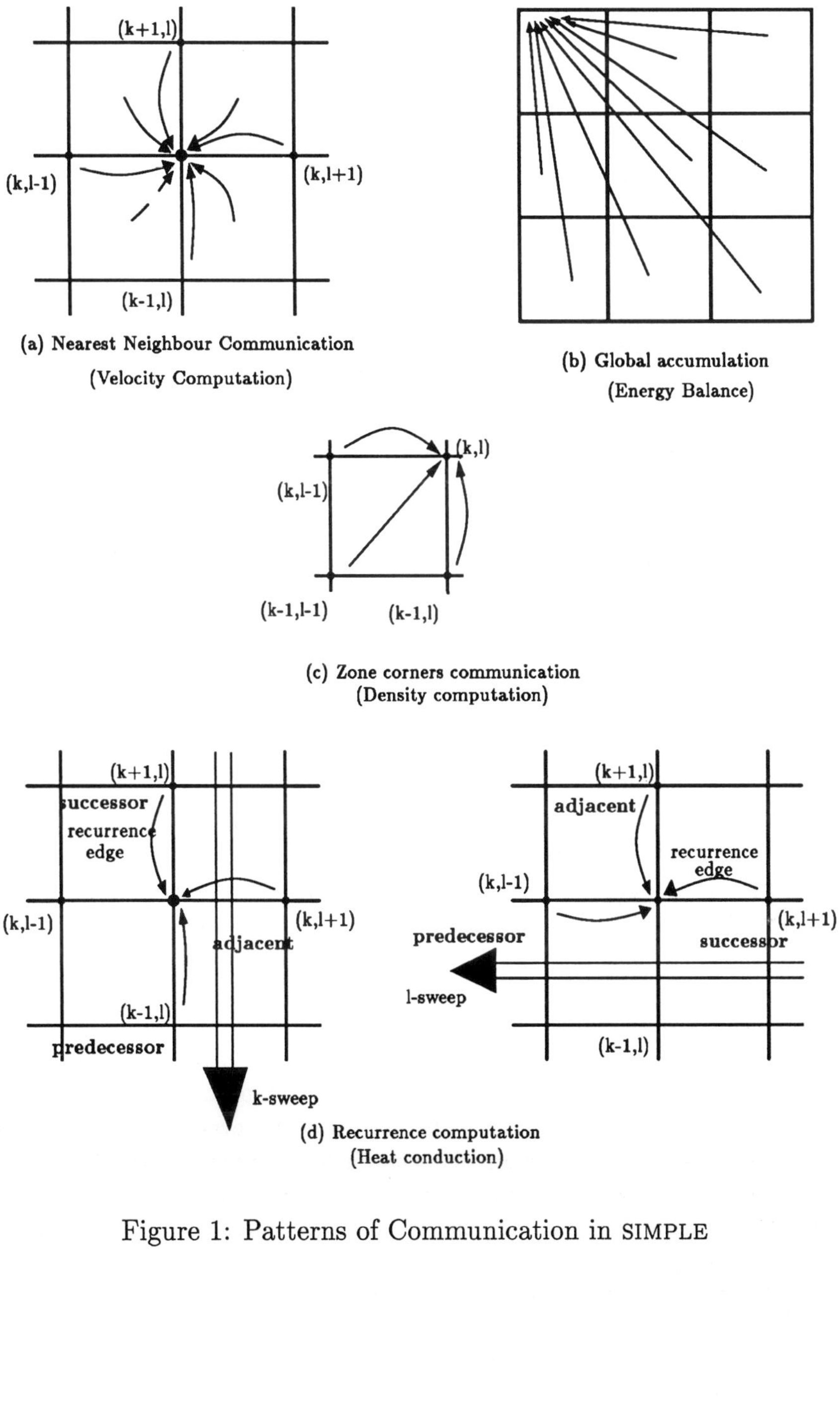

Figure 1: Patterns of Communication in SIMPLE

The order that messages arrive at a process is determined by the order in which they are sent but also on how they collide with other messages in transit. Mailbox numbers let the receiving process focus its attention on a message of a particular type from a particular process rather than having to look at the first message that comes along. Mailbox numbers also make it easier to reorder sends within a process. As long as two sends have either different destinations or the same destinations but different mailbox numbers, they may be reordered. Each textual reference in the program has a number associated with it and all communication that arises from a given reference is tagged with both the associated number and the process name. Therefore messages arising from different array references can always be reordered.

Long messages are automatically broken into packets by the underlying implementation. Packet reassembly is handled similarly. In most message passing systems sending one long message is less expensive than sending several small ones. We assume this in our model.

The examples in the next section are written in C. They were generated by our compiler and then cleaned-up to make them more readable. The loops have been unnormalized and the temporary variable names have been shortened. **Mynode()** is a system routine that returns the name of the executing process.

4 Data Distribution

The data distributions supported in our system are a compromise between generality and regularity. As we discuss in Section 5, we can support very general, irregular data distributions in the sense that our compiler can generate correct code regardless of how complex the program or the data distribution is. However, irregular data distributions are not amenable to compile time analysis and the performance of the generated code may leave much to be desired. A regular data distribution offers more opportunities for optimization. Two such distributions for SIMPLE are wrapped rows/columns and blocks.

Given P processes, a wrapped row distribution of an array would assign the rows of the array to processors in a round-robin way – thus, process 1 would get row 1, (P+1), (2P+1) etc. A wrapped column distribution is similar except that columns are distributed rather than rows. For a block distribution, the array is divided into P blocks and each process is assigned one block. Blocks need not have the same length in every dimension. For example, one possible block decomposition of a 100 by 100 array among 10 processes is to assign the first 10 rows to process 1, the next 10 rows to process 2 and so on. The matrices in SIMPLE are mapped into blocks with approximately the same number of blocks in each dimension.

5 Code Generation

The difficulty of code generation arises from the need to generate code even for programs that cannot be analyzed well by the compiler such as programs with complex array subscripts – after all, it is not acceptable for a compiler to reject a program simply

```
def Make_AB_North R_bar:realarray@block(32, 32)
                  Sigma:realarray@block(32, 32)
                  a:realarray@block(32, 32)
                  :void =
{ /* Fill in boundary elements */
  call set_boundary_zones A 0.0;
  { for l = 3 to 63 do
      { for k = 3 to 63 do
          d:real@SameAs(A, (k, l)) = Sigma[k,l] + R_bar[k-1, l] * (1 - A[k-1, l]);
          A[k, l] = R_bar[k,l]/d; } }
}
```

Figure 2: Make_AB_North from SIMPLE

because it is too complex! Just as vector compilers generate scalar code as a fall-back position, our compiler must be able to generate some code that is guaranteed to run correctly, if not at blinding speed, for any program. When we started this research, it was not immediately obvious that we would be able to do this. In the absence of a single address space, it is crucial for both the process that needs a data value and the process that owns that data value to know about each other so that communication can take place. This information may not be available at compile-time in programs that are hard to analyze. Our first code generation strategy, called *run-time resolution*, resolves these issues at run-time. Once we have such a fall-back position, we can improve on the quality of code for programs whose communication-computation patterns can be analyzed by the compiler.

In this section we first discuss *run-time resolution* which is a simple but fairly inefficient code generation strategy that is guaranteed to work for any program, no matter how complex. Next, we show how this code can be improved by *partial evaluation* at compile-time – the resulting code generation strategy is called *compile-time resolution.* We also point out some connections between this problem and the problem of code generation for languages with overloaded operators. Even though the results of compile-time resolution are superior to those of run-time resolution, there is still room for improvement. We discuss two extensions, *vectorization* of messages and *accumulation*, that are required to parallelize SIMPLE successfully. We motivate both the code generation schemes and the extensions with examples taken from SIMPLE.

5.1 Example

We use the procedure `Make_AB_North`, from the heat conduction phase of SIMPLE, to illustrate our methods (see Figure 2). Notice that all of the arrays are to be decomposed into four blocks of size 32 by 32. Three functions are associated with a block mapping: *BM* determines the owner of an array element from the index expressions of the reference, *BL* computes the offset into the local portion of an array from the index expressions of the reference, and *BA* allocates the local portion of an array.

5.2 Run-time Resolution

Run-time resolution produces one program that is executed by all processes. At run-time every process will examine each statement to determine its role in the computation. The principle that guides the assignment of work to processes is that the owner of a variable (or array reference) must participate in any computation that involves that variable. The owner is responsible for computing the variable's defining expression and for recording its value, as well as for communicating its value to any process that needs it. Conditionals, loops, and function calls are executed by all processes. Due to lack of space we have not included the run-time resolution code for our example.

5.3 Compile-time resolution

Run-time resolution generates inefficient code. Techniques similar to those used to resolve overloading in conventional compilers can be used to generate better code. When compiling languages like Lisp, an overloaded operator like + is usually compiled into a case statement that tests the type of the arguments and dispatches to the appropriate type specific addition routine. The naive code generated by this strategy can be improved considerably if the compiler knows the types of the arguments or the result (for example, through type declarations) since the case statement can be replaced by a dispatch to the relevant addition routine. This kind of code improvement through 'specialization' of generic code can be used profitably in our context as well. The code generated by run-time resolution is like generic code that can be specialized to each process by using the mapping information. This approach is called *compile-time resolution.*

When generating code for each process using compile-time resolution, the compiler examines each statement to determine the process's role in the evaluation of that statement. This is done in two stages. The compiler uses conventional abstract syntax trees as the internal representation of programs. In the first stage, the user's mapping information is propagated through the program's abstract syntax tree. In the second stage, this information is used to generate code. Each node of the abstract syntax tree has two attributes named *evaluators* and *participants.* The *evaluators* of a node in the abstract syntax tree is the set of processes that perform the operation defined by the node. The *participants* of a node, n, in the abstract syntax tree is the set of processes that must participate in the evaluation of some node in the subtree rooted at the node. For lack of space, we do not give the details of the determination of the evaluators and participants attributes. For the most part, these rules are quite straight-forward; the only complication is that the set of participants is used to determine the evaluators for some types of nodes, such as conditionals – the union of the participants of the then-branch and else-branch defines the evaluators for the boolean test in a conditional expression.

The information collected in the first phase is used to generate code. Given a process name and a tree node, the compiler tries to determine if the process is a member of the evaluators of the node. Three outcomes are possible: true, false, and inconclusive. True means that the process must perform the operation defined by the node. False means

```
Make_AB_North(R_bar, Sigma, a)
real_istructure A, Sigma, R_bar;

{ int k, l;

  double t29, t30, t31, t32, t44, t45,

  set_boundary_zones(A, 0.0) ;

  for ( l= 3; l<= 32; l= l+ 1)
      { double d;
        for ( k= 3; k<= 32; k= k+ 1)
          { t29 = Sigma[BL(k, l)];
            t30 = R_bar[BL(k-1, l)];
            t31 = A[BL(k-1, l)];
            d = t29 + t30 * (1 - t31);
            t32 = R_bar[BL(k, l)];
            A[BL(k, l)] = t32 / d);
          } ;
        k = 33;
        t44 = R_bar[BL(k-1, l)];
        send(13, &t44, sizeof(double ), BM(k, l));
        t45 = A[BL(k-1, l)];
        send(16, &t45, sizeof(double ), BM(k, l)); }
}
```

Figure 3: Compile-time resolution code for Make_AB_North for Process 0

it need not. Inconclusive means that run-time resolution must be applied because the compiler cannot analyze the mappings sufficiently. This evaluation will require techniques such as subscript analysis that are commonly used in vectorizing compilers [8]. The code generation phase produces code for each process by walking the annotated abstract syntax tree while applying this evaluation scheme at each node.

The code generated for our example for Process 0 using compile-time resolution is shown in Figure 3. Notice that the loops are restricted to those iterations in which Process 0 needs to be involved. Since Process 0 owns rows 1 to 32 and columns 1 to 32 of matrices `A`, `R_bar`, and `Sigma`, it owns the locations to be updated and all the values required for iterations $(3 \leq l \leq 32, 3 \leq k \leq 32)$. In addition, Process 0 owns two values that are needed for iteration 33 of the inner loop. To determine which iterations a given process must participate in, the set $\{i|f(i) = p \, for \, f \in evaluators\}$ is computed. Computing this inverse is nontrivial; the subset of the evaluators set that is equal to p for a given iteration, i, is associated with that iteration and is what determines the work done during that iteration. Also notice that, the code for Process 0 contains a call to `Set_boundary_zones`. The code for this function is not shown. It just fills in the boundary elements for the rows and columns that Process 0 owns.

For details concerning the how loops and procedure calls are handled and for all of the rules for computing evaluators and participants, we refer the interested reader to the dissertation of one of the authors[11].

5.4 Message Optimizations

Programmers carefully hand optimize their programs to decrease the cost of messages and increase parallelism. A compiler must be able to do the same kinds of optimizations to produce good code. We have implemented two of these optimizations in our compiler: *pipelining* and *vectorization* of messages. Message vectorization is crucial for generating good code for SIMPLE.

Using compile-time resolution, the send and receive commands for a non-local reference are inserted into the generated code where the value is needed. This is a fine place for the receive but a non-optimal place for the send. The receiving process can be delayed unnecessarily if the sending process has work to do between when the value is available and when the send is executed. A better scheme would execute the send as soon as the value is available. The optimization that moves the send to the earliest possible point in the generated code is called *pipelining.* We discuss the need for pipelining in detail in an earlier paper [12].

Vectorization combines messages with a similar source and destination into a single message to reduce overhead. Each message sent incurs a fixed overhead plus a cost per message byte. In most message passing systems the fixed overhead dominates, making it sensible to try to pack messages together. The compiler optimization to accomplish this is performed before code generation and may be thought of as *vectorization* of a read operation. Just as with any potentially vectorizable operation, the operands (in this case, the referenced array element) must be checked to ensure that there is no cycle of data dependencies within the loop. If no such cycle of dependencies exists, the read may be converted to a vector read. This in turn will be converted during code generation to block sends and receives.

The code in Figure 4 results from applying compile-time resolution augmented with vectorization to our example. Notice that the last row of the block of `R_bar` on Process 0 is packed into a vector and sent to Process 2 . Also notice that in the situation where Process 0 owns both `A[k, l]` and `R_bar[k-1, l]` the code is the same as the straight compile-time resolution code even though this reference arises from the same original reference as the values being sent.

5.5 Accumulation

The code generation methods presented above implement "do-across" style parallelism. To generate efficient code for all of SIMPLE, a programming paradigm known as *accumulation* or *global combine* is required. Accumulation is used to apply a commutative and associative operator (such as sum) to the elements of a matrix. Each process examines its local data to compute the local contribution and sends that value to a central

```
Make_AB_North(R_bar, Sigma, a)
real_istructure A, Sigma, R_bar;

{ int k, l, t4;

  double t29, t30, t31, t32, t45, T8[30]

  for ( t4= 3; t4 <= 32; t4 = t4+ 1)
    { t7= R_bar[BL(32, t4)];
      T8[VEC_SEND_Local(t4-3)] = t7; };
  send(13, T8, 30* sizeof(double), 2);

  for (l = 3; l<= 32; l = l+ 1)
      { double d;
        for (k = 3; k<= 32; k = k+ 1)
          { t29 = Sigma[BL(k, l)];
            t30 = R_bar[BL(k-1, l)];
            t31 = A[BL(k-1, l)];
            d = t29 + t30 * (1 - t31);
            t32 = R_bar[BL(k, l)];
            A[BL(k, l)] = t32 / d);
          };
        k – 33,
        t45 = A[BL(k-1, l)];
        send(16, &t45, sizeof(double ), BM(k, l)); }
}
```

Figure 4: Compile-time resolution augmented with Vectorization of Messages for Process 0

location where the final value is computed. The data distribution determines which process will examine a particular element of the matrix. Compile-time resolution has been augmented to handle accumulators efficiently.

5.6 Scatter-gather

The pressure/temperature/energy computations in SIMPLE use coefficient tables that are accessed through another table. This raises a subtle issue regarding the distribution of the coefficient tables. If a table is large in size, it may have to be distributed across the processes. If so, it will not be possible to predict precisely which processes will need access to which coefficients. This means that send/receive pairs cannot be programmed into the code and it is necessary to simulate shared memory. Since the tables are read-only, a second possibility is to give a copy of each table to each process. This is particularly useful when the tables are small, which is the case in SIMPLE (12x15). We chose this solution in our implementation.

A second possibility is to perform a gather phase in which processes send requests for the coefficients they want to appropriate processes and respond to requests from other processes for the coefficients they happen to own. It is necessary for processes to synchronize before entering and leaving the gather phase.

5.7 Discussion

We have presented two code generation methods. *Run-time resolution* produces inefficient code but guarantees that we can generate code for any program. *Compile-time resolution* uses partial evaluation to produce more efficient code. A natural question is, "Are there any places in SIMPLE where run-time resolution is needed?" The answer is no. The reason is that except in a few limited situations the array subscripts are very simple. Only the accesses to the coefficient tables in the pressure/temperature/energy computation are too complex for the compiler to analyze. Fortunately, these tables are small enough to place a copy on each process, which solves the problem.

The computation of the boundary elements is another issue that might cause concern. The program we started with separated the boundary element computations from the interior element computations. The result was more straight-forward inner loops. The quality of the input code definitely affects the quality of the generated code.

6 Results and Analysis

Carefully tuned, handwritten programs provide the best comparison for any parallelizing compiler. Unfortunately, we have been unable to locate a handwritten implementation of SIMPLE for the Intel iPSC/2. This is not surprising; decomposing SIMPLE by hand would be a tedious process. The next best alternative is to develop a model that estimates the behavior of a good handwritten program. In this section we present our experimental results, a model for a handwritten implementation, and a comparison of the two.

We ran a set of experiments using an implementation of one iteration of SIMPLE for a 64 by 64 grid. With the exception of the coefficient matrices, all of the matrices in the program were decomposed into roughly square blocks. Our compiler generates C code[4] for the Intel iPSC/2.

The graph in Figure 5 displays the timing results from our experiments. The implementation for the one process case was obtained by mapping of each matrix into a single block of size 64 by 64. The resulting program has no communication statements and looks like the original sequential program.

[4]The C programs were compiled using the -O option of the Greenhills C compiler.

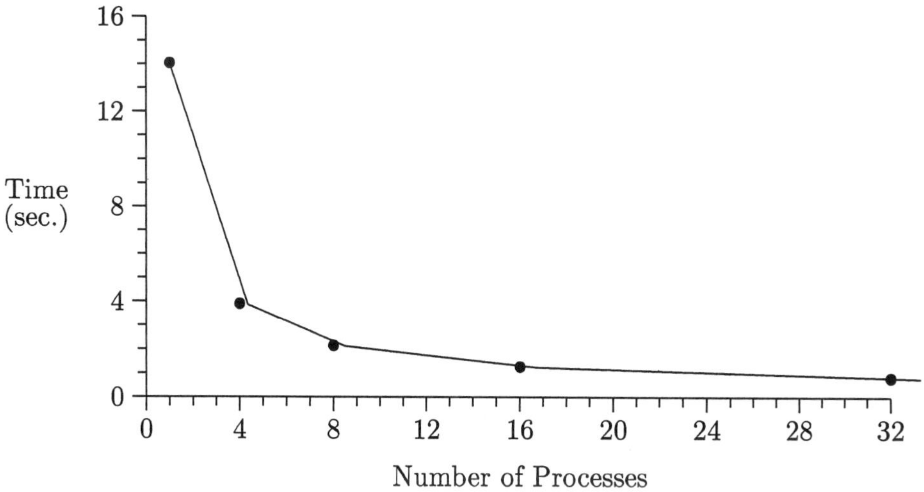

Figure 5: Running times for SIMPLE on a 64 by 64 grid

6.1 Model of a handwritten implementation

How do we model the total amount of work done by a parallel system? The total parallel time can be represented by the formula

$$TPT = \sum_{i=1}^{n} T^i_{comp} + \sum_{i=1}^{n} T^i_{msg} + \sum_{i=1}^{n} T^i_{system} + \sum_{i=1}^{n} T^i_{idle}$$

where T^i_{comp} is the computation time for the ith process, T^i_{msg} is the time spent by process i in sending/receiving messages, T^i_{system} is the time spent by process i doing system chores like paging and context switching, and T^i_{idle} is the time process i spends waiting for messages. Some of these quantities are difficult to obtain because of the primitive nature the time measurement tools on the iPSC/2. Our goal is to develop a model that estimates the running time of a hand-written program. With this goal in mind we can safely ignore the two parameters that are hardest to measure, namely system time and idle time. The resulting model is still valid being on the conservative side of less accurate.

For our particular problem, $\sum_{i=1}^{n} T^i_{comp}$ can be estimated by the number of floating point operations[5] necessary times the cost of an average floating point operation, $\sum_{i=1}^{n} T^i_{comp} = 1,552,883 * C$. About one third of the operations are multiplies, the rest are adds, compares etc. We estimate the cost of a floating point operation as $C = .33 * 8.52 + .66 * 6.64$. The operation costs used are the costs reported for a the multiplication/addition of two double length floating point numbers[3]. This estimate of the floating point work does not taken into account pipelining.

Communication overhead must be measured with respect to a particular mapping. To estimate this overhead, we counted the number of messages and the size of each

[5]The count of the number of floating point operations was obtained by Jamey Hicks using the MIT Gita dataflow simulator.

message in a four process system. The cost of a message of length k*4 bytes is defined by the following equation:

$$cost(k) = t_{startup} + k * t_{send}$$

For the iPSC/2, $t_{startup} = 350\mu s$ and $t_{send} = 0.8\mu s$ for message under 100 bytes and $t_{startup} = 660\mu s$ and $t_{send} = 1.44\mu s$ for longer messages[3]. From this we can extrapolate to estimate the communication cost for larger numbers of processes. Our four process estimate is $\Sigma_{i=1}^{n} T_{msg}^{i} = 207.305ms$. This estimate assumes that a value is sent from a one process to another process at most once and all the values from a row/column of a matrix are transmitted as one message (except in the sweep phases). Values from different arrays are assumed to be sent in separate messages.

System costs are not completely unmeasurable. We can measure the cost of allocating space for arrays. Many functions return arrays as results, so the matrices are stored on the heap instead of the stack. To reduce the cost of allocation, a large chunk of space is allocated at the beginning. Each individual array allocation requires only a few pointer operations. The allocation cost for a four block configuration is $482ms$ per process.

Once we have an estimate for the total work done in the system, it is easy to model parallel time and expected speed-up. The best possible situation would result in a perfect division of the work. Parallel time, PT, is therefore estimated as $PT = TPT/N$ where N is the number of processes. Speed-up is sequential time divided by parallel time:

$$speed - up = (1,552,883 * C + 1760)/PT$$

Sequential time is the cost of floating point operations plus the allocation cost (1760). The graph in Figure 6 displays three curves: perfect speed-up, the speed-up projected by the model, and our speed-up using the roughly square block decomposition.

6.2 Comparison of the Results

There is a substantial gap between the speed-up projected by the model and the speed-up obtained by the programs the compiler generates. Three factors account for the discrepancy. First, our programs send more messages than the projected number. We do not do interprocedural common subexpression elimination to determine when to combine sends of the same value from different procedures. Second, the model assumes that the workload is perfectly balanced. It is not, so all of the processes slow down to the wait for the one with the most work. The blocks on the perimeter have less work than internal blocks because in most cases the work associated with the boundaries is trivial. Also, the southern and western perimeter blocks have more work than the northern and eastern blocks because of the way nodes and zones fit into a matrix. The third factor comes from idle time introduced by the sweep phases in heat conduction. This is unavoidable and is not factored into the model.

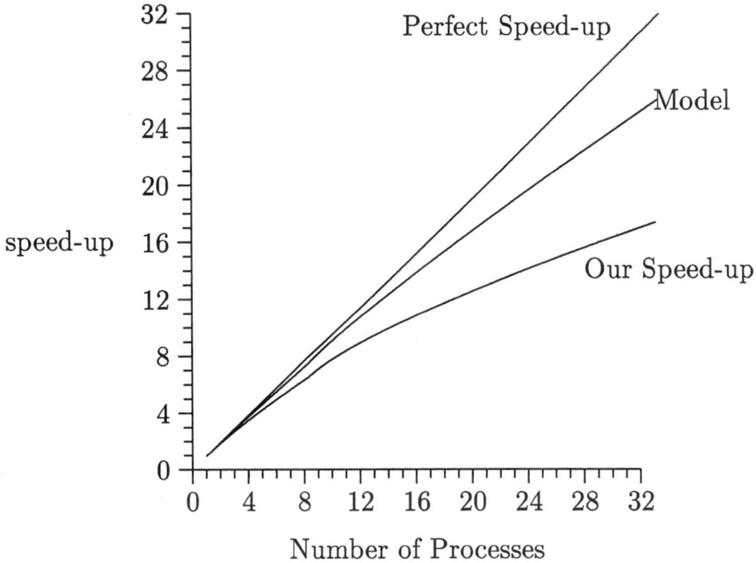

Figure 6: SIMPLE Speed-up

7 Summary

Our experiments with SIMPLE have been very beneficial. Our basic methods have been validated on a large program and we have gained insight into how to expand our system to generate better code. The paradigms that programmers employ by hand such as accumulation and scatter-gather are very useful. As we discussed, accumulation fits naturally into our scheme. We have not yet implemented scatter-gather as we do not yet understand where the cross-over point between replicating arrays and using scatter-gather lies.

We have implemented some techniques that reduce the number of messages in the system. Vectorization of messages is the most notable for SIMPLE. Reducing the number of messages sent still requires work. A handwritten program would send fewer messages than the code we currently generate. Programmers easily recognize that if a value is used by a process in several different procedures it need only be transmitted once. A compiler must perform interprocedural common subexpression recognition to be able to come the same conclusion.

As we have seen, the heat conduction routines throw a wrench into the nice regular pattern of most of SIMPLE. The amount of work done in this phase is small enough that we decided not to try to shuffle the data around to get better performance. However, it is not hard to imagine cases where the work load involved would be large enough that the cost of data movement would be worth the gain in efficiency. Efficient remapping routines need to be added to our system.

A number of other groups are taking approaches similar to ours. Other chapters in this volume describe the work of these groups.

Acknowledgements We would like to thank Kattamuri Ekanadham for the original Id version of SIMPLE, Jamey Hicks for running SIMPLE on Gita for us, and the Cornell Theory Center for use of the iPSC/2.

References

[1] F. Berman et al. Prep-P: a mapping preprocessor for CHiP architectures. In *Proceedings of the International Conference on Parallel Processing*, 1985.

[2] S. Bokhari. *Assignment Problems in Parallel and Distributed Computing.* Kluwer Academic Publishing, 1987.

[3] L. Bomans and D. Roose. Benchmarking the iPSC/2 hypercube multiprocessor. *Concurrency Practice and Experience*, 1(1), September 1989.

[4] W.P. Crowley, C.P. Hendrickson, and T.E. Rudy. The SIMPLE code. Technical Report UCID-17715, Lawrence Livermore Laboratory, 1978.

[5] K. Ekanadham and Arvind. SIMPLE Part I: An exercise in future scientific programming. Technical Report RC12686, IBM, April 1987.

[6] T. Hoshino. Invitation to the world of Pax. *Computer*, 19(5), May 1986.

[7] R. Nikhil, K. Pingali, and Arvind. Id Nouveau. Technical Report CSG Memo 265, MIT Laboratory for Computer Science, 1986.

[8] D. Padua and M. Wolfe. Advanced compiler optimizations for supercomputers. *Communications of the ACM*, 29(12), December 1986.

[9] J. Peir and D. Gajski. Towards computer-aided programming for multi-processors. *Parallel Algorithms and Architectures*, 1986.

[10] K. Pingali and A. Rogers. Compiler parallelization of SIMPLE for a distributed memory machine. Technical Report 90-1084, Department of Computer Science, Cornell University, 1990.

[11] A. Rogers. *Compiling for Locality of Reference.* PhD thesis, Cornell University, August 1990.

[12] A. Rogers and K. Pingali. Process decomposition through locality of reference. In *Proceedings of the SIGPLAN '89 Conference on programming language design and implementation*, 1989.

[13] H. Stone. *High-performance Computer Architecture.* Addison-Wesley, 1987.

[14] M. Wolfe. *Optimizing Supercompilers for Supercomputers.* Pitman Publishing, London, 1989.

Languages, Compilers and Run-Time Environments
for Distributed Memory Machines
J. Saltz and P. Mehrotra (Editors)

Applications of the "Phase Abstractions" for Portable and Scalable Parallel Programming

Lawrence Snyder

University of Washington, Department of Computer Science and Engineering, FR-35, Seattle, Washington 98195, USA

Abstract

Recently developed parallel programming abstractions are illustrated in a complete example by programming the Jacobi iterative approximation computation. The program, written in pseudocode, is designed to illustrate the way in which the new concepts can assist scaling and portability. The specific abstractions exhibited, collectively called the "phase abstractions," are the data, code and port ensembles and the XYZ programming levels.

1 Introduction

One possible explanation for the observed difficulty programmers encounter using the distributed (nonshared) memory parallel programming model is that there are few programming abstractions to support it. Shared memory parallel models can appropriate (with suitable generalization) most of the abstractions developed over the years for sequential computers since the memory model doesn't differ, i.e. both utilize a flat, uniform memory structure. But distributed memory models with their separate address spaces can only apply standard sequential language concepts within a single address space. Indeed, the only widely used programming abstractions — programming concepts directly supported by language constructs — are *send* and *receive* for messages. With such primitive language support, it is little wonder that the programming task is difficult.

New abstractions have recently been invented. For example, "data blocking" — declaring partitionings of arrays to aid in data allocation — was mentioned repeatedly in the workshop presentations and has appeared in recent papers [Koelbel *et al.* 90, Rosing *et al.* 90]. Data ensembles [Griswold *et al.* 90a] provide the same capability in a somewhat more general way, since they are not limited to arrays. Moreover data ensembles have been augmented with the companion concepts of code ensembles and port ensembles [Alverson *et al.* 90]. These latter three abstractions together with the XYZ programming levels [Snyder 90] have been claimed to be sufficient for writing scalable and portable parallel programs, making them possible candidates for language constructs for distributed memory programming languages.

Like the concept of "blocking," which is independent of the specific syntactic form used to express it in any particular programming language, the ensemble and XYZ abstractions are also semantic ideas not bound to a particular syntactic form. This complicates illustrating them and in the cited papers it has only been possible to give program fragments as illustration. A fully worked example has not previously been presented.

In this paper a program is developed to illustrate the ensemble and XYZ abstractions. The example will provide the basis for discussing important features of the abstractions. The emphasis is on illustrating the scaling capabilities of the abstractions, demonstrating the details of their use and showing how they interact. This paper is self-contained in that all needed concepts are reviewed, though consulting the earlier papers [Griswold *et al.* 90a, Alverson *et al.* 90] will give the rationale, the general formulation of the concepts, and more diverse, though less complete, examples.

2 Preliminaries

This section defines the relevant abstractions. Readers familiar with the data, code and port ensemble concepts and the XYZ programming levels may choose to skip this section.

XYZ Programming Levels. The XYZ classification of parallel programming imposes a structure on parallel computations built from a collection of processes [Griswold *et al.* 90a, Snyder 90]. The levels are, from lowest to highest, the process level, the phase level and the problem level, but since these terms all begin with "p," the X, Y and Z letters have been assigned arbitrarily. Define

- X level (process) — the composition of instructions to form processes,
- Y level (phase) — the parallel composition of processes to form phases,
- Z level (problem) — the composition of phases to solve problems.

Thus, a user's problem is solved by executing a series of parallel phases which are each composed of processes.

Processes are local code that execute in their own address space, sharing data and communicating with other processes using the ensembles mechanisms described below.

A phase corresponds to our intuitive notion of a parallel algorithm. For example, the FFT is a parallel algorithm and hence a phase. It is composed of simple processes (X level components) performing a few scalar instructions and it is a common component of solving user problems (Z level). A phase is characterized by a graph. The graph's vertices are the processes and its edges indicate with which other processes (adjacencies) it communicates. The characteristic graph of the FFT is the butterfly.

The problem level expresses the overall logic of the computation by controlling the invocation of the phases. With the details of the constituent routines encapsulated at the lower levels, i.e. processes and phases, Z should be viewed as the main programming level.

The critical point about the XYZ classification is that a phase (Y level) expresses scalable parallelism in the computation. Additional opportunities for concurrency might exist: Instructions within a process might be executed simultaneously (X level concurrency) or phases within a problem definition might be executed simultaneously (Z level concurrency), but the phase captures the parallelism that defines grain size and largely determines efficiency.

At least a portion of this classification is visible in many programming languages. For example, processes are common to most parallel languages and a means of composing these together into a coherent unit of parallel computation, a phase, is also commonly available: DINO is a distributed memory SPMD example [Rosing *et al.* 90] of X and Y level language constructs, and Poker is a distributed memory MIMD example [Snyder 84]. Poker also exhibits the Z level in its "script" facility. Schedule [Dongarra & Sorensen 87] can be considered a Z language to run BLAS phases if each basic linear algebra subroutine is internally parallel. The controller code for SIMD languages is Z level and the simultaneous execution of the data parallel processes make de facto phases.

That the XYZ levels are visible in parallel languages may be less important than the fact that they are visible in problem solutions. Indeed, parallelism profiles of SIMPLE's data flow execution [Culler & Arvind 88] show the periodic bursts (controlled by Z level logic) of the concurrent activity (Y level) of executing the (trivial process) threads.

Ensembles. Ensembles are used to define phases. An ensemble is a set of names, S, with a partitioning $\pi(S)$ describing entities that are logically related, but physically separated [Griswold *et al.* 90a, Alverson *et al.* 90]. The logical relation is given by the set's structure and the separation is given by the partitioning. The partitions are called *sections* and it is often easier to define π by assigning elements of S to sections than vice versa, i.e. it is easier to specify π^{-1}.

Three kinds of ensembles have been identified as being useful for parallel programming: A *data ensemble* is a data structure with a partitioning; the names of the data structure's elements form the set S and the data structure itself defines the logical relationships. (Notice that the data structure need not be an array.) A *code ensemble* is a set of process instances with a partitioning; in the following there will be no assumed structure among the processes, since we will be simplifying to only one (autonomous) process instance per section, but in general the structure captures control dependence. A *port ensemble* is a set of port names with a partitioning; the structure of the ports is given by a communication graph, corresponding to the graph mentioned in the "Y level" discussion above. The code and port ensembles are closely related, as will be seen in the example below.

A phase is composed of one or more data ensembles, a code ensemble, a port ensemble and the (communication) graph. The data ensemble's partitioning allocates the (global) data structure to individual sections, the code ensemble assigns to each section a process instance, the port ensemble assigns to each section port names and the graph interconnects the ports. Thus, each section has code, data and communication channels defined, implementing a process for a single address space. Collectively these processes form a parallel algorithm.

Concept of a Parallel Program. The preceding concepts are sufficient to structure a parallel program.

The computation as given by a (Z level) program whose primitive operations are either phase invocations or "simple computations" needed to control phase invocation. Phases, generally invoked in sequence, cause the execution of a parallel computation. There can be barrier synchronization after each phase execution or not depending on the programmer's intention. If there is no barrier synchronization, then when the process executing in section S of a phase completes, the process assigned to section S of the next

```
begin
/*-------DEFINE PROCESSES (X LEVEL)------*/
   define process P1() begin ... end;
   ...
   define process Pm() begin ... end;
/*-------DECLARE Global Data-------------*/
   declare global data A, B, ... ;
/*-------DEFINE PHASES (Y LEVEL)---------*/
   define phase Q1 = d.ensemble+c.ensemble+p.ensemble+graph;
   ...
   define phase Qn = d.ensemble+c.ensemble+p.ensemble+graph;
/*-------DEFINE PROBLEM (Z LEVEL)--------*/
      begin declare local data a, b, ... ;
         Q1;
         b := Q2;
         while ~b do {
            Q3(a);
            if a>0 then Q4;
            Q5;
            b := Q2;}
         Q6;
   end;
end.
```

Figure 1: Schematic structure of a parallel program.

phase immediately begins executing, independent of the execution progress of the other processes. These two cases will be illustrated in Section 7.

Structurally, the program begins with process definitions followed by the global data structure declarations. Refer to Figure 1. These could appear in either order since one does not depend on the other. Both constituents are needed to define the ensembles, which in turn are needed to define the phases. Once the phases are defined, the body of the problem solution can be defined.

The logical machine model on which the program runs is the "CTA type architecture" [Snyder 86]. This is an idealized nonshared memory machine with an unspecified, but sparse, communication structure and a global controller. Notice that the features of the CTA type architecture are implementable on all current MIMD machines, whether shared or nonshared memory.

See the references [Griswold *et al.* 90a, Alverson *et al.* 90, Snyder 86] for further discussion of all of these topics.

3 Jacobi Iteration Example

The Jacobi iterative method for solving Laplace's equation on a rectangle assumes an $m \times n$ rectangular array A and proceeds in a series of steps, recomputing each point A_{ij} as the average of its four neighbors,

$$A_{ij} = (A_{i-1j}+A_{ij+1}+A_{ij-1}+A_{i+1j})/4.0$$

until the absolute change between two steps for any point is less than a tolerance, epsilon.

The Jacobi iteration is a very simple parallel computation and in using it we risk making too much and too little of the concepts: It may be that this inherently simple code will seem unnecessarily complex by using the abstractions and it may be that important benefits for large computations will not be exposed. The first concern, though perhaps correct, misses the point that the abstractions, without adding more complexity for larger problems, provide a method of structuring them that is not presently available. The second concern, though perhaps also correct, will be addressed in Section 7.

The problem will be solved by defining an iteration phase (`JI`) to compute a step and a convergence phase (`FindMax`) to find the largest change over the whole array. These two phases will be invoked alternately. The cycle will end when the largest change is less than epsilon.

The computation will be defined bottom-up in order to avoid explaining so many forward references. The program components are as follows:

- Process `Approx`, used by the iteration phase, `JI` [2]
- Process `Max`, used by the convergence phase, `FindMax` [3].
- Global data definition, `A` and `Diff` [4].
- Phase `JI` definition, for computing the iteration step [7].
- Phase `FindMax` definition, for computing convergence [9].
- Program body with Z level code [10].

The numbers in brackets refer to the figures illustrating the component's pseudocode text.

4 Specification of the Processes, Level X

The process definition is essentially a local program with interfaces to two kinds of nonlocal information: globally defined data, accessed through data ensembles, and information computed in other processes, accessed through port ensembles. Conceptually, the data ensembles permit processes to share data over multiple phase invocations while the port ensembles are used for data exchange within a phase invocation.

Approx Code. The process, `Approx`, computes new approximation values for a subarray of the global data matrix, `A`. It is parameterized by `a` and `b`, the number of rows and columns, respectively, of the subarray. This region of `A` will be locally referred to as `LocA`. In addition, a local variable, `LocDiff`, will accumulate the maximum difference between elements of a consecutive pair of iterations over all elements of `LocA`. Since `LocDiff` is input to the `FindMax` phase, it must be bound to an element of a data ensemble, making it a parameter to the Approx process. The pseudocode

```
process Approx(LocA[1:a,1:b], LocDiff);
```

specifies the preamble of the process. The values of a and b are attributes of the LocA parameter and are bound when its actual value becomes available.

Because of the four point stencil, computing the approximation of the edge elements of LocA will require references beyond the edge of the local array. These elements will be read from the appropriate adjacent processes and stored locally. To simplify referencing them in the core of the computation, it is convenient if they are stored in their logical position "around the perimeter" of LocA. Accordingly, the local declaration for LocA is "one element larger along each edge"

```
float array LocA[0:a+1, 0:b+1]; float LocDiff;
```

permitting the same reference pattern to apply at the edges as is used in the center.

The next task is to declare the port names. These will be conveniently named N, E, W and S, mnemonic for north, east, west and south, the directions of the required data exchange relative to the LocA subarray. The declaration specifies type information as well as how the port will be used. The pseudocode

```
float array ports (r, w) N, E, W, S;
```

defines the ports to be used for both reading (r) and writing (w). Later (at phase definition) the ports of each process will be bound either to another process' ports or a value derivative, as explained later.

Having completed the preamble for the process, local data structures can be declared and initialized. The specification

```
begin
  int i,j; float temp;
  LocDiff := SmallestPositive;
```

defines the variables and sets LocDiff to the least floating point value greater than zero.

The computational portion of Approx exchanges edge values with its neighbors via the ports, computes a new value for each point as an average of its neighbors, and accumulates the maximum amount of change between any corresponding new and old value.

The data exchange is performed in two parts, sending

```
N <- LocA[1,1:b]; E <- LocA[1:a,b];
W <- LocA[1:a,1]; S <- LocA[a,1:b];
```

where the port name appears on the left side of the transmit arrow (<-), followed by receiving

```
LocA[0,1:b] <- N; LocA[1:a,b+1] <- E;
LocA[1:a,0] <- W; LocA[a+1,1:b] <- S;
```

where the port name appears on the right. (The "colon notation" expresses an index range.) The transmit arrow has asynchronous data driven semantics. That is, sends are transmitted immediately and buffered at their destination (with flow control) and receives either fetch the buffered items in order of arrival or block on an empty buffer.

Computing the new values and determining the difference between new and old values is performed in a doubly nested loop,

```
for i := 1 to a do
  for j := 1 to b do
    begin
    temp := 0.25*(LocA[0,j]+LocA[i,j+1]+LocA[i,j-1]+LocA[i+1,j]);
    LocDiff := max(LocDiff, abs(LocA[i,j]-temp));
    LocA[0,j]:=LocA[i,j];
    LocA[i,j] := temp;
    end;
```

completing the phase definition. Notice the use of the top row of LocA as a temporary. The program without intervening text is shown in Figure 2.

```
process Approx(LocA[1:a,1:b], LocDiff);
float array LocA[0:a+1, 0:b+1]; float LocDiff;
float array ports (r, w) N, E, W, S;
begin
  int i,j; float temp;
  LocDiff := SmallestPositive;
  N <- LocA[1,1:b];     E <- LocA[1:a,b];
  W <- LocA[1:a,1];     S <- LocA[a,1:b];
  LocA[0,1:b] <- N;     LocA[1:a,b+1] <- E;
  LocA[1:a,0] <- W;   LocA[a+1,1:b] <- S;
  for i := 1 to a do
    for j := 1 to b do
      begin
      temp := 0.25*(LocA[0,j]+LocA[i,j+1]+LocA[i,j-1]+LocA[i+1,j]);
      LocDiff := max(LocDiff, abs(LocA[i,j]-temp));
      LocA[0,j]:=LocA[i,j];
      LocA[i,j] := temp;
      end;
end.
```

Figure 2: Specification of the Approx process.

Max Code. Finding the maximum of an ensemble of values is likely to be an operation supported as a primitive in the (Z level) programming language since it is so common. Nevertheless, it will be written explicitly here to provide another illustration.

The process will use a tree-based approach where leaves send their maximum to their parents and the internal nodes, after computing the largest of their local values and their inputs, send their maximum to their parents. The global maximum is emitted by the root, as explained later. In order to give this process a little generality, the degree, d+1, $0 \leq$ d, of the tree, will be a parameter. In addition, even though the `Approx` process only produces a single local maximum per section — the value named `LocDiff` — it is assumed for generality that each `Max` process accepts a linear array, `LocVal`, of local values. Thus, the preamble

```
process Max(LocVal[size]);
float array LocVal[1:size];
float ports (w) PARENT, (r) CHILD[1:d];
```

establishes these conditions for the local computation. As with `a` and `b` above, `size` and `d` are attributes of their respective arrays which are bound when the actual parameters are available. The binding of `d` will be explained below, but note that `d` will not be the same for each process, since some processes are leaves, i.e. d=0.

The declarations

```
begin
  int i; float big; float array kidval[1:d];
```

include an indexing variable, a variable temporarily storing the current maximum and an array to store temporarily the input read from the child(ren). Assuming at least one local value, i.e. `size`$\geq$1, the initialization

```
big := LocVal[1];
```

establishes an intermediate maximum. The processing is straightforward. The local maximum is determined

```
for i := 2 to size do big := max(big, LocVal[i]);
```

followed by receiving the values (if any) from descendants

```
for i := 1 to d do kidval[i] <- CHILD[i];
```

Since the transmission and buffering of the data between processes are performed asynchronously, the sequential receiving does not cause a bottleneck as long as all values are required before processing continues. Notice that depending on the values of `size` and `d`, either loop could fall through.

With the local maximum computed and the input values available, one more iteration

```
for i := 1 to d do big := max(big, kidval[i]);
```

produces the largest value. This iteration could have been combined with the previous loop to remove somewhat more overhead. The result is then sent

```
PARENT <- big;
```

to the parent. The program without intervening text is shown in Figure 3.

Notice that both processes can be written in isolation with little consideration for the processing context except that expressed by the interfaces of the data and port ensembles.

```
process Max(LocVal[size]);
float array LocVal[1:size];
float ports (w) PARENT, (r) CHILD[1:d];
begin
  int i; float big; float array kidval[1:d];
  big := LocVal[1];
  for i := 2 to size do big := max(big, LocVal[i]);
  for i := 1 to d do kidval[i] <- CHILD[i];
  for i := 1 to d do big := max(big, kidval[i]);
  PARENT <- big;
end.
```

Figure 3: Pseudocode for Max Process.

5 Global Data Declaration

Two data structures will be needed. The `m`×`n` array `A` will define the problem data and the array `Diff` will hold the maximum difference for each subarray between successive iterations. The pseudocode

```
float array A[0:m-1,0:n-1];
```

specifies the array `A`.

Since the definition of `Diff` depends on knowing the number of the subarrays in the partitioning of `A`, it is necessary before specifying `Diff` to consider how `A` will become a data ensemble. Suppose `A` is partitioned into a $\rho \times \sigma$ array of subarrays. Because these numbers are to be set by the programmer or the user when tuning the program, they must be parameters to it. But they are also the values needed to define `Diff`,

```
float array Diff[0:rho-1,0:sigma-1];
```

since there is to be one value for each subarray.

Additional values must be defined in anticipation of converting `A` into a data ensemble. Specifically, the subarrays of the partitioning must have a size. So, define the number of rows and columns of subarrays as

```
alpha = ceiling(m/rho);
beta = ceiling(n/sigma);
```

where the "=" can be taken either as an assignment or a constraint, depending on whether the definitions are construed as imperative or declarative.

Figure 4 shows the global data definitions, and the `alpha` and `beta` definitions.

```
float array A[0:m-1,0:n-1];
float array Diff[0:rho-1;0:sigma-1];
alpha = ceiling(m/rho);
beta = ceiling(n/sigma);
```

Figure 4: Global data declarations.

6 Phase Definitions, Y Level

With the `Approx` and `Max` processes defined and global data available it is a straightforward matter to specify the iteration and convergence phases for the Jacobi computation. Recall that a phase specification is defined by

- data ensembles,
- a code ensemble,
- a port ensemble and
- a graph possibly with some value derivatives,

all having the same partitioning.

The best place to begin is by defining the data ensemble, since its partitioning tends to determine the structure for the other ensembles. For the Jacobi Iteration the two global data structures required are `A`, used to define the problem state, and `Diff`, used to store the maximum difference of a subarray between two iterations. Partitioning them defines a data ensemble. Accordingly, the data ensemble definition becomes

```
A.section[i,j]=A[i*alpha:(i+1)*alpha-1,j*beta:(j+1)*beta-1]
  0≤i<rho,0≤j<sigma
```

slicing the array into a `rho`×`sigma` array of subarrays of size `alpha`×`beta`. `A` is now an ensemble. Figure 5 shows the relationship between the data structure and the data ensemble.

The `Diff` array should be similarly partitioned

```
Diff.TD.section[i,j] = Diff[i,j] 0≤i<rho,0≤j<sigma
```

where one element is assigned per section. The "`TD`," mnemonic for two-dimensional,

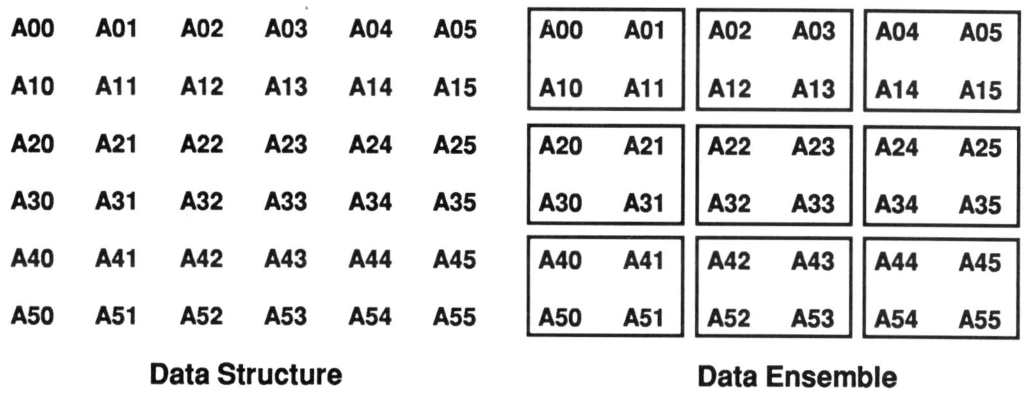

Figure 5: Data Structure and Data Ensemble for `A; m=n=6, alpha=beta=2, rho=sigma=3`.

names the partitioning that will be used for the iteration phase. A second partitioning of `Diff`,

```
Diff.OD.section[i*sigma+j]=Diff[i,j]     0≤i<rho,0≤j<sigma
```

has a linear (one-dimensional) structure and will be used later in the convergence phase. Only one instance of the `Diff` array will exist; it is just differently partitioned in the two ensembles.

The arrays `A` and `Diff`, though thought of as monolithic data structures, have been embellished with a partitioning into sections. The partitioning enables the compiler to allocate the sections to separate address spaces. These separate address spaces can either be allocated to separate processors in nonshared memory machines or perhaps be used in cache management for shared memory machines. In either case the programmer thinks of `A` and `Diff` as single coherent units.

JI Phase. The Jacobi iteration phase is to be called `JI`. The phase specification has a total of four components, data, code, port and graph, corresponding to the items required to define a phase. The previously defined data ensembles

```
JI[i,j].data=A.section[i,j],Diff.TD.section[i,j]     0≤i<rho,0≤j<sigma
```

can be included.

The code ensemble, a set of process instances with a partitioning, is easily defined for the Jacobi iteration. However, rather than first creating a set of process instances and then partitioning them, we proceed directly to incorporating the instances into the definition of the phase. The pseudocode

```
JI[i,j].code = Approx(A,Diff)    0≤i<rho,0≤j<sigma
```

assigns one instance of the **Approx** process to each section. This is a shorthand way of stating "the code ensemble component of the **JI** phase is that ensemble with a **rho**×**sigma** array of sections each containing an instance of **Approx**." The data ensemble arguments to the phase are generally presented at invocation time, but are bound now, "Curried," since they do not change.[1]

For each section the subarray of **A** local to that section will be bound to the **LocA** formal parameter of **Approx**; this will cause the **alpha** and **beta** values to be bound to **a** and **b** identifiers of the processes. Similarly the element of **Diff** local to a section will be bound to the **LocDiff** formal parameter of **Approx**. Notice that although the **JI** phase happens to be an example of a Single Program, Multiple Data (SPMD) computation, code ensembles permit multiple processes to be defined, i.e. MIMD execution.

The port ensemble, a set of port names with a partitioning, can be defined by giving the set and partitioning it, as was done with the data ensemble, or by directly assigning them to the phase, as was done with code ensembles,

```
JI[i,j].port = {N, E, W, S}    0≤i<rho,0≤j<sigma
```

or by inheriting them from the code ensemble. This latter is possible because the port names are defined in the process definition and instances of it have already been assigned to the sections in the code ensemble, so port names can be inherited by the sections. Regardless of which method is used, each section receives the four port names.

Figure 6 illustrates the resulting ensembles of the **JI** phase.

The port names provide the means by which the logical relationships between sections are established. Specifically, by associating port names from different sections, we establish the neighbor relationship. So, the mesh connection induced by the four-point stencil is defined[2] for the sections by the graph

```
JI.graph = {(JI[i,j].S,JI[i+1,j].N) | 0≤i<rho-1,0≤j<sigma}
  ∪ {(JI[i,j].E,JI[i,j+1].W) | 0≤i<rho,0≤j<sigma-1}
```

where the south ports of all sections (but the last row) are associated with the north ports of the section below them; the east/west edges are defined analogously. This association assures that the transmitted data is exchanged by the appropriate processors to implement the computation.

The definition of the graph binds some, but not all, of the ports. The ports around the edge are unassigned. Normally, these ports are exceptional because they must express the boundary conditions of the computation, and it is often the case that describing this processing introduces a substantial number of conditional tests into the program. However, the port ensemble assists in removing many of these conditional tests by permitting ports to be bound to *value derivatives*. These are locally computed functions that sub-

[1]For interest the **FindMax** phase will take its data ensemble as an argument presented at invocation time. See Section 8 for further discussion of argument bindings.

[2]It is sufficient when defining the graph that the edge set be defined and that it be possible to bind edges to port names. There are a multitude of ways of establishing these bindings, including declarative (used here), procedural, graphical, grammatical [Bailey & Cuny 90] and libraries.

Figure 6: Data, code and port ensembles of the Jacobi Iteration.

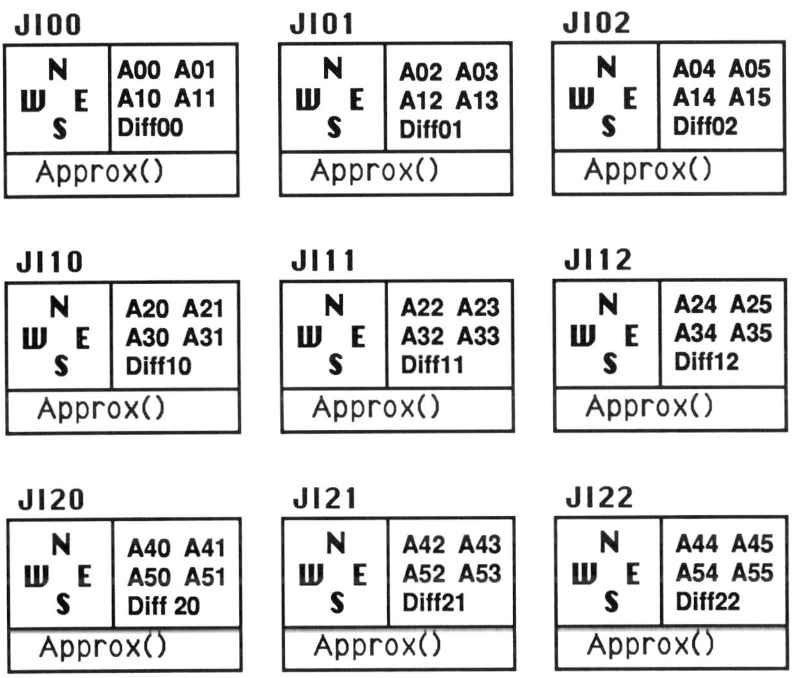

stitute for communication. To illustrate, suppose the north, west and south boundary values are to be zero. Then the specification

```
JI.graph={JI[0,j].N=const(0.0)[0:b-1]|0≤j<sigma}
         ∪ {JI[i,0].W=const(0.0)[0:a-1]|0≤i<rho}
         ∪ {JI[rho-1,j].S=const(0.0)[0:b-1]|0≤j<sigma}
```

causes receives from ports along the north, west and south edges to yield a vector of zeros of the proper length; sends to these ports are simply lost. Notice that the value derivative expression is evaluated locally in the appropriate sections, where the values of the `a` and `b` variables are known.

Another way to use value derivatives is to compute a function using local values to substitute for a communication. For example, suppose the Jacobi iteration is to be symmetric with respect to the east edge, i.e. values received from the east are simply the values stored along the east edge of the array. The specification

```
JI.graph={JI[i,sigma-1].E = reflect() | 0≤i<rho}
```

invokes the function **`reflect`** (defined local to the section) on each send to and receive from an east port on the edge; this function would return the values in `LocA[0:a-1,b-1]`

```
A.section[i,j]=A[i*alpha:(i+1)*alpha-1,j*beta:(j+1)*beta-1]
                                          0≤i<rho,0≤j<sigma
Diff.TD.section[i,j] = Diff[i,j]          0≤i<rho,0≤j<sigma
Diff.OD.section[i*sigma+j]=Diff[i,j]      0≤i<rho,0≤j<sigma

JI[i.j].data=A.section[i,j],Diff.TD.section[i,j]
                                          0≤i<rho,0≤j<sigma
JI[i,j].code = Approx(A,Diff)             0≤i<rho,0≤j<sigma
JI[i,j].port = {N, E, W, S}               0≤i<rho,0≤j<sigma

JI.graph = {(JI[i,j].S,JI[i+1,j].N) |     0≤i<rho-1,0≤j<sigma}
         ∪ {(JI[i,j].E,JI[i,j+1].W) |     0≤i<rho,0≤j<sigma-1}
JI.graph={JI[0,j].N=const(0.0)[0:beta-1]|0≤j<sigma}
         ∪ {JI[i,0].W=const(0.0)[0:alpha-1]|0≤i<rho}
         ∪ {JI[rho-1,j].S=const(0.0)[0:beta-1]|0≤j<sigma}
JI.graph={JI[i,sigma-1].E = reflect() | 0≤i<rho}
```

Figure 7: The Jacobi Iteration phase definition.

for receives and ignore sends. Notice that another possibility for symmetric reflection might simply be to connect the east port with itself making a loop.

The JI phase definition without intervening text is given in Figure 7; a schematic of the phase specification is given in Figure 8.

FindMax Phase. Logically, this phase is structured as a d-ary tree, with each section having d descendants. It is convenient, therefore, to use a linear naming scheme for the sections so as to simplify communication graph definition. The ensemble declaration given at the beginning of this section

```
Diff.OD.section[i*sigma+j] = Diff[i,j]    0≤i<rho,0≤j<sigma,
```

accomplishes this by enumerating the elements in row major order.

Next, the sections need to be assigned a copy of the Max process,

```
FindMax[i].code = Max()    0≤i<rho*sigma.
```

The Diff.OD ensemble will be presented at invocation time.

We consider here how port bindings are made. Recall that the number, d, of children of a node was unbound in the process definition. There is an option of whether to declare the parent and child ports explicitly or inherit them from their definition in the codes assigned in the code ensemble. If ports are explicitly defined in a phase, say by

```
(*) FindMax[i].port={PARENT,CHILD[1:2]} 0≤i<rho*sigma
```

Figure 8: Contents of Section JI22 of the Jacobi Iteration and induced structures.

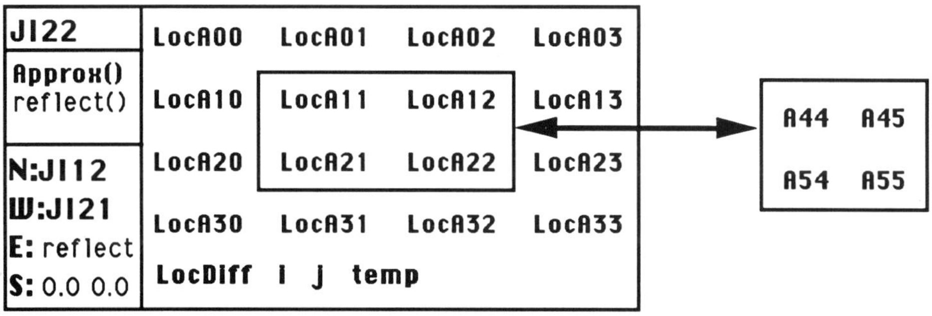

for a binary tree, then d is automatically defined for every node. If a port definition is inherited, then d remains unbound until the graph is specified, when each process has d defined from the node corresponding to it.

Notice that regardless of how the ports are defined, d need not be the same for every node. For example, rather than (∗) above which assigns each node a parent and two child ports, the port definition

```
FindMax[0].port={PARENT, CHILD[1:3]}
FindMax[i].port={PARENT, CHILD[1:2]} 1≤i<rho*sigma/2-1
FindMax[i].port={PARENT} rho*sigma/2-1≤i≤rho*sigma-1
```

specifies, assuming **rho∗sigma** is a power of 2, a complete binary tree with the root (node 0) being ternary so the "extra node" is its child. The graph can express the same information.

```
FindMax.graph={(FindMax[i].CHILD[1],FindMax[2*i].PARENT)
                    | 0≤i<rho*sigma/2-1 }
               ∪ {(FindMax[i].CHILD[2],FindMax[2*i+1].PARENT)
                    | 0≤i<rho*sigma/2-1 }
               ∪ {(FindMax[0].CHILD[3],FindMax[rho*sigma-1].PARENT)}
```

In either case the value of d will differ from process instance to process instance.

The key difference between the fixed and variable degree definitions is that in the fixed degree case some nodes, e.g. leaves, will have ports defined with no descendants bound to them. This is not a problem, since the nonexistent descendants can be assigned, using value derivatives, the SmallestPositive value. For example, assuming the definition (∗) above, the child ports of leaves can be defined

```
FindMax.graph={FindMax[i].CHILD[1]=const(SmallestPositive)
               | rho*sigma/2-1≤i<rho*sigma}
               ∪ {FindMax[i].CHILD[2]=const(SmallestPosititve)
               | rho*sigma/2-1≤i<rho*sigma}.
```

This produces the right result, of course, but it introduces some unneeded computation. Accordingly, the variable degree solution is the slightly preferred solution.

In all of the solutions discussed so far, the root node has an unassigned port, its `PARENT`. The value produced is used in determining whether the iterations have converged, so the value is needed in the Z level control logic of the computation. Accordingly, the value is returned as the result of the phase computation by the value derivative mechanism,

```
FindMax.graph = {FindMax[0].PARENT=return},
```

making the value available for the convergence test, and completing the definition of the `FindMax` phase. The phase definition without intervening text is shown in Figure 9.

```
FindMax[i].code = Max() 0≤i<rho*sigma.
FindMax.graph = {(FindMax[i].CHILD[1],FindMax[2*i].PARENT)
      | 0≤i<rho*sigma/2-1}
   ∪ {(FindMax[i].CHILD[2], FindMax[2*i+1].PARENT)
      | 0≤i<rho*sigma/2-1}
   ∪ {(FindMax[0].CHILD[3],FindMax[rho*sigma-1].PARENT)}
FindMax.graph = {FindMax[0].PARENT=return},
```

Figure 9: The FindMax Phase.

7 Main Program Body, Z Level

Recall that the Z level expresses the top-level logic of the computation by invoking processes. Computations of interest to users, like weather prediction and seismic modeling, will generally be complex. Much of the low level detail will have been encapsulated in the previously defined processes and phases. The user's interest, therefore, can be focused on the Z level code, where the programming is performed in "large units." Unfortunately, the Jacobi is a trivial computation, and so does not illustrate well the characteristics of Z level programming. Hence, to display more of this flavor, we will first solve the Jacobi in the straightforward, naive way, and then consider optimizations of it.

The program, shown in Figure 10, is obvious. Beginning with the previously given definitions and declarations for processes, global data and phases, it reads in the `A` array, applies the `JI-FindMax` phase pair until the maximum error is sufficiently small, and it writes out the result.

There are four logical parameters to the program: `A`, the input array, `epsilon`, the tolerance, and `rho` and `sigma`, the number of sections in each dimension of the partitioning. `A` and `epsilon` have been given as parameters, since it is assumed that the program will be applied to a variety of inputs with differing accuracy. `Rho` and `sigma` are also given explicitly as parameters so the programmer can tune the concurrency. The product `rhosigma` is the amount of phase level concurrency available in the algorithm. The

```
program Jacobi(A,epsilon,rho,sigma);
<declarations and definitions>
  begin float err;
  Read(A);
  do begin
    JI;
    err := FindMax(Diff.OD);
  until err < epsilon;
  Write(A);
  end;
end.
```

Figure 10: The naive Jacobi program.

values assigned to `rho` and `sigma` will often be such that the `rhosigma` product equals the number of physical processors, but they can be set to other values when the program is tuned [Griswold *et al.* 90a].

The number of rows and columns of `A` are attributes of the array. Their values were defined when the array was created and stored with it when it was originally written out by the system-provided Write phase. When the system-provided Read phase inputs `A`, the values of `m` and `n` are bound and from these can be computed `alpha` and `beta`. Notice that if `alpha` does not divide `m` or `beta` does not divide `n` then the subarrays assigned to sections along the edge may not be "full" `alpha`×`beta` subarrays. Nevertheless, the size of the actual subarray, `a`×`b` will be known to the process code.

When the `JI` phase is invoked the array `A` is recomputed and the values of the `Diff` array are updated. The default barrier synchronization requires that each process of `JI` complete prior to the invocation of `FindMax`. When `FindMax` completes, the root process (the one executing in section `FindMax[0]`) emits a value by writing to its `PARENT` port. This value is returned, as a result of the "return" value derivative specification, and is assigned to `err`. This value, a local value to the Z computation and not part of any phase or process, controls the continuation of the iteration. When convergence is achieved, the final values stored in the array `A` are written out by the system-provided Write phase.

Notice that if there are Π=`rhosigma` processors, numbered 0 to Π-1 and they are assigned one section to one processor in row-major order for `JI` and in sequence in `FindMax`, then it happens that the `LocDiff` value produced by the section assigned to any processor is the `LocVal` required by the `FindMax` section running on that processor. This is not an accident. It is a result of using the same sequence (rmo) to enumerate elements of `Diff.OD` for `FindMax` as is used to assign processors to sections of `JI`. Of course, it needn't always work out so well. Analyzing these situations, however, is beyond the scope of this example.

The naive Jacobi is perhaps not the best solution. For example, it is probably unlikely that the computation will converge after the first iteration, yet convergence is always tested after an approximation step. Since the convergence tests represent a nontrivial fraction of the total work, it would improve the program to eliminate some of them.

```
program Jacobi(A,epsilon,rho,sigma);
<declarations and definitions>
  begin
  <define function f>
  float err; int q;
  Read(A);
  JI;
  q := f(FindMax(Diff.OD),epsilon);
  JI<<q-1>>;;
  do { JI;
    err := FindMax(Diff.OD);}
  until err < epsilon;
  Write(A);
  end;
end.
```

Figure 11: Revised Jacobi with reduced convergence tests.

Postulating a function, `f`, that can make an estimate of the number of iterations required for convergence based on the size of the initial error, the program might be revised as shown in Figure 11.

After an initial iteration, the `FindMax` phase is invoked. The value returned is used to estimate the number of iterations as `q`. Then the approximation phase is invoked `q-1` times without synchronization by the construction:

```
JI<<q-1>>;;
```

which is intended to denote $\mathtt{JI}^{q-1}$. The fact that the consecutive invocations of the `JI` phase produce the correct result without the synchronization is a consequence of the way the program was written and the data driven semantics of the communication. It is not a property of every phase, but it is clearly a property programmers should try to achieve. There is no need for a barrier synchronization after the multiple invocation statement, since the next phase to be invoked is also a `JI` phase, so the nonsynchronizing double semicolon notation is used. Barrier synchronization is thus deferred until the `FindMax`. This modification eliminates both the overhead of `q-1` barrier synchronizations as well as `q-1` convergence tests. Performance is presumably improved.

8 Commentary on the Program and Abstractions

In this section we review the program, noting aspects of its organization not previously mentioned and illustrating the benefits of the phase abstractions.

Memory Model. Observe that ensemble data is persistent across phase invocations while local variables are not. Thus, in Figure 8 the `LocA` values in the box remain between invocations as does `LocDiff`. The other variables are *logically* reallocated, making their values undefined with each invocation.

Scaling. Clearly, as the problem size changes, `m` and `n` will change. Assuming `rho` and `sigma` remain fixed, `alpha` and `beta` change, causing the array `A` to be properly partitioned to form a `rho`×`sigma` array of subarrays. This is what is expected from flexible data structures.

When additional processors become available the amount of physical parallelism, Π, increases and this should probably cause an increase of logical parallelism, i.e. increasing the `rhosigma` product. This might be done transparently if the programmer has specified constraints on the relationship between `rho`, `sigma` and Π, say `rho=sigma=`$\pi=\Pi^{1/2}$.

Alternatively, the logical parallelism parameters to the program can simply be given explicitly, as is likely when the program is being tuned. As an example, suppose that by experimentation it has been determined that the architecture is more efficient when there are 4 processes per processor rather than one. Then, assuming a sufficiently large problem, binding `rho` and `sigma` to 2π achieves the desired objective of making the logical parallelism 4 times the physical parallelism. No changes are required of the program. There are simply more sections in the ensembles.

The essential point is that ensembles allow the end user to control the granularity of the computation after the program is written. Different size problems, different amounts of physical parallelism and various operating systems characteristics affect how large the grain size of the computation should be. Since they change over time, programs must be able to adapt.

Structural Conformance. Clearly, the organization chosen for a data ensemble is that scheme maximizing locality and simplifying the programming of the phase. But what guarantee is there that when two phases operate on the same data, e.g. `Diff`, that they will prefer the same or a compatible structure? Of course, there is none. In general, one ensemble structure can be mapped to another by the system shipping the data from the memories representing one structure to the memories representing another. However, it is often possible to make a compromise between competing structures.

For example, suppose that the block structure of the `A` array was to be used with a phase that prefers strips of columns. Then, the square blocks might be converted into tall blocks by setting `rho=1` and `sigma` to the desired concurrency, e.g. Π. This solution fails to exploit the good perimeter to area ratio of square blocks, but the overall efficiency of the combined program might be improved. Also, it might be that the "strips" algorithm could be customized to use stacks of a few "tallish" blocks, helping one phase at perhaps only a modest cost to the other.

Composing Phases. The composition of two phases is a phase. Thus, phase procedures can be anticipated in Z level languages. This also makes it possible to consider `JI<<q-1>>` as one phase. The benefit is that phase invocation overhead can be removed, since the compiler can decentralize the loop control.

This raises an important, and often missed, point about the phase abstraction. The phase graph is a communication graph and as such is undirected. This should be contrasted with most other systems using graphs to represent parallel computations, where the directed graphs express dependence. Code [Browne 90] is a good example. Communication graphs are somewhat more general in that connected processes may or may not depend upon one another; in Jacobi, there is no dependence between **Approx** processes, there is between **FindMax** processes. One place where this distinction becomes important is phase composition.

Consider the composition of phases. In the communication graph, the boundaries between phase invocations, as in `JI<<q-1>>`, are decentralized and handled locally. It is only the invocation delimiter (;) that causes the barrier synchronization. In the dependence graph case, the barrier between two phases would seem always to have to be honored, because the processes of the later phase(s) may actually depend on the earlier phase(s). By having somewhat more general semantics, the communication graph encourages solutions that are somewhat more flexible, offering opportunities for more efficiency, as in the revised program.

Communication. In programming the Jacobi it has been assumed that the communication facilities needed to implement sends and receives are available. That is, when the process executing in section JI00 sends elements out its east port to the process in section JI01, it is assumed that the communication can be implemented, regardless of where that section resides in the machine. Of course, this can be implemented by whatever scheme is suitable for the architecture: Shared memory machines can use queues in shared memory, message passing machines can use their general routing mechanism. But if there are qualities of the architecture that can be exploited to improve the performance, say point-to-point mesh communication, then the availability of the graph information enables the program to be customized to the machine. Notice that the Jacobi might run best on an architecture containing point-to-point communication support for both arrays and trees, which might not always be the available. The way to solve this is considered in "Portability" below.

Shared Memory. The phase abstractions approach should be compared with the shared memory model. Like shared memory, it permits the global data to be viewed monolithically, as a single shared entity. This is presumably compatible with the conceptual view of the computation. The ensembles, however, give the partitioning and communication structure, which can be the basis of efficient implementations on both shared and nonshared memory machines. Most importantly, the use of explicit partitioning and communication structures allows the programmer to have an accurate model of the execution costs of the program: Data references within a section are always unit-cost local references; references implemented via sends and receives are usually much more expensive. An accurate cost model is essential for writing efficient programs [Snyder 86].

Portability. There has been no concern in programming the problem for the mapping of the processes on to the architecture. This is appropriate for portable programs, since it must be assumed that the architecture will change and thus mapping must a seen as a tuning or customizing operation. But, one of the chief benefits of the phase abstraction approach is that it greatly assists in this customization.

Specifically, postulate a mesh architecture. Then the processes of the `JI` phase will have an obvious efficient direct mapping onto the target machine. The processes of the **FindMax** phase do not, however, because of the impossibility of a dilation=1 embedding of a tree into a mesh [Rosenberg & Snyder 78]. The program will work, because of the general communication provided, but it is possible and straightforward to improve the **FindMax** phase. One technique is to use the mesh structure directly, having the local

Figure 12: Mesh tree alternate for FindMax.

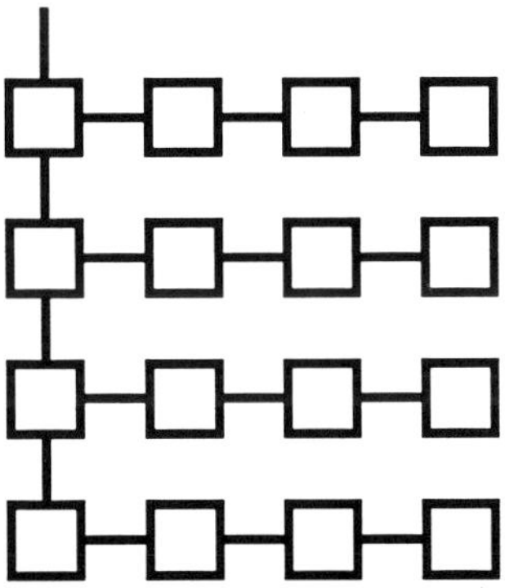

maxima shift left to the first column and then shift up to the corner. This is still a binary tree, as Figure 12 shows. The only modification to the program is the obvious change to the `FindMax.graph`. The improvement is impressive: For a 16×16 mesh the embedding used in Figure 9 requires 56 communication steps, using the Manhattan distance between adjacent nodes as the (contention free) communication cost, while the time for the alternate embedding of Figure 12 is only 30. More complex `FindMax` alternatives have been considered [Griswold *et al.* 90b].

Binding time. It is a maxim of computing that the earlier values can be bound the more efficient the resulting computation can be. Many of the parameters of the Jacobi computation, like other large numerical computations, can be bound early. Certainly, Π changes very infrequently and so, once a program is tuned, `rho` and `sigma` tend to remain fixed. It is also common for the problem size to change only infrequently, because repeated computations are made within the same problem setting. And finally, many numerical algorithms, even if thought of as "dynamic" admit good static solutions.

This advanced information about the computation is extremely useful to the compiler for creating efficient code. Accordingly, the phase abstractions are most effective if they are used in an *environment* where such information is known at compile time, Poker [Snyder 84] is an example, rather than in an "offline compile" system where all the parameters are unbound. Such an environment doesn't require the user to bind any of the information, but if it is known, better results can be obtained.

As a related specificational matter, notice that in the `JI` example, the ensembles, graph and value derivatives were all specified at phase declaration time. This was pedagogically useful, but not semantically necessary. The code ensemble must be bound to the phase name,

```
JI[i,j].code=Approx()        0≤i<rho, 0≤j<sigma
```

but all other constituents can be expressed at invocation time. Assuming for simplicity that `MESH` has been defined,

```
JI(A,Diff.TD)[MESH]{unbound(N,S)=const(0.0)[0:sigma-1],
  unbound(W)=const(0.0)[0:rho-1],unbound(E)=reflect()}
```

is the same invocation as the `JI` invocation of Figure 10. Though such inline specifications are useful, they are cumbersome and most programmers will balance generality with clarity.

9 Conclusions

The Jacobi iterative computation has been programmed using the XYZ and ensemble abstractions with the result that the program is extremely malleable. With simple changes to parameters — or if parameters were not planned then declarations — the program can easily accommodate larger problems, greater physical parallelism and variously structured inputs. Though not evident in the Jacobi example, such considerations can lead to programs with better asymptotic performance than conventional, less malleable programs [Alverson *et al.* 90].

The essential accomplishment of the XYZ programming levels and the ensembles concepts is that they structure a parallel computation to expose those features that seem likely to be changed in response to a new computing setting. An example of such a feature is the amount of logical parallelism available in the algorithm, or control of the "grain size." In many programming systems the maximum parallelism is specified, which for the Jacobi case would result in "one point per process." This will incur significant overhead in process multiplexing unless it is possible to increase the grain size automatically [Socha 90], which is generally impossible. In those few systems that promote large grain size, e.g. Poker, the adaptation of the program to different amounts of logical parallelism requires detailed program changes. Using the phase abstractions — specifically, partitioning the ensembles — causes the programmer to consider (and to say) what the grain size is, and if done properly, how it should change.

Considering the diversity of parallel machines available and proposed, such malleability would seem to be mandatory if parallel programs are to have a long lifetime, spanning many machines, and thus justify the investment needed to create them.

10 Acknowledgments

The XYZ and ensemble concepts have received all but their earliest development in a collaboration with Gail A. Alverson, William G. Griswold and David Notkin. It is a pleasure to have worked with these fine scientists on the phase abstractions and to thank them. James Ahrens has also contributed to these ideas while he has been implementing the phase abstractions. Conversations with Jan Cuny, Scott Hauck, Calvin Lin and Dennis Gannon have also been very helpful. Judy Watson's preparation of this difficult manuscript is greatly appreciated. This research was funded in part by the Office of Naval Research contract N00014–89–J–1368.

References

G. A. Alverson, William G. Griswold, David Notkin and Lawrence Snyder (1990), "A Flexible Communication Abstraction for Nonshared Memory Parallel Computing," *Proceedings of Supercomputing '90*, (to appear)

Duane A. Bailey and Janice E. Cuny (1990), "Visual Extensions to Parallel Programming Languages," in David Gelernter, Alexandru Nicolau and David Padua (editors), *Language and Compilers for Parallel Computing*, MIT Press

James C. Browne (1990), "Software Engineering of Parallel Programs in a Computationally Oriented Display Environment," in David Gelernter, Alexandru Nicolau and David Padua (editors), *Languages and Compilers for Parallel Computing*, MIT Press, pp. 75–94

David E. Culler and Arvind (1988), "Resource Requirements of Dataflow Programs," *Proceedings of International Symposium on Computer Architecture*, IEEE, pp. 141–150

J. J. Dongarra and D. C. Sorensen (1987), "SCHEDULE: Tools for Developing and Analyzing Parallel Fortran Programs," in L. H. Jamieson, D. B. Gannon and R. J. Douglass (editors), *The Characteristics of Parallel Algorithms*, MIT Press

William G. Griswold, Gail A. Harrison, David Notkin and Lawrence Snyder (1990a), "Scalable Abstractions for Parallel Programming," *Proceedings 5th Distributed Memory Computer Conference*, (to appear)

William G. Griswold, Gail A. Harrison, David Notkin and Lawrence Snyder (1990b), "How Port Ensembles Aid the Efficient Retargeting of Reduction Algorithms," *Proceedings International Conference on Parallel Processing*, Penn State, pp. 286–7

Charles Koelbel, Piyush Mehrotra and John van Rosendale (1990), "Supporting Shared Data Structures on Distributed Memory Architectures," *Proceedings of the 2nd Principles and Practice of Parallel Programming Symposium*, ACM, pp. 177–186

Arnold L. Rosenberg and Lawrence Snyder (1978), "Bounds on the Cost of Data Encodings," *Mathematical Systems Theory*, 12:9–39

Matthew Rosing, Robert B. Schnabel and Robert P. Weaver (1990), "The DINO Parallel Programming Language," Technical Report CU-CS-457-90, University of Colorado

Lawrence Snyder (1984), "Parallel Programming and the Poker Environment," *Computer* 17(7):26-36

Lawrence Snyder (1986), "Type Architecture, Shared Memory and the Corollary of Modest Potential," *Annual Review of Computer Science*, Vol. 1, pp. 289–318

Lawrence Snyder (1990), "The XYZ Abstraction Levels of Poker-like Languages," in David Gelernter, Alexandru Nicolau and David Padua (editors), *Language and Compilers for Parallel Computing*, MIT Press, pp. 470–489

David Socha (1990), "Compiling Single-point Iterative Programs for Distributed Memory Computers," *Proceedings of the 5th Distributed Memory Computing Conference*, IEEE, (to appear)

Languages, Compilers and Run-Time Environments
for Distributed Memory Machines
J. Saltz and P. Mehrotra (Editors)

Nicke – C Extensions for Programming on Distributed-Memory Machines

Dalia Malki
IBM Israel Scientific Center

Marc Snir
IBM Research, T. J. Watson Research Center

Abstract

This document describes the Nicke programming language. Nicke is an extension of C for programming distributed-memory machines. It supports both message-passing and shared-memory parallelism. We present the rationale for Nicke and describe the main features of the language. The Nicke language has been implemented on the 8CE machine under the Mach Operating System, [6], and is being ported to the Victor machine under the Trollius kernel [11, 5]. The language is supported by a preprocessor that translates Nicke code into standard C, and by a run-time library.

1 Introduction

1.1 Environment

The language *Nicke* is a parallel programming language that extends C. It is targeted for distributed memory multiprocessors, in particular, for the Victor prototype developed at IBM research [11]. It is equally well suited for other multicomputers, such as Ncube, iSPC2, etc. [2]. These are machines consisting of a large number of processors (256, for Victor), each executing its own independent code. Each processor has its own local memory, and communication between processors is done via message passing. Special hardware and firmware provide efficient support for message passing: In many of these machines, source to destination routing of messages is done transparently from the user, and the physical location of the communicating nodes has a relatively small effect on message transfer time. (This is not true for the Victor system, where message passing is handled in software) Still, interprocess communication is one or two orders of magnitude slower than access to local memory. Also, context switching is a relatively expensive operation: Fast microprocessors tend to have large "contexts" (register files, pipelines, on-chip caches, status registers, etc.) The explicit overhead of saving and restoring such information, and the implicit overhead of reduced cache performance, extract a large penalty from code with fine granularity.

In addition to this hardware environment, we also assume software that provides a few basic functions: Message transfer between physical nodes, memory allocation, and process spawning. These functions are supported by the Trollius kernel on Victor; similar functions are available on most commercial multicomputers.

The Nicke language supports the shared memory paradigm, in addition to the message passing paradigm. The Nicke language has been implemented to run under Mach, and is running on a shared memory multiprocessor, the 8CE machine [6]. However, most attention has been given in the design of Nicke to message passing support, and the current version of Nicke may not make the most efficient use of shared memory.

1.2 Rationale

The design of Nicke has been affected by many considerations, many of them mundane (such as the desire to implement the language using a simple preprocessor). However, the design broadly reflects our understanding of what is a reasonable high level language for the design and implementation of parallel algorithms. One obviously desires such language to be as high level as possible, abstracting as much as possible from the concrete details of the underlying machine. It is presumably easier to code correct programs in higher-level languages, because it is easier for the user to specify and understand the logical, *qualitative* effect of a computation. However, since performance matters to us, there is another iron-clad requirement: The high-level language should allow the user to easily specify and understand *quantitative* performance aspects of a computation, such as running time. Such is the case, for example, for sequential imperative languages such as Fortran or C: It is reasonably easy to estimate the number of instructions executed by a program; and computation time is approximately proportional to the number of high-level instructions executed. The frequent choice of Fortran or C for algorithm implementation (rather than languages with higher level operations or non-imperative languages) is due in large part to that *transparency* of the language. Similar considerations mandate that some features of parallel computations be explicit and easily quantifiable in Nicke.

The first such feature is parallelism itself, which we make explicit. There should be an obvious difference between code that is inherently sequential and code that can be executed in parallel, otherwise the programmer has scant support in designing *parallel* algorithms. A sequential language, with an underlying parallelizing compiler, will not do: The programmer would need a detailed understanding of the compiler in order to estimate performance.

The second such feature is communication. Communication is a severe bottleneck on the performance of large-scale multiprocessors. In order to achieve good performance it is important to optimize the computation to communication ratio. Such optimization sometimes require algorithm redesign, and can not be achieved by compiler alone. Thus, the programming language must distinguish between local communication (e.g., between a processor and its local memory), and global communication. In the shared memory paradigm, the local-to-global distinction is reflected by a distinction between private and shared variables. In the message passing paradigm this distinction is reflected by using message passing operations for interprocess communication. Nicke supports both paradigms, and makes global communication explicit.

The third feature is synchronization. Large MIMD machines are not synchronous, and synchronization is an explicit, and often expensive operation. This is especially true is arbitrary subsets of processors are to synchronize.

Theoretical and pragmatical considerations indicate that other, more detailed features of a parallel computation can, ideally, be hidden from the user, and handled by compiler, run-time resource manager, or firmware, with a predictable and acceptable effect on performance. For example, it is feasible to ignore the precise number of physical processors, and program for "virtual processors" (processes). This holds true when the program has *slack*, i.e. the amount of available parallelism is larger than the number of physical processors, the overhead of time multiplexing each processor is acceptable, and sufficient memory is available at each node. (The time-multiplexing of several virtual processors on one physical processor may be programmed at compile time, with very small overhead [7]; it may even be supported by hardware [9].) It is possible to generate dynamically processes, and allocate them to physical processors, at a cost similar to the cost of a global synchronization. It is feasible to ignore the detailed topology of the interconnection mechanism, and merely distinguish "local" from "global". This assumes again that the program has slack, and that communication latency can be hidden by time-multiplexing each processor.

Thus, in an ideal world, a programming language with explicit parallelism and dynamic process creation, global vs local distinction, and explicit synchronization operations, would be sufficient for the design and implementation of efficient parallel algorithms. However, we do not live in an ideal world, and current system support for parallelism leaves much to be desired. Moreover, even in an ideal world it is often necessary to do low-level tuning, and exercise more explicit control on physical resources. We desire to do such low-level tuning within the same programming environment that is used for "high-level" programming. However, we wish to keep the distinction between the high-level, machine-independent, virtual model used for algorithm design, and the low-level, machine-dependent, physical model used for performance tuning.

To support this point of view, Nicke is designed to consist of two layers: The virtual layer and the physical layer. At the virtual layer a computation is expressed in terms of processes that can be spawned dynamically. These processes communicate via messages or shared variables. At the physical layer, the user may control which physical processors are allocated to each process, and may control the policy that is used to emulate shared memory. A user may totally ignore the physical layer, and code his or her application entirely in the virtual layer; some default resource allocation mechanisms will be used. It may then improve the performance of the code by exercising more control on resource allocation. This, ideally, will not change the outcome of the computation, but will just reduce its cost. (In practice, a different outcome may occur if the code is nondeterministic, or if an exception occurs because the program exhausts some resource.)

This two-layered approach is not new. This is the essence of metaprogramming in logic or functional programming [8, 3]. Similar goals are achieved by pragmas, or compiler directives in many parallel programming languages. Our system is somewhat more flexible in that its pragmas are executable at run time.

2 Basic Constructs

2.1 Processes

2.1.1 Process declaration

The basic unit of execution in Nicke is the *process*. Nicke processes are defined as C functions with the additional keyword procdef, designating them as processes. Process functions may not have parameters. Here is an example of a process declaration (the body omitted):

```
procdef F()
{
        ...
}
```

2.1.2 Process creation

Processes are created in two ways: by process declaration and by dynamic process generation.

A process declaration creates a *process group*, and assigns a name to each process in the group. The processes are instantiated when the declaration is elaborated: global processes are created at startup and automatic processes within functions are created upon function invocation. For example, the following declaration instantiates a group of 100 processes of the above type F():

```
procreate <F f[100]>;
```

The procreate declaration may also be used to create non-homogeneous groups of processes, as in the following *tuple* declaration:

```
procreate <F f1, G g1, H h1>;
```

Process generation statements are used for dynamic creation of processes. They appear in the code and are evaluated at runtime. Following are examples of the two forms of calls:

```
parc(F[100]);

parw(F, G, H);
```

In the parc version the parent (calling) process continues executing with the created processes, while in the parw version it waits for their termination. The runtime call permits any runtime computable expression to be used as array dimension, allowing calls of the form:

```
parw(F[n]);
```

The local constant INDEX is initialized to the index of the process within its group when the process is created. Thus, siblings can immediately proceed to perform distinct computing tasks, according to the value of their index, without further coordination. This is in contradistinction to the situation in Ada [12].

2.1.3 Remote references

A reference to a process is, in effect, a network-wide logical address that can be used to communicate with this process; each process that has a copy of that reference can communicate with the referenced process. A process declaration associates a name with each declared process. This variable refers to the process. Code within the scope of this declaration can use this reference to communicate with the referenced process. In a process generation statement, no names are assigned with the created processes; however the statement returns a reference (pointer) to the process group. The function `member(group-ptr,i)` returns a pointer to the *i*th process in the group referenced by `group-ptr`. Thus, the parent of a process group can communicate with each process it spawns. The constants `GROUP`, `ME` and `PARENT` are initialized at process creation to refer to the process group, the process itself, and the process parent, respectively. Thus, a process can communicate with its parent, and with any of its siblings.

References to processes and process groups have type `remptr` (remote pointer). A Nicke program can declare variables of this type and can assign them values; references to processes or process groups can be communicated by passing the value of such remote pointer.

2.2 Interprocess Communication

2.2.1 Scoping rules and sharing

The regular scoping rules of C apply to Nicke. In particular, a process can refer to any externally declared variable within its scope. However, the basic paradigm of Nicke is that of distributed memory: each process has its own address space. Externally declared variables are not truly shared: each process may have its own copy of such variables. If an external variable is initialized when declared, and is not modified anywhere during execution, then any access to this variable will return the correct, initial value. The effect of updates to external variables is undefined. Thus, external variables can not be used for interprocess communication, but only as system-wide constants.

2.2.2 Synchronization

Nicke provides several operations to synchronize siblings within a group. The sync instruction implements a *barrier synchronization*: each sibling reaching a `sync` suspends until all siblings have reached a `sync`, or have terminated. a `pbreak` instruction allows to terminate execution of all processes in a group.

2.2.3 Messages

The basic communication mechanism between processes is asynchronous message passing. Messages are addressed to *processes* via *process pointers*. The sending command is nonblocking. The parameters of a `send()` are the addressee, a message tag and a variable list. The variable list contains any legal expression passable as a parameter to function. The message also carries the sender address.

There is a blocking `receivew()` command, where the receiving process suspends until a suitable message is available, and a non-blocking `receivec()` command, where a zero value is returned if no suitable message is available. The parameters are a *receive condition* and a list of reception variables. The list of reception variables may include any legal *l-value*. The sending list and the receiving list must match in length and types (the results in the case of nonmatching lists are undefined). The receive condition is an arbitrary expression that may involve the constants TAG (the message tag) and SENDER (the message sender). (The current implementation supports only a restricted form of conditions.)

Various communication mechanisms (synchronous message passing, remote procedure call) can be implemented on top of this simple message-passing mechanisms. It is expected that these will be supported by library extensions.

2.3 Example

The constructs introduced in this section are sufficient to program nontrivial parallel applications. The following is an example of the obvious (and inefficient) parallel version of the sieve of Erasthotenes, coded in Nicke. A `sieve` process tests successive numbers for division by a prime p. The sieve processes are linked in a chain, and each number is passed along this chain. A number p that survives all tests is a prime. A new process is appended to the end of the chain to test for division by p, and p is sent to the `print` server process. The program has no termination condition, and will end when running out of resources.

```
procdef PRINT()
{
...
}

procreate <PRINT print>;          /* create print server */

procdef SIEVE()
{
  int i,p;
  remptr next;

  next = NULL;
  receivew(1, p);

  while(1) {
    receivew(1, i);                        /* receive new candidate */
    if ((i%p) != 0) {                       /* local test succeeds */
      if(next == NULL) {                        /* new prime found */
        send(print,1,i);     /* send new prime to print process */
        next = group(parc(SIEVE),0);     /* create next process */
```

```
        }
        send(next,1,i)
      }
   }
}

procreate <SIEVE head>;          /* create first sieve process */

main()
{
   int j;

   send(print,1,2);
   for(j=2; ; j++)
      send(head,1,j); /* send numbers thru sieve */
}
```

2.4 Processor Allocation

A Nicke program can specify which processor is to run a process by adding a `place(exp)` statement to the process generating declaration or instruction. This expression may involve the pseudo constant `INDEX`. The placement expression is evaluated once for each generated process in the process group, with `INDEX` set to the process index. The resulting value is the index of the processor that is allocated to the process. If `place()` occurs in a process declaration, then the place instruction should be a constant expression; if it occurs in a process generation statement, then it can be an arbitrary expression.

For example, assume that the system has `NUMPROC` processors, numbered from 0 to `NUMPROC-1`, and that processor i is close to processors $i-1$ and $i+1$. Then it would be advantageous, in the previous example, to allocate successive sieve processes at successive processors (with wraparound). The statement that spawns new sieve processes is modified accordingly:

```
next = parc(SIEVE) place((Location(ME) + 1)%NUMPROC)
```

Alternatively, we might want to use random placement, to achieve better load balancing. This would be achieved by a place statement of the form

```
next = parc(SIEVE) place(random()%NUMPROC)
```

3 Shared Variables

3.1 Rationale

Shared variables are a very natural idiom for the expression of many parallel algorithms. Think about the simulation of a large physical system (or, equivalently, of the evolution of a PDE solver). A large, shared data structure represents the state of this system at a particular time; a (parallel) computation pushes simulated time ahead (possibly, at different rates at different places). One thinks of such algorithms as performing a coordinated computation on a representation of the data domain of the problem. The possible partition of this representation into pieces allocated to distinct processors, so as to decrease communication, is accessory. The first, natural encoding of the algorithm would use a shared data structure to represent the global data domain. A language that does not support this idiom seriously handicaps its user.

However, efficient partition of data is essential to performance on a multicomputer where inter-process communication is orders of magnitudes slower then local memory access. Thus, we would like to preserve the paradigm of shared data structures, in particular shared arrays, while providing means to optimize access to such shared structures. The goal is to provide mechanisms to support shared data structures on a multicomputer such that:

- Access to shared variables is always "correct" (i.e., serializable).
- Access to shared variables is efficient when the algorithm exhibits much locality.

Caching techniques are very efficient in exploiting temporal locality of accesses; however, by themselves, they do no lead to a good exploitation of spatial locality. The long latencies in message-passing multicomputers imply that data must be transferred in large chunks (hundreds or thousands of bytes), to amortize the fixed overheads. Such chunking can be often achieved by partitioning the data correctly. However, the basic chunks will often not reside in contiguous segments (for example, they may be submatrices of a two dimensional array). In such case, hardware blocking techniques are inefficient. For many interesting numerical algorithms computation is not evenly spread over all the data domain: adaptive algorithms spend more computing time in "interesting" parts of the domain; sparse arrays may be used to delete from the data representation "uninteresting" parts of the data domain. The correct domain partition, in such cases, is irregular and data dependent. Such partitions do not have a simple syntactic description, nor can such partition be derived by compile time analysis. Thus, we want to allow the user more flexibility in specifying partitions of shared data structures in an algorithm dependent manner. For a similarly motivated research, see [10].

3.2 Shared arrays

Nicke currently support one type of shared data structure: shared arrays. Shared arrays are declared in the same way as regular C arrays, except that the declaration is prefixed by the keyword `shared`, must be external and can not be initialized. Thus

```
shared int a[100][100]
```

creates a two dimensional, 100×100 shared array of integers. The elements of the array are regular C variables (of type integer, in this example). However, the shared array has a very different structure from a regular C array. In particular, one can not use pointers to access elements of a shared array, as usually done in C – entries are always accessed by their indices.

An array entry can be assigned a value, by a regular assignment, e.g.

```
a[i][j] = 5
```

or by an assigment operator, e.g.

```
a[i][j] += 3
```

Thich increments the value of a[i] [j] by 3. An array entry can be used like any other C variable of the corresponding type. (To simplify preprocessing, the current version of Nicke uses distinct separators for operations on shared variables.)

Assignments are executed atomically. Consider, for example the following code.

```
shared int a;

procdef SILLY()
{
printf("%d",a);
a += 1;
}

main()
{
a = 0;
parw(SILLY[3]);  /* spawn three processes that each increments a by 1 */
}
```

The variable a is thrice incremented atomically by one. It successively assumes the values 0, 1, 2 and 3. This code will print the three values 000, 001, 011, or 012, in some permuted order.

3.3 Shared array partition

The Nicke language provides several tools to help the user specify a partition of a shared array, and specify a protocol for shared data access.

3.3.1 Windows

A shared array can be partitioned into (typically disjoint) *windows*. A window can be thought as of a cache line, storing part of the array. Remote accesses that involve data transfer will usually move the entire window data. The partition of a shared array into windows is specified when the array is declared by appending a *window type* to this declaration. Thus, the declaration

```
shared int a[100][100] subarray(2,5)
```

specifies that the array a[100] [100] is partitioned into windows each consisting of a 2×5 submatrix. Syntactically, the window type is a function which includes constant parameters. Nicke has a library of predefined window types, corresponding to the most usual array partitions. The (expert) user may add new window types to this library. For each added window type, the user has to a supply a set of routines for the initialization of the window structure, and for the access of elements. Basically, array entries are stored in a "window major" order; an entry is accessed by its window index, and its displacement within the window. The window access routines compute the window index and displacement from the array indices. Typically, these will be simple, inlined routines, so that the overhead per entry access is small, when the entry is available locally. However, the user may specify more complex partitions; in particular there are no impediments to the use dynamically changing partitions, or overlapping partitions, other that the potentially large overhead of window routines for such partitions.

3.3.2 Caching protocols

Each window in a partitioned shared array is managed by a fixed processor, the window manager. The user may specify the location of the window manager for each window, by adding a placement expression to the shared array declaration; this expression has the same syntax and semantics as the placement expression for processes. One simple use of partition and placement is to statically allocate each window to a fixed processor in the network. An access to a shared variable within a window will involve a few instructions, if the window is at the node where the access is done; it will require a message exchange with the window manager, otherwise. Nicke also supports various caching policies for windows. One can have a single copy caching protocol (which we call `erew`): whenever a processor accesses a shared variable then the (unique) copy of the window containing this variable is moved to the accessing processor. Typically, this requires a protocol where the requester communicates with the window manager, and next with the processor currently holding the window. Another supported protocol (`crew`) allows multiple copies per window: whenever a processor accesses a shared variable, it receives a copy of the window containing the variable; if it is a write access, then all other copies are invalidated. Other caching protocols (including "non consistency check", called `chaos`) are also supported. The type of protocol to be used may be specified when the shared array is declared.

3.3.3 Explicit window manipulation

Clearly, indiscriminate use of window caching protocols may result in high overheads. It is expected that tolerably low overheads will be obtained by tailoring the data partition and the caching protocol to the communication pattern of the algorithm. As a last resort, Nicke also allows explicit manipulation of windows by the user, with instructions such as `fetch`, `flush` and `invalidate`.

4 Implementation

The implementation of Nicke consists of two parts:

- The preprocessor that translates a Nicke program into standard C code, containing additional calls to system and library functions.

- The run-time support, which consists of a set of functions providing various communication and resource allocation functions.

The Nicke language supports global object spaces for processes, process groups and shared arrays. Nicke processes may require services from any network location using remote reference pointers. A set of data structures link between the program level and the runtime support: they are recognized by the preprocessor and manipulated by the runtime *servers*. The servers are resident at each node in the network and provide network-wide services.

4.1 Preprocessor

4.1.1 Data Structures

The basic structure used to access any remote object is the *remote pointer structure*, called `remptr`. The referred object type is determined by the `mode` field. The structure is of the following type:

```
typedef struct {
        t_location          location;
        union {
                int         pid;
                int         gid;
                int         tag;
                char        *addr;
        }       id;
        int                 mode;
} remptr;
```

A *process environment structure* accompanies each Nicke process. It holds Nicke-specific context information for the process. The preprocessor passes down this structure through every function call as an additional parameter, and makes the following information available for the process:

```
typedef struct {
        remptr      e_parent;
        remptr      e_me;
        remptr      e_group;
        int         e_groupsize;
        int         e_groupind;
} processenv;
```

References to all the constants `INDEX`, `ME`, `GROUP`, `PARENT`, etc., are replaced by the preprocessor with the appropriate fields in the environment structure.

4.1.2 Parallel Constructs

The preprocessor translates most Nicke constructs into library routine calls that implement the services directly.

Processes

Declarations that create processes are translated into code that creates the process group and spawns these processes. A process array declaration is translated into a for-loop; a process tuple declaration is translated into a sequence of statements. Externally declared processes are spawned by the `main` process that executes on processor `HOST`.

Nicke processes are always created within *process groups*. The spawning of a child proceeds as follows:

- The user code allocates a new process group of the appropriate size and receives back a remote pointer for the group.
- For each process in the group, the `N_RemSpawn()` routine is called. If allocation and/or placement occur in the declaration, they are computed here and passed as parameters to `N_RemSpawn`. The routine prepares an environment structure for the new process containing the group pointer, the parent (calling) process pointer, the group size and the process' index in the group. It calls the remote kernel which determines the local process id and adds it to the environment before invoking the actual process body function. The remote kernel returns the process id in a message. `N_RemSpawn()` finally returns the caller a remote pointer to the newly created process.
- The kernel at the child node spawns the child process.
- The remote pointer returned by `N_RemSpawn()` is assigned to the process array variable and the process is added to its group via the `N_AddMember()` call.

Process Groups

All the group operations are implemented via single library routine calls:

- The barrier synchronization `sync` is handled by calling `N_Synch()` from all the processes in the group.
- Similarly, `pbreak` is handled by `N_Pbreak()`.
- The `parw` call incurs an implicit call to `N_WaitGroup()` which blocks until all the children have terminated.
- A new process group is created by first allocating it via the `N_NewGroup()` call and then adding the members one by one via `N_AddMember()`.

Messages

A message *send* operation encapsulates the data in a buffer and calls the sending routine; a complement *receive* operation moves the data into the variables in the receive list.

Shared Arrays

The declaration of a shared memory array is translated in two parts:

- A declaration of a global window descriptor structure of the appropriate type, declared in all the nodes.
- The initialization of the window descriptor structure and allocation of the actual memory portions for it. The initialization routine is invoked concurrently on all nodes, each allocating the local portions and assigning global pointers accordingly.

Accessing a shared memory element may be either for read or for write. In both cases, the preprocessor calls the *index* and *offset* macros of the given window type to attain a window handle and an offset within it. It invokes either `N_ShGet()` or `N_ShPut()` with a buffer address and a length parameter to perform the copy in/out.

4.1.3 Compile Time Tags

Nicke allows declaration of processes and shared arrays in the global program scope. The variables associated with these objects should be valid in all the network nodes. These variable are remote pointers, and their values are bound at *runtime*, after the appropriate resource allocation occurs (and at the location of allocation). Nicke uses remote *tags* as the valid values for pointers. The tags are determined at compile time, and are used locally for tagging objects. Since the location is known at compile time, the pointers are valid everywhere once the resource is allocated and tagged.

4.2 Nicke kernel

The runtime library and resident kernel support the compound operations required by the preprocessor.

The underlying kernel layer is assumed to support certain, basic intra-node primitives. If the target system contains a compatible version of these services, they may be used. Otherwise, they need to be implemented for the Nicke library to run with. The required services consist of a local process spawner that maintains information about the living processes and provides the process control operations *yield*, *terminate*, *sleep*, *wakeup* (in any form). It includes a memory manager that manages the entire local memory space. And it includes a router that forwards messages to any node in the network. (This layer is given as a standard part of the Trollius system; the Trollius version of Nicke uses Trollius processes for each Nicke process.)

On top of this layer, the Nicke kernel maintains its own notion of processes, provides a memory tagging facility, and provides network wide services through memory resident servers.

The spawning of remote processes is carried out by the *spawner server*. The server prepares the Nicke context for new processes and supports running of program parts as separate processes.

The *group server* maintains group information at the parent location. It provides the group operations like member queries and barrier synchronization.

The *window server* manipulates memory *windows* and provides *software caching* operations. These include caching, replication, locking and overlap handling. All shared array operations are carried out through the window interface and allow the system to modify the window information internally (while the user only maintains a *window handle* for reference). In this way, the system may operate with a limited amount of memory, swap window contents to disk and perform periodic garbage collection.

The Nicke library interface routines invoke the operations supported by the servers. The library interface routines perform the encapsulation of parameters needed for the service requests into messages and the message exchange. For instance, whenever a response is required from the server the appropriate interface routine automatically attaches the "return-address" to the request.

5 Conclusion

The runtime support package for Nicke has been implemented on 8CE, an experimental shared bus multiprocessor workstation built at the IBM T. J. Watson Research Center [6]. The Mach [1] operating system runs on 8CE and provides multithreads support and shared memory handling at the kernel level. The Nicke runtime package uses the Mach C Threads facility for multiprocessing [4].

The preprocessor can run on any Unix machine, and produces standard C code with library routine calls. The current implementation of the preprocessor poses some restrictions on the Nicke syntax.,

The Victor V256 system has been the first target, message passing machine for Nicke [11]. Victor is a 256 Tranputer machine, interconnected in a mesh topology and connected to an IBM RT serving as host. The Trollius system provides basic operating system services on Victor [5]. The Trollius kernel is loaded from the host onto every node in the network. The resident kernel supports asynchronous message passing and routing, process spawning and memory handling. The Nicke runtime support package has been implemented on top of Trollius, using a Trollius process for each Nicke process and using the Trollius message passing system for interaction.

As can be inferred from this paper, our goal is not the design of the most clean, elegant, high-level language for parallelism (an extension of C can not possibly be clean and elegant). Rather, we try to create a flexible tool for experimenting with algorithmic aspects of parallel computation.

A language with better typing and better extensibility than C would provide a better basis to our work. At present, constraints of the C language prevents us from making process types, processes and shared variables first-class citizens in Nicke. The use of C++ would improve, but not completely solve this problem. Also, several compromises were made in the current prototype to avoid the need for a full Nicke compiler (the preprocessor does not create a symbol table). While not affecting the semantics of the language, these make the syntax bulkier, and introduce annoying restrictions.

The Nicke kernel has not been optimized for performance, and we expect much work to be involved in kernel tuning. The kernel is parallel in that servers may run concurrently at each processor; however, each kernel call is executed sequentially, by one server. Further parallelism could by applied to distribute execution of kernel calls. Also, the design of efficient window management algorithms for shared arrays is a challenging research issue.

We have not given so far any attention to I/O. Standard Unix I/O services will not be appropriate for a large scale parallel machine with massively parallel I/O. New paradigms for parallel I/O need to be developed and reflected at the programming language level (or the metaprogramming level).

Finally, the two-layered approach exemplified by Nicke may offer a useful direction for the (semi) standardization of parallel programming languages, e.g. for the definition of a standard parallel C language. At present, parallel architectures are too different to hope that a unique parallel language will map equally well say, on a Victor machine or an IBM 3090. However, this does not preclude the use of a common, core language that would be appropriate for a wide variety of parallel machines. This core corresponds to the virtual layer of Nicke. In order to achieve good performance it would be nessessary to annotate the code, providing more machine-specific information. The annotation language may differ from one type of architecture to another (but not necessarily from one machine to another, when the machines are broadly similar). This annotation mechanism corresponds to the physical layer of Nicke. With such approach, code can be ported from one machine to another by mere recompilation. The code can then be tuned for improved performance, without affecting the computation outcome.

References

[1] M. Accetta, R. Baron, D. Golub, R. Rashid, A. Tevanian, and M. Young. Mach: A new kernel foundation for unix development. Technical report, Carnegie Mellon University, August 1986.

[2] William C. Athas and Charles L. Seitz. Multicomputers: Message-passing concurrent computers. *IEEE Computer*, pages 9–24, 1988.

[3] K. A. Bowen and R. A. Kowalski. Amalgamating language and metalanguage in logic programming. In *Logic Programming*. Academic Press, 1982.

[4] E. C. Cooper and R. P. Draves. C threads. Draft of Technical Report, July 1987.

[5] Cornell Theory Center. *Trollius User's Reference Manual*, 1989.

[6] Armando Garcia, David J. Foster, and Richard F. Freitas. The advanced computing environment multiprocessor workstation. Technical Report TR 14491, IBM Research, T. J. Watson Research center, 1989.

[7] David A. George. Epex – environment for parallel execution. Technical Report TR 13158, IBM Research, T. J. Watson Research center, 1987.

[8] Paul Hudak, Jean-Marc Delosme, and Ilse C.F. Ipsen. Parlance: A para-functional programming environment for parallel and distributed computing. Technical Report YALEU/DCS/RR-524, Yale University, dept. of Computer Science, 1987.

[9] James T. Kuehn and Burton J. Smith. The horizon supercomputing system: Architecture and software. In *Proc. Supercomputing'88*, pages 28–34, 1988.

[10] Piyush Mehotra and John Van Rosendale. Parallel language constructs for tensor product computations on loosely coupled architectures. In *Proc. Supercomputing'89*, pages 616–626, 1989.

[11] F. T. Tong, R. C. Booth, D. G. Shea, W. W. Wilcke, and D. J. Zukowski. The victor project. Technical Report TR 13040, IBM Research, T. J. Watson Research center, 1987.

[12] Shaula Yemini. On the suitability of ada multitasking for expressing parallel algorithms. In *Proc. of the AdaTEC Conference on Ada*, 1982.

Languages, Compilers and Run-Time Environments
for Distributed Memory Machines
J. Saltz and P. Mehrotra (Editors)

A Static Performance Estimator in the Fortran D Programming System

Vasanth Balasundaram[a], Geoffrey Fox[b], Ken Kennedy[c] and Ulrich Kremer[c]

[a]IBM T.J. Watson Research Center, P.O. Box 218, Yorktown Heights, NY 10598, USA (affiliated with Caltech during this work)

[b]Syracuse University, Depts. of Computer Science and Physics, 111 College Place, Syracuse, NY 13244-4100, USA (affiliated with Caltech during this work)

[c]Rice University, Dept. of Computer Science, P.O. Box 1892, Houston, TX 77251, USA

Abstract
The choice of the data decomposition scheme is an important factor in determining the available parallelism and hence the performance of an application on a distributed memory multiprocessor. In this paper, we present a performance estimator and discuss its role in the interactive Fortran D programming system. The estimator statically evaluates the relative efficiency of different data decomposition schemes for any given program on any given distributed memory multiprocessor. Our method is not based on a theoretical machine model, but instead uses a set of kernel routines to "train" the estimator for each target machine. We also describe a prototype implementation of this technique and discuss an experimental evaluation of its accuracy.

1. INTRODUCTION

A major goal of the Center for Research on Parallel Computation (CRPC), a research consortium consisting of several universities and national research labs, is to develop a machine-independent parallel programming model usable for both shared and distributed-memory SIMD/MIMD architectures. Initial efforts have been directed towards the design of a language that is powerful enough to express data parallel computations, yet also simple enough that a sophisticated compiler can produce efficient programs for different parallel architectures. The resulting language proposal, called Fortran D [7], extends Fortran by introducing constructs that specify data decompositions.

At Rice, the Fortran D implementation group is building a system to compile Fortran D to efficient code for distributed-memory multiprocessors [9]. The efficiency of the compiler-generated program will depend on the ability of the compiler to minimize communication and load imbalance in the resulting program. A major objective of the project is to show that Fortran D programs can be translated into efficient code for distributed memory machines, assuming that the original program is structured according to a *data-parallel programming style.* Programs written in such a style allow the user to take full advantage of the compiler without intolerable loss of efficiency in the compiler-generated code.

One of the reasons for the success of vector supercomputers is the availability of compilers that allowed machine-independent vectorizable programs to be written. Such automatic vectorization and other compiler technologies have made it possible for the scientist to structure Fortran loops according the well-understood rules of "vectorizable style" and expect the resulting program to be compiled to efficient code on any vector machine [5, 15]. It is an open question whether distributed-memory machines and their compilers can repeat such a success.

A compiler is in general better suited for inserting the necessary communication induced by a decomposition, which is a straightforward, but tedious and error prone task. In contrast, we expect most compilers not to do well when loops contain control flow, index arrays, or I/O-operations. In these situations, the user might be able to restructure the program in a fashion that will avoid the compiler's "deficiencies" or isolate the "problematic" code, allowing the compiler to perform well on the rest of the program. We call this the *data-parallel programming style.*

We will consider the compiler project as successful if for most scientific applications written in a data-parallel programming style the compiler will generate code that is within a factor of two of the speed of a corresponding hand-coded, message-passing version of the program. Details on the compiler validation strategy for the Fortran D compiler can be found in [9].

1.1. Why a Static Performance Estimator?

Perhaps the most important intellectual step in preparing a program for execution on a distributed-memory parallel computer is to choose a decomposition for the fundamental data structures used in the program. Once selected, this data domain decomposition scheme often completely determines the parallelism in the resulting program. Unfor-

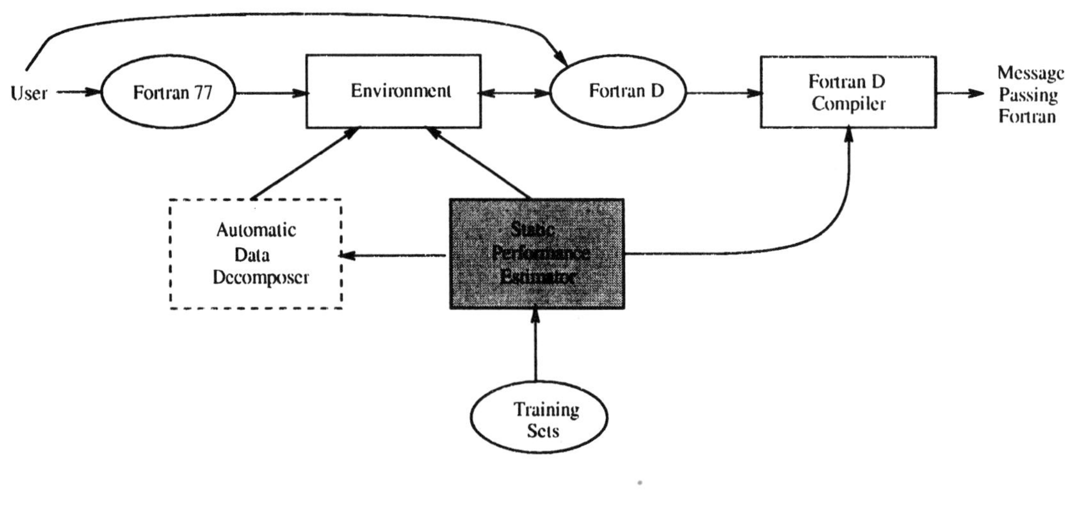

FIGURE 1: The Fortran D programming system

tunately, there are no existing tools to help the programmer make this important step correctly. As of today, the programmer must guess a data decomposition, compile, and run the resulting program to determine its effectiveness. Comparing two different data decomposition schemes requires implementing and running both versions of the program, a tedious task at best.

It turns out, however, that data dependency information is often sufficient to make predictions about the relative efficiencies of different data decomposition schemes. Let us illustrate this with a simple example. Consider the following program segment:

```
do j = 2, n
    do i = 2, n
        A(i, j) = 𝓕( A(i−1, j) )
        B(i, j) = 𝓕'( A(i, j), B(i, j−1), B(i, j) )
    enddo
enddo
```

$\mathcal{F}$ and $\mathcal{F}'$ are linear functions whose exact nature is irrelevant to this discussion. There is a data dependence carried by the i loop: the dependence of A(i, j) on A(i−1, j). This dependence indicates that the computation of an element of A cannot be started until the element immediately above it in the previous row has been computed. There is also a data dependence carried by the j loop: that of B(i, j) on B(i, j−1). This dependence indicates that the computation of an element of B cannot be started until the computation of the element immediately to the left of it in the previous column has been computed.

This pattern of data dependences between references to elements of an array gives us some clues as to how we ought to decompose the array. It is usually a good strategy to decompose an array in a manner that internalizes the maximum number of data dependences within each partition, so that there is no need to move data between the different partitions that are stored on different processors; this avoids expensive communication via messages. For example, the data dependence of A(i, j) on A(i−1, j) can be satisfied by decomposing A in a column-wise manner, so that the dependences are "internalized"within each partition. The data dependence of B(i, j) on B(i, j−1) can be satisfied by decomposing B row-wise, since this would internalize the dependences within each partition.

However, it is not enough to examine only the dependences that arise due to references to the same array. In some cases, the data flow in the program implicitly couples two different arrays together, so that the decomposition of one affects that of the other. In our example, each point B(i, j) also requires the value A(i, j). Let us treat this as a special data dependence called a *value* dependence (read "B is value dependent on A"), to distinguish it from the traditional data dependence that is defined only between references to the same array. This value dependence must also be satisfied either by internalization or by communication. Internalization of the value dependence is possible only by decomposing B in the same manner as A, so that each B(i, j) and the A(i, j) value required by it are in the same partition.

By looking at the data dependences in the program segment, we can come up with the following list of data decomposition schemes for the arrays A and B:

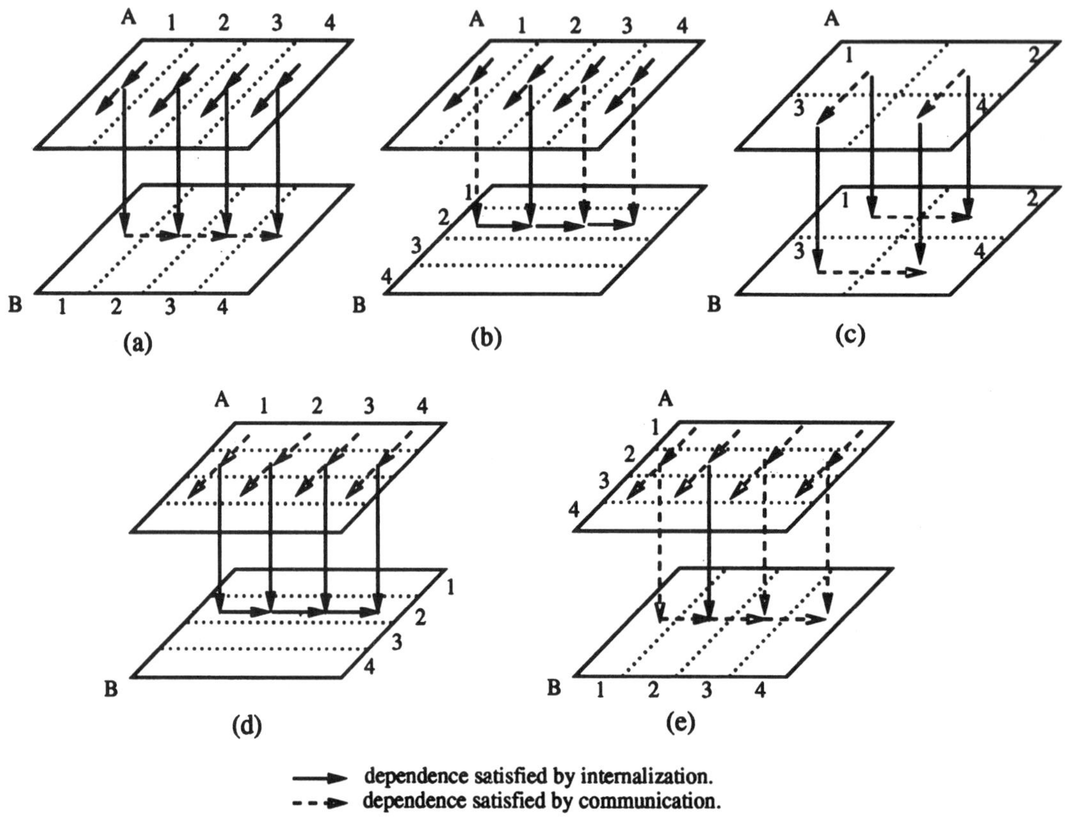

FIGURE 2: Data dependences satisfied by internalization and communication for different data decomposition schemes of arrays A and B. For clarity, only a few of the dependences are shown.

(a) Decompose A by column and B by column. This satisfies the dependences within A and the value dependences of B on A by internalization but communication is required to satisfy the data dependences within B (Figure 2(a)).

(b) Decompose A by column and B by row. Dependences within B are now satisfied by internalization, but communication is needed to satisfy the value dependence of B on A (Figure 2(b)).

(c) Decompose both A and B as 2 dimensional blocks. This would result in communication to satisfy dependences within both A and B, while the value dependence of B on A is satisfied by internalization (Figure 2(c)).

(d) Decompose A by row and B by row. This case is analogous to (a), except that now we would require communication to satisfy dependences within A.

(e) Decompose A by row and B by column. Very few dependences are internalized within partitions in this case, which would result in substantial communication.

Communication overhead is a major cause of performance degradation on most machines, so a reasonable first choice would be the data decomposition scheme that requires the least communication. By looking at the diagram in Figure 2, we can immediately rule out case (e), because it requires "too much communication compared to the other cases" However, making a similar comparison between (a), (b), (c) and (d) is not so straightforward, because it is not immediately clear as to which one is better. Here is where the static performance estimator comes in. The estimator is designed to evaluate different data decomposition schemes statically, by using the data dependence information about the program segment. The estimator can make a better evaluation of a data decomposition scheme than the programmer, by doing a more rigorous analysis based on the data dependences.

We have taken this idea a step further, and integrated the performance estimator into an interactive programming environment that helps the user to understand the effect of a given data decomposition and program structure on the efficiency of the *compiler-generated* code running on a given target machine [3]. Figure 1 shows the structure of our proposed Fortran D programming system. The programming system is built around the stand-alone Fortran D compiler. In contrast to other parallel programming environments [4, 14, 16], the user does not take active part in the compilation process itself. The main components of the environment are a static performance estimator and an automatic data partitioner. In addition, the programming environment will provide program transformations and editing capabilities that allow the users to restructure their programs according to a data-parallel programming style.

Our static performance estimator consists of two separate modules, a *machine module* and a *compiler module*. The machine module predicts the performance of a node program with explicit communication (message-passing Fortran program), while the compiler module estimates the performance of a program annotated with data decompositions (i.e., a Fortran D program).

If efficient enough, the machine module can be used by the compiler to make decisions on different communication alternatives. The programming environment can use an efficient compiler module to predict the implications of decomposition decisions. However, to be effective, the performance estimator needs to be able to accurately predict when the performance of one data decomposition strategy becomes preferable to those of the alternatives.

1.2. Automatic Data Decomposition

Before the user invokes the performance estimator, the data domain must first be decomposed. The automatic data decomposition tool in the environment provides a starting point for the user in choosing a good data decomposition, and the automatic data decomposer then converts the input Fortran program into a Fortran D program. The analysis performed by the data decomposer is divided into two phases — alignment analysis and decomposition analysis.

Alignment analysis is used to prune the search space of possible arrays alignments by selecting only those alignments that minimize data movement. Alignment analysis is machine-independent; it is performed by analyzing the array access patterns of computations in the program [11, 10].

Decomposition analysis follows alignment analysis. It applies heuristics to prune unprofitable choices in the search space of possible decompositions of the data structures. The efficiency of a data decomposition is determined by machine-dependent aspects such as interconnection topology, number of processors, and communication costs. The automatic data decomposer uses the final set of alignments and decompositions to generate a set of reasonable data decomposition schemes. In the worst case, the set of decompositions is the cross product of the alignment and decomposition sets.

In addition to determining a static global data decomposition, the automatic data decomposer will also perform local and global analysis to determine the profitability of redistributing arrays at various points in the program. The system finally selects the decomposition with the best predicted performance.

We believe that for a common class of scientific problems, known as *loosely synchronous* problems [8], the automatic data decomposer can determine the most efficient data decomposition scheme without further user interaction, assuming the original Fortan program is written in a data-parallel programming style.

2. DISTRIBUTED MEMORY PROGRAMMING MODEL

We assume that the distributed memory program is written using the *loosely synchronous* model as defined by Fox, et.al. [8]. The salient features of this programming model are outlined below.

All processor nodes execute the *same* node program. The programmer therefore only writes a single generic node program (and perhaps a host program that executes on some front-end machine).

All computation within a processor's node program can only involve data items contained in the processor's local memory. Non-local data items must be accessed through inter-processor communication, which is assumed to be implemented via message-passing.

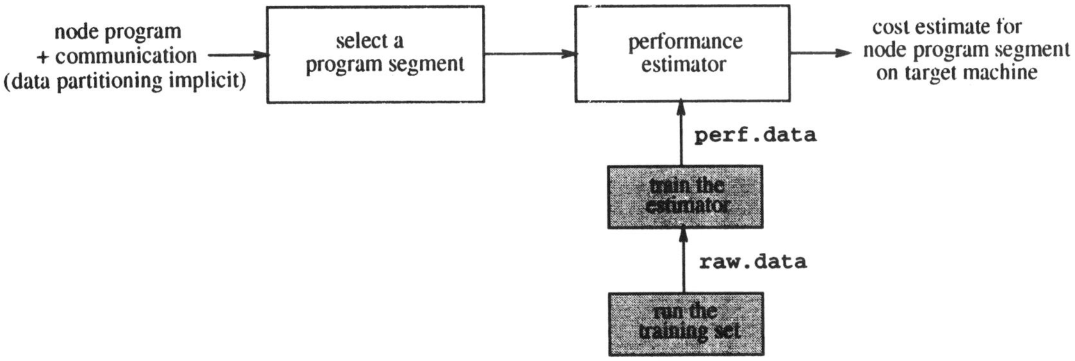

FIGURE 3: The performance estimation process.

Thus, *the writing of the node program implicitly defines the decomposition of the data domain.*

Communication between a group of processors imposes a synchronizing condition among all the processors. This implies that *all the processors operate in a loose lockstep, consisting of alternating phases of parallel asynchronous computation and synchronous communication.*

The previous feature is an important property of the loosely synchronous distributed memory programming model: any data transfer among processors occurs simultaneously in concert, with all processors participating within a well-defined phase. This allows any inherent regularity in the communication pattern to be exploited for maximum efficiency on the target machine. Experiments conducted on a wide variety of real applications has shown that a large class of regular problems and some spatially irregular problems are very well suited for the loosely synchronous model [8].

One disadvantage of this model is that it may not be well suited for temporally irregular problems. However, in this paper we restrict ourselves to problems with regular geometries whose data dependency graphs can be computed statically (i.e., spatially and temporally regular problems), so that the loosely synchronous model is well suited to our needs.

3. CHOOSING THE DATA DECOMPOSITION SCHEME

Let us consider the problem of deriving a distributed memory node program (specified according to the loosely synchronous model) from a sequential program. This requires three steps: (1) identify opportunities for data parallelism in the sequential program, (2) decompose the data domain across the processors, and (3) generate the node program (with loosely synchronous communication), which, when executed in parallel by all the processors, exploits the available data parallelism.

Step (3) involves the specification of the program that operates on a generic data partition, and also the specification of the loosely synchronous inter-processor communication. This can be done automatically by a "distributed memory compiler" as mentioned earlier. Such a compiler would typically use the *data dependence graph* of the sequential program, along with the data decomposition information, to derive the node program and the communication. For the purposes of this paper, we will assume that steps (1) and (2) are the programmer's responsibility, and step (3) is performed by a distributed memory compiler.

Experiments with preliminary implementations of such compilers have indicated that the choice of the data decomposition strategy strongly influences the performance of the parallel program on the distributed memory machine. This is not surprising, since it is the data decomposition scheme that ultimately determines how much of the available data parallelism in the application can be effectively exploited on the target machine.

In an attempt to better understand how the data decomposition strategy affects the performance of the generated node program, we decided to build an interactive data decomposition tool. Our idea was to use this data decomposition tool to statically explore different data decomposition schemes without having to run the node program each time on the machine. Details of this tool are described in an earlier work [3].

The techniques discussed in that earlier work focussed on the derivation of the node program and the inter-processor communication in response to the user's choice of a particular data decomposition scheme. We wanted to add to the tool the ability to statically determine which choice of data decomposition was best for a given target machine. In order to do this, we needed a scheme for comparing several different data decomposition schemes statically. Providing a measure for comparing different data decomposition schemes statically would be very useful in a data decomposition tool, as well as in sophisticated distributed memory compilers that attempt to derive the data decomposition

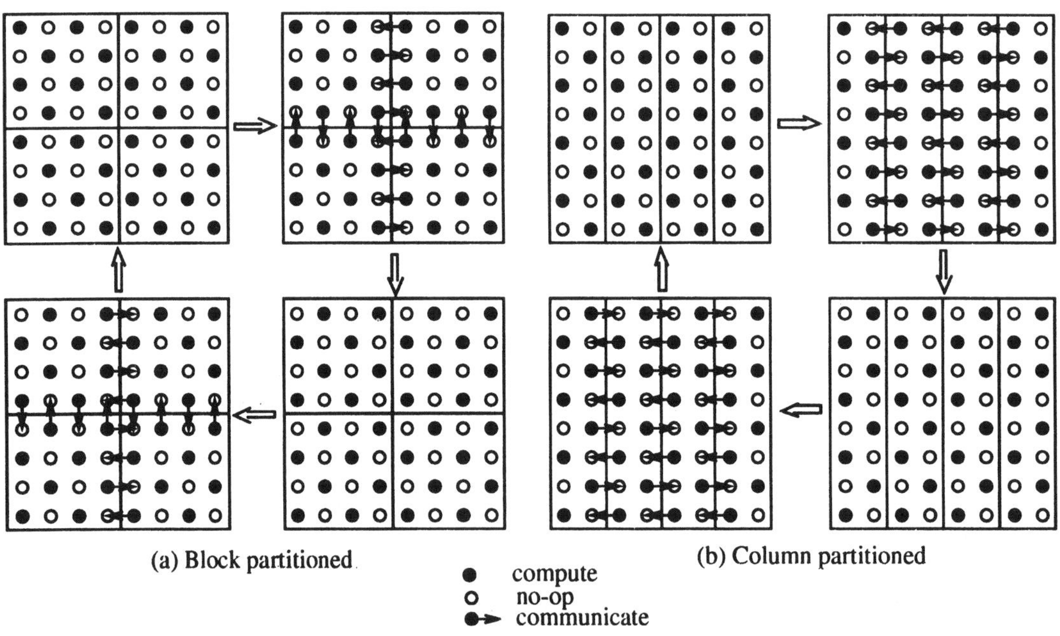

FIGURE 4: Two possible data decomposition schemes for program REDBLACK.

scheme automatically. Clearly, any relative evaluation of data decomposition schemes will depend not only on the nature of data dependences in the program, but also on several target machine specific parameters. To make our job easier, we will restrict ourselves to data partitions that are rectangular, and also assume that the data domain is decomposed uniformly (i.e., all partitions are of the same shape). Extending our techniques for more general cases is a topic of future research.

4. AN EXAMPLE

To better motivate the relationship between the data decomposition scheme and factors such as communication overhead, data domain size, execution time and number of processors used, let us consider an example. Program REDBLACK, listed below, is a segment of the node program for a pointwise relaxation using the "red-black" checkerboard algorithm.

The original data domain for this problem is a 2 dimensional grid, which must be appropriately decomposed across the processors. In the following node program segment, (idim $\times$ jdim) is the size of each processor's data partition. This local data is stored within each processor's local memory as an array val(0:idim+1, 0:jdim+1). The interior of the array val(1:idim, 1:jdim) contains the actual elements of the processor's local partition of the data domain, while the borders val(0, 1:jdim), val(idim+1, 1:jdim), val(1:idim, 0) and val(1:idim, jdim+1) are used to store boundary data elements that are received from the neighboring processors.

```
program REDBLACK

do k = 1, ncycles
   //Compute the RED points in my partition.
   do j = 1, jdim, 2
      do i = 1, idim, 2
         val(i,j) = a*(val(i,j-1) + val(i-1,j)
                    + val(i,j+1) + val(i+1,j)) + b*val(i,j)
      enddo
   enddo
   do j = 2, jdim, 2
      do i = 2, idim, 2
         val(i,j) = a*(val(i,j-1) + val(i-1,j)
                    + val(i,j+1) + val(i+1,j)) + b*val(i,j)
      enddo
   enddo
   //Communicate RED points on my partition
   //boundary to the neighboring procs.
   call communicate (val, RED, neighbors)
   //Compute the BLACK points in my partition.
   do j = 1, jdim, 2
      do i = 2, idim, 2
         val(i,j) = a*(val(i,j-1) + val(i-1,j)
                    + val(i,j+1) + val(i+1,j)) + b*val(i,j)
      enddo
   enddo
   do j = 2, jdim, 2
      do i = 1, idim, 2
         val(i,j) = a*(val(i,j-1) + val(i-1,j)
                    + val(i,j+1) + val(i+1,j)) + b*val(i,j)
      enddo
   enddo
   //Communicate BLACK points on my partition
   //boundary to the neighboring procs.
   call communicate (val, BLACK, neighbors)
enddo
```

The node program given above is the code that is executed by each processor, on its local partition of the data domain. Depending on the values of idim and jdim, the size of the partition can be varied. This lets us change the data decomposition scheme by merely changing the loop bounds, and without having to make any extensive modifications to the node program.

For example, Figure 4 shows two possible data decomposition schemes of a 2 dimensional data domain of size 8×8. The two data decomposition schemes shown in the figure are block-partitioning and column-partitioning. When idim $= 4$, jdim $= 4$ each partition is a 4×4 block, and we get the block-partitioned case. When idim $= 8$, jdim $= 2$, each partition is an 8×2 strip, and we get the column-partitioned case. In both cases, four partitions of equal size are created, which are assigned to four processors of the target distributed memory machine.

Figure 4 also illustrates the compute-communicate sequence for the block-partitioned and column-partitioned schemes. There are several methods for performing the communication between neighboring processors (indicated in the figure by arrows that cross partition boundaries). In most existing distributed memory machines, message startup cost is usually an important factor in determining the particular communication strategy to employ. A useful rule of thumb is: communicating a small number of large messages is more efficient than communicating a large number of small messages. Program REDBLACK achieves larger size messages by performing the communication outside the do j loop, so that all the boundary elements can be communicated together as a vector, instead of individually.

We wrote the REDBLACK node program in Fortran, using the EXPRESS[1] programming environment. EXPRESS is a commercially available package, that extends Fortran 77 with a portable communication library, and is based on the loosely synchronous programming model [6]. The program was executed on the NCUBE, and execution times were determined for increasing data domain sizes and number of processors. Figure 5 shows the graph of data domain size (i.e., size of the original 2 dimensional problem grid) versus average execution time for a single iteration of the do k loop. For a data domain of size $N \times N$, and P processors, the logical processor interconnection topology for the block-partitioned case is assumed to be a $\sqrt{P} \times \sqrt{P}$ 2 dimensional grid, with each processor getting a block partition of size $N/\sqrt{P} \times N/\sqrt{P}$ data elements, and for the column-partitioned case it is assumed to be a linear array of size P with each processor getting a column partition of size $N \times N/P$ data elements.

For example, when $P = 16$ and $N = 32$, block-partitioning assigns to each processor a partition of size 8×8, while column-partitioning assigns to each processor a partition of size 32×2.

It is interesting to note the crossover point of the curves for the block-partitioned and column-partitioned cases. It indicates that the efficiency of a data decomposition scheme is dependent on the data domain size as well as number of processors used. For 16 processors, column partitioning is more efficient than block partitioning for data domain sizes less than 180×180, whereas for 64 processors, the critical domain size is 128×128.

The steps in the curves are caused by load imbalance effects. When the data domain size N is not exactly divisible by the number of processors P, some processors are assigned an extra data partition to work on. The load imbalance created due to this is greater for the column-partitioned scheme compared to the block-partitioned scheme, resulting in larger step sizes for the column-partitioned case.

5. THE TRAINING SET METHOD OF PERFORMANCE ESTIMATION

The REDBLACK example illustrates some of the subtleties involved in trying to compare different data decomposition schemes. We experimented with different decomposition strategies on several distributed memory machines, including the NCUBE, Symult S2010

[1]EXPRESS is a copyright of ParaSoft Corporation.

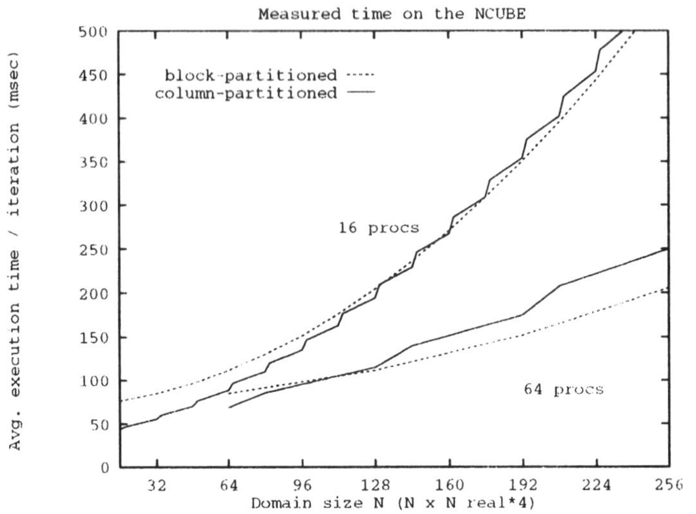

FIGURE 5: Graphs of data domain size vs. average measured execution time of the main loop for program REDBLACK on the NCUBE.

and the Meiko transputer array[2], and attempted to derive a theoretical performance model based on our observations. Our attempts were based on published techniques for developing performance evaluation models, such as [13, 1] for example. We found that it was difficult to derive a single theoretical model that could predict the experimentally observed behavior of the node program on different data decomposition schemes.

Although the theoretical model could predict overall program execution time with a fair degree of accuracy, it failed to predict the *crossover point* (see Figure 5) of the curves with consistent accuracy. Several other effects such as the undulations (or change in slope) of the curve were also difficult to predict. The accuracy of estimating the overall execution time did not matter so much to us as the accuracy of estimating the crossover point at which one data decomposition scheme is preferable over another.

Note that it in general it may be impossible to specify the "crossover point" in terms of data domain size alone, as suggested by the graphs in Figure 5. The crossover point may shift depending on the particular communication routines used for message-passing, hardware and operating system peculiarities of the target machine and on the implementation of the low-level software layer. It could also be affected by minor algorithmic changes to the program.

We were eventually convinced that a purely theoretical model was too general for our purposes, and attempting to refine the theoretical prediction techniques would only result in increasingly complex models with little improvement in accuracy. We began experimenting with alternative methods of performance estimation that are more directed to our specific needs. The resulting technique, called the *Training Set Method*, will now be described.

[2]All programs were written in EXPRESS.

The Training Set Method consists of two initialization steps that must be performed once for each target machine (see Figure 3), and an estimation algorithm that can be invoked by an interactive tool or a distributed memory compiler on any node program to be run on the specified target machine.

In the first initialization step, a set of routines called the *training set* is run on the target machine. The training set is a node program that performs a sequence of basic arithmetic and control flow operations, followed by a sequence of communication calls. The average execution time of the arithmetic and control flow operations are measured on the target machine, and the data is written out to a `raw.data` file. The communication calls are designed to test several data movement patterns using all possible combinations of the various message-passing utilities supported on the target machine. The average times taken for each communication is measured for increasing data sizes and processor numbers, as well as for unit and non-unit data strides (e.g., communicating a column of data vs. communicating a row of data in Fortran). This data is also written out to the `raw.data` file as a set of (x, y) points, where x is the message size in bytes and y is the average time that *one processor* spends in participating in the loosely synchronous communication. In the present version of this system, the training set is written in EXPRESS, and the communication calls use the loosely synchronous message-passing utilities provided by EXPRESS.

In the second initialization step, the performance data in the `raw.data` file is analyzed and the raw performance data is converted into a more compact and usable form. Functions are fitted to the communication performance data and average values are computed for the execution times of the arithmetic and control operations. The functions and the average values are then written out to a `perf.data` file. The `perf.data` file is a compressed form of the `raw.data` file. On the NCUBE for example, our preliminary implementation resulted in a `raw.data` file that was several tens of Mbytes in size, while the size of the `perf.data` file was around a Kbyte. The functions in `perf.data` will be used by the performance estimation algorithm to reconstruct the communication performance data in the `raw.data` file.

A variant of the chi-squared fit method [12] is used to fit functions to the communication data in the `raw.data` file. The communication data however, are piecewise linear functions, and the chi-squared fit can only be applied to continuous linear functions (see Figure 6). The discontinuities arise due to packetization costs incurred by the need to pad the message so that it can be sent as a whole number of packets. To get around this caveat, we use the chi-squared fit to fit a function of the form $y = a + bx$ only to the continuous linear segments of the piecewise linear curve. In addition, the step size between the adjacent linear line segments is also determined. Knowing the function $y = a + bx$ for a continuous line segment, the step size between adjacent line segments and the packet size on the machine, we can reconstruct a close approximation to the original piecewise linear curve of the communication performance data as specified in the `raw.data` file. Further details on the construction of the training set are given in [2].

The graph in Figure 6 shows the actual communication performance data for some data movement patterns on a 64 processor NCUBE. Although this is only a small sample of the data obtained using the training set, it is illustrative of the unusual behavior of different communication patterns. The curves in the graph correspond to the following

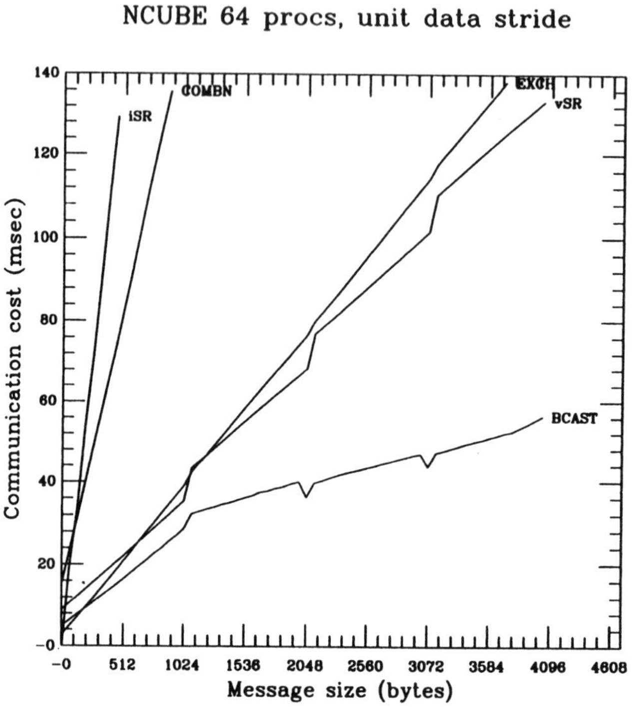

FIGURE 6: A sample of the communication performance data for the NCUBE.

communication patterns, all written using EXPRESS:

- `iSR`: circular shift using individual element send/receive. All processors send data to their right neighbor and then receive data from their left neighbor.

- `vSR`: same as above, except that the data is communicated as a vector instead of element by element.

- `EXCH`: synchronous circular shift (also called "exchange"). The communication is done in two stages. During the first stage, all even numbered processors send data to the right, while all odd numbered processors receive data from the left. In the second stage, all odd processors send to the right while the even processors receive from the left. Contrary to vSR, the `EXCH` mechanism of pairing of sends and receives between neighboring processors ensures that the receiving processor is always prepared to receive the message, regardless of its size.

- `BCAST`: one to all broadcast. Note that it is incorrect to conclude from the graph that "broadcast is faster than circular shift". This is because the graph shows the time that each processor contributes (measured as an average across all the processors) towards the overall data movement, and *not* the time for the completion of the communication call itself.

- `COMBN`: the "combine" operation, where a global reduction is performed using some associative and commutative operator, after which the results of the reduction are communicated to all the processors. This is equivalent to performing a tree reduction over the processors while applying the reduction operator at each node, and then broadcasting the result computed at the root of the tree to all the processors.

6. THE PERFORMANCE ESTIMATION ALGORITHM

Procedure ESTIMATE shown in Figure 7 implements the performance estimation algorithm. The algorithm uses the arithmetic/control and communication performance data stored in the `perf.data` file to determine an execution and communication time estimate. The procedure takes as input a node program statement, which can be either a *simple* statement or a *compound* statement. A compound statement is one which consists of other compound and simple statements, while a simple statement does not. An assignment is an example of a simple statement; do loops, subroutine calls, if-then, etc., are examples of compound statements. The `program` statement in Fortran is a special case of a compound statement: it consists of the entire body of the program. The execution time estimate etime and the communication time estimate ctime are assumed to be initialized to zero.

Procedure ESTIMATE allows us to estimate the execution time and communication time of any selected node program segment, regardless of its size. The branch probability is assumed to be 0.5 by default, but the user is allowed to override it. Note that this algorithm is best used for *comparing* two different data decomposition schemes (i.e., two different node programs for the same application). The etime and ctime values for the different data decomposition schemes can then be compared to get a fairly good estimate of what their relative performance on the target machine would be.

7. A PROTOTYPE IMPLEMENTATION

We implemented a prototype version of the estimator in the ParaScope interactive parallel programming environment [4]. Figure 9 shows a screen snapshot during a typical performance estimation session.

The user can edit the distributed memory node program within ParaScope, and make appropriate changes to it to reflect a particular data decomposition scheme. A statement such as a do loop can then be selected, and the performance estimator invoked by clicking on the `estimate` button. ParaScope responds with an execution time estimate of the selected segment on the target machine, and also the communication time estimate given as a percentage of the execution time. In this way, the effect of different data decomposition strategies can be evaluated on any part of the node program.

If the selected program segment contains symbolic variables, for instance in the upper and lower bounds of a do loop, the user is prompted for the values or value ranges of these variables, since they are necessary for applying procedure ESTIMATE. Once the value of a symbolic variable is supplied, some limited constant propagation is automatically done so that all other occurrences of that variable within the selected program segment also get the value. In addition, the user is also prompted for a branch probability when an if-then statement is encountered by procedure ESTIMATE. The user can optionally accept the default branch probability which is assumed to be between 0.25 and 0.75. The current

```
procedure ESTIMATE (S, etime, ctime)

//Input: a node program statement S.
//Output: the execution time estimate (etime) and communication
//time estimate (ctime) for S on the target machine.

if (S is a simple statement) {
    for (each arithmetic operation α in S) {
        let t(α) be its avg. execution time as specified in the perf.data file;
        etime += t(α);
    }
    for (each load/store operation λ in S) {
        let t(λ) be its avg. execution time as specified in the perf.data file;
        etime += t(λ);
    }
}
else if (S is a compound statement) {
    let B be the body of S;
    etemp = 0.0;  ctemp = 0.0;
    for (each statement b ∈ B) {
        ESTIMATE (b, etemp, ctemp);
    }
    if (S is a do loop) {
        etime += etemp * # of iterations of loop;
        ctime += ctemp * # of iterations of loop;
    }
    if (S is an if-then branch) {
        etime += etemp * probability of branch;
        ctime += ctemp * probability of branch;
    }
    if (S is a subroutine call) {
        let σ be the cost of a subroutine call as specified in the perf.data file;
        etime += etemp + σ;
        ctime += ctemp;
    }
    if (S is a communication call) {
        let δ be the message size in bytes;
        compute the time estimate t(δ) for this msg using the method outlined in Sec. 5;
        ctime += t(δ);
        etime += t(δ);
    }
}
```

FIGURE 7: The performance estimation algorithm.

implementation only handles structured control flow in the node program, and arbitrary branching using goto is prohibited.

We used this prototype implementation to test the accuracy of the estimation technique for several problems. Figure 8 shows the results of the estimator when applied to the do k loop of program REDBLACK, compared to actual measurements on the target machine. The error in the estimation of execution and communication time is approximately 5-10%, but the "crossover point" of the block and column partition curves is predicted quite accurately. Note that besides indicating the crossover point at which one data decomposition is preferable over another, the estimator also gives us a measure of the difference in performance between the two strategies. This may be very useful to the user in making several tradeoff decisions.

8. CONCLUSION AND FUTURE WORK

We have proposed a method for discriminating between different data decomposition choices in a distributed memory parallel program. Our technique, the Training Set Method, is inspired by the observation that it is very hard to build a parameterized model that can help make a comparison of different data distribution strategies across a wide range of communication patterns, problem sizes and target machines. The Training Set Method bases its estimation not on a "hard-wired" theoretical model, but rather on a "training" mechanism that uses a carefully written program (called the training set) to train the model for a particular target machine. This training procedure needs to be done only once for each target machine, during the environment or compiler installation time.

Although the use of a training set simplifies the task of performance estimation significantly, its complexity now lies in the design of the training set program, which must be able to generate a variety of computation and data movement patterns to extract the effect on performance of the hardware/software characteristics of the target machine. Fortunately, real applications (especially the regular and spatially irregular ones) rarely show random data movement patterns; there is often an inherent regularity in their behavior. We would therefore conjecture that the training set program that we designed will probably give fairly accurate estimates for a large number of real applications, even though it tests only a small (regular) subset of all the possible communication patterns. We are planning to investigate how neural networks in conjunction with a test suite of programs and the training set can be used to identify computation or communication patterns where the performance estimation is imprecise and help adapt the performance estimator accordingly.

While creating a machine-level training set seems to be fairly straightforward, a compiler-level training set will be much more difficult to construct and use. Representative program kernels such as the Livermore loops must be created and their performance measured for different data decompositions, numbers of processors, and array sizes. Estimating the performance of a Fortran D program then requires matching computations in the program with kernels from the training set.

Since it is not possible to incorporate all possible computation patterns in the compiler-level training set, the performance estimator will encounter code fragments that cannot be matched with existing kernels. To estimate the performance of these codes, the compiler

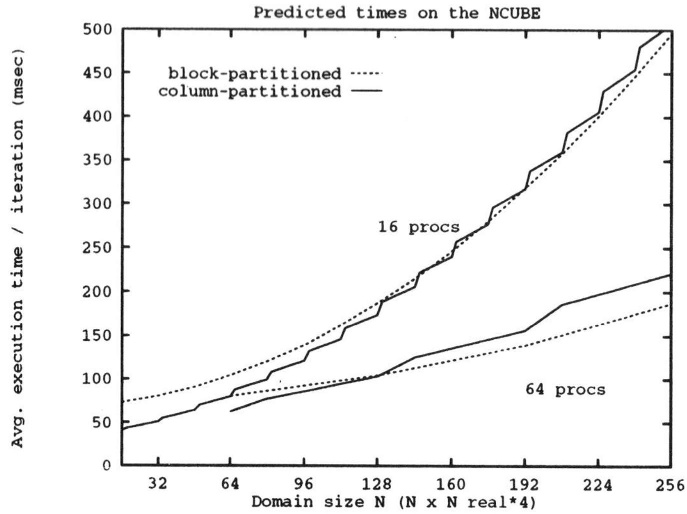

FIGURE 8: Predicted average execution times for column and block partitioned REDBLACK for the NCUBE.

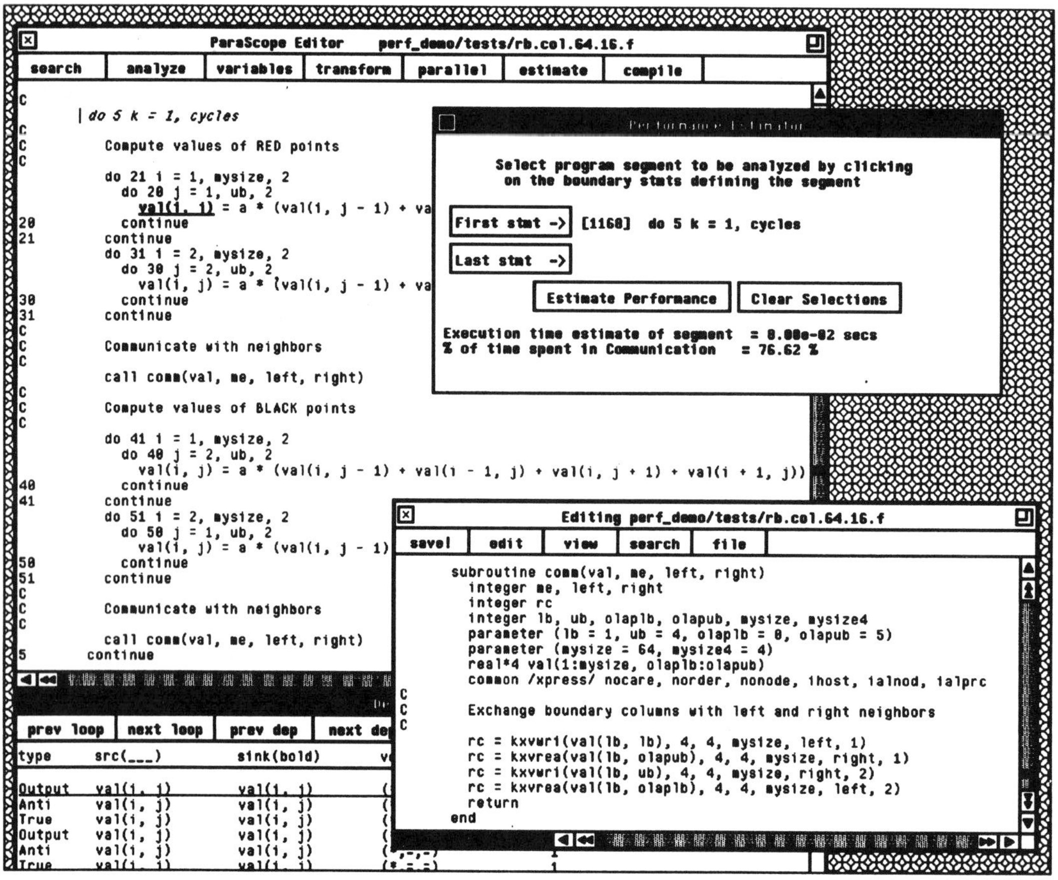

FIGURE 9: Screen snapshot of the performance estimator in ParaScope.

module must rely on the machine-level training set. We plan to incorporate elements of the Fortran D compiler in the performance estimator so that it can mimic the compilation process. The compiler module can thus convert any unrecognized Fortran D program fragment into an equivalent node program, then invoke the machine module to estimate its performance.

An appealing feature of this approach is that changes in the compiler will require only rerunning the training sets to initialize the tables for the new performance estimator, in the same way that changing the target machine requires rerunning the training set described in this paper.

References

[1] M. Annaratone, C. Pommerell, and R. Rühl. Interprocessor communication and performance in distributed memory parallel processors. *Proceedings of the 16th Symposium on Computer Architecture, Jerusalem*, pages 315–324, May 1989.

[2] V. Balasundaram. A static performance estimator. Technical Report C3P-941, Caltech Concurrent Computation Program, Caltech, Pasadena, CA, August 1990.

[3] V. Balasundaram, G. Fox, K. Kennedy, and U. Kremer. An interactive environment for data partitioning and distribution. *Proceedings of the Fifth Distributed Memory Computing Conference, Charleston, S. Carolina*, April 1990.

[4] V. Balasundaram, K. Kennedy, U. Kremer, K. McKinley, and J. Subhlok. The ParaScope editor: an interactive parallel programming tool. *Supercomputing 89, Reno, Nevada*, November 1989.

[5] D. Callahan, K. Kennedy, and U. Kremer. A dynamic study of vectorization in PFC. Technical Report 89-97, Rice University, Houston, TX, July 1989.

[6] ParaSoft Corporation. EXPRESS user manual. 1989.

[7] G. Fox, S. Hiranandani, K. Kennedy, C. Koelbel, U. Kremer, C. Tseng, and M. Wu. Fortran D language specification. Technical Report TR90-141, Dept. of Computer Science, Rice University, December 1990.

[8] G. Fox, M. Johnson, G. Lyzenga, S. Otto, J. Salmon, and D. Walker. *Solving Problems on Concurrent Processors, Vols. 1 and 2.* Prentice Hall, Englewood Cliffs, NJ, 1988.

[9] Seema Hiranandani, Ken Kennedy, and Chau-Wen Tseng. Compiler support for machine-independent parallel programming in Fortran D. In *Compilers and Run-Time Software for Scalable Multiprocessors, eds. J. Saltz and P. Mehrotra.* Elsevier, Amsterdam, The Netherlands, To appear in 1991.

[10] K. Knobe, J. Lukas, and G. Steele, Jr. Data optimization: Allocation of arrays to reduce communication on SIMD machines. *Journal of Parallel and Distributed Computing*, 8(2):102–118, 1990.

[11] J. Li and M. Chen. Synthesis of explicit communication from shared-memory program references. Technical Report YALEU/DCS/TR-755, Yale University, May 1990.

[12] W.H. Press, B.P. Flannery, S.A. Teukolsky, and W.T. Vetterling. *Numerical recipes in C: the art of scientific computing.* Cambridge University Press, 1988.

[13] V. Sarkar. Determining average program execution times and their variance. *Proceedings of the SIGPLAN 89 conference on programming language design and implementation*, pages 298–312, July 1989.

[14] R. Sawdayi, G. Wagenbreth, and J. Williamson. MIMDizer: Functional and data decomposition. In J. Saltz and P. Mehrotra, editors, *Compilers and Runtime Software for Scalable Multiprocessors.* Elsevier, Amsterdam, The Netherlands, to appear in 1991.

[15] M. Wolfe. Semi-automatic domain decomposition. *In proceedings of the Fourth Conference on Hypercubes, Concurrent Computers, and Applications, Monterey, CA*, pages 75–81, March 1989.

[16] H.P. Zima, H.J. Bast, and M. Gerndt. SUPERB: A tool for semi-automatic SIMD/MIMD parallelization. *Parallel Computing*, 6:1–18, 1988.

Languages, Compilers and Run-Time Environments
for Distributed Memory Machines
J. Saltz and P. Mehrotra (Editors)

Compiler Support for Machine-Independent Parallel Programming in Fortran D

Seema Hiranandani, Ken Kennedy, and Chau-Wen Tseng

Department of Computer Science, Rice University, P.O. Box 1892, Houston, TX 77251-1892

Abstract

Because of the complexity and variety of parallel architectures, an efficient machine-independent parallel programming model is needed to make parallel computing truly usable for scientific programmers. We believe that Fortran D, a version of Fortran enhanced with data decomposition specifications, can provide such a programming model. This paper presents the design of a prototype Fortran D compiler for the iPSC/860, a MIMD distributed-memory machine. Issues addressed include data decomposition analysis, guard introduction, communications generation and optimization, program transformations, and storage assignment. A test suite of scientific programs will be used to evaluate the effectiveness of both the compiler technology and programming model for the Fortran D compiler.

1 Introduction

It is widely recognized that parallel computing represents the only plausible way to continue to increase the computational power available to computational scientists and engineers. However, it is not likely to be a success unless parallel computers are as easy to use as the conventional vector supercomputers of today. A major component of the success of vector supercomputers is the ability to write machine-independent vector programs in a subdialect of Fortran. Advances in compiler technology, especially automatic vectorization, have made it possible for the scientist to structure Fortran loops according the rules of "vectorizable style" [Wol89, CKK89], which are well understood, and expect the resulting program to be compiled to efficient code on any vector machine.

Compare this with the current situation for parallel machines. The scientist wishing to use such a machine must rewrite the program in some dialect of Fortran with extensions that explicitly reflect the architecture of the underlying machine, such as message-passing primitives for distributed-memory machines or multidimensional vector operations for synchronous data-parallel machines. In addition to being a lot of work, this conversion is daunting because the scientist risks losing his investment when the next high-end parallel

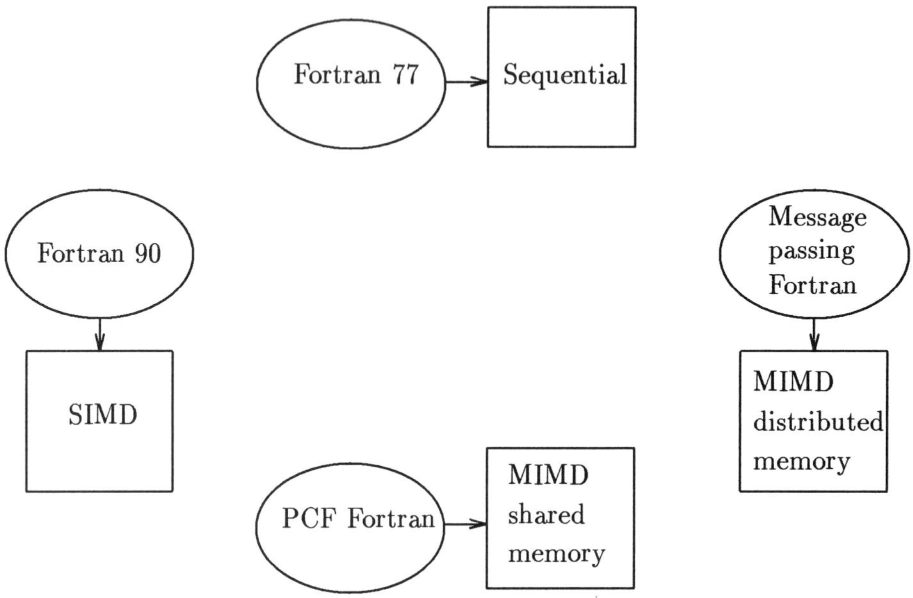

Figure 1: Fortran Dialects and Machine Architectures

machine requires a different set of extensions.

We are left with the question: Can this problem be overcome? In other words, is it possible to identify a subdialect of Fortran from which efficient parallel programs can be generated by a new and possibly more sophisticated compiler technology? Researchers working in the area, including ourselves, have concluded that this is not possible in general. Parallel programming is a difficult task in which many tradeoffs must be weighed. In converting from a Fortran program, the compiler simply is not able to always do a good job of picking the best alternative in every tradeoff, particularly since it must work solely with the text of the program. As a result, the programmer may need to add additional information to the program for it to be correctly and efficiently parallelized.

But in accepting this conclusion, we must be careful not to give up prematurely on the goal of supporting machine-independent parallel programming. In other words, if we extend Fortran to include information about the parallelism available in a program, we should not make those extensions dependent on any particular parallel machine architecture. From the compiler technologist's perspective, we need to find a suitable language for expressing parallelism and compiler technology that will translate this language to efficient programs on different parallel machine architectures.

Parallel Programming Models

Figure 1 depicts four different machine types and the dialect of Fortran commonly used for programming on each of them: Fortran 77 for the sequential machine, Fortran 90 for the SIMD parallel machine (*e.g.,* the TMC Connection Machine), message-passing Fortran for the MIMD distributed-memory machine (*e.g.,* the Intel iPSC/860) and Parallel Computer

Forum (PCF) Fortran [Lea90] for the MIMD shared-memory machine (*e.g.*, the BBN TC2000 Butterfly). Each of these languages seems to be a plausible candidate for use as a machine-independent parallel programming model.

Research on automatic parallelization has already shown that Fortran is unsuitable for general parallel programming. However, message-passing Fortran looks like a promising candidate—it should be easy to implement a run-time system that simulates distributed memory on a shared-memory machine by passing messages through shared memory. Unfortunately, most scientific programmers reject this alternative because programming in message-passing Fortran is difficult and tedious. In essence, this would be reduction to the lowest common denominator: programming every machine would be equally hard.

Starting with PCF Fortran is more promising. In targeting this language to a distributed-memory machine, the key intellectual step is determining the data decomposition across the various processors. It seems plausible that we might be able to use the parallel loops in PCF Fortran to indicate which data structures should be partitioned across the processors—data arrays accessed on different iterations of a parallel loop should probably be distributed. So what is wrong with starting from PCF Fortran? The problem is that the language is nondeterministic. If the programmer inadvertently accesses the same location on different loop iterations, the result can vary for different execution schedules. Hence PCF Fortran programs will be difficult to develop and require complex debugging systems.

Fortran 90 is more promising, because it is a deterministic language. The basic strategy for compiling it to different machines is to block the multidimensional vector operations into submatrix operations, with different submatrices assigned to different processors. We believe that this approach has a good chance of success. In fact, we are participating in a project with Geoffrey Fox at Syracuse to pursue this approach. However, there are questions about the generality of this strategy. SIMD machines are not yet viewed as general-purpose parallel computers. Hence, the programs that can be effectively represented in Fortran 90 may be only a strict subset of all interesting parallel programs. We would still need some way to express those programs that are not well-suited to Fortran 90.

Machine-Independent Programming Strategy

For these reasons, we have chosen a different approach, one that introduces a new set of language extensions to Fortran. We believe that specifying the data decomposition is the most important intellectual step in developing large data-parallel scientific programs. Most parallel programming languages, however, are inadequate in this regard because they only provide constructs to express functional parallelism [PB90]. Hence, we designed a language that extends Fortran by introducing constructs that specify data decompositions. We call the extended language Fortran D, for obvious reasons. Figure 2 shows our plan to use Fortran D as our machine-independent programming model. We should note that our goal in designing Fortran D is not to support the most general data decompositions possible. Instead, our intent is to provide data decompositions that are both powerful enough to express data parallelism in scientific programs, and simple enough to permit the compiler to produce efficient programs.

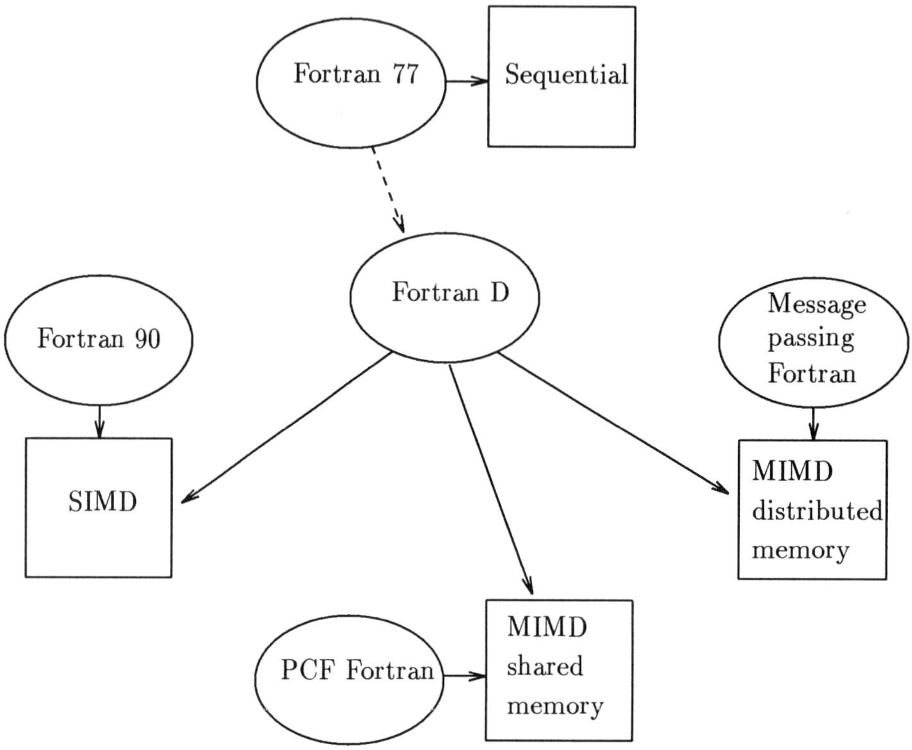

Figure 2: Machine-Independent Programming Strategy Using Fortran D

A Fortran D program is a Fortran program augmented with a set of data decomposition specifications. If these specifications are ignored the program can be run without change on a sequential machine. Hence, the meaning of the program is exactly the meaning of the Fortran program contained within it—the specifications do not affect the meaning, they simply advise the compiler. Compilers for parallel machines can use the specifications not only to decompose data structures but also to infer parallelism, based on the principle that only the owner of a datum computes its value. In other words, the data decomposition also specifies the distribution of the work in the Fortran program.

In this paper we describe a project to build and evaluate a Fortran D compiler for a MIMD distributed-memory machine, namely the Intel iPSC/860. If successful, the result of this project will go a long way toward establishing that machine-independent parallel programming is possible, since it is easy to target a MIMD shared-memory machine once we have a working system for a MIMD distributed-memory machine. The only remaining step would be the construction of an effective compiler for a SIMD machine, like the Connection Machine. Such a project is being planned and will be the subject of a future paper.

The next section presents an overview of the data decomposition features of Fortran D. Section 3 discusses the compiler strategy for a single loop nest, and Section 4 looks at compilation issues for whole programs. Section 5 describes our approach to validating this work on a collection of real application programs. In Section 6 we describe the relationship of this project to other research in the area. We conclude in Section 7 with a discussion of future work.

2 Fortran D

The data decomposition problem can be approached by noting that there are two levels of parallelism in data-parallel applications. First, there is the question of how arrays should be *aligned* with respect to one another, both within and across array dimensions. We call this the *problem mapping* induced by the structure of the underlying computation. It represents the minimal requirements for reducing data movement for the program, and is largely independent of any machine considerations. The alignment of arrays in the program depends on the natural fine-grain parallelism defined by individual members of data arrays.

Second, there is the question of how arrays should be *distributed* onto the actual parallel machine. We call this the *machine mapping* caused by translating the problem onto the finite resources of the machine. It is dependent on the topology, communication mechanisms, size of local memory, and number of processors in the underlying machine. Data distribution provides opportunities to reduce data movement, but must also maintain load balance. The distribution of arrays in the program depends on the coarse-grain parallelism defined by the physical parallel machine.

Fortran D is a version of Fortran that provides data decomposition specifications for these two levels of parallelism. First, the `DECOMPOSITION` statement is used to declare a problem domain for each computation. The `ALIGN` statement is then used to describe a problem mapping. Finally, the `DISTRIBUTE` statement is used to map the problem and its associated arrays to the physical machine. We believe that our two phase strategy for specifying data decomposition is natural for the computational scientist, and is also conducive to modular, portable code.

2.1 Alignment and Distribution Specifications

Here we give a quick summary of some basic data decompositions supported in Fortran D. The `DECOMPOSITION` statement simply declares the name, dimensionality and size of the decomposition. The `ALIGN` statement specifies how arrays should be *aligned* with respect to one another, both within and across array dimensions. It represents the minimal requirements for reducing data movement for the program, and is largely independent of any machine considerations. The alignment of arrays in the program depends on the natural fine-grain parallelism defined by individual members of data arrays

Arrays mapped to the same decomposition are automatically aligned with each other. There are two types of alignment. Intra-dimensional alignment specifies the alignment within each dimension. Inter-dimensional alignment takes place between dimensions. The alignment of arrays to decompositions is specified by placeholders in the subscript expressions of the array and decomposition. In the following example:

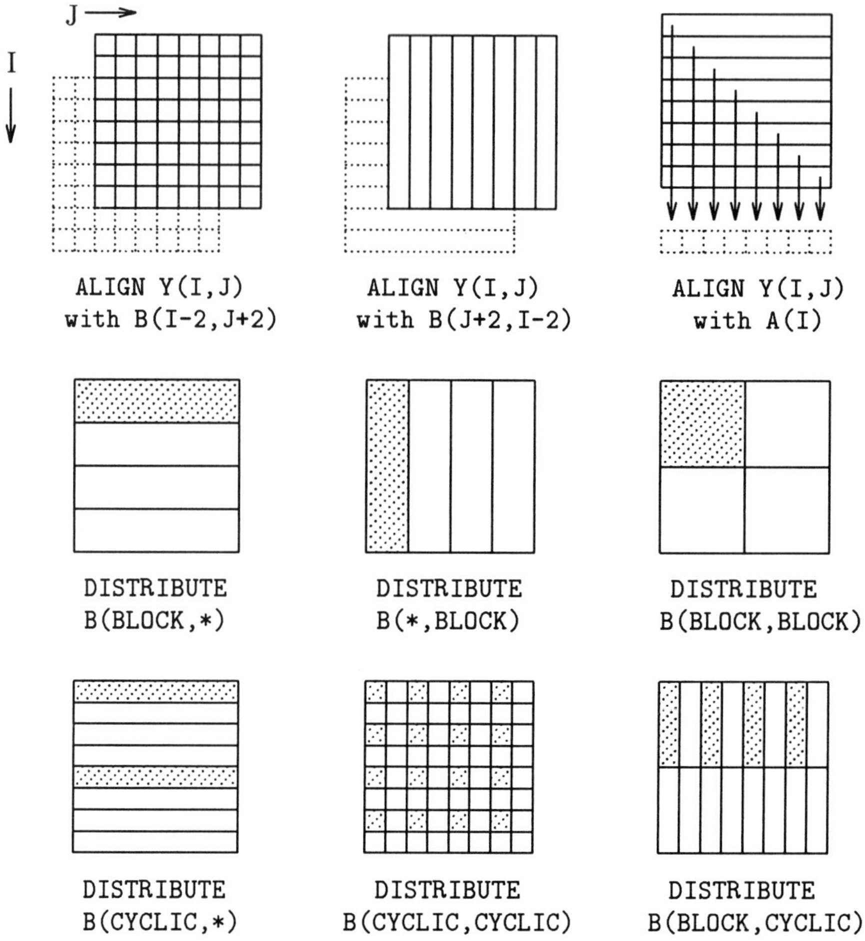

Figure 3: Fortran D Data Decomposition Specifications

```
REAL X(N), Y(N,N)
DECOMPOSITION A(N), B(N,N)
ALIGN X(I) with A(I-1)
ALIGN Y(I,J) with B(J, I)
```

A and B are declared to be decompositions of size N and $N \times N$, respectively. Array X is aligned with respect to A with an offset of -1, and array Y is aligned with the transpose of B.

After arrays have been aligned with a decomposition, the DISTRIBUTE statement maps the decomposition to the finite resources of the physical machine. Data distribution provides opportunities to reduce data movement and load imbalance within the constraints specified by data alignment. Data distribution takes advantage of the coarse-grain parallelism, but its effectiveness is dependent on the topology, communication mechanisms, size of local memory, and number of processors in the underlying machine.

Data distribution is specified by assigning an independent *attribute* to each dimension of a decomposition. Predefined attributes are BLOCK, CYCLIC, and BLOCK_CYCLIC. The symbol * marks dimensions that are not distributed. Once a distribution is chosen for the decomposition, all the arrays aligned with the decomposition can be mapped to the machine. The following program fragment demonstrates Fortran D syntax, the data decompositions are shown in Figure 3.

```
REAL X(N), Y(N,N)
DECOMPOSITION A(N), B(N,N)
ALIGN X(I) with A(I-1)
ALIGN Y(I,J) with B(I-2,J+2)
ALIGN Y(I,J) with B(J+2,I-2)
ALIGN Y(I,J) with A(I)
DISTRIBUTE A(CYCLIC)
DISTRIBUTE B(BLOCK,*)
```

2.2 Regular and Irregular Distributions

In addition, data parallelism may either be regular or irregular. Regular data parallelism can be effectively exploited through the data decompositions shown. Irregular data parallelism, on the other hand, requires irregular data decompositions and run-time processing to manage the parallelism. In Fortran D, irregular distributions are defined by the user through an explicit data array, as shown in the example below.

```
INTEGER MAP(N)
DECOMPOSITION IRREG(N)
DISTRIBUTE IRREG(MAP)
```

In this example, the elements of MAP must contain valid processor numbers. IRREG(i) will be mapped to the processor indicated by MAP(i). MAP may be either distributed or replicated; distributed MAP arrays will consume less memory but may require extra communication to determine location. Fortran D also supports dynamic data decomposition, *i.e.,* changing the decomposition at any point in the program. The complete Fortran D language is described in detail elsewhere [FHK+90].

2.3 Distribution Functions

Distribution functions specify the mapping of an array or The ALIGN and DISTRIBUTE statements in Fortran D specify how distributed arrays are mapped to the physical machine. The Fortran D compiler uses the information contained in these statements to construct *distribution functions* that can be used to calculate the mapping of array elements to processors. Distribution functions are also created for decompositions and are used during the actual distribution of arrays onto processors.

The distribution function μ, defined below,

$$\mu_A(\vec{i}) \;=\; (\delta_A(\vec{i}), \alpha_A(\vec{i})) \;=\; (p, \vec{j})$$

is a mapping of the global index $\vec{i}$ of a decomposition or array A to a local index $\vec{j}$ for a unique processor p. Each distribution function has two component functions, δ and α.

$$\begin{aligned}
\mu_A^{(block,*)}(i,j) &= (\lceil i/BlockSize \rceil, ((i-1) \bmod BlockSize + 1, j)) \\
\mu_B^{(cyclic,*)}(i,j) &= ((i-1) \bmod P + 1, (\lceil i/P \rceil, j)) \\
\mu_X(i,j) &= (\lceil i/BlockSize \rceil, ((i-1) \bmod BlockSize + 1, j+1)) \\
\mu_Y(i,j) &= ((j-1) \bmod P + 1, (\lceil j/P \rceil, i))
\end{aligned}$$

Figure 4: Distribution Functions

These functions are used to compute ownership and location information. For a given decomposition or array A, the owner function δ_A maps the global index $\vec{i}$ to its unique processor owner p, and the local index function α_A maps the global index $\vec{i}$ to a local index $\vec{j}$.

2.3.1 Regular Distributions

The formalism described for distribution functions are applicable for both regular and irregular distributions. An advantage of the simple regular distributions supported in Fortran D is that their corresponding distribution functions can be easily derived at compile-time. For instance, given the following regular distributions,

```
REAL X(N, 0:N-1), Y(N,N)
DECOMPOSITION A(N,N), B(N,N)
ALIGN X(I,J) with A(I, J+1)
ALIGN Y(I,J) with B(J, I)
DISTRIBUTE A(BLOCK, *);
DISTRIBUTE B(CYCLIC, *);
```

the compiler automatically derives the distribution functions in Figure 4. In the figure, the 2-D decompositions A and B are declared to have size (N, N). The number of processors is P. For a block distribution, $BlockSize = \lceil N/P \rceil$.

2.3.2 Irregular Distributions

For an irregular distribution, we use an integer array to explicitly represent the component functions $\delta_A(\vec{i})$ and $\alpha_A(\vec{i})$. This is the most general approach possible since it can support any arbitrary irregular distribution. Unfortunately, the distribution must now be evaluated at run-time. In the following 1-D example,

```
INTEGER MAP(N), X(N)
DECOMPOSITION A(N)
ALIGN X(I) with A(I)
DISTRIBUTE A(MAP)
```

the irregular distribution for decomposition A is stored in the integer array `MAP`. The distribution functions for decomposition A and array X are then computed through run-time preprocessing techniques [SBW90, MV90].

3 Basic Compilation Strategy

In this section we provide a formal description of the general Fortran D compiler strategy. The basic approach is to convert Fortran D programs into *single-program, multiple-data* (SPMD) node programs with explicit message-passing. The two main concerns for the Fortran D compiler are 1) to ensure that data and computations are partitioned across processors, and 2) to generate communications where needed to access nonlocal data.

The Fortran D compiler is designed to exploit large-scale data parallelism. Our philosophy is to use the *owner computes* rule, where every processor only performs computation for data it owns [ZBG88, CK88, RP89]. However, the owner compute rule is relaxed depending on the structure of the computation. However, in this paper we concentrate on deriving a functional decomposition and communication generation by applying the owner computes rule.

We begin by examining the algorithm used to compile a simple loop nest using the owner computes rule. Correct application of the rule requires knowledge of the data decomposition for a program. As previously discussed, in Fortran D information concerning the ownership of a particular decomposition or array element is provided by the `ALIGN` and `DISTRIBUTE` statements.

3.1 Some Notation

We begin by describing some notation we will employ later in this paper.

DO $\vec{k} = \vec{l}$ to $\vec{m}$ by $\vec{s}$

  $X(g(\vec{k})) = Y(h(\vec{k}))$

ENDDO

In the example loop nest above, $\vec{k}$ is the set of loop iterations. It is also displayed as as the triplet $[\vec{l} : \vec{m} : \vec{s}]$. In addition, X and Y are distributed arrays, and g and h are the array subscript functions for the left-hand side (lhs) and right-hand side (rhs) array references, respectively.

3.1.1 Image

We define the *image* of an array X on a processor p as follows:

$$image_X(p) \;=\; \{\vec{i} \mid \delta_X(\vec{i}) = p\}$$

The *image* for a processor p is constructed by finding all array indices that cause a reference to a local element of array X, as determined by the distribution functions for the array. As a result, *image* describes all the elements of array X assigned to a particular processor p. We also define t_p as *this processor*, a unique processor identification representing the local processor. Thus the expression $image_X(t_p)$ corresponds to the set of all elements of X owned locally.

3.1.2 Iteration Sets

We define the *iteration set* of a reference R for a processor p to be the set of loop iterations $\vec{j}$ that cause R to access data owned by p. Each element of the iteration set corresponds

```
FOR each loop nest k⃗ = l⃗ to m⃗ by s⃗ DO
  reduced_iter_set = ∅
  FOR each statement_i in loop with lhs = X_i(g_i(k⃗))
    iter_set = g_i^{-1}(image_{X_i}(t_p)) ∩ [l⃗ : m⃗ : s⃗]
    reduced_iter_set = reduced_iter_set ∪ iter_set
  ENDFOR
  reduce bounds of loop nest to those in reduced_iter_set
ENDFOR
```

Figure 5: Reducing Loop Bounds Using Iteration Sets

to a point in the iteration space, and is represented by a vector containing the iteration number for each loop in the loop nest.

The iteration set of a statement can be constructed in a very simple manner. Our example loop contains two references, $X(g(\vec{k}))$ and $Y(h(\vec{k}))$. The iteration set for processor p with respect to reference $X(g(\vec{k}))$ is simply $g^{-1}(image_X(p))$, the inverse subscript function g^{-1} applied to the image of the array X on processor p. Similarly, the iteration set with respect to reference $Y(h(\vec{k}))$ can be calculated as $h^{-1}(image_Y(p))$.

This property will be used in several algorithms later in the paper. In particular, notice that when using the owner computes rule, the iteration set of the *lhs* of an assignment statement for processor p is exactly the iterations in which that statement must be executed on p. For example, in the simple loop above, the function $g^{-1}(image_X(t_p))$ may be used to determine when t_p, the local processor, should execute the statement.

3.2 Guard Introduction

The guard introduction phase of the compiler ensures that computations in a program are divided correctly among the processors according to the owner computes rule. This may be accomplished by a combination of reducing loop bounds and guarding individual statements. Both approaches are based on calculating *iteration sets* for statements in a loop.

3.2.1 Loop Bounds Reduction

Since evaluating guards at run-time increases execution cost, the Fortran D compiler strategy is to reduce loop bounds where possible for each processor to avoid evaluating guard expressions. Figure 5 presents a straightforward algorithm for performing simple loop bounds reduction. The algorithm works as follows. First, the iteration sets of all the *lhs* are calculated for the local processor t_p. These sets are then unioned together. The result represents all the iterations on which a assignment will need to be executed by the processor. The loop bounds are then reduced to the resulting iteration set.

```
FOR each loop nest k⃗ = l⃗ to m⃗ by s⃗ DO
  previous_iter_set = [l⃗ : m⃗ : s⃗]
  FOR each statement_i in order DO
    IF statement_i = assignment AND lhs = global array X_i(g_i(k⃗)) THEN
      iter_set = g_i^{-1}(image_{X_i}(t_p)) ∩ [l⃗ : m⃗ : s⃗]
    ELSE
      iter_set = [l⃗ : m⃗ : s⃗]
    ENDIF
    IF iter_set = previous_iter_set THEN
      insert statement_i after statement_{i-1}
    ELSE
      terminate previous mask if it exists
      create new mask for iter_set and insert statement_i inside mask
      previous_iter_set = iter_set
    ENDIF
  ENDFOR
ENDFOR
```

Figure 6: Generating Statement Masks Using Iteration Sets

3.2.2 Mask Generation

In the case where all assignment statements have the same iteration set, loop bounds reduction will eliminate any need for masks since all statements within the reduced loop bounds always execute. However, loop bound reduction will not work in all cases. For instance, loop nests may contain multiple assignment statements to distributed data structures. The iteration set of each statement for a processor may differ, limiting the number of guards eliminated through bounds reduction. The compiler will need to introduce masks for the statements that are conditionally executed.

Figure 6 presents a simple algorithm to generate masks for statements in a loop nest. Each statement is examined in turn and its iteration set calculated. If it is equivalent to the iteration set of the previous statement, then the two statements may be guarded by the same mask. Otherwise, any previous masks must be terminated and a new mask created. We assume the existence of functions to generate the appropriate guard/mask for each statement based on its iteration set.

3.3 Communication Generation

Once guards have been introduced, the Fortran D compiler must generate communications to preserve the semantics of the original program. This can be accomplished by calculating SEND and RECEIVE iteration sets. For simple loop nests which do not contain *loop-carried* (inter-iteration) true dependences [AK87], These iteration sets may also be used to generate IN and OUT array index sets that combine messages to a single processor into one message. We describe the formation and use of these sets in more detail in the following sections.

3.3.1 Regular Computations

LOCAL, SEND, and RECEIVE Iteration Sets

We describe as *regular computations* those computations which can be accurately characterized at compile-time. In these cases the compiler can exactly calculate all communications and synchronization required without any run-time information. The first step is to calculate the following iteration sets for each reference R in the loop with respect to the local processor t_p:

- LOCAL – Set of iterations in which R results in an access to data local to t_p.
- SEND – Set of iterations in which R results in an access to data local to t_p, but the statement containing R is executed on a different processor.
- RECEIVE – Set of iterations in which the statement containing R is executed on t_p, but R results in an access to data not local to t_p.

The LOCAL, SEND, and RECEIVE iteration sets can be generated using the owner computes rule. Figure 7 shows the algorithm for regular computations. It starts by first calculating the iteration set for the lhs of each assignment statement with respect to the local processor t_p; this determines the LOCAL iteration set.

The iteration sets for each rhs of the statement are then constructed with respect to the t_p. Any element of the LOCAL iteration set that does not also belong to the iteration set for the rhs will need to access nonlocal data; it is put in the RECEIVE iteration set. Conversely, any elements in the iteration set for the rhs not also in the LOCAL iteration are needed by some other processor; it is put into the SEND iteration set. These iteration sets complete specify all communications that must be performed.

IN and OUT Index Sets

For loop nests which do not contain loop-carried true dependences, communications may be moved entirely outside of the loop nest and blocked together. In addition, messages to the same processor may also be combined to form a single message. These steps are desirable when communication costs are high, as is the case for most MIMD distributed-memory machines. The following array index sets are utilized for these optimizations:

- IN – Set of array indices that correspond to nonlocal data accesses. These data elements must be received from other processors in order to perform local computations.
- OUT – Set of array indices that correspond to local data accessed by other processors. These data elements must be sent to other processors in order to permit them to perform their computations.

```
FOR each statement_i with lhs = X_i(g_i(k⃗)) in loop nest k⃗ = l⃗ to m⃗ by s⃗ DO
  local_iter_set^{tp}_{X_i} = g_i^{-1}(image_{X_i}(t_p)) ∩ [l⃗ : m⃗ : s⃗]
  FOR each rhs reference to a distributed array Y_i(h_i(k⃗)) DO
    local_iter_set^{tp}_{Y_i} = h_i^{-1}(image_{Y_i}(t_p)) ∩ [l⃗ : m⃗ : s⃗]
    receive_iter_set^{tp}_{Y_i} = local_iter_set^{tp}_{X_i} − local_iter_set^{tp}_{Y_i}
    send_iter_set^{tp}_{Y_i} = local_iter_set^{tp}_{Y_i} − local_iter_set^{tp}_{X_i}
  ENDFOR
ENDFOR
```

Figure 7: Generating SEND/RECEIVE Iteration Sets (for Regular Computations)

```
FOR each statement_i with lhs = X_i(g_i(k⃗)) in loop nest k⃗ = l⃗ to m⃗ by s⃗ DO
  FOR each rhs reference to a distributed array Y_i(h_i(k⃗)) DO
    {* initialize IN and OUT index sets *}
    FOR proc = 1 to numprocs DO
      in_index_set^{(tp,proc)}_{Y_i} = ∅
      out_index_set^{(tp,proc)}_{Y_i} = ∅
    ENDFOR
    {* compute OUT index sets *}
    FOR each j⃗ ∈ send_iter_set^{tp}_{Y_i} DO
      send_p = δ_{X_i}(g_i(h_i^{-1}(μ_{Y_i}^{-1}(t_p, α_{Y_i}(h_i(j⃗))))))
      out_index_set^{(tp,send_p)}_{Y_i} = out_index_set^{(tp,send_p)}_{Y_i} ∪ {α_{Y_i}(h_i(j⃗))}
    ENDFOR
    {* compute IN index sets *}
    FOR each j⃗ ∈ receive_iter_set^{tp}_{Y_i} DO
      recv_p = δ_{Y_i}(h_i(j⃗))
      in_index_set^{(tp,recv_p)}_{Y_i} = in_index_set^{(tp,recv_p)}_{Y_i} ∪ {α_{Y_i}(h_i(j⃗))}
    ENDFOR
  ENDFOR
ENDFOR
```

Figure 8: Generating IN/OUT Index Sets (for Regular Computations)

The calculation of IN and OUT index set for regular computations is depicted in Figure 8. The algorithm works as follows. Each element in the SEND and RECEIVE iteration sets is examined. Some combination of the subscript, mapping, alignment, and distribution functions and their inverses are applied to the element to determine the source or recipient of each message. The message to that processor is then stored in the appropriate IN or OUT index set, effectively blocking it with all other messages to the same processor.

More complicated algorithms are needed for loops with loop-carried dependences, since not all communication can be moved outside of the entire loop nest. To handle loop-carried dependences, IN and OUT index sets need to be constructed at each loop level. Dependence information may be used to calculate the appropriate loop level for each message, using the algorithms described by Balasundaram et al. and Gerndt [BFKK90, Ger90]. Messages in SEND and RECEIVE sets can then be inserted in the IN or OUT set at that loop level.

3.3.2 Irregular Computations

Irregular computations are computations that cannot be accurately characterized at compile-time.[1] It is not possible to determine the SEND, RECEIVE, IN, and OUT sets at compile-time for these computations. However, an *inspector* [MSS+88, KMSB90] may be constructed to preprocess the loop body at run-time to determine what nonlocal data will be accessed. This in effect calculates the IN index set for each processor. A global transpose operation between processors can then be used to calculate the OUT index sets as well.

An inspector is the most general way to generate IN and OUT sets for loops without loop-carried dependences. Despite the expense of additional communications, experimental evidence from several systems [KMV90, WSBH91] proves that it can improve performance by blocking together communications to access nonlocal data outside of the loop nest. In addition it also allows multiple messages to the same processor to be blocked together. The Fortran D compiler plans to automatically generate inspectors where needed for irregular computations.

The structure of an inspector loop is shown in Figure 9. For compatibility with our treatment of regular computations, the Fortran D inspector also generates the LOCAL and RECEIVE iteration sets. In the first part of the inspector, the LOCAL iteration set is calculated for each statement based on the *lhs*. The *rhs* is examined for each element in the LOCAL iteration set. Any nonlocal references cause the iteration to be added to the RECEIVE iteration set. The owner and local index of the nonlocal reference are then calculated and added to the IN index set.

After the local IN sets have been calculated, a global transpose is performed in the remainder of the inspector. Each processor sends its IN index set for a given processor to that processor. Upon receipt, they become OUT index sets for the receiving processor.

[1]Irregular computations are different from irregular distributions, which are irregular mappings of data to processors.

```
FOR each statement_i with lhs = X_i(g_i(k⃗)) in loop nest k⃗ = l⃗ to m⃗ by s⃗ DO
  local_iter_set^{tp}_{X_i} = g_i^{-1}(image_{X_i}(t_p)) ∩ [l⃗ : m⃗ : s⃗]
  receive_iter_set^{tp}_{Y_i} = ∅
  FOR each rhs reference to a distributed array Y_i(h_i(k⃗)) DO
    {* calculate IN index sets for this processor *}
    FOR each j⃗ ∈ local_iter_set^{X_i}_{t_p} DO
      IF (δ_{Y_i}(h_i(j⃗))) ≠ t_p) THEN
        receive_iter_set^{tp}_{Y_i} = receive_iter_set^{tp}_{Y_i} ∪ {j⃗}
        recv_p = δ_{B_i}(h_i(j⃗))
        in_index_set^{(t_p,recv_p)}_{Y_i} = in_index_set^{(t_p,recv_p)}_{Y_i} ∪ {α_{Y_i}(h_i(j⃗))}
      ENDIF
    ENDFOR
    {* send IN index sets to all other processors *}
    FOR recv_p = 1 to numprocs DO
      IF (recv_p ≠ t_p) THEN
        send(in_index_set^{(t_p,recv_p)}_{Y_i}, recv_p)
      ENDIF
    ENDFOR
    {* receive IN index sets, convert into OUT index sets *}
    FOR send_p = 1 to numprocs DO
      IF (send_p ≠ t_p) THEN
        receive(out_index_set^{(t_p,send_p)}_{Y_i}, send_p)
      ENDIF
    ENDFOR
  ENDFOR
ENDFOR
```

Figure 9: Inspector to Generate IN/OUT Index Sets (for Irregular Computations)

```
{* original loop to be transformed into send, receive, and compute loops *}
DO k⃗ = l⃗ to m⃗ by s⃗
  X(g(k⃗)) = Y(h(k⃗))
ENDDO
{* send loop *}
FOR send_p = 1 to numprocs DO
  IF (out_index_set_Y^(t_p,send_p) ≠ ∅) THEN
    buffer_values(out_value_set_Y^(t_p,send_p), out_index_set_Y^(t_p,send_p))
    send(out_value_set_Y^(t_p,send_p), send_p)
  ENDIF
ENDFOR
{* local compute loop *}
FOR each j⃗ ∈ {local_iter_set_X^t_p − receive_iter_set_Y^t_p} DO
  X(α_A(g(j⃗))) = Y(α_B(h(j⃗)))
ENDFOR
{* receive loop *}
FOR recv_p = 1 to numprocs DO
  IF (in_index_set_Y^(t_p,recv_p) ≠ ∅) THEN
    receive(in_value_set_Y^(t_p,recv_p), recv_p)
    store_values(in_value_set_Y^(t_p,recv_p), in_index_set_Y^(t_p,recv_p))
  ENDIF
ENDFOR
{* nonlocal compute loop *}
FOR each j⃗ ∈ receive_iter_set_Y^t_p DO
  X(α_X(g(j⃗)))) = get_value(Y(h(j⃗)))
ENDFOR
```

Figure 10: Send, Receive, and Compute Loops Resulting from IN/OUT Index Sets

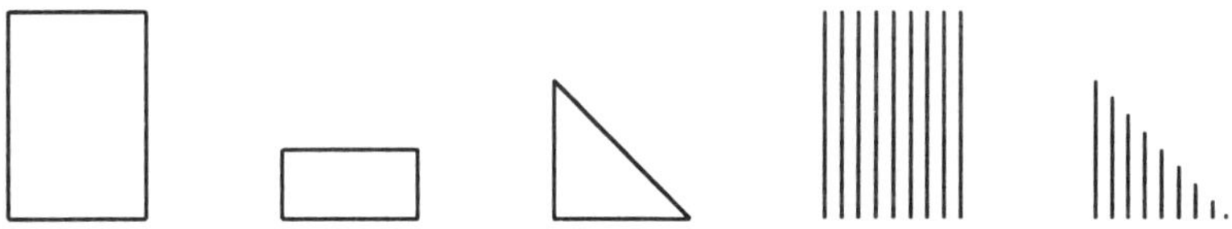

Figure 11: Regular Section Descriptors (RSDs)

3.3.3 Resulting Program

Once the SEND and RECEIVE sets have been calculated, the example loop nest is transformed into the loops pictured in Figure 10 [KMSB90]. In the *send* loop, every processor sends data they own to processors that need the data. The OUT index set for *rhs* of the statement in the example loop has already been calculated. However, the function *buffer_values()* must be used to actually collect the values at each index and the OUT set. The resulting values are then sent to the appropriate processor.

Next, in the *local compute* loop, loop iterations that assign and use only local data may be executed. These are elements that are in the LOCAL but not RECEIVE iteration sets. These iterations are executed immediately following the send loop to take advantage of communication latency.

In the *receive* loop, every processor receives nonlocal data sent from their owners in the send loop. The values received are mapped to their designated storage locations using the function *store_values()*. The indices corresponding to these values have already been calculated and stored in the IN index sets. Finally, in the *nonlocal compute* loop every processor performs computations for loop iterations that also require nonlocal data. The function *get_value()* is used to fetch nonlocal data from their designated storage locations.

3.4 Regular Sections

For the sake of efficiency, when generating communications the Fortran D compiler constructs approximations of the *image* for each distributed array using *regular section* or *data access descriptors* [CK87, BK89, HK90]. A regular section descriptor (RSD) is a compact representation of rectangular or right-triangular array sections and their higher dimension analogs. They may also possess some constant step. The union and intersection of RSDs can be calculated inexpensively, making them highly useful for the Fortran D compiler. RSDs have also proven to be quite precise in practice, due to the regular computation patterns exhibited by scientific programs [HK90]. Figure 11 shows some examples of regular section descriptors.

4 Compilation of Whole Programs

We have shown how the Fortran D compiler introduces guards and generates communications for a simple loop nest. When compiling whole programs containing multiple loop nests or procedures, the compiler faces much more complex problems, as well as many opportunities for optimization. Here we present a brief overview of the issues facing the Fortran D compiler.

4.1 Data Decomposition Analysis

Researchers have found that the computation structure may often change between different phases of a program. Relying on a single static data decomposition for these programs will result in excessive data movement [KLS90, KN90]. To overcome this problem, Fortran D permits data decomposition specifications to be inserted at any point in a program, providing dynamic data decompositions. However, to support a modular programming style, we restrict the scope of dynamically declared data decompositions to that of the current procedure. When a procedure returns, any dynamic data decompositions declared locally are restored to the values they possessed before the procedure was called.

Dynamic data decompositions complicate the job of the Fortran D compiler, since it needs to know how an array is decomposed in order to generate the proper guards and communications. We define the *reaching* data decompositions at a point P in the program to be the set of data decompositions that have a path to P not *killed* by another decomposition statement. In order to generate the correct code for each reference to a distributed array, the Fortran D compiler must perform global dataflow analysis to solve the reaching data decomposition problem. When there are multiple reaching decompositions, the compiler must either insert run-time routines to handle each decomposition, or apply node splitting techniques to allow compile-time resolution.

4.2 Program Transformations

One of the features of the Fortran D compiler is that it utilizes the results of dataflow and dependence analysis to apply program transformations that eliminate guards or improve communications. Transformations must be performed after decomposition analysis, since their profitability depend on the data decomposition present. The following sections show examples of a few transformations. We are investigating the usefulness of other transformations such as loop skewing and peeling. In the following examples, for the sake of clarity we ignore guards and assume that all arrays are identically aligned and have `BLOCK` distributions.

4.2.1 Loop Interchanging

Loop interchange can be used to move dependences to outer loops, enabling vector communications.

```
{* dependence on loop j *}
do i = 1, n
   do j = 1, n
       perform_send(X(i,j-1))
       perform_recv(X(i,j-1))
       X(i,j) = X(i,j-1)
   enddo
enddo
```

```
{* after loop interchange *}
do j = 1, n
   perform_send(X(1:n,j-1))
   perform_recv(X(1:n,j-1))
   do i = 1, n
      X(i,j) = X(i,j-1)
   enddo
enddo
```

4.2.2 Strip Mining

Strip mine can be used to simplify guard introduction, reduce size of messages, and improve load balance.

```
{* original message too large *}
perform_send(X(1:n))
perform_recv(X(1:n))
do i = 1, n
    ... = X(i)
enddo
```

```
{* strip mine reduces message size *}
do i = 1, n, strip
    perform_send(X(i:i+strip-1))
    perform_recv(X(i:i+strip-1))
    do i$ = i, i+strip-1
        ... = X(i$)
    enddo
enddo
```

4.2.3 Loop Distribution

Loop distribution can be used to simplify guard introduction and enable other transformations such as loop interchange.

```
{* dependences on both loops *}
do i = 1, n
   perform_send(X(i-1,1:n))
   perform_recv(X(i-1,1:n))
   do j = 1, n
       perform_send(Y(i,j-1))
       perform_recv(Y(i,j-1))
       X(i,j) = X(i-1,j)
       Y(i,j) = Y(i,j-1)
   enddo
enddo
```

```
{* after distribution & interchange *}
do i = 1, n
   perform_send(X(i-1,1:n))
   perform_recv(X(i-1,1:n))
   do j = 1, n
      X(i,j) = X(i-1,j)
   enddo
enddo
do j = 1, n
   perform_send(Y(1:n,j-1))
   perform_recv(Y(1:n,j-1))
   do i = 1, n
     Y(i,j) = Y(i,j-1)
   enddo
enddo
```

4.2.4 Align

Loop alignment [ACK87] can improve guard introduction.

```
{* statements require masks *}
do i = 1, n
   X(i) = i
   Y(i+1) = i
enddo
```

```
{* alignment eliminates masks *}
X(1) = i
do i = 2, n
   X(i) = i
   Y(i) = i-1
enddo
Y(n+1) = n
```

4.3 Communications Optimization

A major goal of the Fortran D compiler is to aggressively optimize communications. We describe some techniques we will attempt in order to eliminate or combine messages.

4.3.1 Vectorize Messages

Generating communications for loops containing loop-carried true dependences is complex. A simple solution is to insert all communications at the deepest loop nesting level. directly preceding each reference to a nonlocal memory reference. Unfortunately, this approach generates large numbers of small messages that may prove inefficient because of high communications overhead and latency. Algorithms developed by Balasundaram *et al.* and Gerndt employ data dependence information to insert communications at the outermost loop allowable, without violating dependences [BFKK90, Ger90]. This enables messages to be vectorized, as in the following example:

```
{* dependence on loop j *}
do i = 1, n
   do j = 1, n
      perform_send(X(i,j-1))
      perform_recv(X(i,j-1))
      X(i,j) = X(i,j-1)
   enddo
enddo
```

```
{* dependence on loop i *}
do i = 1, n
   perform_send(X(i-1,1:n))
   perform_recv(X(i-1,1:n))
   do j = 1, n
      X(i,j) = X(i-1,j)
   enddo
enddo
```

Vectorizing messages are desirable because they combine many small messages into one large message, reducing message overhead. The Fortran D compiler will use the algorithm *comm* from [BFKK90] for determining the loop level for inserting communications.

Message vectorization is a special case of *prefetching* data; *i.e.,* fetching nonlocal data before it is used in a computation. More general data prefetching optimizations are possible. Like *instruction scheduling* or *software prefetching*, the goal of data prefetching is to reduce apparent latency by performing useful computation while waiting for expensive memory accesses. The KALI compiler, developed by Koelbel *et al.*, utilizes this strategy for individual parallel loops by computing loop iterations that access only local data while waiting for data from other processors [KMV90].

4.3.2 Utilize Collective Communications

Li and Chen showed that the compiler can take advantage of the highly regular communication patterns displayed by many computations [LC90a]. Rather than generating a large number of individual send and receive communication primitives, the compiler can instead take advantage of efficient collective communications libraries such as EXPRESS [EXP89], CRYSTAL_ROUTER [FJL+88], CRYSTAL communications [CCL89], and PARTI [SBW90]. The compiler will exploit these routines to reduce the cost of communications. The guiding principles are:

- Apply program analysis to identify communications patterns
- Utilize collective communications routines where profitable, even if *overcommunication*) result; *e.g.*, extra data/messages
- Recognize and replace reductions; *e.g.*, sum reductions

4.3.3 Global Dataflow Analysis

Communications may be optimized further by considering interactions between all the loop nests in the procedure. Global dataflow analysis can show that an assignment to a variable is *live* at a point in the program if there are no intervening assignments to that variable. For instance, assume that messages in previous loop nests have already retrieved nonlocal elements for a given array. If those values are *live*, messages in succeeding loop nests may be eliminated or reduced. The precision of such analyses can be improved by using regular section descriptors to analyze liveness for array sections.

4.3.4 Combine or Eliminate Messages

The algorithms for generating communications described in Section 3 consider each statement individually. When compiling loop nests containing multiple statements, communications may be optimized by combining or eliminating messages based on other messages in the loop nest. The Fortran D compiler will examine the messages generated for each array at each loop level, starting at the most deeply nested loop. The compiler needs to determine whether any of the messages may be:

- Subsumed by other messages at that loop level
- Combined with other messages at that loop level
- Subsumed or reduced by messages at inner loops

In addition, if a processor is sending several messages for different arrays to the same processor, they may be combined into the same message.

4.3.5 Relax Owner Computes Rule

The *owner computes* rule provides the basic strategy of the Fortran D compiler. We may also relax this rule, allowing processors to compute values for data they do not own. For instance, suppose multiple *rhs* of an assignment statement are owned by a processor that is not the owner of the *lhs*. Computing the result on the processor owning the *rhs* and then sending the result to the owner of the *lhs* could reduce the amount of data communicated. Consider the following loop:

```
do i = 1, n
  A(i) = B(i) + C(i)
enddo
```

Assume that B(i) and C(i) are mapped together to a processor different from the owner of A(i). The amount of data communicated may be reduced by half if the computation is first performed by the processor owning B and C, then sent to the processor owning A. This optimization is a simple application of the "owner stores" rule proposed by Balasundaram [Bal91].

In particular, it may be desirable for the Fortran D compiler to partition loops amongst processors so that each loop iteration is executed on a single processor, such as in KALI and ARF [KMV90, WSBH91]. This technique may improve communication and provides greater control over load balance, especially for irregular computations. It also eliminates the need for individual statement masks and simplifies handling of control flow within the loop body. The Fortran D compiler will detect phases of the computation where the owner computes rule may be relaxed to improve communications or load balance.

4.3.6 Replicate Computation

The Fortran D compiler considers scalar variables to be replicated. All processors thus perform computations involving assignments to scalar variables. This causes redundant computation to be performed, but is profitable because it significantly reduces communication costs. A similar approach may be taken for computations on elements of distributed arrays. It may be more efficient to replicate computation on multiple processors, rather than incur the expense of communicating the value from the owner of that element. Consider the following loop:

```
do i = 3, n
  X(i) = f(i)
  Y(i) = (X(i-1) + X(i-2)) / 2
enddo
```

Assume that arrays X and Y are distributed arrays aligned identically onto the same decomposition, and that f is a function performing computation that does not require values from other processors. Straightforward compilation of this loop would cause messages to be generated, communicating the new values of X(i-1) and X(i-2) to the processor performing the assignment to Y(i). However, if the Fortran D compiler replicates the computation of X(i-1) and X(i-2) on the receiving processor, it eliminates the need for any communications.

4.3.7 Eliminate Dead Computation

A side effect of replicating all scalar variables is that naive compilation frequently results in computations that generate processor-specific dead values, *i.e.,* values that are not used by the local processor. In these cases an obvious optimization is to not compute the scalar value. For instance, consider the following loop:

```
do i = 1, n
  sum = Y(i-1) + Y(i+1)
  X(i) = sum / 2
enddo
```

The Fortran D compiler must determine that the scalar variable **sum** is only used locally by the assignment to `X(i)` and guard it appropriately. Otherwise it will waste computation by calculating **sum** on all processors for all loop iterations. Worse yet, the compiler may generate communications to fetch nonlocal values of `Y`, adding significant communication costs!

4.3.8 Block Messages

The goal of many communication optimizations is reduce communications overhead by combining small messages together to form larger messages. However, the Fortran D compiler needs to be careful since physical machines have local memory and message buffering limits. Excessively large or long-lived messages may cause memory and buffer overflows that will abort or deadlock the program.

If information concerning the limits of the system can be fed to the compiler, it may block large messages by strip mining the loops containing communications. Messages may then be broken up and moved to the strip mined loop. The compiler would need to calculate a blocking factor that remains within the physical limits of the underlying parallel machine. Blocking is also useful as a means of compromising between communications and load balance.

4.4 Storage Management

Once guards and communications have been calculated, the Fortran D compiler must still select and manage storage for all nonlocal array references. The simplest approach is to allocate full-sized arrays on each processor. This requires the least change to the program, but may waste tremendous amounts of memory. More sophisticated storage management techniques manipulate both the location and lifetimes of nonlocal storage in order to reduce memory use and code complexity. Storage management may be separated into two phases, selection of the desired storage types, and coordinating their usage.

4.4.1 Determine Storage of Nonlocal Data

First, analysis must be performed to choose a storage type for nonlocal access of each array. There are several different storage types, described below:

- *Overlaps* are expansion of local array sections to accommodate neighboring nonlocal elements [Ger90]. Overlaps are useful for regular computations because they allow the generation of clear and readable code. However, for certain computations storage may be wasted because all array elements between the local section and the one accessed must also be part of the overlap. Storage is also wasted because overlaps are assigned to individual arrays, and cannot be reused for other arrays later in the program.

- *Persistent buffers* are designed to overcome the contiguous nature of overlaps. They are useful when the size of the nonlocal data is fixed, but is not necessarily in a neighboring area. For instance, a persistent buffer can be used to store the pivot for Gaussian elimination.

- *Temporary buffers* are used for nonlocal data with short live ranges. They may be reused after the loop, or even within the loop.
- *Hash tables* are mainly used to store nonlocal data for irregular distributions. They provide a nonlocal value cache that allows quick lookup for nonlocal values [MSMB90].

4.4.2 Maintain Overlap Areas, Temporaries, and Hash Tables

Once the type of storage is chosen, the compiler needs to perform analysis to determine the total amount of storage needed as overlaps, persistent buffers, or temporary buffers. It also needs to change all nonlocal array references assigned to buffers so that they access the appropriate buffer instead.

4.5 Interprocedural Issues

The presence of procedures adds significantly to the complexity of the compilation process, especially for data decomposition analysis. Just as within a procedure, we need to calculate which data decompositions reach every reference to a distributed array. If multiple decompositions reach a procedure, either run-time routines or interprocedural node splitting techniques such as *cloning* or *inlining* may be required to handle the code. Since Fortran D semantics limit the scope of all decompositions to the procedure in which they are declared, this can be solved as a forward interprocedural dataflow problem, using the techniques developed for the ParaScope environment [CKT86].

Unfortunately, the same semantics also require the compiler to insert calls to run-time data decomposition routines to restore the original data decomposition upon procedure return. Since dynamic data decomposition is an expensive operation, these calls should be eliminated where possible. We define a data decomposition specification to be *live* if it has a *reachable use*; *i.e.,* if there is a path from the specification to a reference to a distributed array that is not killed by a different specification. The live data decomposition problem may be solved as a backward interprocedural problem. Many compiler inserted run-time data decompositions can then be determined to be not *live*, and may be safely eliminated. It may also be possible to hoist dynamic data decompositions out of loops, dramatically improving the performance of loops containing data decomposition statements.

4.6 Compiler Architecture

In review, the primary goal of the Fortran D compiler is to produce a correct distributed-memory program based on the *owner computes* rule. To do this, the compiler introduces guards and generates communications to access nonlocal data. Information from dataflow, dependence, and interprocedural analysis is applied to enhance each phase of compilation. Another important goal of the compiler is to optimize communications and minimize load imbalance. The basic architecture of the compiler is shown below:

1. Data Decomposition Analysis
   (a) Determine reaching decompositions
   (b) Determine live decompositions

   (c) Optimizing decompositions

2. Program Transformations
   (a) Loop interchanging
   (b) Strip mining
   (c) Loop distribution
   (d) Align

3. Guard Introduction
   (a) Calculate SEND & RECEIVE iteration sets
   (b) Loop bounds reduction
   (c) Mask generation

4. Communication generation
   (a) Calculate SEND & RECEIVE index sets
   (b) Calculate IN & OUT index sets
   (c) Generate inspector/executors

5. Communication optimization
   (a) Vectorize messages
   (b) Utilize collective communications
   (c) Global dataflow analysis
   (d) Combine/eliminate messages
   (e) Relax owner computes rule
   (f) Replicate computation
   (g) Eliminate dead computation
   (h) Block messages

6. Storage Assignment
   (a) Determine storage of nonlocal data
   (b) Maintain overlap areas, temporaries, and hash tables

4.7 Fortran D Programming Environment

The compiler is a key element of the Fortran D programming system being developed at Rice University [HKK+91]. The structure of the programming system is shown in Figure 12. It is being developed in the context of the ParaScope parallel programming environment [CCH+88], and will take advantage of its analysis and transformation abilities [CKT86, KMT91]. Another part of the Fortran D system is a static performance estimator that will take as input a Fortran D or message-passing Fortran program and predicts its performance on the target machine [BFKK90, BFKK91]. The performance estimation is based on *training sets*, programs containing kernel computation and communications that can be executed on the target machine. The automatic data partitioner is the final component of the Fortran D programming system. It will utilize both the performance estimator and Fortran D compiler to automatically select and predict the performance of different data decompositions on the target machine.

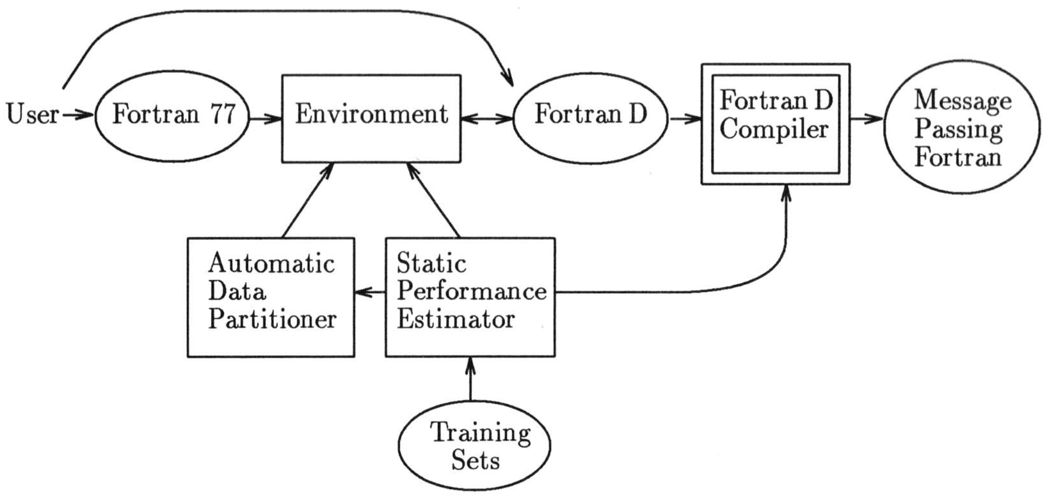

Figure 12: Fortran D Programming Environment

5 Validation

We plan to establish whether our compilation scheme for Fortran D can achieve acceptable performance on the iPSC/860, a representative MIMD distributed-memory machine. We will use a benchmark suite currently being developed by Geoffrey Fox at Syracuse. This suite will consist of a collection of Fortran programs. Each program in the suite will have five versions:

(v1) the original Fortran 77 program,

(v2) the best hand-coded message-passing version of the Fortran program,

(v3) a "nearby" Fortran 77 program,

(v4) a Fortran D version of the nearby program, and

(v5) a Fortran 90 version of the program.

The "nearby" version of the program will utilize the same basic algorithm as the message-passing program, except that all explicit message-passing and blocking of loops in the program are removed. The Fortran D version of the program consists of the nearby version plus appropriate data decomposition specifications. The purpose of the program suite is to provide a fair test of the prototype compiler that does not depend on high-level algorithm changes, but does exercise its ability to optimize whole programs based on the structure of the computation and machine-dependent issues such as the number and speed of processors in the parallel machine.

Our validation strategy is depicted in Figure 13. We will compare the running time of the best hand-coded message-passing version of the program (v2) with the output of the Fortran D compiler for the Fortran D version of the nearby program (v4) We will view the project as successful if the Fortran D version is within a factor of two for

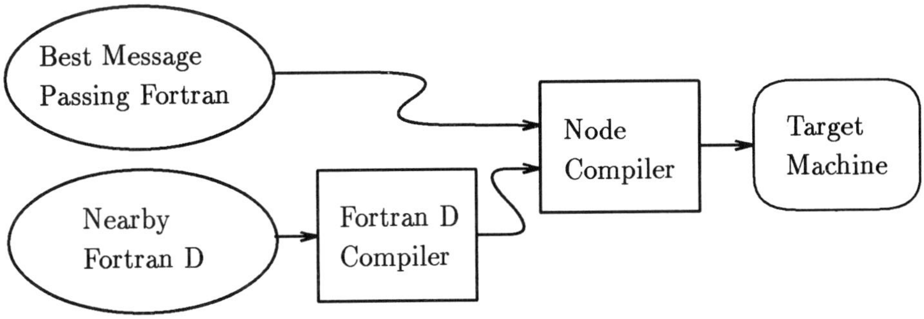

Figure 13: Fortran D Validation Strategy

approximately 75% of the programs in the validation suite. In effect we will be testing the limits of our machine-independent Fortran D programming model, as well as the efficiency and capabilities of our compiler technology. Future experiments will also compare the Fortran 90 compiler and programs for SIMD machines.

6 Relationship to Other Research

6.1 Programming Models and Languages

The proliferation of parallel architectures has focused much attention on machine-independent parallel programming. Some researchers have proposed elegant architecture-independent programming models such as *Bird-Meertens formalism* [Ski90] and the *Bulk-Synchronous* bridging model [Val90]. However, their suitability for scientific programming is unclear, and they also lack language or compiler support.

High-level parallel languages such as Linda [CG89], Strand [FT90, FO90], and Delirium [LS91] are valuable when used to *coordinate* coarse-grained functional parallelism. However, they tend to be inefficient for capturing fine-grain data parallelism of the type described by Hillis and Steele [HS86], because they lack both language and compiler support to assist in efficient data placement. Parallelism must also be explicitly specified when using these languages. As a result, language and compiler support is needed to automatically detect and exploit fine-grained data parallelism.

6.2 Compilation Techniques

The Fortran D compiler borrows heavily from previous research on compiling data-parallel application codes for distributed-memory machines. In the following sections, we look at related systems and their contributions to our Fortran D compilation strategy. First we look at some compilation techniques, then we examine existing compilation systems.

Gupta and Banerjee [GB91] propose a constraint-based approach to automatically calculate suitable data decompositions. They use simple alignments and distributions similar to those in Fortran D. Prins [Pri90] utilizes *shape refinement* in conjunction with linear transformations to specify data layouts and guide resulting data motion. These researchers do not discuss providing compiler support to generate communications.

Some researchers concentrate on computations within loops that only involve a single array. Ramanujam and Sadayappan [RS89] examine both the data and iteration space to derive a combined task and data partition of the loop nest. Hudak and Abraham [HA90] find a stencil-based approach useful for analyzing communications and deriving efficient rectangular or hexagonal data distributions. These researchers do not discuss generating communication for these complex distributions. They also make simplifying assumptions about the effects of the underlying processor topology, and do not consider collective communications.

Wolfe [Wol89, Wol90] describes transformations such as *loop rotation* for distributed-memory programs with simple BLOCK distributions. Callahan and Kennedy [CK88] propose methods for compiling programs with user-specified data distribution functions and using compiler inserted *load* and *store* commands to support nonlocal memory accesses. They also demonstrate how such programs can be optimized using transformations such as loop distribution, loop peeling, etc. The Fortran D compiler will apply many of the same transformations. BOOSTER [PvGS90] provides user-specified distribution functions defined as *program views*, but does not generate or optimize communications.

6.3 SIMD Compilation Systems

6.3.1 CM Fortran

CM Fortran [AKLS88, TMC89] is a version of Fortran 77 extended with vector notation, alignment, and data layout specifications. Programmers must explicitly specify data-parallelism in CM FORTRAN programs by marking certain array dimensions as parallel. The operating system of the underlying SIMD distributed-memory machines provides the illusion of infinite machine size through the use of virtual processors. This greatly simplifies the data distribution and communication generation responsibilities of the compiler, and has freed researchers to concentrate on techniques to automatically derive both static and dynamic data alignments [KLS88, TMC89, KLS90, KN90]. More recently, researchers have also begun to study *strip mining* and other techniques to avoid the inefficiencies of using virtual processors [Wei91].

6.3.2 C*

C* [RS87] is an extension of C similar to C++ that supports SIMD data-parallel programs. C* labels data as *mono* (local) or *poly* (distributed). There are no alignment or distribution specifications; the compiler automatically chooses the data decomposition. Parallel algorithms are specified as *actions* on a *domain*, an abstract data type implementation based on the C++ class. Communications are automatically generated by the compiler. As with CM Fortran, virtual processors are generated for each element of a domain and mapped to each physical processor. Researchers have also examined synchronization problems when translating SIMD programs into equivalent SPMD programs, as well as several communication optimizations [QH90].

6.3.3 DINO

DINO [RSW89, RSW90, RW90] is an extended version of C supporting general-purpose distributed computation. DINO supports BLOCK, CYCLIC, and special stencil-based data distributions with overlaps, but provides no alignment specifications. A DINO program contains a virtual parallel machine declared to be an *environment*. Parallelism is explicitly specified by *composite functions*. Nonlocal memory references must be annotated with the "#" operator. The DINO compiler then translates these references into communications. Passing distributed data as parameters to composite functions also generates nonlocal memory accesses. Special DINO language constructs are provided for reductions. DINO programs are deterministic unless special asynchronous distributed arrays are used. As with CM Fortran, DINO programs generate multiple processes per physical processor when large numbers of virtual processors are declared in the environment.

6.3.4 Paragon

PARAGON [CR89, Ree90] is a programming environment targeted at supporting SIMD programs on MIMD distributed-memory machines. It provides both language extensions and run-time support for task management and load balancing. Data distribution in PARAGON may either be performed by the user or the system. Parallel arrays are mapped onto *shapes* that consist of arbitrary rectangular distributions. Only the first two dimensions of each array may be distributed, and alignment is not supported. The location of each array element may be determined at run-time by checking the *distribution map* stored on each processor. Redistribution and replication of arrays and subarrays, as well as permutation and reduction mechanism are supported. Irregular distributions and run-time preprocessing support is being planned. PARAGON does not perform analysis or transformations to detect or enhance parallelism.

6.3.5 SPOT

SPOT [SS90, Soc90] is a point-based SIMD data-parallel programming language. Distributed arrays are defined as *regions*. Computations are specified from the point of view of a single element in the region, called a *point*. Locations relative to a given point are assigned symbolic names by *neighbor* declarations. An *iteration index* operator allows the programmer to specify whether nonlocal values from neighbors are from the current or previous iteration. This stencil-based approach allows the SPOT compiler to derive efficient *near-rectangular* data distributions. The compiler then generates computation and communication by expanding the single point algorithm to cover all points distributed onto a node. No alignment and or distribution specifications are provided. It is not clear how SPOT will support computation patterns that cannot be described by stencils, or those involving multiple arrays.

6.4 MIMD Compilation Systems

6.4.1 Crystal

CRYSTAL [CCL89, LC90b, LC90a] is a high-level functional language. The CRYSTAL compiler targets distributed-memory machines, performing both automatic data decomposition and communications generation. Programs are first separated into *phases*. Each phase has a different computation structure, represented by an *index domain*. Heuristics are employed to align data arrays with the index domain, both within and across dimensions, then the control structure of the program is derived. Communication patterns are synthesized from the computation, evaluated for a variety of block distributions, then matched with CRYSTAL collective communication routines. Later phases of the compiler generate message-passing C programs for the physical machine. Because it targets a functional language, CRYSTAL does not possess program analysis techniques for imperative languages such as Fortran. It is currently unclear whether the CRYSTAL language can express all scientific computations. Work in progress to adapt the CRYSTAL compiler for scientific Fortran codes will help answer this question.

6.4.2 Id Nouveau

ID NOUVEAU [RP89] is a functional language extended with single assignment arrays called *I-structures*. User-specified BLOCK distributions are provided. The basic *run-time resolution* algorithm is similar to the guard and message introduction phases of the Fortran D compiler, but without any attempt to eliminate redundant guards. Guard elimination is described as *compile-time resolution*; it is performed by calculating the set of *evaluators* and *participants* for each statement. Message presending and blocking optimizations are performed using vectorization transformations such as loop fusion and strip mining. Global accumulates are also supported.

6.4.3 SUPERB

SUPERB [ZBG88, Ger90] is a semi-automatic parallelization tool that supports arbitrary user-specified contiguous rectangular distributions. It performs dependence analysis to guide interactive program transformations in a manner similar to the ParaScope Editor [KMT91]. SUPERB originated the *overlap* concept as a means to both specify and store nonlocal data accesses. Once program analysis and transformation is complete, communication is automatically generated and blocked utilizing data dependence information. Some interprocedural analysis is supported. The Fortran D compiler uses overlaps for storing certain classes of nonlocal data. Major differences between SUPERB and the Fortran D compiler include support for data alignment, automatic compilation, collective communications, dynamic data decomposition, and storage choices for nonlocal values.

6.4.4 ASPAR, Express

ASPAR [IFKF90] is a compiler that performs automatic data decomposition and communications generation for loops containing a single distributed array. It utilizes collective communication primitives from the EXPRESS run-time system for distributed-memory machines [EXP89]. ASPAR performs simple dependence analysis using *A-lists* to detect parallelizable loops. The structure of the loop computation may be recognized as a *reduction* operation, in which case the loop is parallelized by replacing the reduction with the appropriate EXPRESS *combine* operation. If the loop performs regular computations on a distributed array, a *micro-stencil* is derived and used to generate a *macro-stencil* to identify communication requirements. Communications utilizing EXPRESS primitives are then automatically generated. ASPAR automatically selects BLOCK distributions; no alignment or distribution specifications are provided.

6.4.5 MIMDizer

MIMDIZER is an interactive parallelization system for MIMD shared and distributed-memory machines. Based on FORGE, it performs dataflow and dependence analyses and also supports loop-level transformations. Associated tools also graphically display call graph, control flow, dependence, and profiling information. When programming for distributed-memory machines, users interactively select BLOCK or CYCLIC distributions for selected array dimensions. *Code spreading* is applied interactively to loops to introduce parallelism. Alignment is not provided. MIMDIZER automatically generates communications corresponding to nonlocal memory accesses at the end of the parallelization session.

6.4.6 Pandore

PANDORE [APT90] is a compiler for distributed-memory machines that takes as input C programs extended with BLOCK, CYCLIC, and overlapping data distributions. Distributed arrays are mapped by the compiler onto a user-declared *virtual distributed machine* that may be configured as a vector, ring, grid, or torus. The compiler then outputs code in the *vdm_l* intermediate language. Calls to the PANDORE communication library to access nonlocal data is also automatically generated by the compiler. Guard introduction and communications optimization techniques are under development.

6.4.7 AL

AL [Tse90] is a language designed for the Warp distributed-memory systolic processor. The programmer utilizes DARRAY declarations to mark parallel arrays. The AL compiler then applies *data relations* to automatically align and distribute each DARRAY, detect parallelism, and generate communication. Only one dimension of each DARRAY may be distributed, and computations must be *linearly related.*

6.4.8 Oxygen

OXYGEN [RA90] is a compiler for the K2 distributed-memory machine. Unlike systems discussed previously, OXYGEN follows a functional rather than data decomposition strategy. Task-level parallelism is specified by labeling each parallel block of code with a *p_block* directive. Loop-level parallelism is specified by labeling parallel loops with either *split* or *scatter* directives. Decompositions are mapped onto the K2 architecture as *ring*, *rowwise*, or *colwise.* Distributed data arrays may be declared as *local*, *multicopy*, or *singlecopy*, corresponding to private, replicated, and distributed, respectively. Explicit communications directives for reductions and broadcast are also provided. The OXYGEN compiler then converts Fortran code with user directives into C++ node programs with communications. Messages are inserted at points in the program called *checkpoints* to enforce coarse-grain synchronization. Work is in progress to automatically generate OXYGEN directives for functional and data decomposition.

6.4.9 PARTI, ARF

PARTI [SBW90] is a set of run-time library routines that support irregular computations on MIMD distributed-memory machines. PARTI is first to propose and implement user-defined irregular distributions [MSS+88] and a hashed cache for nonlocal values [MSMB90]. PARTI has also motivated the development of ARF [WSHB91], a compiler designed to interface Fortran application programs with PARTI run-time routines. ARF provides BLOCK and CYCLIC distributions, and is the first compiler to support user-defined irregular distributions. It also generates *inspector* and *executor* loops for run-time preprocessing [KMSB90, WSBH91]. The goal of ARF is to demonstrate that inspector/executors can be automatically generated by the compiler. It does not currently generate messages at compile-time for regular computations.

6.4.10 Kali

KALI [KMV90, MV90] is the first compiler system that supports both regular and irregular computations on MIMD distributed-memory machines. Programs written for KALI must specify a virtual processor array and assign distributed arrays to BLOCK, CYCLIC, or user-specified distributions. Instead of deriving a functional decomposition from the data decomposition, KALI requires that the programmer explicitly partition loop iterations onto the processor array. This is accomplished by specifying an *on clause* for each parallel loop. Communication is then generated automatically based on the on clause and data distributions. An *inspector/executor* strategy is used for run-time preprocessing of communication for irregularly distributed arrays [KMSB90]. Major differences between KALI and the Fortran D compiler include mandatory on clauses for parallel loops, support for alignment, collective communications, and dynamic decomposition.

7 Conclusions and Future Work

An efficient yet usable machine-independent parallel programming model is needed to make large-scale parallel machines useful for scientific programmers. We believe that Fortran D, a version of Fortran enhanced with data decompositions, provides such a programming model. This paper presents the design of a compiler that translates Fortran D to distributed-memory parallel machines, as well as a strategy for evaluating its effectiveness.

The major features of the Fortran D compiler include a rich set of data decomposition specifications, sophisticated intraprocedural and interprocedural analyses, dynamic data decomposition, program transformation, communication optimization, and support for both regular and irregular problems. We expect to be able to generate efficient code for a large class of programs with only minimal effort from the scientific programmer.

The current version of the compiler generates code for a subset of the decompositions allowed in Fortran D, namely unaligned block decompositions. We are extending the implementation to handle other data decompositions. Significant work remains to develop and implement decision algorithms for the optimizations presented in this paper, as well as a whole program compilation algorithm.

8 Acknowledgements

The authors wish to thank Vasanth Balasundaram, Marina Kalem, and Uli Kremer for inspiring many of the ideas in this work. Our research group was formed largely due to their efforts. We also wish to acknowledge the assistance of Chuck Koelbel, especially in the area of irregular distributions. Finally, we are grateful to the ParaScope research group for providing the underlying software infrastructure for the Fortran D compiler.

References

[ACK87] J. R. Allen, D. Callahan, and K. Kennedy. Automatic decomposition of scientific programs for parallel execution. In *Proceedings of the Fourteenth Annual ACM Symposium on the Principles of Programming Languages*, Munich, Germany, January 1987.

[AK87] J. R. Allen and K. Kennedy. Automatic translation of Fortran programs to vector form. *ACM Transactions on Programming Languages and Systems*, 9(4):491–542, October 1987.

[AKLS88] E. Albert, K. Knobe, J. Lukas, and G. Steele, Jr. Compiling Fortran 8x array features for the Connection Machine computer system. In *Symposium on Parallel Programming: Experience with Applications, Languages and Systems*, New Haven, CT, July 1988.

[APT90] F. André, J. Pazat, and H. Thomas. Pandore: A system to manage data distribution. In *Proceedings of the 1990 ACM International Conference on Supercomputing*, Amsterdam, The Netherlands, June 1990.

[Bal91] V. Balasundaram. Translating control parallelism to data parallelism. In *Proceedings of the Fifth SIAM Conference on Parallel Processing for Scientific Computing*, Houston, TX, March 1991.

[BFKK90] V. Balasundaram, G. Fox, K. Kennedy, and U. Kremer. An interactive environment for data partitioning and distribution. In *Proceedings of the 5th Distributed Memory Computing Conference*, Charleston, SC, April 1990.

[BFKK91] V. Balasundaram, G. Fox, K. Kennedy, and U. Kremer. A static performance estimator to guide data partitioning decisions. In *Proceedings of the Third ACM SIGPLAN Symposium on Principles and Practice of Parallel Programming*, Williamsburg, VA, April 1991.

[BK89] V. Balasundaram and K. Kennedy. A technique for summarizing data access and its use in parallelism enhancing transformations. In *Proceedings of the SIGPLAN '89 Conference on Program Language Design and Implementation*, Portland, OR, June 1989.

[CCH+88] D. Callahan, K. Cooper, R. Hood, K. Kennedy, and L. Torczon. ParaScope: A parallel programming environment. *The International Journal of Supercomputer Applications*, 2(4):84–99, Winter 1988.

[CCL89] M. Chen, Y. Choo, and J. Li. Theory and pragmatics of compiling efficient parallel code. Technical Report YALEU/DCS/TR-760, Dept. of Computer Science, Yale University, New Haven, CT, December 1989.

[CG89] N. Carriero and D. Gelernter. Linda in context. *Communications of the ACM*, 32(4):444–458, April 1989.

[CK87] D. Callahan and K. Kennedy. Analysis of interprocedural side effects in a parallel programming environment. In *Proceedings of the First International Conference on Supercomputing*. Springer-Verlag, Athens, Greece, June 1987.

[CK88] D. Callahan and K. Kennedy. Compiling programs for distributed-memory multiprocessors. *Journal of Supercomputing*, 2:151–169, October 1988.

[CKK89] D. Callahan, K. Kennedy, and U. Kremer. A dynamic study of vectorization in PFC. Technical Report TR89-97, Dept. of Computer Science, Rice University, July 1989.

[CKT86] K. Cooper, K. Kennedy, and L. Torczon. The impact of interprocedural analysis and optimization in the $\mathbb{R}^n$ programming environment. *ACM Transactions on Programming Languages and Systems*, 8(4):491–523, October 1986.

[CR89] A. Cheung and A. Reeves. The Paragon multicomputer environment: A first implementation. Technical Report EE-CEG-89-9, Cornell University Computer Engineering Group, Ithaca, NY, July 1989.

[EXP89] Parasoft Corporation. *Express User's Manual*, 1989.

[FHK+90] G. Fox, S. Hiranandani, K. Kennedy, C. Koelbel, U. Kremer, C. Tseng, and M. Wu. Fortran D language specification. Technical Report TR90-141, Dept. of Computer Science, Rice University, December 1990.

[FJL+88] G. Fox, M. Johnson, G. Lyzenga, S. Otto, J. Salmon, and D. Walker. *Solving Problems on Concurrent Processors*, volume 1. Prentice-Hall, Englewood Cliffs, NJ, 1988.

[FO90] I. Foster and R. Overbeek. Bilingual parallel programming. In *Proceedings of the Third Workshop on Languages and Compilers for Parallel Computing*, Irvine, CA, August 1990.

[FT90] I. Foster and S. Taylor. *Strand: New Concepts in Parallel Programming.* Prentice-Hall, Englewood Cliffs, NJ, 1990.

[GB91] M. Gupta and P. Banerjee. Automatic data partitioning on distributed memory multiprocessors. In *Proceedings of the 6th Distributed Memory Computing Conference*, Portland, OR, April 1991.

[Ger90] M. Gerndt. Updating distributed variables in local computations. *Concurrency—Practice & Experience*, 2(3):171–193, September 1990.

[HA90] D. Hudak and S. Abraham. Compiler techniques for data partitioning of sequentially iterated parallel loops. In *Proceedings of the 1990 ACM Inter-*

national Conference on Supercomputing, Amsterdam, The Netherlands, June 1990.

[HK90] P. Havlak and K. Kennedy. Experience with interprocedural analysis of array side effects. In *Proceedings of Supercomputing '90*, New York, NY, November 1990.

[HKK+91] S. Hiranandani, K. Kennedy, C. Koelbel, U. Kremer, and C. Tseng. An overview of the Fortran D programming system. Technical Report TR91-154, Dept. of Computer Science, Rice University, March 1991.

[HS86] W. Hillis and G. Steele, Jr. Data parallel algorithms. *Communications of the ACM*, 29(12):1170–1183, 1986.

[IFKF90] K. Ikudome, G. Fox, A. Kolawa, and J. Flower. An automatic and symbolic parallelization system for distributed memory parallel computers. In *Proceedings of the 5th Distributed Memory Computing Conference*, Charleston, SC, April 1990.

[KLS88] K. Knobe, J. Lukas, and G. Steele, Jr. Massively parallel data optimization. In *Frontiers88: The 2nd Symposium on the Frontiers of Massively Parallel Computation*, Fairfax, VA, October 1988.

[KLS90] K. Knobe, J. Lukas, and G. Steele, Jr. Data optimization: Allocation of arrays to reduce communication on SIMD machines. *Journal of Parallel and Distributed Computing*, 8(2):102–118, 1990.

[KMSB90] C. Koelbel, P. Mehrotra, J. Saltz, and S. Berryman. Parallel loops on distributed machines. In *Proceedings of the 5th Distributed Memory Computing Conference*, Charleston, SC, April 1990.

[KMT91] K. Kennedy, K. S. McKinley, and C. Tseng. Analysis and transformation in the ParaScope Editor. In *Proceedings of the 1991 ACM International Conference on Supercomputing*, Cologne, Germany, June 1991.

[KMV90] C. Koelbel, P. Mehrotra, and J. Van Rosendale. Supporting shared data structures on distributed memory machines. In *Proceedings of the Second ACM SIGPLAN Symposium on Principles and Practice of Parallel Programming*, Seattle, WA, March 1990.

[KN90] K. Knobe and V. Natarajan. Data optimization: Minimizing residual interprocessor data motion on SIMD machines. In *Frontiers90: The 3rd Symposium on the Frontiers of Massively Parallel Computation*, College Park, MD, October 1990.

[LC90a] J. Li and M. Chen. Generating explicit communication from shared-memory program references. In *Proceedings of Supercomputing '90*, New York, NY, November 1990.

[LC90b] J. Li and M. Chen. Index domain alignment: Minimizing cost of cross-referencing between distributed arrays. In *Frontiers90: The 3rd Symposium on the Frontiers of Massively Parallel Computation*, College Park, MD, October 1990.

[Lea90] B. Leasure, editor. *PCF Fortran: Language Definition, version 3.1.* The Parallel Computing Forum, Champaign, IL, August 1990.

[LS91] S. Lucco and O. Sharp. Parallel programming with coordination structures. In *Proceedings of the Eighteenth Annual ACM Symposium on the Principles of Programming Languages*, Orlando, FL, January 1991.

[MSMB90] S. Mirchandaney, J. Saltz, P. Mehrotra, and H. Berryman. A scheme for supporting automatic data migration on multicomputers. In *Proceedings of the 5th Distributed Memory Computing Conference*, Charleston, SC, April 1990.

[MSS+88] R. Mirchandaney, J. Saltz, R. Smith, D. Nicol, and K. Crowley. Principles of runtime support for parallel processors. In *Proceedings of the Second International Conference on Supercomputing*, St. Malo, France, July 1988.

[MV90] P. Mehrotra and J. Van Rosendale. Programming distributed memory architectures using Kali. ICASE Report 90-69, Institute for Computer Application in Science and Engineering, Hampton, VA, October 1990.

[PB90] C. Pancake and D. Bergmark. Do parallel languages respond to the needs of scientific programmers? *IEEE Computer*, 23(12):13–23, December 1990.

[Pri90] J. Prins. A framework for efficient execution of array-based languages on SIMD computers. In *Frontiers90: The 3rd Symposium on the Frontiers of Massively Parallel Computation*, College Park, MD, October 1990.

[PvGS90] E. Paalvast, A. van Gemund, and H. Sips. A method for parallel program generation with an application to the Booster language. In *Proceedings of the 1990 ACM International Conference on Supercomputing*, Amsterdam, The Netherlands, June 1990.

[QH90] M. Quinn and P. Hatcher. Data parallel programming on multicomputers. *IEEE Software*, 7(5):69–76, September 1990.

[RA90] R. Ruhl and M. Annaratone. Parallelization of FORTRAN code on distributed-memory parallel processors. In *Proceedings of the 1990 ACM International Conference on Supercomputing*, Amsterdam, The Netherlands, June 1990.

[Ree90] A. Reeves. The Paragon programming paradigm and distributed memory compilers. Technical Report EE-CEG-90-7, Cornell University Computer Engineering Group, Ithaca, NY, June 1990.

[RP89] A. Rogers and K. Pingali. Process decomposition through locality of reference. In *Proceedings of the SIGPLAN '89 Conference on Program Language Design and Implementation*, Portland, OR, June 1989.

[RS87] J. Rose and G. Steele, Jr. C*: An extended C language for data parallel programming. In L. Kartashev and S. Kartashev, editors, *Proceedings of the Second International Conference on Supercomputing*, Santa Clara, CA, May 1987.

[RS89] J. Ramanujam and P. Sadayappan. A methodology for parallelizing programs for multicomputers and complex memory multiprocessors. In *Proceedings of Supercomputing '89*, Reno, NV, November 1989.

[RSW89] M. Rosing, R. Schnabel, and R. Weaver. Expressing complex parallel algorithms in DINO. In *Proceedings of the 4th Conference on Hypercube Concurrent Computers and Applications*, Monterey, CA, March 1989.

[RSW90] M. Rosing, R. Schnabel, and R. Weaver. The DINO parallel programming language. Technical Report CU-CS-457-90, Dept. of Computer Science, University of Colorado, April 1990.

[RW90] M. Rosing and R. Weaver. Mapping data to processors in distributed memory computations. In *Proceedings of the 5th Distributed Memory Computing Conference*, Charleston, SC, April 1990.

[SBW90] J. Saltz, H. Berryman, and J. Wu. Multiprocessors and runtime compilation. ICASE Report 90-59, Institute for Computer Application in Science and Engineering, Hampton, VA, September 1990.

[Ski90] D. Skillicorn. Architecture-independent parallel computation. *IEEE Computer*, 23(12), December 1990.

[Soc90] D. Socha. Compiling single-point iterative programs for distributed memory computers. In *Proceedings of the 5th Distributed Memory Computing Conference*, Charleston, SC, April 1990.

[SS90] L. Snyder and D. Socha. An algorithm producing balanced partitionings of data arrays. In *Proceedings of the 5th Distributed Memory Computing Conference*, Charleston, SC, April 1990.

[TMC89] Thinking Machines Corporation, Cambridge, MA. *CM Fortran Reference Manual*, version 5.2-0.6 edition, September 1989.

[Tse90] P. S. Tseng. A parallelizing compiler for distributed memory parallel computers. In *Proceedings of the SIGPLAN '90 Conference on Program Language Design and Implementation*, White Plains, NY, June 1990.

[Val90] L. Valiant. A bridging model for parallel computation. *Communications of the ACM*, 33(8):103–111, August 1990.

[Wei91] M. Weiss. Strip mining on SIMD architectures. In *Proceedings of the 1991 ACM International Conference on Supercomputing*, Cologne, Germany, June 1991.

[Wol89] M. J. Wolfe. Semi-automatic domain decomposition. In *Proceedings of the 4th Conference on Hypercube Concurrent Computers and Applications*, Monterey, CA, March 1989.

[Wol90] M. J. Wolfe. Loop rotation. In D. Gelernter, A. Nicolau, and D. Padua, editors, *Languages and Compilers for Parallel Computing.* The MIT Press, 1990.

[WSBH91] J. Wu, J. Saltz, H. Berryman, and S. Hiranandani. Distributed memory compiler design for sparse problems. ICASE Report 91-13, Institute for Computer Application in Science and Engineering, Hampton, VA, January 1991.

[WSHB91] J. Wu, J. Saltz, S. Hiranandani, and H. Berryman. Runtime compilation methods for multicomputers. In *Proceedings of the 1991 International Conference on Parallel Processing*, St. Charles, IL, August 1991.

[ZBG88] H. Zima, H.-J. Bast, and M. Gerndt. SUPERB: A tool for semi-automatic MIMD/SIMD parallelization. *Parallel Computing*, 6:1–18, 1988.

Languages, Compilers and Run-Time Environments
for Distributed Memory Machines
J. Saltz and P. Mehrotra (Editors)

PANDORE: A System to Manage Data Distribution

Françoise André, Jean-Louis Pazat and Henry Thomas

IRISA, Campus de Beaulieu, 35042 Rennes Cedex, FRANCE

Abstract

We investigate here the implementation of "high level" languages on Distributed Memory Parallel Computers (DMPCs). The Pandore system provides a language, a compiler and a run-time support which allows to use DMPCs with a sequential language including data distribution statements. In Pandore, code parallelization is achieved according to data distribution. No explicit process definition nor interprocess communications are needed at the user level. One of the main features of our approach is that data distribution do not modify the result of the program in any case; on the contrary, efficiency is closely related to data distribution.

1. INTRODUCTION

Today, many programming models are investigated in order to provide the user an easy way for programming DMPCs.

In all cases the major issue is not to hide totally the distributed structure of the memory, but to allow the user to express local and distant accesses in the same way without any message passing mechanism. This can be achieved by providing a global name space to the user but it is different from implementing a shared virtual memory as described in [1] or using it into a specific algorithm [2]. The first difference is that in our approach, the user is in charge of the mapping of data; the second difference is that data do not migrate from one processor to another during the program execution.

The main field of applications for DMPCs is scientific programming which involves large data structures such as matrices. To parallelize these applications on DMPCs it seems very efficient to rely on methods based on data partitioning. For writing a *data parallel algorithm*, the user first defines how the data structures are partitioned, so that each process of the parallel program works on different parts of data. Then the work of the programmer is:

1. To restrict the data domain accesses of each process to the exact part of data it works on.

2. To map the partitioned data onto the local memories.

3. To implement local and remote accesses to variables according to the local names of variables, using message passing procedures and local temporary storage.

Presently, logical data decomposition through fully automatic partitioning methods seems to be intractable in many cases. On the contrary, compilers are being defined to solve most of the problems due to the generation of low level code.

As most of scientific codes are already written in sequential languages (most of them in Fortran) , compiling sequential programs for DMPCs is an important issue. Superb [3], Parascope [4] and our project Pandore [5] are based on a sequential language with new constructs and statements to allow the user to express data distribution. In other approaches parallel constructs are added to a sequential language such as the *forall* statement in KALI [6] or the composite procedures of DINO [7]. Some other projects in this field not presented in this volume are Aspar [8], Booster [9] and Oxygen [10].

2. OVERVIEW OF THE PANDORE SYSTEM

In order to specify the potential parallelism of a sequential program, the user decomposes data structures in sub-structures. In the Pandore system the user task is to annotate data structures in order to define a regular decomposition among them. For example, assuming A is an array of $N \times M$ elements, the statement

```
partition(A,Block(K,L))
```

partitions the array Win in $\lceil N/K \rceil \times \lceil M/L \rceil$ subarrays of size $K \times L$. In order to map the partitioned structure, the user specifies a virtual processor domain (Virtual Distributed Machine VDM) which corresponds to some ideal distributed memory parallel architecture. For example the declaration:

```
processor mygrid[10][10]
```

defines a grid of 100 processors.

Accesses to different sub-structures can be achieved in parallel in the object code if no dependencies exists in the source code. The Pandore compiler automatically generates distributed processes and manages with data distribution through consistent local or distant accesses.

In the first step the Pandore Compiler produces a parallel SPMD program which consists in a set of processes. Each process is associated with a virtual processor and executes the part of the original program related to the local data.

An intermediate language is used for the resulting object code (Virtual Distributed Machine Language Vdm_l) which is then expanded into specific machine code. In our actual implementation we produce code for the iPSC2.

3. THE PANDORE LANGUAGE

A source language for the Pandore system can be built upon any sequential language (Pascal, Fortran, C,...). For our first investigation, we have implemented Pandore upon an extended subset of the C language (C_Pandore). We have added new keywords and constructs in order to express:

- the data partitioning,
- the mapping of partitioned data (VDM definition),
- the different phases of a program.

3.1 Data partitioning

If we want to partition and distribute a variable, it must be declared as "distributed", for example:

```
distributed int A[N][M]
```

declares an array of `N x M` integers which may later be partitionned using the statement:

```
partition(A,Block(k,l))
```

The `partition` statement allows to decompose an n-dimensional array into n-dimensional sub-blocks using the `Block` function. For example the 2-dimension array T is partitioned into blocks ofsize $k \times l$. If $N \bmod k \neq 0$, the last blocks in the first dimension are of size $N \bmod k$. If $M \bmod l \neq 0$, the last blocks in t he second dimension are of size $M \bmod l$.

When the computation associated with one sub-block refers to boundary elements of the other sub-blocks, it is convenient to use the `Block_overlap` function, which allows to duplicate boundary slices of neighboring sub-blocks. For each dimension, the overlap parameters specify:

- The size of the slice of the previous block in the current dimension which is duplicated,
- The size of the slice of the next block in the current dimension which is duplicated,
- The optional overlap for the extreme blocks.

For example, the statement

```
partition(T,Block_overlap((k,1,1,None) (l,1,1,None)))
```

partitions the array `T` into blocks of size $k \times l$ with an overlap of a slice of size one, in each direction except for the extreme blocks.

Presently we only offer these two partitioning functions. User–defined partitioning functions are envisaged for a next version of the system.

3.2 Virtual Distributed Machines

In C_Pandore, a VDM is a set of interconnected virtual processors with local memories. A VDM must be declared like other variables before being used.

The keyword `processor` introduces a new type which allows to define VDMs as arrays of processors. A qualifier is used to specify particular topologies. At present it is only possible to define the following VDM topologies: vector, ring, grid and torus.

A VDM is in use for the duration of one computational phase corresponding to the execution of a parallelized block. Only one VDM may be "opened" at a time; if no VDM is explicitely opened, the current VDM is a single processor and the computation is sequential. The statement :

```
vdm my_vdm(<parameters>){<parallelized VDM- block>}
```

opens the virtual machine `my_vdm` as a target machine for the distribution of the data structures specified in `<parameters>` and for the parallel execution of the block of instructions.

3.3 Data distribution over VDMs

The data distributed over the current VDM are indicated at the opening of the VDM as a list of items `((<variable>,<mode>))`.

The first parameter of an item specifies the name of the variable to distribute . The partitioning mode for the variable must be given before the VDM–block. No partitioning statement is allowed inside a VDM–block.

The second parameter (`IN`, `OUT` or `INOUT`) indicates:

- that the values of the distributed structure are significant at the entry of the block (`IN`) and that the structure will recover the initial values at the end of the block,
- that the modified values of the structure are significant after the end of the block (`OUT`),
- or that they are significant before and after the block execution (`INOUT`).

The value of the `<mode>` parameter allows to know if it is necessary to distribute (to collect) the actual content of the data structure at the beginning (at the end) of a VDM-block or not.

The distribution is realized by the Pandore system in the following way :

- If the variable is a partitioned array :
  The distribution of the data structure is chosen according to the topology of the current VDM. If there are less blocks in the partitioned array than processors in the VDM, only the first processors of the VDM receive a block. If the partitioned array is too large, block assignation is made by folding (on vector and grid VDMs) or in a modulo fashion (on ring and torus VDMs).
- If the distributed variable is of a basic data type (or an unpartitioned array) :
  A single processor (chosen by the system) owns the variable (the entire array).
- If a variable is declared inside a VDM :
  Each processor owns an independent copy of the variable.

Figure 1 gives a short example of a C_Pandore program.

3.4 Compilation and run-time support

The Pandore compiler generates a SPMD program in an intermediate level language. Each processor executes the same code (SPMD) but the data distribution induces a conditional execution for each statement.

The basic scheme is defined for the assignment between distributed variables ($A[i] := B[j]$). In this case, one processor must execute the code and at most one processor must send the value of $B[j]$. the SPMD program is the following:

```
if Owner(A[i]) = myself
  then
        if Owner(B[j]) = myself
          then
                tmp := B[j]
          else
                tmp := recv(Owner(B[j]))
        endif ;
        A[i] := tmp
  else
        if Owner(B[j]) = myself
          then
                send(Owner(A[i]), B[j])
        endif
endif
```

Where

- *myself* is the name of the current process,
- *Owner(x)* is the name of the process where x is mapped,
- *tmp* is a temporary local storage managed by the compiler,
- communication between processes is FIFO,
- *recv(P)* waits for a value to be received from the process P
- *send(P,V)* sends the value of V to the process P but does not wait for V to be received by P

In the case of the assignment of a distributed variable to a local variable (`a :=A[i]`) the scheme is more simple: each processor must execute the code and at most one processor must send the value of A.

```
if Owner(A[i]) = myself
  then
        tmp := A[i];
        send(others, A[i])
  else
        tmp := recv(Owner(A[i]))
endif
a := tmp ;
```

Where *others* stands for the set of processes of the Vdm except the process which sends the value.

In the case of the assignment of a local variable to a distributed variable (`A[i] := a`), one processor must execute the code and the value of a has not to be sent.

if *Owner(A)* = *myself* **then** *A[i]* := a **endif**

The case of the assignment between local variables is trivial: each process executes the same code.

This basic scheme is similar to the scheme proposed in [4]. It is now implemented as run-time resolution and is quite inefficient because the conditional execution creates an overhead for the execution of each instruction on each processor. Though this overhead does not depend on the number of processors, it is the major limitation of this scheme.

The problem of a conditional execution is treated in a three phases mechanism. For example:

if A[i]=0 then goto etiq

is transformed into:

Test:=(A[i]=0); if Test then goto etiq

where *Test* is a unique variable localized on some processor of the VDM chosen by the compiler.

In this case, the scheme is the following:

```
(* Phase 1 Condition evaluation *)
        if Owner(Test)= myself
          then
              if Owner(A[i]) = myself
                then
                    tmp := A[i]
                else
                    tmp := recv(Owner(A[i]))
              endif ;
              Test :=(tmp = 0 )
          else
              if Owner(A[i]) = myself
                then
                    send(Owner(Test), A[i])
              endif
        endif ;
(* Phase 2 Broadast *)
        if Owner(Test) = myself
          then
              tmp2 := Test;
              send(OTHERS, Test)
          else
             tmp2:= recv(Owner(Test))
        endif ;
(* Phase 3 Conditional execution *)
        if tmp2 then goto etiq endif ;
```

In the scheme proposed by Kennedy et al [4], each data item of the condition is broadcasted and each process evaluates the condition. In our scheme, data item of the condition are sent to one processor which evaluates the condition, then the result is broadcasted. Our scheme generates less communication than Kennedy's when many data elements forms the condition as in:

if (A[i]=B[i]+C[i])

This scheme can be improved in some simple cases, as for example in *if A[i]=0 then B[j]:=0*, no broadcast is needed and *tmp* should reside on the processor which owns *B[j]*.

Loops are treated with a simple combination of these basic rules. One must note that the use of a *local* variable is necessary in *for* loops to avoid a sequentialization of iterations due to the accesses to the loop index: this corresponds to the behavior of the `forall` statement if no dependancies exist.

4. FURTHER WORK

We are now working on a more formal expression of the execution scheme; in particular variables accesses should be treated separately from conditional execution of statements for clearness.

The main improvements of our system rely on compile-time analysis of iterations and data accesses domains. Such an analysis will allow us to reduce significantly the overhead due to the run-time evaluation of locality of reference.

Another improvement of the execution scheme will be achieve by packing communications and allow processes to send value as soon as possible to avoid unnecessary synchronizations between processes. This requires analysis of data domains and data dependences.

```
...
distributed int Win[N] , Wout[N];
processor row[4];
main()
{ ...
 /* parallelized phase */
  partition (Win, block_overlap(100,1,1));
  partition (Wout, block(100));
  vdm row ( (Win, IN), (Wout, OUT)) {
    int i ;
    for(i=1; i<N-1; i++) Wout[i]= A*Win[i-1] + B*Win[i] + C*Win[i+1];
  }
  ...
}
```

Figure 1: Convolution in C_Pandore

References

[1] K. Li and R. Schaefer. A hypercube shared virtual memory system. In *1989 International Conference on Parallel Processing*, pages 125–132, 1989.

[2] D. Badouel, K. Bouatouch, and T. Priol. Ray tracing on distributed memory parallel computers: strategies for distributing computations and data. In S. Whitman, editor, *Parallel Algorithms and architectures for 3D Image Generation*, pages 185–198, ACM Siggraph'90 Course 28, August 1990.

[3] H. P. Zima, H.-J. Bast, and M. Gerndt. SUPERB: a tool for semi-automatic MIMD /SIMD parallelization. *Parallel Computing*, (6):1–18, 1988.

[4] D. Callahan and K. Kennedy. Compiling programs for distributed-memory multiprocessors. *Journal of Supercomputing*, 2:151–169, 1988.

[5] F. André, J.-L. Pazat, and H. Thomas. PANDORE: a system to manage data distribution. In *Int. Conf. on Supercomputing*, pages 380–388, June 1990.

[6] C. Koebel and P. Mehrotra. *Supporting Shared Data Structures on Distributed Memory Architectures.* Technical Report csd-tr 915, Department of Computer Science, Purdue University, 1990.

[7] M. Rosing, R. B. Schnabel, and R. P. Weaver. *The DINO Parallel Programming Language.* Technical Report CU-CS-457-90, University of Colorado at Boulder, 1990.

[8] K. Ikudome, G. C. Fox, A. Kolawa, and J. W. Flower. An automatic and symbolic parallelization system for distributed memory parallel computers. In *5' Distributed Memory Computing Conference*, April 1990.

[9] E. M. Paalvast and A. J. Van Gemund. A method for parallel program generation with an application to the *Booster* language. In *Int. Conf. on Supercomputing*, pages 457–469, June 1990.

[10] R. Ruhl and M. Annaratone. Parallelization of FORTRAN Code on distributed memory parallel processors. In *Int. Conf. on Supercomputing*, pages 342–353, June 1990.

Languages, Compilers and Run-Time Environments
for Distributed Memory Machines
J. Saltz and P. Mehrotra (Editors)

DISTRIBUTED MEMORY COMPILER METHODS FOR IRREGULAR PROBLEMS – DATA COPY REUSE AND RUNTIME PARTITIONING[1]

Raja Das[a], Ravi Ponnusamy[b], Joel Saltz[a] and Dimitri Mavriplis[a]

[a]ICASE, MS 132C, NASA Langley Research Center, Hampton VA. 23666 USA

[b]Department of Computer Science, Syracuse University , Syracuse, NY 13244-4100

Abstract

This paper outlines two methods which we believe will play an important role in any distributed memory compiler able to handle sparse and unstructured problems. We describe how to link runtime partitioners to distributed memory compilers. In our scheme, programmers can *implicitly* specify how data and loop iterations are to be distributed between processors. This insulates users from having to deal explicitly with potentially complex algorithms that carry out work and data partitioning.

We also describe a viable mechanism for tracking and reusing copies of off-processor data. In many programs, several loops access the same off-processor memory locations. As long as it can be verified that the values assigned to off-processor memory locations remain unmodified, we show that we can effectively reuse stored off-processor data. We present experimental data from a 3-D unstructured Euler solver run on an iPSC/860 to demonstrate the usefulness of our methods.

1 Introduction

Over the past few years, we have developed methods needed to generate efficient distributed memory code for a large class of sparse and unstructured problems. In sparse and unstructured problems, the dependency structure is determined by variable values

[1]This work is supported by NASA contract NAS1-18605 while the authors were in residence at ICASE, NASA Langley Research Center. In addition, support for author Saltz was provided by NSF from NSF grant ASC-8819374. The authors assume all responsibility for the contents of the paper.

known only at runtime. In these cases, effective use of distributed memory architectures is made possible by a runtime preprocessing phase. This preprocessing is used to partition work, to map data structures and to schedule the movement of data between the memories of processors. The code needed to carry out runtime preprocessing can be generated by a distributed memory compiler in a process we call *runtime compilation* [39].

This paper presents two new runtime compilation methods. In this paper, we describe:

how to link runtime partitioners to distributed memory compilers, and

how to reduce interprocessor communication requirements by eliminating redundant off-processor data accesses.

A *compiler-linked* runtime partitioner uses dynamic data dependency information to decompose data structures and to partition loop iterations. The compiler produces code that at runtime generates a standardized representation of the dependency graph that arises from one or more loop nests. This dependency graph representation is then passed to a compiler embedded data structure partitioner. The compiler also generates code that at runtime produces a graph that is used in a compiler embedded loop iteration partitioner. Programmers use Fortran extensions to specify which loops and which distributed arrays should be used to derive data structure partitions. Consequently, programmers *implicitly* specify how data and loop iterations are to be distributed between processors. The idea of developing a set of widely applicable partitioners has been pursued by G. Fox for many years (see for instance [15] and [16]), and a general scheme for linking such partitioners to compilers was outlined in [33]. In this paper we describe some of the runtime support and the language extensions that are allowing us to develop the software required to realize some of these ideas. In the interest of casting our vote for standardization in the development of languages and extensions for distributed memory MIMD and SIMD machines, we present our work in the context of a pre-existing language, Fortran D [17].

Once data structure and loop iteration partitioning have been determined, we carry out further preprocessing to generate communication calls needed to efficiently transport data between processors. In sparse and unstructured computations, distributed arrays are typically accessed using indirection. Runtime preprocessing is used to generate a small number of communications calls to carry out the required data transport. In many cases, several loops access the same off-processor memory locations. As long as it is known that the values assigned to off-processor memory locations remain unmodified, it is possible to reuse stored off-processor data. A mixture of compile-time and run-time analysis can be used to recognize these situations. Compiler analysis determines when it is safe to assume that the off-processor data copy remains valid. Software primitives generate communications calls which selectively fetch only those off-processor data, which are not available locally. We will call a communications pattern that eliminates redundant off-processor data accesses an *incremental schedule.* The preprocessing described here builds on the work described in [6], [22] and [46].

We will set the context of the work in Section 2. In Section 3.1, we will describe primitives that produce incremental schedules. In Section 3.2 we will describe the primitives used to couple data and loop iteration partitioners to compilers. In Section 4 we will present an overview of our compiler effort. We describe the transformations which generate incremental inspectors and executors, and describe the language extensions we use to control compiler-linked runtime partitioning. Finally, in Section 5 we will present performance data to characterize the performance of our methods.

2 Overview

2.1 Overview of Fortran D

We will present our runtime-compilation methods in the context of Fortran D. Fortran D is a version of Fortran 77 enhanced with a rich set of data decomposition specifications, a definition of the language extensions may be found in [17], a less detailed description of Fortran D is given in the article by Hiranandani et. al., found in this book. Fortran D as currently specified requires that users explicitly define how data is to be distributed. Many researchers have explored the problem of specifying data decompositions, and FortranD has drawn extensively on this work (e.g. [46], [25], [36] and [11], [34], [7, 27, 26, 28]) While our work will be presented in the context of Fortran D, the same optimizations and analogous language extensions could be used for a wide range of languages and compilers.

Fortran D can be used to explicitly specify an irregular inter-processor partition of distributed array elements. In Figure 1, we present an example of such a Fortran D declaration. In Fortran D, one declares a template called a *distribution* used to characterize the significant attributes of a distributed array. The distribution fixes the size, dimension and way in which the array is to be partitioned between processors. A distribution is produced using two declarations. The first declaration is *decomposition.* Decomposition fixes the name, dimensionality and size of the distributed array template. The second declaration is *distribute.* Distribute is an executable statement and specifies how a template is to be mapped onto processors. Fortran D provides the user with a choice of several regular distributions, in addition, a user can explicitly specify how a distribution

```
....
S1 REAL*8 x(N),y(N)
S2 INTEGER map(N)
S3 DECOMPOSITION reg(N),irreg(N)
S4 DISTRIBUTE reg(block)
S5 ALIGN map with reg
S6 ... set values of map array using some mapping method ..
S7 DISTRIBUTE irreg(map)
S8 ALIGN x,y with irreg
....
```

Figure 1: Fortran D Irregular Distribution

is to be mapped onto processors. A specific array is associated with a distribution using the Fortran D statement *align*. In statement S3, Figure 1, two size `N`, one dimensional decompositions are defined. In statement S4, decomposition `reg` is partitioned into equal sized blocks with a block assigned to each processor. In statement S5, array `map` is aligned with distribution `reg`. Array `map` will be used to specify (in statement S8) how distribution `irreg` is to be partitioned between processors. An irregular distribution is specified using an integer array; when $map(i)$ is set equal to p, element i of the distribution `irreg` is assigned to processor p.

The current Fortran D syntax requires programmers to *explicitly* define irregular data decompositions. As we shall illustrate in the following sections, our new language extensions and compiler techniques make it possible for programmers to *implicitly* specify how data and loop iterations are to be distributed between processors.

2.2 Overview of PARTI

In this section, we will give an overview of the functionality of the PARTI primitives described in previous publications ([46], [6], [39]). In many algorithms, data produced or input during a program's initialization plays a large role in determining the nature of the subsequent computation. In the PARTI approach, when the data structures that define a computation have been initialized, a preprocessing phase follows. Vital elements of the strategy used by the rest of the algorithm are determined by this preprocessing phase.

In distributed memory MIMD architectures, there is typically a non-trivial communications latency or startup cost. For efficiency reasons, information to be transmitted should be collected into relatively large messages. The cost of fetching array elements can be reduced by precomputing what data each processor needs to send and receive.

In irregular problems, such as solving PDEs on unstructured meshes and sparse matrix algorithms, the communication pattern depends on the input data. This typically arises due to some level of indirection in the code. In this case, it is not possible to predict at compile time what data must be prefetched. To deal with this lack of information the original sequential loop is transformed into two constructs namely, the *inspector* and the *executor*.

During program execution, the *inspector* loop examines the data references made by a processor, and calculates what off-processor data needs to be fetched and where that data will be stored once it is received. The *executor* loop then uses the information from the inspector to implement the actual computation. We have developed a suite of primitives that can be used directly by programmers to generate inspector/executor pairs.

These primitives are named PARTI (Parallel Automated Runtime Toolkit at ICASE) [12], [6]; they carry out the distribution and retrieval of globally indexed but irregularly distributed data-sets over the numerous local processor memories. Each inspector produces a set of *schedules*, which specify the communication calls needed to either:

a obtain copies of data stored in specified off-processor memory locations (i.e. *gather*) or,

b modify the contents of specified off-processor memory locations (i.e. *scatter*), or

c accumulate (e.g. add or multiply) values to specified off-processor memory locations, (i.e. *accumulate*).

Schedulers use hash tables to generate communication calls that, for each loop nest, transmit only a single copy of each off-processor datum [22], [46]. The schedules are used in the executor by PARTI primitives to gather, scatter and accumulate data to/from off-processor memory locations. In this paper, the idea of eliminating duplicates has been taken a step further. If several loops require different but overlapping data references we can now avoid communicating redundant data (See Section 3.1 and Section 4.1.3).

In distributed memory machines, large data arrays need to be partitioned between local memories of processors. These partitioned data arrays are called *distributed arrays*.

Long term storage of distributed array data is assigned to specific memory locations in the distributed machine. It is frequently advantageous to partition distributed arrays in an irregular manner. For instance, the way in which the nodes of an irregular computational mesh are numbered frequently does not have a useful correspondence to the connectivity pattern of the mesh. When we partition the data structures in such a problem in a way that minimizes interprocessor communication, we may need to be able to assign arbitrary array elements to each processor.

Each element in a distributed array is assigned to a particular processor, and in order for another processor to be able to access a given element of the array we must know the processor in which it resides, and its local address in this processor's memory. We thus build a *translation table* which, for each array element, lists the host processor address.

For a one-dimensional array of N elements, the translation table also contains N elements, and therefore must be itself be distributed over the local memories of the processors. This is accomplished by putting the first N/P elements on the first processor, the second N/P elements on the second processor, etc ..., where P is the number of processors. If we are required to access the mth element of the array, we look up its address in the distributed translation table, which we know can be found in the $(m/N) * P + 1^{th}$ processor. One of the PARTI primitives handles initialization of distributed translation tables, and other primitives are used to access the distributed translation tables.

3 The PARTI Primitives

This section describes the primitives which schedule and then carry out movement of data between processors, along with the primitives that couple partitioners to compilers. The primitives that couple partitioners to compilers are entirely new. The data movement and scheduling primitives are related to the PARTI primitives described earlier ([6] and [46]) but incorporate a number of new insights we have had about sparse and unstructured computations. These primitives differ in a number of ways from those described earlier in that the new primitives:

eliminate redundant off-processor references and

make it simple to produce parallelized loops that are virtually identical in form to the original sequential loops.

To explain how the primitives work, we will use an example which is similar to loops found in unstructured computational fluid dynamics (CFD) codes. In most unstructured CFD codes, a mesh is constructed which describes an object and the physical region in which a fluid interacts with the object. Loops in fluid flow solvers sweep over this

```
      real*8 x(N),y(N)
C     Loop over edges involving x, y
L1    do i=1,n_edge
      n1 = edge_list(i)
      n2 = edge_list(n_edge+i)
S1    y(n1) = y(n1) + ...x(n1) ... x(n2)
S2    y(n2) = y(n2) + ...x(n1) ... x(n2)
      end do
C     Loop over Boundary faces involving x, y
L2    do i=1,n_face
      m1 = face_list(i)
      m2 = face_list(n_face+i)
      m3 = face_list(2*n_face + i )
S3    y(m1) = y(m1) + ...x(m1) ... x(m2) ... x(m3)
S4    y(m2) = y(m2) + ...x(m1) ... x(m2) ... x(m3)
      end do
```

Figure 2: Sequential Code

mesh structure. The two loops shown in Figure 2 represent a sweep over the edges of an unstructured mesh followed by a sweep over faces that define the boundary of the object. Since the mesh is unstructured, an indirection array has to be used to access the vertices during a loop over the edges or the boundary faces. In loop L1, a sweep is carried out over the edges of the mesh and the reference pattern is specified by integer array **edge_list**. Loop L2 represents a sweep over boundary faces, and the reference pattern is specified by **face_list**. The array **x** only appears in the right hand side of expressions in Figure 2, (statements S1 through S4), so the values of **x** are not modified by these loops. In Figure 2, array **y** is both read and written to. These references all involve accumulations in which computed quantities are added to specified elements of **y** (statements S1, S2, S3 and S4).

3.1 Primitives for Communications Scheduling

In this section we use a running example derived from Figure 2 in order to present the runtime support we need to eliminate redundant off-processor references. As was the case with our earlier suite of primitives described in [6], this runtime support can be used either by a complier or can be embedded into distributed memory codes manually by programmers. Our new primitives carry out preprocessing that make it straightforward to produce parallelized loops that are virtually identical in form to the original sequential loops. The importance of this is that it will be possible to generate the same quality object code on the nodes of the distributed memory machine as could be produced by the sequential program running on a single node.

Our primitives make use of hash tables [22] to allow us to recognize and exploit a number of situations in which a single off-processor distributed array reference is used several times. In such situations, the primitives only fetch a single copy of each unique off-processor distributed array reference.

3.1.1 PARTI Executor

Figure 3 depicts the *executor* code with embedded fortran callable PARTI procedures *dfmgather*, *dfscatter_add* and *dfscatter_addnc*. Before this code is run, we have to carry out a preprocessing phase, to be described in Section 3.1.2. This executor code changes significantly when non-incremental schedules are employed. An example of the executor code when the preprocessing is done without using incremental schedules is given in [41].

The arrays **x** and **y** are partitioned between processors, each processor is responsible for the long term storage of specified elements of each of these arrays. The way in which **x** and **y** are to be partitioned between processors is determined by the inspector. In this example, elements of **x** and **y** are partitioned between processors in exactly the same way. Each processor is responsible for *n_on_proc* elements of **x** and **y**.

It should be noted that except for the procedure calls, the structure of the loops in Figure 3 is identical to that of the loops in Figure 2. In Figure 3, we again use arrays named **x** and **y**; in Figure 3, **x** and **y** now represent arrays defined on a single processor of a distributed memory multiprocessor. On each processor P, arrays **x** and **y** are declared to be larger than would be needed to store the number of array elements for which P is responsible. We will store copies of off-processor array elements beginning with local array elements `x(n_on_proc+1)` and `y(n_on_proc+1)`.

The PARTI subroutine calls depicted in Figure 3 move data between processors using a precomputed communication pattern. The communication pattern is specified by either a single *schedule* or by an array of schedules. *dfmgather* uses communication schedules to fetch off-processor data that will be needed either by loop L1 or by loop L2. The schedules specify the locations in distributed memory from which data is to be obtained. In Figure 3, off-processor data is obtained from array **x** defined on each processor. Copies of the off-processor data are placed in a buffer area beginning with `x(n_on_proc+1)`.

The PARTI procedures *dfscatter_add* and *dfscatter_addnc*, in statement S2 and S3 Figure 3, accumulate data to off-processor memory locations. Both *dfscatter_add* and *dfscatter_addnc* obtain data to be accumulated to off processor locations from a buffer area that begins with `y(n_on_proc+1)`. Off-processor data is accumulated to locations of **y** between indices 1 and `n_on_proc`. The distinctions between *dfscatter_add* and *dfscatter_addnc* will be described in Section 3.1.3.

In Figure 3, several data may be accumulated to a given off-processor location in loop L1 or in loop L2.

3.1.2 PARTI Inspector

In this section, we will outline how we carry out the preprocessing needed to generate the arguments needed by the code in Figure 3. This preprocessing is depicted in Figure 4.

The way in which the nodes of an irregular mesh are numbered frequently do not have a useful correspondence to the connectivity pattern of the mesh. When we partition such a mesh in a way that minimizes interprocessor communication, we may need to be able to assign arbitrary mesh points to each processor. The PARTI procedure *ifbuild_translation_table* (S1 in Figure 4) allows us to map a globally indexed distributed array onto processors in an arbitrary fashion. Each processor passes the procedure *ifbuild_translation_table* a list of the array elements for which it will be responsible (**myvals** in S1, Figure 4). If a given processor needs to obtain a datum that corresponds to a particular global index i for a specific distributed array, the processor can consult the

```
real*8 x(n_on_proc+n_off_proc)
real*8 y(n_on_proc+n_off_proc)

S1 dfmgather(sched_array,2,x(n_on_proc+1),x)

     C  Loop over edges involving x, y
     L1 do i=1,local_n_edge
          n1 = local_edge_list(i)
          n2 = local_edge_list(local_n_edge+i)
     S1   y(n1) = y(n1) + ...x(n1) ... x(n2)
     S2   y(n2) = y(n2) + ...x(n1) ... x(n2)
        end do

S2 dfscatter_add(edge_sched,y(n_on_proc+1),y)

     C  Loop over Boundary faces involving x, y
     L2 do i=1,local_n_face
          m1 = local_face_list(i)
          m2 = local_face_list(local_n_face+i)
          m3 = local_face_list(2*local_n_face + i )
     S3   y(m1) = y(m1) + ...x(m1) ... x(m2) ... x(m3)
     S4   y(m2) = y(m2) + ...x(m1) ... x(m2) ... x(m3)
        end do

S3 dfscatter_addnc(face_sched,y(n_on_proc+1),
   buffer_mapping,y)
```

Figure 3: Parallelized Code for Each Processor

```
S1 translation_table = ifbuild_translation_table(1,myvals,n_on_proc)

S2 call flocalize(translation_table,edge_sched,part_edge_list, local_edge_list,2*n_edge,n_off_proc)

S3 sched_array(1) = edge_sched

S4 call fmlocalize(translation_table,face_sched,

   incremental_face_sched, part_face_list,local_face_list,

   4*n_face, n_off_proc_face,

   n_new_off_proc_face, buffer_mapping, 1,sched_array)

S5 sched_array(2) = incremental_face_sched
```

Figure 4: Inspector Code for Each Processor

distributed translation table to find the location of that datum in distributed memory.

The PARTI procedures *flocalize* and *fmlocalize* carry out the bulk of the preprocessing needed to produce the executor code depicted in Figure 3. We will first describe *flocalize*, (S2 in Figure 4). On each processor P, flocalize is passed:

1. a pointer to a distributed translation table (translation_table in S2),
2. a list of globally indexed distributed array references for which processor P will be responsible, (**edge_list** in S2), and
3. number of globally indexed distributed array references (2*n_edge in S2).

Flocalize returns:

1. a *schedule* that can be used in PARTI gather and scatter procedures (edge_sched in S2),
2. an integer array that can be used to specify the pattern of indirection in the executor code (**local_edge_list** in S2), and
3. number of distinct off-processor references found in edge_list (n_off_proc in S2).

A sketch of how the procedure *flocalize* works is shown in Figure 5. The array **edge_list** shown in Figure 2 is partitioned between processors. The **part_edge_list** passed to *flocalize* on each processor in Figure 4 is a *subset of* **edge_list** depicted in Figure 2. We cannot use **part_edge_list** to index an array on a processor as **part_edge_list**

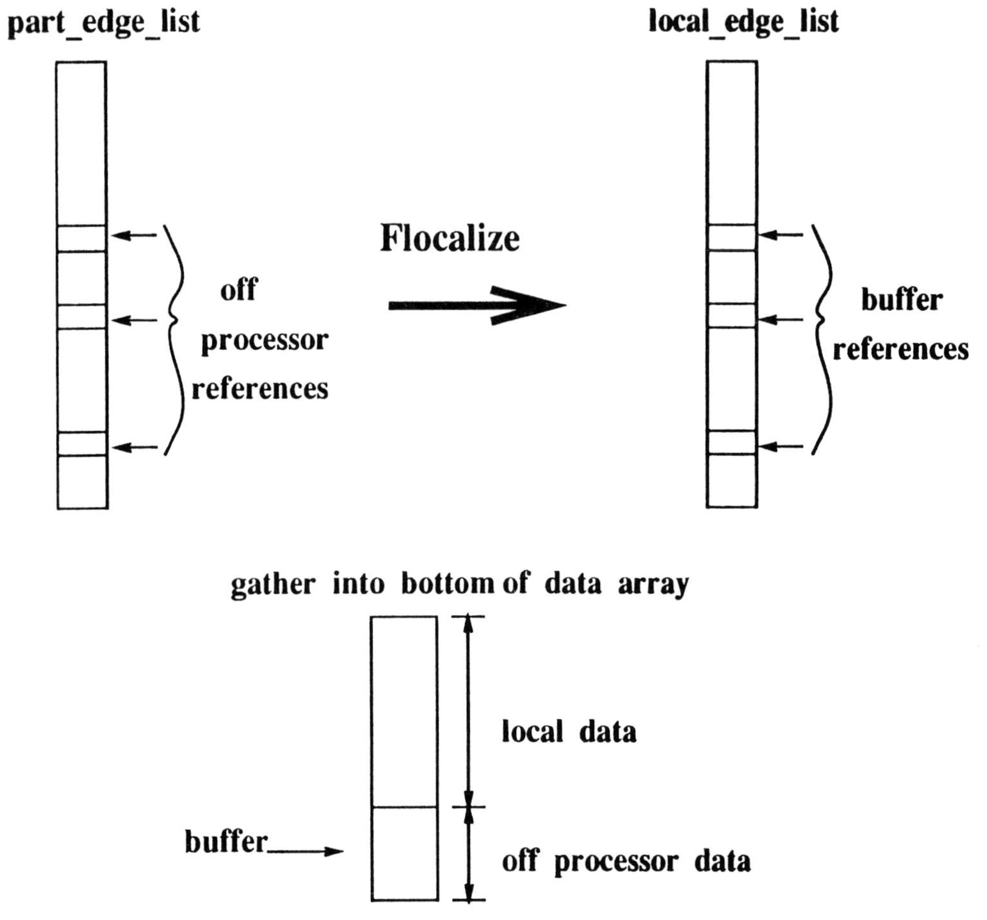

Figure 5: Flocalize Mechanism

refers to globally indexed elements of arrays **x** and **y**. *Flocalize* changes this **part_edge_list** so that valid references are generated when the edge loop is executed. The buffer for each data array is placed immediately following the on-processor data for that array. For example, the buffer for data array **x** starts at **x(n_on_proc+1)**. Hence, when *flocalize* changes the **part_edge_list** to **local_edge_list**, the off-processor references are changed to point to the buffer addresses. When the off processor data is collected into the buffer using the *schedule* returned by *flocalize*, the data is stored in a way such that execution of the edge loop using the **local_edge_list** accesses the correct data.

There are a variety of situations in which the same data need to be accessed by multiple loops (Figure 2). In Figure 2, no assignments to **x** are carried out. In the beginning of Figure 3, each processor can gather a single copy of every distinct off-processor value of **x** referenced by loops L1 or L2. The PARTI procedure *fmlocalize* (S4 in Figure 4) makes it simple to remove these duplicate references. *fmlocalize* makes it possible to obtain only those off-processor data not requested by a given set of pre-existing schedules. The procedure *dfmgather* in the executor in Figure 3 obtains off-processor data using *two schedules*; *edge_sched* produced by *flocalize* (S2 Figure 4) and *incremental_face_sched* produced by *fmlocalize* (S4 Figure 4).

The pictorial representation of the *incremental schedule* is given in Figure 6. The schedule to bring in the off-processor data for the edge_loop is given by the *edge schedule* and is formed first. During the formation of the schedule to bring in the off-processor data for the face_loop we remove the duplicates shown by the shaded region in Figure 6. Removal of duplicates is achieved by using a hash table. The off-processor data to be accessed by the edge schedule is first hashed using a simple hash function. Next all the data to be accessed during the face_loop is hashed. At this point the information that exists in the hash table allows us to remove all the duplicates and form the *incremental schedule*. In Section 5 we will present results showing the usefulness of incremental schedule.

To review the work carried out by fmlocalize, we will summarize the significance of all but one of the arguments of this PARTI procedure. On each processor, fmlocalize is passed:

1. a pointer to a distributed translation table (translation_table in S4),
2. a list of globally indexed distributed array references. (face_list in S4),
3. number of globally indexed distributed array references (4*n_face in S4),
4. number of pre-existing schedules that need to be taken into account when removing duplicates (1 in S4), and

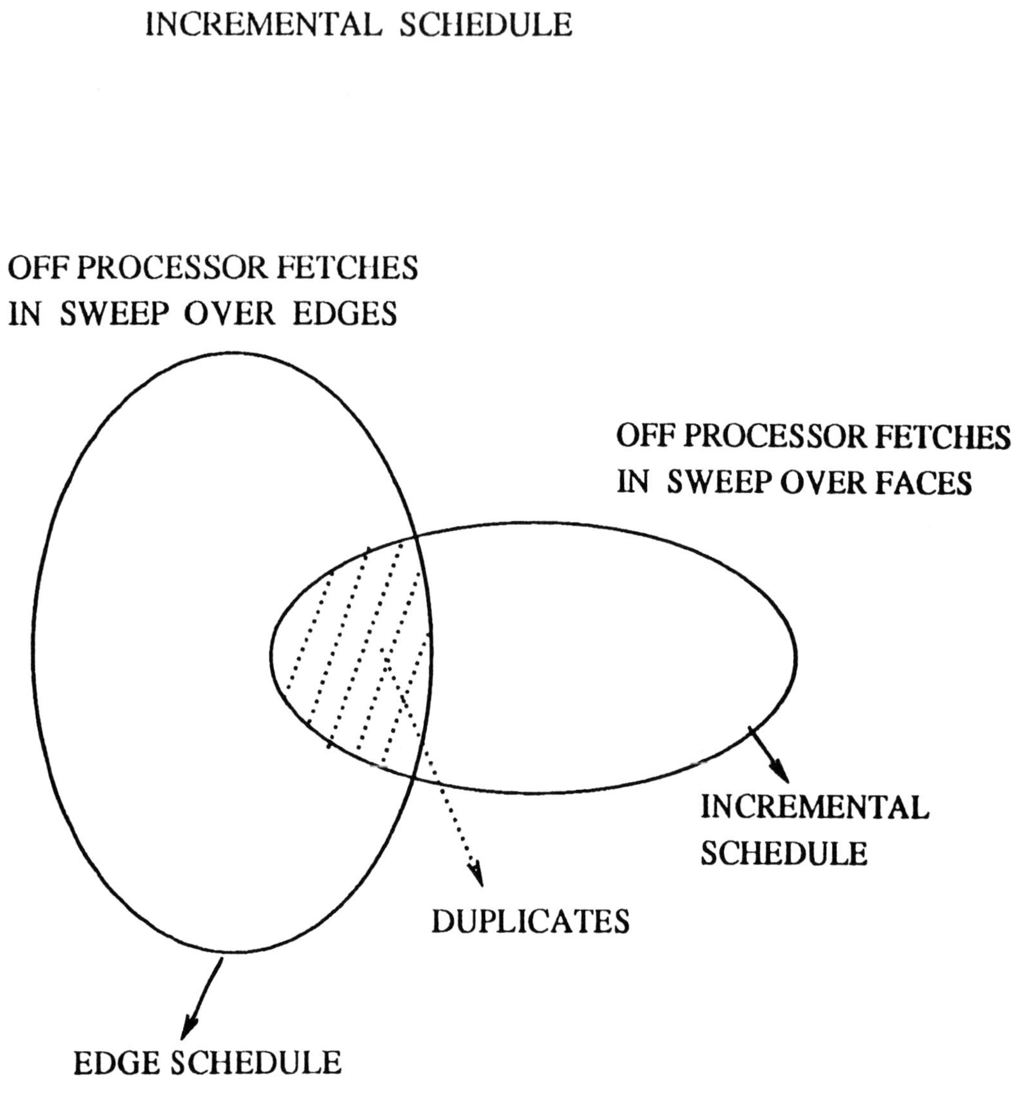

Figure 6: Incremental Schedule

5. an array of pointers to pre-existing schedules (sched_array in S4).

Fmlocalize returns:

1. a *schedule* that can be used in PARTI gather and scatter procedures. This schedule *does not take any pre-existing schedules into account* (face_sched in S4),
2. an *incremental schedule* that includes only off-processor data accesses not included in the pre-existing schedules (incremental_face_sched in S4),
3. a list of integers that can be used to specify the pattern of indirection in the executor code (local_face_list in S4),
4. number of distinct off-processor references in face_list (n_off_proc_face in S4).
5. number of distinct off-processor references not encountered in any other schedule (n_new_off_proc_face in S4).
6. buffer_mapping - to be discussed in Section 3.1.3.

3.1.3 A Return to the Executor

We have already discussed *dfmgather* in Section 3.1.1 but we have not said anything so far about the distinction between *dfscatter_add* and *dfscatter_addnc*. When we make use of incremental schedules, we assign a single buffer location to each off-processor distributed array element. In our example, we carry out separate off-processor accumulations after loops L1 and L2. As we will describe below, in this situation, our off-processor accumulation procedures may no longer reference consecutive elements of a buffer.

We assign copies of distinct off-processor elements of **y** to buffer locations, to handle off-processor accesses in loop L1, Figure 3. We can then use a schedule (edge_sched) to specify where in distributed memory each consecutive value in the buffer is to be accumulated. PARTI procedure *dfscatter_add* can be employed; this procedure uses schedule *edge_sched* to accumulate to off-processor locations consecutive buffer locations beginning with **y(n_on_proc + 1)**. When we assign off-processor elements of **y** to buffer locations in L2, some of the off-processor copies may already be associated with buffer locations. Consequently in S3, Figure 3, our schedule (face_sched) must access buffer locations in an irregular manner. The pattern of buffer locations accessed is specified by integer array *buffer_mapping* passed to *dfscatter_addnc* in S3, Figure 3. (*dfscatter_addnc* stands for dfscatter_add non-contiguous)

3.2 Mapper Coupler

In irregular problems, it is frequently desirable to allocate computational work to processors by assigning all computations that involve a given loop iteration to a single processor [6]. We consequently partition *both* distributed arrays and loop iterations. Our approach is to first partition distributed arrays and then, based on distributed array partitionings, partition loop iterations. This appears to be a practical approach as in many cases, the same set of distributed arrays are used by many loops.

When we partition distributed arrays, we have not yet assigned loop iterations to processors. We do assume that we will partition loop iterations so as to attempt to minimize non-local distributed array references. Our approach to data partitioning makes an implicit assumption that most (although not necessarily all) computation will be carried out in the processor associated with the variable appearing on the left hand side of each statement.

There are many partitioning methods available, [42], [15], [5] [9] but currently partitioners must be coupled to user programs in a manual fashion. This manual coupling is particularly troublesome when we wish to make use of parallelized partitioners. Here, we introduce a new notion of linking partitioners with programs by producing a generic data structure at run time, which is independent of the problems. For this purpose, we have developed primitives which can generate a standardized input format for the partitioners. In our approach the standardized data structure is generated from the loops in the problem specified by users using certain language extensions to be discussed in Section 4.1.

We now outline what needs to be done to link a data partitioner with a program in which a specific loop has been specified using the language extensions described in Section 4.1. We first consider loops in which all distributed arrays appearing in a loop conform in size and are to be distributed in an identical manner. We also restrict ourselves to loops without loop carried dependencies (this restriction will be relaxed slightly later in this section). We define a statement *bipartite runtime dependency graph* (statement BRDG) to represent the dependencies between the index of a distributed array element defined on the left hand side of a loop statement **S** and the indices of all distributed array elements on the right hand side of **S**. As the name implies, statement BRDG is a bipartite directed graph. We merge the statement BRDG associated with each statement **S** in a loop to form a *loop* **BRDG**. When we merge l links we associate a weight l with the merged vertex. Most data partitioners make use of undirected connectivity graphs. When all distributed arrays appearing in a statement conform, we can collapse the loop **BRDG** into a undirected graph, the loop *runtime dependence graph* or the loop **RDG**. The weight associates with each edge of the loop **RDG** is the sum of the weights of the two collapsed **BRDG** edges.

A loop **RDG** is constructed by adding edge $< i, j >$ between nodes i and j either when

> a reference to array index i appears on the left side of an expression and a reference to j appears on the right side, or
>
> a reference to array index j appears on the left side of an expression and a reference to i appears on the right side.

Each time edge $< i, j >$ is encountered, we increment a counter associated with $< i, j >$. Accumulation type output dependency edges of type $< i, i >$ are ignored in the graph generation process as the presence of such dependencies do not induce inter-processor communication. The loop **RDG** is currently represented by a distributed data structure [31], this data structure is closely related to Saad's Compressed Sparse Row (CSR) format (see [38]).

Data partitioning is carried out as follows. We assume **P** processors.

1. At *compile time* a *dependency coupling code* is generated. This code produces a loop **RDG** at runtime,
2. The loop **RDG** is passed to a *data partitioning* procedure that partitions the loop **RDG** into **P** subgraphs. The **RDG** vertices assigned to each subgraph correspond to a distributed array distribution.
3. The output of the partitioning procedure is a distributed translation table. This translation table is associated with each of the identically distributed arrays referenced in the loop.

Once we have partitioned data, we must partition computational work. One convention is to compute a program statement S in the processor associated with S's left hand side distributed array element. (If the left hand side of **S** references a replicated variable then the work is carried out in all processors). Were we to assign work in this manner, we would want to partition the **RDG** for statement **S** in a way that would correspond to reducing the combined cost of load imbalance and the cost of interprocessor communication. Each **RDG** edge to cross a boundary between partitions would correspond to either a unidirectional or bidirectional data communication. Instead of assigning work to the processor associated with S's left hand distributed array element, we partition distributed arrays and loop iterations separately. Our motivation for using the loop **RDG** as an input to a data partitioner comes from our decision to attempt to partition loop iterations so as to minimize off-processor distributed array references.

To partition loop iterations, we use a graph called the *runtime iteration graph* or **RIG**. The **RIG** associates with each loop iteration i, all indices of each distributed array accessed during iteration i. The **RIG** is generated for every loop that references at least one irregularly distributed array. The *runtime iteration processor assignment graph* or **RIPA** lists, for each loop iteration, the number of distinct data references associated with each processor.

We partition loop iterations in the following manner:

1. The **RIG** is generated for each loop in which distributed arrays are referenced.

2. The processor assignment is found for for each distributed array reference appearing in a **RIG**. If the distributed array is irregularly distributed, this information is obtained using the array's distributed translation table (Section 2.2). The processor assignments are used to generate the **RIPA** graph.

3. Loop iterations are partitioned using an *iteration partitioning procedure* which makes use of the **RIPA** graph.

Just as there are many possible strategies that can be used to partition data, there are also many strategies that could be used to partition loop iterations. We currently employ strategies that assign loop iterations to the processor associated with the largest number of distributed array references in the **RIG**.

3.3 Compiler-linked Mapping: Runtime Support

In this section we outline the primitives employed to carry out compiler-linked data and loop iteration partitioning.

We begin each compiler-linked mapping with an initial distribution of loop iterations and of integer indirection arrays needed to determine distributed array references. The object of this initial preprocessing is to extract information needed for mapping. In many cases, the initial distribution of loop iterations I_{init}, will be a simple default distribution. In some situations (e.g. adaptive codes), preprocessing to support irregular array mappings may have already been carried out. Thus integer indirection arrays may have already been irregularly distributed when we begin our derivation of a compiler-linked mapping. Our runtime support will handle either regular or irregular initial loop iteration distributions I_{init}. The *local* loop **RDG** is defined as the restriction of the loop **RDG** to a single processor. The local loop **RDG** includes only distributed array elements associated with I_{init}.

Procedure *eliminate_dup_edges* uses a hash table to store unique directed dependency edges, along with a count of the number of times each edge has been encountered. Once

---

partition loop iterations between processors in blocks

partition integer indirection array **edge_list** so that if iteration i is assigned to processor **P**, **edge_list(i)** and **edge_list(n_edge+i)** are on **P** (methods needed to carry out this preprocessing are described in [46]).

> do i=1,n_edge
>
> pass dependency edges (n1,n2), (n2,n1) to procedure *eliminate_dup_edges*
>
> end do
>
> obtain loop **RDG** data structure from hash table using procedure *edges_to_RDG*
>
> loop **RDG** is passed to *RDG_partitioner.* A pointer is returned to a distributed translation table which describes the new mapping.

Figure 7: Runtime Support for Deriving Irregular Data Distributions

all edges in a loop have been recorded, **edges_to_RDG** generates the local loop **RDG** and then merges all local loop **RDG** graphs to form the loop **RDG**. The data structures that describe the loop **RDG** graph are passed to a data partitioner *RDG_partitioner. RDG_partitioner.* returns a pointer to a distributed translation table that describes the new mapping. Note that *RDG_partitioner.* can use any heuristic to partition the data, the only constraint is that the partitioners have the correct calling sequence.

We consider the sequential code depicted in Figure 2 to illustrate how the primitives can be used to link partitioners with programs. We assume that the user has specified using the language extensions that arrays **x** and **y** are to be partitioned based the loop L1 in a conforming manner. At *compile time*, a sequence of calls to a set of mapper coupler primitives are embedded as shown in Figure 7.

The partitioning of loop iterations is supported by two primitives, *deref_rig* and *partition_rig.* The **RIG** is generated by code transformed by a compiler. The primitive *deref_rig* inputs the **RIG**. This primitive accesses distributed translation tables to find the processor assignments associated with each distributed array reference. *deref_rig* returns the **RIPA**. The **RIPA** is partitioned using the iteration partitioning procedure, *iter_partition.*

4 PARTI Compiler

In this section we first describe language extensions which allow a programmer to implicitly specify how data and loop iterations are to be partitioned between processors. We then outline compiler transformations used to carry out this implicitly defined work and data mapping. The compiler transformations generate code which embeds the mapper coupler primitives described in Section 3.2. In addition we outline compiler transformations needed to take advantage of the incremental scheduling primitives described in Section 3.1.

4.1 Compiler-Linked Problem Mapping

4.1.1 Overview

The current Fortran D syntax outlined in Section 2.1 requires programmers to *explicitly* define irregular data decompositions.

In Figure 1, we align real arrays **x** and **y** with the decomposition *irreg* (statement S5). The array **map** is used to specify the distribution of **irreg**. Integer array **map** is aligned with decomposition *reg* (statement S4) and then *reg* is distributed by amoung the processors blocks (statement S6). The meaning of the statement S7 is that the distribution of decomposition *irreg* is determined by *values* assigned to **map**. For example, if the value map(100) is 10, this indicates that both x(100) and y(100) are assigned to processor 10.

The difficulty with the declarations depicted in Figure 1 is that *it is not obvious how one would partition the irregularly distribute array.* The *map* array which gives the distribution pattern of irreg has to be generated separately by running a partitioner. The Fortran-D constructs are not rich enough for the user to couple the generation of the map array to the program compilation process. While there are a wealth of partitioning heuristics available (see for instance [42], [15], [5]), coding such partitioners from scratch can represent a significant effort. There is no standard interface between the partitioners and the different problems. The partitioners described in the literature typically operate on data structures whose physical interpretation is known to the programmer (e.g. meshes in finite difference equations, sparse matrices in sparse linear systems solvers, etc).

Our approach is to identify a nest of loops L that involves each irregularly distributed array we will need to partition. From the loop L, we produce at compile time a mapper coupler (see Section 3.2)

Figure 8 is derived from the sequential code in Figure 2. The code in Figure 8 contains loops L1 and L2 from the code in Figure 2. To simplify presentation, only L1 is depicted explicitly in Figure 8.

```
    ....
    real*8 x(N),y(N)
    decomposition coupling(N)
S1  if(remap.eq.yes) then
S2  distribute coupling(implicit using edges)
    endif
S3  align x,y with coupling
    ....
S4  implicitmap(x,y) edges
C   Loop over edges involving x, y
L1  do i=1,n_edge
    n1 = edge_list(i)
    n2 = edge_list(n_edge+i)
S1  y(n1) = y(n1) + ...x(n1) ... x(n2)
S2  y(n2) = y(n2) + ...x(n1) ... x(n2)
    end do
    ....
    L2 Loop over faces involving x, y
```

Figure 8: Example of Implicit Mapping

We use statement S4 to designate loop `L1` as the loop that will be used to generate a mapper coupler. **implicitmap**(x,y) indicates that an **RDG** graph is to be generated based on the dependency relations between distributed arrays `x` and `y` in loop `L1`. We assume that all arrays listed in an implicitmap statement are to be identically distributed and that the loop in question parallelizes, except for possible accumulation type output dependencies (If the compiler cannot determine that these assumptions are valid, an error is reported).

In many codes used to solve mesh based problems, we can specify a nest of loops so that the **RDG** will represent the original mesh. For instance, in Figure 8, loop L1 represents a sweep over the edges of a mesh. The **RDG** obtained from statement S4 recaptures the original mesh topology.

It is easy to generalize the language extensions described here so that we specify an implicit mapping using more than one loop. In this case, a multiple loop **RDG** is generated based on merged dependency patterns arising from the loops.

4.1.2 Embedding Mapper Coupler Primitives

We use the example in Figure 8 to show how the compiler primitives are embedded in the code. When the statement **distribute ... implicit using** is encountered in the code, the compiler locates the loop L specified by the user. The indirection pattern in this loop will be used to generate the **RDG**. In order for the executable statement **distribute ... implicit using** to make sense, we must be able to anticipate how the distributed arrays in L will be indexed. when L is next encountered. We need to be able to determine that all relevant reference patterns in L can be predicted when **distribute ... implicit using** executes. In our simple example (Figure 8), the implicit distribution statement is located in the same procedure as the user specified loop. The compiler must identify all variables V that determine the subscript functions of distributed arrays in L and must determine whether there is any chance that any members of V could be killed between **distribute ... implicit using** and loop L. In this case, standard data flow analysis can determine whether any assignment has been made to a member of V. In many cases, the implicit distribution statement might not be placed in the same procedure as L. In this case, we will require the results of interprocedural analysis.

When L is identified and indexing information pertaining to L is obtained, a transformed loop L' is generated. L' contains the calls to *eliminate_dup_edges* that will be needed to generate the local loop **RDG** (see Section 3.2). Recall from Section 3.2 that *eliminate_dup_edges* produces a hash table. A pointer to this hash table is passed to procedure *edges_to_RDG*. This procedure produces a loop **RDG** which is passed to a data partitioner, *RDG_partitioner*.

Loop iterations are partitioned at runtime whenever a loop accesses at least one irregularly distributed array. Corresponding to each such loop L is generated a loop L" which generates the **RIG**. As described in Section 3.2, the **RIG** is passed to *deref_rig* to produce the **RIPA**. The **RIPA** in turn is partitioned using the iteration partitioning procedure, *iter_partition.*

4.1.3 Inspector/Executor Generation for Incremental Scheduling

Inspectors and executors must be generated for loops in which distributed arrays are accessed via indirection. Inspectors and executors are also needed in most loops that access irregularly distributed arrays. In this section we outline what must be done to generate distributed memory programs which make effective use of incremental and non-incremental schedules. Most of what we describe is as yet unimplemented, although we have constructed and benchmarked a simple compiler capable of carrying out local transformations to embed non-incremental schedules. This work is described in [46].

We first outline what must be done to generate an inspector and an executor for a program loop L. We assume that dependency analysis has determined that L either has no loop carried dependencies, or has only the simple accumulation type output dependencies of the sort exemplified in Figure 2. It should be noted that the calling sequences of the compiler-embeddable PARTI primitives differ somewhat from the primitives described in Section 3. The functionality described in primitives *flocalize* and *fmlocalize* are each implemented as a larger set of simpler primitives.

We scan through the loop and find the set of distributed arrays A that are irregularly distributed or are indexed using indirection. Information needed to generate a schedule for a given distributed array reference, can be produced from the subscript function of the reference along with knowledge of an array's distribution. We must check to make sure that the the subscript functions of all members of A are loop invariant as the methods described in this paper do not address cases in which indexing patterns are modified by computations carried out within the loop. As long as a distributed array's indexing pattern is not modified by computations carried out within a loop, a compiler can generate preprocessing code that can be hoisted out of L. This preprocessing code produces a representation of the distributed array's indexing pattern. For instance, consider the following loop:

```
do i=1,n
n1 = nde(2*i)
n2 = nde(2*i-1)
```

```
.. = x(n1) ... y(n2)

.. = ... z(n2)

end do
```

The subscript function of **y** and **z** (using notation from the Fortran 90 array extensions) is nde(2:2*n:2), and the subscript function of **x** is nde(1:2*n-1:2). Recall from Section 2.2, that schedules specify communication *patterns* and are not bound to a specific distributed array. We can avoid having to compute redundant schedules when we know that the same communication pattern will reoccur in more than one place in a loop. For instance, if **y** and **z** in the above loop are partitioned in a conforming manner, we need only to compute a single schedule to bring in off-processor elements of **y** and **z**.

Optimizations that reduce the number of schedules reduce the preprocessing time required by the *inspector*. Obviously, the elimination of redundant schedules also has a favorable impact on storage requirements. Minor modifications of common subexpression elimination should be reasonably effective in identifying redundant schedules. In [46] we describe a compiler that carries out this optimization in a rudimentary manner.

The use of incremental schedules, (Section 3.1), make it possible to avoid retransmission of unchanged distributed array. As we will show in Section 5, proper use of incremental schedules can have a marked effect on the time spent on communication. In order to make use of previously stored copies of distributed array elements, we must ensure that the off-processor copies are still valid. Recall that we assumed that loop L had no loop carried dependencies. Thus our decision to assign each loop iteration to a single processor ensures that off-processor data obtained immediately before entering L will continue to be valid in L. The generation of incremental schedules can be carried out in two passes. A compiler first generates an inspector and executor for L with full schedules. During the second pass, some full schedules will be replaced with incremental schedules. In order to replace a full schedule with an incremental schedule, we need to know which schedules will have already caused the storage of off-processor data within L.

Generation of efficient inspectors and executors for loop L requires us to obtain information about a program as a whole. When L is called multiple times we attempt to reuse previously computed schedules. Each time L is called, we need to determine whether it is possible that the subscript functions or loop distributions in the set of distributed arrays A have been modified since the last call to L.

Analysis must also be carried out if we are to use incremental schedules to eliminate duplicate data communications between loops. We need rather comprehensive information about the program behavior. Consider a right hand side reference to distributed array **x** in program statement S for which we would like to use an incremental schedule. We will need to know

> when off-processor data copies of values of **x** become invalidated by new assignments, and
>
> which communications schedules will have already been invoked by the time we reach **x**,

Methods exist which appear likely to allow us to be able to do a reasonable job of achieving both of these objectives for many irregular scientific codes. A program dependence graph (e.g. [13], [10]) is a directed graph whose vertices represent the assignment statements and control predicates that occur in a program. The edges represent *dependences* among program components. An edge represents either a control dependence or a data dependence. Each time a schedule is used, new copies of off-processor array elements become available. In order to generate an incremental schedule for **x** at S, we need to know which schedules have already caused the storage of potentially reusable off-processor data. We can view this off-processor data reuse as a type of dependence and represent this dependence as a specific type of edge in a program dependence graph. We will call this kind of dependence edge a *reuse* edge. Using *slicing* methods, [44], [23] we can find all statements and predicates of a program that might affect the values of the distributed array reference to **x** in statement S. In ongoing joint work with Kennedy's group at Rice, we are currently developing a variant of slicing methods which will allow us to automate the use of incremental schedules. The results of this work will be implemented as part of the Fortran D compiler being developed at Rice [21].

5 Experimental Results

5.1 Timing Results from the Euler Equation Solver

The PARTI procedures described in Section 3 were used to port a 3-D unstructured mesh Euler solver [32]. The Euler code iterates until it has computed a steady state solution on a given mesh. Two versions of the Euler solver were tested, one version used the primitive *flocalize* and *fmlocalize* to generate incremental schedules (Section 3.1), the other used only the primitive *flocalize* and generated only non-incremental schedules (Section 3.1.2). The 3-D unstructured mesh Euler solver was tested using a sequence of structurally similar meshes of varying sizes. The smallest mesh used had 3.6K vertices, the largest mesh had 210K vertices and 1.2 million edges. Figure 9 depicts a surface view of the 210K vertex mesh. The unstructured meshes were partitioned by the method described in [42].

Table 1 shows the timings obtained using non-incremental communication scheduling and Table 2 were obtained using *incremental schedules.* The single node code for these meshes run at approximately 4 Megaflops. We conjecture that the single node performance is relatively poor because the data access patterns in unstructured mesh computations are highly irregular and the number of memory references per floating point operation is very high. Both of these characteristics make it difficult for the Intel 80860 architecture to keep the processor supplied with data.

The use of incremental scheduling had a significant impact on communications costs. For instance, on the 26K mesh, the communications cost per iteration on 16 processors was 2.0 seconds when we did not employ incremental schedules. The communications cost dropped to 1.1 seconds when we used incremental schedules. On the 210K mesh on 64 processors the communications cost per iteration dropped from 3.7 seconds to 2.3 seconds when we employed incremental schedules.

Since the form of the sequential code and the parallelized code is virtually identical, we did not expect the parallelization process to introduce any new inefficiencies beyond those exacted by the preprocessing and by the calls to the primitives. We compared the parallel code running on a single node with the sequential code and found only a 2 % performance degradation. In the parallelized Euler codes, the total cost of all preprocessing was insignificant compared to the execution times required to solve the problems. The program typically requires at least 100 iterations to converge, and the preprocessing times were less than 3 % of the parallel execution times.

5.2 Timing Results using the Mapper Coupler

In this section, we present data that indicates that the costs incurred by the mapper coupler primitives were roughly on the order of the cost of a single iteration of our unstructured mesh code. We also show that the mapper coupler costs are quite small compared to the cost of partitioning the data.

In Table 3, *graph generation* depicts the time required by the mapper interface to generate the runtime dependence graph (**RDG**) data structure (Section 3.2. These timings involve a loop over edges that is functionally equivalent to loop L1 in Figure 2. The graph generation time includes the time required to call *eliminate_dup_edges* and the time required to call *edges_to_RDG* (Section 3.3)

In Table 3, *mapper* depicts the time needed to partition the **RDG** using using a parallelized version of Simon's eigenvalue partitioner [42]. We partitioned the **RDG** into a number of subgraphs equal to the number of processors employed. The cost of the

Size	Number of Processors					
Mesh		1	2	8	16	64
3.6K	Mflops	4.1	6.0	12.0	14.4	-
	Time/iter(s)	4.6	3.1	1.5	1.3	-
	comm/iter(s)	-	0.5	0.9	0.9	-
26K	Mflops	-	-	19.2	29.9	
	Time/iter(s)	-	-	7.1	4.5	
	comm/iter(s)	-	-	2.3	2.0	
210K	Mflops	-	-	-	-	118.6
	Time/iter(s)	-	-	-	-	8.4
	comm/iter(s)	-	-	-	-	3.7

Table 1: Timings from Intel iPSC/860 : Unstructured, Irregular Mesh Using Non-Incremental Schedule

Size	Number of Processors					
Mesh		1	2	8	16	64
3.6K	Mflops	4.1	7.1	16.9	17.4	-
	Time/iter(s)	4.6	2.6	1.1	1.1	-
	comm/iter(s)	-	0.3	0.5	0.7	-
26K	Mflops	-	-	23.8	38.8	
	Time/iter(s)	-	-	5.6	3.4	
	comm/iter(s)	-	-	1.1	1.1	
210K	Mflops	-	-	-	-	144.3
	Time/iter(s)	-	-	-	-	7.1
	comm/iter(s)	-	-	-	-	2.3

Table 2: Timings from Intel iPSC/860 : Unstructured, Irregular Mesh Using Incremental Schedule

Table 3: Mapper Coupler Timings from Intel iPSC/860

Number of Vertices	Number of Processors	2	4	8	16	32	64
3.6K	graph generation (secs.)	0.34	0.24	0.21	0.20	-	-
	mapper (secs)	15.92	11.50	12.11	14.92	-	-
	iter partitioner (secs)	0.94	0.57	0.42	0.34	-	-
	comp/iter (secs)	2.4	1.31	0.6	0.34	-	-
9.4K	graph generation (secs.)	-	0.86	0.69	0.53	0.35	-
	mapper (secs)	-	70.96	62.3	65.2	89.7	-
	iter partitioner (secs)	-	1.19	0.82	0.60	0.43	-
	comp/iter(secs)	-	4.83	2.35	1.1	0.67	-
54K	graph generation (secs.)	-	-	-	-	1.50	0.94
	mapper (secs)	-	-	-	-	544.81	673.14
	iter partitioner (secs)	-	-	-	-	3.30	3.03
	comp/iter(secs)	-	-	-	-	6.06	3.81

partitioner is relatively high both because of the partitioner's high operation count and because only a modest effort was made to produce an efficient parallel implementation. It should be noted that any parallelized graph partitioner could be used as a mapper. The *iter partitioner* time shown in Table 3 gives the time needed to partition loop iterations among processors. The table also includes the time needed for a single iteration of the Euler code for different problem sizes.

6 Conclusions

Programs designed to carry out a range of irregular computations including sparse direct and iterative methods require many of the optimizations described in this paper. Some examples of such programs are described in [2], [29], [4], [45] and [18].

Several researchers have developed programming environments that are targeted towards particular classes of irregular or adaptive problems. Williams [45] describes a programming environment (DIME) for calculations with unstructured triangular meshes using distributed memory machines. Baden [3] has developed a programming environment targeted towards particle computations. This programming environment provides facilities that support dynamic load balancing. DecTool [9] is an interactive environment designed to provide facilities for either automatic or manual decompositions of 2-D or 3-D discrete domains.

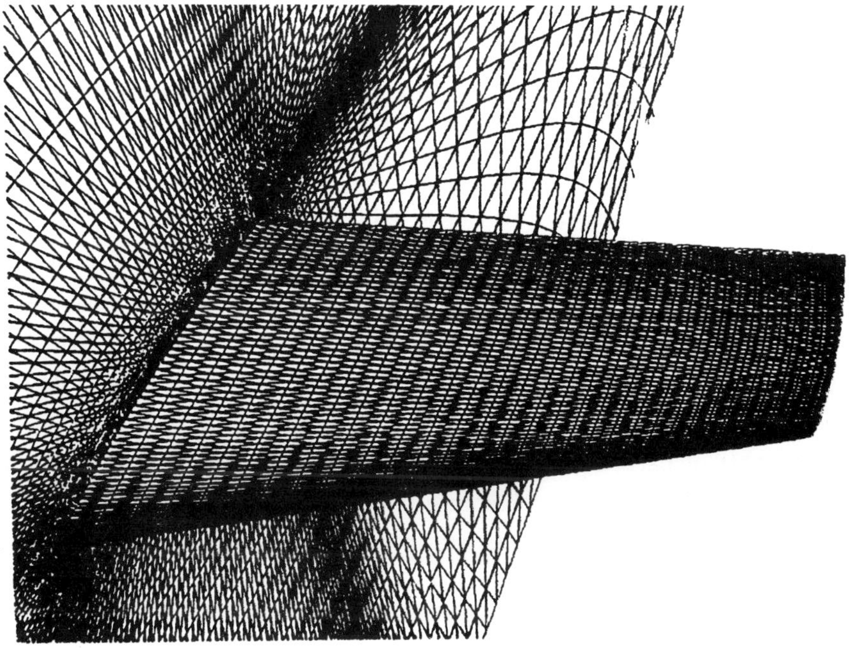

Figure 9: Surface View of Unstructured Mesh Employed for Computing Flow over ONERA M6 Wing , Number of nodes = 210K

There are a variety of compiler projects targeted at distributed memory multiprocessors [47], [8], [37], [35], [1], [43], [14], [19], [20], [24], [7, 27, 26, 28] [25], [21], [46]. Runtime compilation methods are employed in four of these projects; the Fortran D project [21], the Kali project [25], Marina Chen's work at Yale [30] and our PARTI project [33], [40], [46], and [39]. The Kali compiler which was the first compiler to implement inspector/executor type runtime preprocessing [25] and the ARF compiler which was the first compiler to support irregularly distributed arrays [46]. In related work, Lu and Chen have reported some encouraging results on the potential for effective runtime parallelization of loops in distributed memory architectures [30].

This paper has presented two new runtime compilation methods, and described in detail the required runtime support. We described how to design distributed memory compilers capable of carrying out dynamic workload and data partitions. We also described how to reduce interprocessor communication requirements by eliminating redundant off-processor data accesses. This runtime support required for this methods has been implemented in the form of PARTI primitives. We first described the design of the PARTI primitives, and then outlined the compiler transformations that embed these primitives.

We implemented a full unstructured mesh computational fluid dynamics code by embedding our runtime support by hand and have presented our performance results. These performance results demonstrated that our method for eliminating redundant off-processor communication had a significant impact on communications costs. Our performance results also demonstrated that the costs incurred by the mapper coupler primitives were roughly on the order of the cost of a single iteration of our unstructured mesh code and were quite small compared to the cost of the partitioner itself. We did not compare the time required by the PARTI primitives to Intel send and receive calls in this paper. In [6] we presented such a comparison and found that overheads incurred by using PARTI appear to be quite modest (no more than 20 %).

We have joined forces with the Fortran D group in compiler development and are implementing the methods described in this paper in the context of Fortran D in cooperation with Kennedy's group at Rice.

The non-incremental PARTI primitives described in Section 3.1 are available for public distribution and can be obtained from netlib or from the anonymous ftp cite ra.cs.yale.edu. The incremental PARTI primitives and the Mapper coupler primitives described in Section 3.2 will be released soon and will be available through the same sources.

Acknowledgements

The authors would like to thank Geoffrey Fox for many enlightening discussions about universally applicable partitioners; we would also like to thank Ken Kennedy, Chuck Koelbel and Seema Hiranandani for many useful discussions about integrating into Fortran-D runtime support for irregular problems.

The authors would also like to thank: Dennis Gannon for the use of his Faust system and his help in getting us started with Faust, Horst Simon for the use of his unstructured mesh partitioning software; and Venkatakrishnan for useful suggestions for low level communications scheduling.

References

[1] F. André, J.-L. Pazat, and H. Thomas. PANDORE: A system to manage data distribution. In *International Conference on Supercomputing*, pages 380–388, June 1990.

[2] C. Ashcraft, S. C. Eisenstat, and J. W. H. Liu. A fan-in algorithm for distributed sparse numerical factorization. *SISSC*, 11(3):593 599, 1990.

[3] S. Baden. Programming abstractions for dynamically partitioning and coordinating localized scientific calculations running on multiprocessors. *To appear, SIAM J. Sci. and Stat. Computation.*, 1991.

[4] D. Baxter, J. Saltz, M. Schultz, S. Eisentstat, and K. Crowley. An experimental study of methods for parallel preconditioned krylov methods. In *Proceedings of the 1988 Hypercube Multiprocessor Conference, Pasadena CA*, pages 1698,1711, January 1988.

[5] M.J. Berger and S. H. Bokhari. A partitioning strategy for nonuniform problems on multiprocessors. *IEEE Trans. on Computers*, C-36(5):570–580, May 1987.

[6] H. Berryman, J. Saltz, and J. Scroggs. Execution time support for adaptive scientific algorithms on distributed memory architectures. *Concurrency: Practice and Experience*, 3(3):159–178, June 1991.

[7] M. C. Chen. A parallel language and its compilation to mulitprocessor archietctures or vlsi. In *2nd ACM Symposium on Principles Programming Languages*, January 1986.

[8] A. Cheung and A. P. Reeves. The paragon multicomputer environment: A first implementation. Technical Report EE-CEG-89-9, Cornell University Computer Engineering Group, Cornell University School of Electrical Engineering, july 1989.

[9] N.P. Chrisochoides, C. E. Houstis, E.N. Houstis, P.N. Papachiou, S.K. Kortesis, and J.R. Rice. Domain decomposer: A software tool for mapping pde computations to parallel architectures. Report CSD-TR-1025, Purdue University, Computer Science Department, September 1990.

[10] K. Cooper and K. Kennedy. Interprocedural side-effect analysis in linear time. In *Proceedings of the ACM SIGPLAN 88 Conference on Programming Language Design and Implementation, ACM SIGPLAN Not. 23,7*, pages 57–66, July 1988.

[11] Thinking Machines Corporation. CM Fortran reference manual. Technical Report version 1.0, Thinking Machines Corporation, Feb 1991.

[12] R. Das, J. Saltz, and H. Berryman. A manual for parti runtime primitives - revision 1 (document and parti software available through netlib). Interim Report 91-17, ICASE, 1991.

[13] J. Ferrante, K. Ottenstein, and J. Warren. The program dependence graph and its use in optimization. *ACM TOPLAS*, 1987.

[14] I. Foster and S. Taylor. *Strand: New Concepts in Parallel Programming.* Prentice-Hall, Englewood Cliffs, NJ, 1990.

[15] G. Fox. A graphical approach to load balancing and sparse matrix vector multiplication on the hypercube. In *The IMA Volumes in Mathematics and its Applications. Volume 13: Numerical Algorithms for Modern Parallel Computer Architectures Martin Schultz Editor.* Springer-Verlag, 1988.

[16] G. Fox and W. Furmanski. Load balancing loosely synchronous problems with a neural network. In *Third Conf. on Hypercube Concurrent Computers and Applications*, pages 241–27278, 1988.

[17] G. Fox, S. Hiranandani, K. Kennedy, C. Koelbel, U. Kremer, C. Tseng, and M. Wu. Fortran D language specification. Department of Computer Science Rice COMP TR90-141, Rice University, December 1990.

[18] G. Fox, M. Johnson, G. Lyzenga, S. Otto, J. Salmon, and D. Walker. *Solving Problems on Concurrent Computers.* Prentice-Hall, Englewood Cliffs, New Jersey, 1988.

[19] H. M. Gerndt. Automatic parallelization for distributed memory multiprocessing systems. Report ACPC/ TR 90-1, Austrian Center for Parallel Computation, 1990.

[20] P. Hatcher, A. Lapadula, R. Jones, M. Quinn, and J. Anderson. A production quality C* compiler for hypercube machines. In *3rd ACM SIGPLAN Symposium on Principles Practice of Parallel Programming*, pages 73–82, April 1991.

[21] S. Hiranandani, K. Kennedy, and C. Tseng. Compiler support for machine-independent parallel programming in Fortran D. In *Compilers and Runtime Software for Scalable Multiprocessors, J. Saltz and P. Mehrotra Editors*, Amsterdam, The Netherlands, To appear 1991. Elsevier.

[22] S. Hiranandani, J. Saltz, P. Mehrotra, and H. Berryman. Performance of hashed cache data migration schemes on multicomputers. *Journal of Parallel and Distributed Computing, to appear*, 12, August 1991.

[23] S. Horwitz, T. Reps, and D. Binkley. Interprocedural slicing using dependence graphs. *ACM TOPLAS*, 12(1):26–60, January 1990.

[24] K. Ikudome, G. Fox, A. Kolawa, and J. Flower. An automatic and symbolic parallelization system for distributed memory parallel computers. In *DMCC5*, pages 1105–1114, Charleston, SC, April 1990.

[25] C. Koelbel, P. Mehrotra, and J. Van Rosendale. Supporting shared data structures on distributed memory architectures. In *2nd ACM SIGPLAN Symposium on Principles Practice of Parallel Programming*, pages 177–186. ACM SIGPLAN, March 1990.

[26] J. Li and M. Chen. Generating explicit communication from shared-memory program references. In *Proceedings Supercomputing '90*, November 1990.

[27] J. Li and M. Chen. Index domain alignment: Minimizing cost of cross-reference between distributed arrays. In *Proceedings of the 3rd Symposium on the Frontiers of Massively Computation*, October 1990.

[28] J. Li and M. Chen. Automating the coordination of interprocessor communication. In *Programming Languages and Compiler for Parallel Computing*, Cambridge Mass, 1991. The MIT Press.

[29] J. W. Liu. Computational models and task scheduling for parallel sparse cholesky factorization. *Parallel Computing*, 3:327–342, 1986.

[30] L. C. Lu and M.C. Chen. Parallelizing loops with indirect array references or pointers. In *Proceedings of the Fourth Workshop on Languages and Compilers for Parallel Computing, to appear*, Santa Clara, CA, August 1991.

[31] Parti runtime primitives for compilers, in progress. Interim report, ICASE, 1991.

[32] D. J. Mavriplis. Three dimensional unstructured multigrid for the euler equations, paper 91-1549cp. In *AIAA 10th Computational Fluid Dynamics Conference*, June 1991.

[33] R. Mirchandaney, J. H. Saltz, R. M. Smith, D. M. Nicol, and Kay Crowley. Principles of runtime support for parallel processors. In *Proceedings of the 1988 ACM International Conference on Supercomputing , St. Malo France*, pages 140–152, July 1988.

[34] M. J. Quinn and P. J. Hatcher. Data-parallel programming on multicomputers. *IEEE Software*, pages 69–76, September 1990.

[35] A. Rogers and K. Pingali. Process decomposition through locality of reference. In *Conference on Programming Language Design and Implementation.* ACM SIGPLAN, June 1989.

[36] M. Rosing and R. Schnabel. An overview of Dino - a new language for numerical computation on distributed memory multiprocessors. Technical Report CU-CS-385-88, University of Colorado, Boulder, 1988.

[37] M. Rosing, R.W. Schnabel, and R.P. Weaver. Expressing complex parallel algorithms in Dino. In *Proceedings of the 4th Conference on Hypercubes, Conurrent Computers and Applications*, pages 553–560, 1989.

[38] Y. Saad. Sparsekit: a basic tool kit for sparse matrix computations. Report 90-20, RIACS, 1990.

[39] J. Saltz, H. Berryman, and J. Wu. Runtime compilation for multiprocessors, to appear: Concurrency, Practice and Experience, 1991. Report 90-59, ICASE, 1990.

[40] J. Saltz, K. Crowley, R. Mirchandaney, and Harry Berryman. Run-time scheduling and execution of loops on message passing machines. *Journal of Parallel and Distributed Computing*, 8:303–312, 1990.

[41] J. Saltz, R. Das, R. Ponnusamy, D. Mavriplis, H Berryman, and J. Wu. Parti procedures for realistic loops. In *Proceedings of the 6th Distributed Memory Computing Conference*, Portland, Oregon, April-May 1991.

[42] H. Simon. Partitioning of unstructured mesh problems for parallel processing. In *Proceedings of the Conference on Prallel Methods on Large Scale Structural Analysis and Physics Applications*. Permagon Press, 1991.

[43] P. S. Tseng. *A Parallelizing Compiler for Distributed Memory Parallel Computers*. PhD thesis, Carnegie Mellon University, Pittsburgh, PA, May 1989.

[44] M. Weiser. Program slicing. *IEEE Trans. on Software Eng.*, SE-10(4):352–357, July 1984.

[45] R. D. Williams and R. Glowinski. Distributed irregular finite elements. Technical Report C3P 715, Caltech Concurrent Computation Program, February 1989.

[46] J. Wu, J. Saltz, S. Hiranandani, and H. Berryman. Runtime compilation methods for multicomputers. In *Proceedings of the 1991 International Conference on Parallel Processing*, pages II–26,II–30, 1991.

[47] H. Zima, H. Bast, and M. Gerndt. Superb: A tool for semi-automatic MIMD/SIMD parallelization. *Parallel Computing*, 6:1–18, 1988.

Languages, Compilers and Run-Time Environments
for Distributed Memory Machines
J. Saltz and P. Mehrotra (Editors)

Scheduling EPL Programs for Parallel Processing *

Balaram Sinharoy, Bruce McKenney and Boleslaw K. Szymanski

Department of Computer Science
Rensselaer Polytechnic Institute
Troy, N.Y. 12180-3590, USA

Abstract

The declarative semantics of the Equational Programming Language EPL allow for parallelization in various forms. As a specific instance, the horizontal partitioning performed by the EPL compiler for the CM style of SIMD machines is presented first. The larger issue of EPL compiler optimization for distributed-memory MIMD machines is discussed next.

For these architectures two problems, viz., data alignment and wavefront computations are investigated. First the complexity of aligning data elements to minimize the communication cost is assesed. Exact algorithms and a polynomial-time approximate algorithm are presented. Finally, the optimum wavefront and the optimum division of tasks to execute a set of recurrence equations are investigated.

1 Introduction

Equational Programming Language, abbreviated EPL, is a simple functional language designed for programming parallel scientific computation. The language is defined in terms of just a few constructs: generalized arrays and subscripts for data structures, recurrent equations for data value definitions, ports for process interactions and virtual processors for execution directives. An EPL program consists of *data declarations* and *annotated conditional equations.* Equations are defined over multidimensional jagged-edge arrays and may be annotated by *virtual processors* on which they are executed. Data declarations are annotated by the *record* and *port* designators which are used to identify interfaces with an external environment and other programs.

In addition to programs, the EPL user can define *configurations* which describe interconnections between ports of different processes. Configurations allow the programmer to reuse the same EPL programs in different computations. They also facilitate computation decomposition. A port creates a fair merge of its input sequences and hence enables an easy expression of non-determinism [5] without changing the functional character of a program definition.

In addition to single-valued data structures, EPL programs contain *subscripts* that assume a range of integers as their values. Subscripts give EPL a dual flavor. In the *definitional view*

*This work was partially supported by the National Science Foundation under grant CCR-8613353, and grant CDA-8805910, the Office of Naval Research under contract N00014-86-K-0442 and by the Army Research Office under contract DAAL03-86-K-0112.

they may be treated as universal quantifiers and equations are then viewed as logical predicates. In the *operational view* they can be seen as loop control variables, and each equation then is seen as a statement nested in loops implied by its subscripts. A more detailed description of the language may be found elsewhere [11].

The basic techniques used in the compilation of EPL programs are data dependence analysis and data attributes propagation. In a single program, the dependencies are represented in a compact form by the *conditional array graph.* This graph associates each dependence with its attributes, such as the distance between dependent elements, conditions under which dependence holds, the subscripts associated with it, etc. Both explicit data dependencies (defined by the usage of one data structure in an equation defining the other) and implicit data dependencies (implied, for example, by the sequentiality of the reading of incoming messages) are represented as various kinds of edges in the conditional array graph. Each node of this graph contains information about the represented entity, such as the number and ranges of its dimensions, its type and class, and conditions guarding its definitions.

The correctness of the program is checked by verifying the consistency of the different attributes of data structures and data dependencies. To accomplish this, the EPL compiler propagates data and dependence attributes along the edges of the graph.

A similar dependence graph is also created for a configuration. It shows the data dependencies among the processes of the computation and is used in scheduling processes and mapping them onto the processors.

The extent of transformation required to generate the object code depends on the architecture at hand. The easiest is the translation for a specialized dataflow architecture that consists of the following functional elements:

token memory A memory in which a subscripted variable ("tagged value") is stored after it has been read in or evaluated.

matching unit A unit that checks that all data values needed for evaluation of an equation instance are present in the token memory.

executing unit One of a number of arithmetic units able to evaluate EPL operators.

The conditional array graph defines the number of copies of a value needed in the token memory for each evaluated subscripted variable (it is simply the number of edges outgoing from the node representing this variable). Each process may have a separate dataflow machine assigned to its execution and the machines have to be connected to enable an exchange of data through the process ports. Alternatively, one dataflow machine may be allocated to the entire computation, and then ports would merely define equivalences of variables in different processes. With a sufficient number of arithmetic units, the dataflow implementation can provide the highest parallelism. However, eager scheduling of EPL computations can easily lead to an excessive demand for the token memory [1].

In the well-known Flynn's classification of parallel computational models [6], the von Neumann model is characterized by a Single stream of Instructions controlling a Single stream of Data (SISD). A first step towards parallelism is to introduce Multiple Data streams (SIMD), and a second step is to add Multiple Instruction streams (MIMD). The last category can be conveniently split on the basis of data access mechanism into shared and distributed memory architectures. In the shared memory architectures, all processors have equal access to the shared memory. In the distributed memory architectures, each process has direct access to its local memory but can access memory of other processors only through a message passing mechanism that enables the processors to communicate with each other.

SIMD machines have historically been represented by the vector and array processors. More recently, the SIMD category has been enriched by an architecture proposed by Hillis [7] and termed the *Connection Machine*, or CM[1]. Like the vector processors, the CM is based on data parallelism, with a single instruction stream acting across an array of data, but the CM's array consists of active elements, CPUs that are capable of holding state and intercommunicating. Vectorization is at this time a fairly well-known art [2]; effective use of the CM's increased flexibility is still being explored.

For the Connection Machine, the major task of the EPL translation is to identify an EPL subscript that will index individual processors (i.e., a subscript that defines a domain of the computation). Equations indexed by the domain subscript will be executed in parallel on different processors. The selection of the domain subscript is influenced by the fact that a reference to an indexing expression (other than a simple domain subscript) implies communication of data from another processor.

Even more involved is the translation for Multiple Data Multiple Instruction machines. For shared memory architectures in this class, only the placement of equations is an issue; ports can be easily and efficiently implemented as blocks of shared memory. Efficient translation requires strong memory optimization to counterweight the effects of 'excessive' dimensions introduced due to the single assignment rule of the language.

For distributed memory machines, additional difficulty arises from data placement. In the current implementation of the EPL code generator for the Intel hypercube, we adopted the expedient of distributing data items together with the equations that define them. Doing this folds the data placement problem back into that of optimal allocation of equations to processors, still a more complex task than equation allocation for shared memory machines.

2 Basic Scheduling in EPL

A schedule of equation evaluation is determined by a topological sort of the array graph. The scheduling starts by creating a component graph that consists of all the maximally strongly connected components (MSCCs) in the array graph and the edges connecting these MSCCs. The component graph is therefore an acyclic directed graph. This graph can typically be topologically sorted in many different ways, each of them resulting in a different object program. It is also necessary to schedule each node that represents a non-singleton MSCC. Thus, the component graph scheduling has to define the schedule for each node in the component graph and, then, to find the topological sort of the whole graph that results in the highest efficiency of the generated code. The details of the component graph node scheduling are presented in [11].

Once all nodes have been scheduled, the architecture-dependent optimizations take place.

[1] Hillis' generic architecture currently has several implementations, the CM-1 and CM-2 (Trademarks of Thinking Machines, Corp), and the MP-1 (Trademark of Maspar, nc.)

MSCC scheduling represents the least restrictive ordering of the computation required to compute the correct result. The resultant component graph contains parallel paths and iterations that may be exploited in parallelization.

Currently, there are three distinct optimizations done in the second stage of scheduling: horizontal partitioning for data parallelism, parallel task selection, and loop merging and nesting for memory optimization.

2.1 Horizontal Partitioning

In horizontal partitioning slices are made across multidimensional structures such that the evaluations of elements along each slice are independent of each other. One dimension of each data structure might be designated to be projected along the processor array, with each processor then holding a single instance of that structure. Operations along that projection dimension take place in parallel [7]. This approach is typical of data parallelism suitable for SIMD machines, particularly for the Connection Machine [7]. In making a choice of a projection dimension for a variable the following criteria are considered.

The best projection dimension of a variable will have the smallest number of expression-type references along it in the program, since each reference of this type would imply a communication step. The respective forms of the expressions are also of interest. A reference which uses expressions of the form `I-k` or `I+k`, where `I` is a subscript and `k` is a constant, is less costly than one which uses a more general form of expression. These special forms of references result in very regular communication patterns ("shift right" and "shift left") which, by avoiding collisions, may be performed very rapidly on the Connection Machine.

The second criterion is the extent to which computations can be merged along the projection dimension, since we want the largest possible part of the program to be parallelized. Currently, the selection of the projection dimension is based on the total number of references made to it in the program. In a future implementation the reference count will be weighted according to the complexity of each reference. We would like also to take advantage of reduce and scan operations[2], either expressed by the EPL `all` operator or recognized from the syntactical pattern in the EPL program.

2.2 Parallel Task Selection

Since the component graph produced in the first stage of the scheduling defines a partial order, it may contain nodes that are not dependent on each other and therefore may be executed in parallel. Parallel tasks are created from an initial set of such nodes. Each task is then enlarged by adding to it nodes that are dependent only on the nodes already in this task. If the extent of parallelism obtained this way exceeds the number of available processors, tasks that require the most communication among themselves are merged together. In the opposite case a form of horizontal partitioning is used, in which intervals of a subscript in an iteration are assigned to different processors. The extent of parallelism and, more importantly, the amount of communication needed are controlled by the size of the subscript interval. This form

[2]reduce applied to a vector produces a scalar result whereas scan results in a vector of partial results. Both operations can be implemented in log time of the number of their arguments on the Connection Machine.

of parallelism is particularly suitable for shared memory architectures, since distributing an iteration does not necessitate distributing data structures. For distributed memory machines that are based on message passing, the EPL compiler assigns data to the processor which produces it (in other words the processor that executes an equation keeps the resulting data structure in its local memory). Thus, distributing an iteration requires distributing instances of a data structure among different processors. This is cost effective only if references to such distributed data structure are simple.[3]

2.3 Memory Optimization

In the memory optimization stage, attempts are made to enlarge the scope of created iterations. Nodes with the same range can be merged to form larger components. Merging scopes of iterations may enable sharing of memory locations by elements of the same or related array variables. Usually, there are many ways in which components can be merged (using different dimensions), each corresponding to a different topological sorting of the component graph. The memory requirements of different candidate scopes of iterations serve as the criteria for selecting the optimal merging. The selection is equivalent to the NP-complete problem of finding a clique with the maximum weight of nodes in an undirected graph [4]. Therefore the EPL compiler uses a heuristic for memory optimization [11].

The memory optimization stage is executed after the parallelization stage (horizontal partitioning, task selection, or both) to further improve the efficiency of the generated code.

3 Case Study: Horizontal Partitioning for the CM

As an example of horizontal partitioning, the machine-dependent EPL postprocessor for the CM (called here the CM scheduler) is discussed. Since the CM CPUs are, on an individual basis, relatively slow, there is a premium on deducing as much data parallelism as possible. The function of the CM Scheduler is to use information in the component graph to select a set of projection dimensions, along with their associated subscripts, for the computation. A goal, though not a requirement, of this selection is to assign a projection dimension to each data node (variable). A restriction is that no data node have more than one projection dimension. A data node may (at a price) be referenced along its projection dimension by a non-projection subscript.

The method used for the selection is based on merging of equations along the projection dimension. It proceeds by propagating projection choices backwards through the dependencies. The choice of projection subscript for the left-hand side of an equation is propagated through its uses on the right-hand side. Though there can be only one projection dimension for a data item, it is possible for the computation as a whole to have multiple projection subscripts, used within groups of equations which are independent.

The selection of projection dimensions consists of multiple propagation stages. In each stage, a projection subscript is chosen. This subscript is then propagated through each equation to designate the projection dimensions for the other data items used in the equation. As noted,

[3]Simple index references do not require any communication whereas general index expressions define complex communication patterns.

each initial choice is currently based on a simple reference count. We plan to replace this criterion by a reference count weighted according to the complexity of the subscript expression in which it is used. Let I denote one of the initially-chosen subscripts. Then each other subscript, say J, which has not been chosen is checked for:

- any reference to a data item A which was defined using I, but referenced using J along a **`different`** dimension; any such reference is killed (marked as no longer relevant), since there can only be one projection dimension per data item.
- any reference to an A which was defined or referenced using I and also defined or referenced using J along the **`same`** dimension; J is marked as a new projection subscript, thus propagating the projection to a new subscript.

Once the propagations are complete, each subscript which has been chosen for projection is marked (along with its associated loop) for projection; for each live variable definition in which that subscript is used, the data node has its corresponding dimension marked as a projection dimension.

The decisions made by the CM scheduler are made concrete by the EPL code generator, as it generates C* (for the CM-2) or MPL (for the MP-1) object code. Projection subscripts are noted when a loop is being opened; projection dimensions are relevant when the data item is being declared; both are important when a data item is referenced in an equation.

When a loop is opened, the code generator checks to see if the loop induction variable has been designated a projection subscript. For this case, a `domain` (C*) or `all` (MPL) is generated rather than a `for` or `while` statement.

When a data item is declared, the code generator looks for a projection dimension for the item. If projection dimension is found, it is dropped from the declaration, and a `domain` (C*) or `plural` (MPL) keyword is prefixed to the declaration statement.

When a data item is referenced, the code generator must consider both the data item dimension being referenced and the subscript being referenced, either or both of which may be projected. These two conditions generate four cases that reduce to the following two rules:

- the actual symbol name of every projection subscript is replaced by the self-referencing subscript `iproc`; this is done by string substitution in the code generator
- every reference to a projection dimension is prefixed by `proc[subscript_expression]`, unless this turns out to be precisely "`proc[iproc]`".

The CM scheduler has been implemented for the Maspar MP-1, generating MPL as object code. The speed of the resulting programs is currently being compared to that of equivalent hand-coded programs.

Directions for future research include investigating criteria for the choice of initial subscripts for projection, and recognizing constructs suitable for execution using reduce and scan operations. There are two parts to such a recognizer. First, a dimension must be recognized along which a simple recurrence is being generated (e.g. `A[I] = f(A[I-1])`. This dimension needs to be recognized anyway, since, in the absence of a reduce or scan operation, the computation along it is completely sequential, making it a poor choice of projection dimension. Second, the right-hand side expression in an equation must match a pattern where the operator (`f` above) is associative, an implicit requirement for scan and reduce. Since there are a number of EPL idioms amenable to computation using scan and reduce operations, such a recognizer should do much to improve programs which are currently only partially parallelizable.

4 Alignment Problem

In this section we discuss the problem of aligning data elements to minimize communication cost when the computation is performed on an array of virtual processors. It is assumed that the data elements are defined by a set of recurrence equations with uncoupled indexes.

Example 1: Suppose that the three two-dimensional arrays A, B and C are defined as

$$A[I,J] = f(B[I-5,J-1], B[I-3,J-1], C[I-2,J-3], C[I-4,J-8])$$
$$B[I,J] = g(A[I-4,J-2], A[I-7,J-4], C[I-2,J-3], C[I-3,J-7])$$
$$C[I,J] = h(A[I-3,J-8], A[I-4,J-5], A[I-6,J], B[I-5,J-7], B[I-4,J-4])$$

If $A[I,J]$ and $B[I-5,J-1]$ are evaluated by the same processor then the first argument of the function "f" is conveniently located in the local memory. However we need to communicate the second argument from the processor two positions away along the dimension I. The question is what instance of each of the arrays A, B and C should be evaluated by the same processor in order to minimize the communication cost.

Section 5.1 gives a mathematical formulation for the alignment problem. The complexity of the problem is investigated in section 5.2. Section 5.3 presents two methods of solving and section 5.4 contains an approximate algorithm with polynomial complexity.

4.1 Mathematical Formulation

Indexes of the set of recurrence equations are assumed to be uncoupled. Thus, each dimension of the data elements can be aligned separately. If in example 1, $A[I,\ldots]$ is aligned with $B[I+x,\ldots]$, the communication cost between A and B (cost to access appropriate elements of the array B to evaluate an element of A and vice versa) is

$$C_{AB}(x_1) = |x_1+5| + |x_1+3| + |x_1-4| + |x_1-7|$$

Similarly,

$$C_{AC}(x_2) = |x_2+2| + |x_2+4| + |x_2-3| + |x_2-4| + |x_2-6|$$
$$C_{BC}(x_3) = |x_3+2| + |x_3+3| + |x_3-5| + |x_3-4|$$

Our objective is to find the vector (x_1, x_2, x_3) that minimizes

$$C = C_{AB}(x_1) + C_{AC}(x_2) + C_{BC}(x_3)$$

which is of the form

$$\sum_i \sum_j |x_i - a_{ij}| \qquad (1)$$

Since aligning B and C with respect to A dictates the alignment between B and C we have also the constraint

$$x_1 = x_2 + x_3$$

This kind of constraint can be used to reduce the number of variables in the problem.

The data alignment problem can be transformed into a set of minimization problems as follows. Consider the undirected graph $G = (V, E)$, where $V = \{v_1, v_2, \ldots, v_n\}$ represents the data elements defined by the set of recurrence equations and $E = \{(v_i, v_j) | v_i$ and v_j appear on opposite sides of an equation$\}$. Let the edges of G be marked using a set of labels $\{x_1, x_2, \ldots\}$. The label x_k assigned to the edge (v_l, v_m), $l \geq m$, represents an alignment of the data element $v_l[I]$ with $v_m[I + x_k]$. The alignment problem can be generalized to allow the same label to appear on more than one edge, indicating that the alignment distance must be the same for the corresponding pairs of data elements.

Each of the connected components of G defines a separate minimization problem. Let $G' = (V', E')$ be a connected component of G, and $T = (V_T, E_T)$ be a spanning tree of G'. Without loss of generality, we can assume that the edges of the spanning tree E_T are marked by the labels $\{x_1, x_2, \ldots, x_k\}$ where $k \leq |E_T|$. Each edge in $E' \setminus E_T$, when added to the spanning tree, produces a distinct cycle, traversal of which yields a constraint. All the cycles of the connected component can be obtained from these fundamental cycles. The constraints are of the form of a dot product defined as

$$x_i = A \cdot X$$

where $i = k + 1, \ldots, n$; $X = [x_1, x_2, \ldots, x_k]$, and $A \in Z^k$.

If all the edges of the spanning tree are labelled distinctly then $A \in \{-1, 0, 1\}^k$. In this case each of the constraints can be used to replace a distinct x_i in (1), thus reducing the number of variables to k. Hence, the alignment problem is equivalent to finding such a vector $[x_1, x_2, \ldots, x_k]$ that minimizes

$$\sum_{i=1}^{k} \sum_{j=1}^{n_i} |x_i - a_{ij}| + \sum_{i=1}^{n} |A_i \cdot X - b_i| \tag{2}$$

where $A_i \in \{-1, 0, 1\}^k$. The above problem is similar to finding the closest vector in a lattice. In [3], [8] this problem is proven NP-hard for an arbitrary lattice. In the next section, following [9], we prove it NP-hard for the special type of lattice defined in (2). It should be noted that if all the edges of the graph G are labeled distinctly then A_i is in a proper subset of $\{-1, 0, 1\}^k$. In this case the complexity of the problem is not known to the authors.

If there are no constraints (i.e, G has no cycles) then the problem reduces to finding such a $X = [x_1, \ldots, x_k]$ that minimizes (1). The following theorem (see [9] for proof) suggests an appropriate algorithm:

Theorem 1 *x minimizes the function*

$$m_0|x - a_0| + m_1|x - a_1| + \ldots + m_n|x - a_n|$$

where $m_i > 0$ for $i \in \{1, 2 \ldots, n\}$ and $a_0 \leq a_1 \ldots \leq a_n$, if and only if $a_l \leq x \leq a_u$, where $l = \max_k(\sum_{i=1}^{k} m_i \leq \frac{\sum_{i=1}^{n} m_i}{2})$ and $u = \min_k(\sum_{i=1}^{k} m_i \geq \frac{\sum_{i=1}^{n} m_i}{2})$.

4.2 The Minimization Problem is NP-hard

We have seen that the optimum alignment can be found if we can find $X \in \{-1, 0, 1\}^k$ which minimizes (2). In this section, first we prove that problem F (defined below) is NP-complete. Then we reduce problem F to the minimization problem.

Problem F: *Is there a vector* $Y = [y_1, y_2, \ldots, y_k] \in \{0,1\}^k$ *such that for a given function* f *and a constant* c,

$$f(y_1, y_2, \ldots, y_k) \leq c$$

where $f = D\bar{Y} + \sum_{i=1}^{n} |A_i\bar{Y} + c_i|$, $D \in Z_+^k$, $-1 \leq c_i \leq 2k-1$ *and* $A_i \in \{-1,0,1\}^k$

Lemma 1 *Problem F is NP-complete.*

Proof: Obviously the problem is in NP. We will reduce the satisfiability problem to problem F. The satisfiability problem is to determine if there is an $X = [x_1, x_2, \ldots, x_k] \in \{0,1\}^k$ for which a given CNF (Conjunctive Normal Form) is satisfiable, i.e.,

$$\prod_{i=1}^{n} \sum_{j=1}^{k} (a_{ij}x_j + a'_{ij}\bar{x}_j) = 1$$

where $a_{ij}, a'_{ij} \in \{0,1\}$ and '+' indicates boolean 'or' and juxtaposition indicates boolean 'and'.

Replacing $\bar{x}_j$ by $(1-x_j)$ and using arithmetic addition we can find c'_i and A'_i and can write that the CNF is satisfiable if and only if there is an $X = [x_1, x_2, \ldots, x_k] \in \{0,1\}^k$ which satisfies the following n inequalities (each inequality corresponds to a clause in the CNF):

$$A'_i \cdot \bar{X} + c'_i \geq 0$$

where $i \in \{1, \ldots, n\}$, $-1 \leq c'_i \leq k-1$, $A'_i \in \{-1,0,1\}^k$,

i.e., if and only if $\sum_{i=1}^{n} |A'_i \cdot \bar{X} + c'_i| \leq \sum_{i=1}^{n} (A'_i \cdot \bar{X} + c'_i)$

Let $\sum_{i=1}^{n} (A'_i \cdot \bar{X} + c'_i) = \sum_{i=1}^{k} d_i x_i + e$. Replacing x_i by $1 - y_i$ for all i's for which $d_i > 0$ and by y_i otherwise, and transferring everything but the constant to the left we get (for appropriate values of the constants)

$$D\bar{Y} + \sum_{i=1}^{n} |A_i \cdot \bar{Y} + c_i| \leq c$$

where $D \in Z_+^k$, $-1 \leq c_i \leq 2k-1$, $A_i \in \{-1,0,1\}^k$ and $Y = [y_1, \ldots y_k] \in \{0,1\}^k$. Thus, for every CNF we can construct an instance of the problem F in polynomial time. Hence, problem F is NP-complete. □

Theorem 2 *The problem of finding the vector of integers* $X = [x_1, x_2, \ldots, x_k]$ *that minimizes*

$$g = \sum_{i=1}^{k} \sum_{j=1}^{n_i} |x_i - b_{ij}| + \sum_{i=1}^{n} |A_i \cdot \bar{X} + c_i|$$

where $a_{ij} \in Z_+, c_i \in Z, b_{ij} \in Z, A_i \in \{-1,0,1\}^k$ *is NP-hard.*

Proof: The problem F can be reduced to the minimization problem. Let

$$f(x_1, x_2, \ldots, x_k) = D \cdot \bar{X} + \sum_{i=1}^{n} |A_i \cdot \bar{X} + c_i|$$

Let $f(l, l, \ldots, l) = p$ for some integer l. Consider the function

$$h = p|x_1 - l| + p|x_1 - u| - p(u - l)$$

where $l \leq u$. Let

$$f'(x_1, x_2, \ldots, x_k) = f(x_1, x_2, \ldots, x_k) + p\sum_{i=1}^{k} |x_i - l| + p\sum_{i=1}^{k} |x_i - u| - kp(u - l).$$

Clearly, $f'(x_1, x_2, \ldots, x_k) = f(x_1, x_2, \ldots, x_k)$ for $l \leq x_i \leq u$, $i \in \{1, 2, \ldots, k\}$

and $f'(x_1, x_2, \ldots, x_k) \geq f(x_1, x_2, \ldots, x_k) + 2kp$, otherwise.

So the minimum of f' is in the domain $l \leq x_1 \leq u, \ldots, l \leq x_k \leq u$. After setting $l = 0$ and $u = 1$, the problem F reduces in polynomial time (since $p = \sum_i |c_i| \leq n(2k-1)$) to a subproblem of the minimization problem, where $b_{ij} = 0$ for all i, j. Hence the minimization problem is NP-hard. □

4.3 Exact Methods of Solution

Although the problem is NP-hard, many EPL program yields small values of the constants making the exact methods of practical interest.

4.3.1 Enumeration

It is not difficult to give an upper and a lower bound for each of the variables within which the minimum must lie. Let

$$p = \sum_{i=1}^{k}\sum_{j=1}^{n_i}|b_{ij}| + \sum_{i=1}^{n}|c_i|\ , \qquad l_i = \min_j(b_{ij}) \ \text{ and } \ u_i = \max_j(b_{ij})$$

If $x_i < -p + u_i$ or $x_i > p + l_i$ then the value of the function is greater than p. So for the minimum point $-p + u_i \leq x_i \leq p + l_i$. A tighter bound is [9]

$$\left\lceil \frac{-p+\sum_{j=1}^{n_i} b_{ij}}{n_i} \right\rceil \leq x_i \leq \left\lfloor \frac{p+\sum_{j=1}^{n_i} b_{ij}}{n_i} \right\rfloor \quad , \quad 1 \leq i \leq n$$

The minimum point(s) can be found by simply enumerating all the points inside the defined upper bounds. The complexity of this method is $O(c^k)$ where c is the largest range of any variable x_i in the domain. It is not unreasonable to expect that for many EPL programs the values of c and k are such that the use of the enumeration method will be cost-effective.

4.3.2 Successive Replacement

The successive replacement method is based on solving $r \leq k$, where r is the rank of (2) linear equations defining *hyperplanes* of (2). Each hyperplane is defined either by an equation $x_i - a_{ij} = 0$, for some i and j such that $1 \leq i \leq k$, $1 \leq j \leq n_i$ or by an equation $A_i \cdot X - b_i = 0$, for some i, $1 \leq i \leq n$. The *rank r of (2)* is equal to the rank of the set of all the above equations (for the alignment problem this is k).

Lemma 2 *There is a minimum point of (2) that lies on one of the hyperplanes of (2).*

Proof Let $X_0 = [x_1^0, x_2^0, \ldots, x_k^0]$ be a minimum point that does not lie on any hyperplane. Thus, all terms in (2) are non-zero. Let d_1 have the smallest absolute value among numbers for which one of the terms in (2) becomes zero at the point $X_1 = [x_1^0 + d_1, x_2^0, \ldots, x_k^0]$. To complete the proof, it is sufficient to notice that X_1 lies on a hyperplane, and since none of the terms of (2) is zero at X_0, then $f(X_1) > f(X_0)$ implies $f(X_0) > f(x_1^0 - d_1, x_2^0, \ldots, x_k^0)$ contradicting our assumption about X_0. □

In [9] it is shown that all the points that minimize (2) form a convex set.

For each instance of the minimization problem with k variables and n terms we can create n reduced problems with $k-1$ variables and $n-1$ terms. The reduction simply eliminates one of the variables by substituting for it an equation derived from one of the terms. Each reduced problem is the restriction of the minimization problem to the corresponding hyperplane of (2). By Lemma 2, minimization in at least one of the reduced problems will yield the solution to the original problem. The reduction step can in turn be applied to each of the reduced problems, until all but one of the variables are eliminated (cf. Theorem 1).

If A_i's in (2) are obtained from a spanning tree with distinctly labeled edges, then successive replacement of variables keeps the new coefficients of the remaining variables in $\{-1, 0, 1\}$ for all the hyperplane equations [9]. Thus, the solutions of the reduced problems, and also of the original problem, are integers.

It is clear that the number of steps of this algorithm is less than $\binom{n}{k}$, hence its complexity can be approximated as $O(2^n)$ or $O(n^k)$. Depending on the number of the hyperplanes and values of constants in (2) this algorithm may be more or less effective than the enumeration method. Generally, the successive replacement is effective if n is close to k, (i.e. the number of cycles in the graph G is small) or k (i.e., the number of data elements to be aligned) is small.

4.4 Approximate Algorithm

In this section we propose a polynomial-time approximate algorithm for the minimization problem and a method for iterative refinement of the result. Suppose we are to minimize

$$g_1 = \sum_{i=1}^{k} \sum_{j=1}^{n_i} |x_i - a_{ij}| + \sum_{i=1}^{n} |A_i \cdot X - b_i|$$

Let

$$g_2 = \sum_{i=1}^{k} \sum_{j=1}^{n_i} (x_i - a_{ij})^2 + \sum_{i=1}^{n} (A_i \cdot X - b_i)^2$$

Let $(x_1^0, x_2^0, \ldots, x_k^0)$ be a solution of the k simultaneous linear equations (assuming it exists)

$$\sum_{j=1}^{n_m} (x_m - a_{mj}) + \sum_{i=1}^{n} a'_{im}(A_i X - b_i) = 0 \quad , \quad 1 \leq m \leq k$$

where a'_{im} is the m-th element of A_i. These equations are obtained by differentiating g_2 with respect to $x_1, \ldots, x_k$. Let the minimum m of the function g_1 be at the point $(\bar{x}_1, \bar{x}_2, \ldots, \bar{x}_k)$ and $M = g_2(x_1^0, x_2^0, \ldots, x_k^0)$. Then, $M \leq g_2(\bar{x}_1, \bar{x}_2, \ldots, \bar{x}_k) \leq m^2$, so we know the lower limit of the solution and therefore can estimate an error of $(x_1^0, x_2^0, \ldots, x_k^0)$ approximation. Since $g_1(x_1^0, x_2^0, \ldots, x_k^0) \leq \sqrt{kM}$, the relative error is never larger than

$$\frac{\sqrt{kM} - \sqrt{M}}{\sqrt{M}} = \sqrt{k} - 1.$$

Often the above result can be improved by the following iterative scheme. We start with the point $(x_1^0, x_2^0, \ldots, x_k^0)$ obtained above. Let the i-th iteration, i=0,1,2,.. results in a point $(x_1^i, x_2^i, \ldots, x_k^i)$. We can evaluate left and right derivatives of our function at this point and select the variable, say x_l (and direction for this variable) with the steepest decline. The new iteration point is defined as: $x_j^{i+1} = x_j^i$, for $j \neq l$ and $x_l^{i+1} = x_l^i + d$, where d is the smallest (largest if $d < 0$) among the numbers that make a new term in (2) equal to zero for $x_l^i + d$. Unfortunately the scheme may not converge to the global minimum (cf. [9] for a discussion).

5 Optimum Direction of Computation

Suppose that we want to compute an array A defined recursively as

$$A[I, J] = f(A[I-5, J], A[I-1, J-2], A[I-1, J+2])$$

Such a definition imposes an order of evaluation on the elements of A, and therefore not all those elements can be evaluated simultaneously. In this section we investigate different orders in which the array elements can be evaluated. Our goal is to find the order which enables the computation to be completed in minimum time.

We restrict our attention to two-dimensional arrays processed on a linear arbitrary large array of processors with an unbounded number of processors (see [10] for higher dimension). Fig. 1 shows the processing of the array A. If at some instance of execution A[I,J] has been evaluated for all indexes (I,J) located above Z, then all the points on the line Z can be computed simultaneously. Such a line Z is termed a *wavefront of computation.* The *direction of computation* is a line perpendicular to the wavefront of computation. If $A[I,J]$ is defined in terms of $A[I-x, J-y]$ then the vector (x,y) is called a *distance vector.* A necessary and sufficient condition for a line to be a wavefront is that all distance vectors attached to a point on that line lie on one side of the wavefront. Evidently, any line between X and Y in Figure 2 can be a wavefront, since for these and only these lines are the distance vectors on one side of the line. We would like to find out the wavefront which results in a computation with minimum execution time.

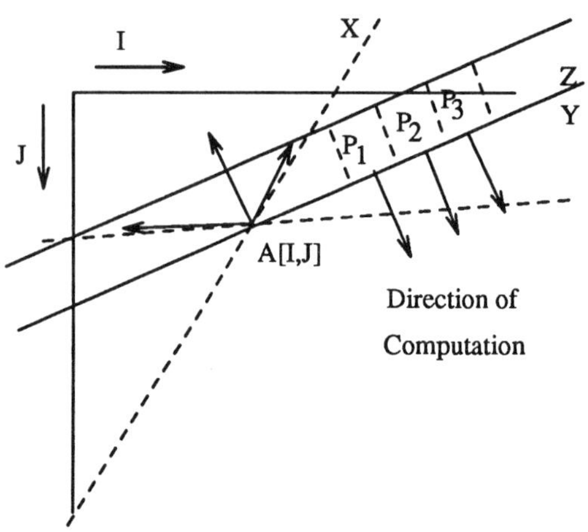

Fig. 1: Distance vectors and the possible wavefronts.

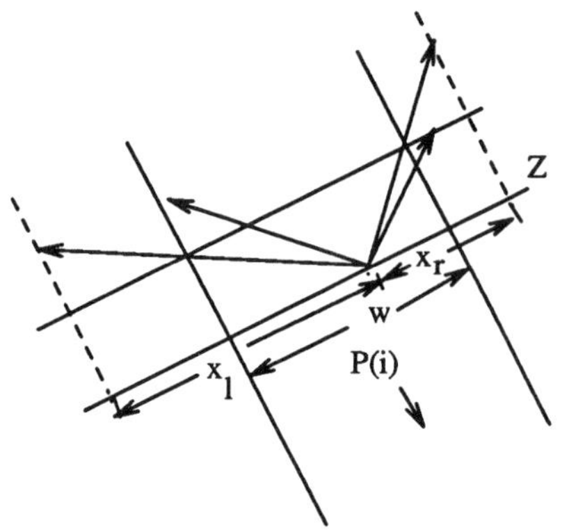

Fig. 2: Longest projections on the Z wavefront.

Suppose that there are n distance vectors, p of them extending to the right and $q = n - p$ to the left of a point on the wavefront Z to which they are attached. Let z_l^i, $i = 1, 2, \ldots, q$ and z_r^i, $i = 1, 2, \ldots, p$ be the projections of the vectors to the left and right of this point, respectively. Let z_l and z_r be the largest of z_r^i's and z_l^i's respectively.

Let's assume first that two processors can communicate with each other directly only when they are neighbors. Under this assumption the minimum width of an index range along the wavefront Z that a processor can be allowed to compute is $max(z_l, z_r)$.

Let's consider the case when each array element computed by the neighboring processor is accessed individually. The total number of elements communicated from the processors at right for a unit of computation along the direction of computation is

$$z_r^1 * p + (z_r^2 - z_r^1) * (p-1) + (z_r^3 - z_r^2) * (p-2) + \ldots + (z_r^p - z_r^{p-1}) = \sum_{i=1}^{p} z_r^i$$

Adding the communication needed from the left neighbor, we obtain:

$$\sum_{i=1}^{p} z_r^i + \sum_{i=1}^{q} z_l^i$$

Let θ be an angle between the optimum direction and the positive x-axis. The sum of the projections of the points $(x_1, y_1), \ldots, (x_n, y_n)$ is

$$C = \sum_{i=1}^{n} |x_i cos\theta + y_i sin\theta|$$

Let α and β denote the minimum and the maximum angles ($\beta < \alpha + \pi$, for a wavefront) that the direction vectors make with the positive x-axis. Our objective is to minimize

$$\sum_{i=1}^{n} |x_i cos\theta + y_i sin\theta| \quad where \quad \beta < \theta < \alpha + \pi \tag{3}$$

It is not very difficult to find θ in $\beta < \theta < \alpha + \pi$ that minimizes (3). Let $\{\gamma_1, \gamma_2, \ldots, \gamma_m\}$ be a sorted list of the angles $\theta_i = arctan(-\frac{x_i}{y_i})$, $1 \le i \le n$, such that $\beta < \theta_i < \alpha + \pi$. Let $\gamma_0 = \beta + \delta$, and $\gamma_{m+1} = \alpha + \pi - \delta$, where δ is defined by the resolution of the implementation. For each range $(\gamma_j,\ \gamma_{j+1})$, $j = 0, 1, \ldots, m$, expression (3) can be written as

$$acos\theta + bsin\theta \tag{4}$$

where $a = \sum_{i=1}^{n} c_i x_i$ and $b = \sum_{i=1}^{n} d_i y_i$, $c_i, d_i \in \{+1, -1\}$ and their exact values depend on the range. The minimum of (4) in a range $\gamma_j \le \theta \le \gamma_{j+1}$ is either at the boundaries of the range or at $\phi = arctan(\frac{a}{b})$, if $\gamma_j \le \phi \le \gamma_{j+1}$. Thus, the best wavefront angle θ which minimizes (3) in the range $\beta < \theta < \alpha + \pi$ can be determined in a linear time.

Usually, array elements are not also accessed individually, but instead several of them are sent in a packet. Typically, packets can be transferred between non-neighboring processors through hopping. Under these assumptions, the minimum width of the wavefront assigned to a processor can be less than $max(z_l, z_r)$. If the width is small, each processor spends less time on computation but more time on communication because not as much relevant information is transferred in each packet. On the other hand, if the width is large, each processor spends more time on computation between data transfers and the communication cost is relatively smaller. However, after a certain width is achieved, the communication cost does not decrease any further with the increase in width. In the following we discuss the selection of the optimal wavefront and width size under the above assumptions.

In fig. 2, $P(i)$ represents the i-th processor that computes a width w of the wavefront. The packets being transferred are rectangular with sides parallel to the wavefront and the direction of computation. Let the packet size be $p = p_h \times p_l$, where p_l stands for the length of the packet along the wavefront and p_h denotes the height of the packet along the direction of computation. The number of packets that pass through $P(i)$ while it computes a strip of the length p_h along the direction of computation is

$$C(w) = \left\lfloor \frac{z_l}{w} \right\rfloor \left\lceil \frac{w}{p_l} \right\rceil + \left\lfloor \frac{z_r}{w} \right\rfloor \left\lceil \frac{w}{p_l} \right\rceil + \left\lceil \frac{z_l (mod\ w)}{p_l} \right\rceil + \left\lceil \frac{z_r (mod\ w)}{p_l} \right\rceil \tag{5}$$

Corollary of the following theorem gives the smallest value of w that minimizes $C(w)$.

Theorem 3 *The minimum value of*

$$C(w) = \lfloor \tfrac{x}{w} \rfloor \lceil \tfrac{w}{p} \rceil + \lceil \tfrac{x(mod\ w)}{p} \rceil$$

is $\lceil \frac{x}{p} \rceil$. *The smallest value of* w *for which* $C(w)$ *reaches the minimum is equal to* $\left\lceil \frac{x}{\lceil \frac{x}{p} \rceil} \right\rceil$.

Proof: The proof is performed by case analysis.

Case 1: $0 < w \le p$

In this case $C(w) = \lceil \frac{x}{w} \rceil \geq \lceil \frac{x}{p} \rceil$, in particular $C(p) = \lceil \frac{x}{p} \rceil$.

Case 2: $mp < w \leq (m+1)p \ , \ m > 0$

$$C(w) = (m+1) \lfloor \tfrac{x}{w} \rfloor + \lceil \tfrac{x (mod\ w)}{p} \rceil$$

Let $x = dw + r$ where $0 \leq r < w$, then

$$C(w) = d(m+1) + \lceil \tfrac{r}{p} \rceil$$

If $r = 0$ then $C(w) = d(m+1)$ and we have

$$\lceil \tfrac{x}{p} \rceil \leq \lceil \tfrac{d(m+1)p}{p} \rceil = d(m+1)$$

So $\lceil \frac{x}{p} \rceil \leq C(w)$. If $np < r \leq (n+1)p$ for some n, then we have

$$C(w) = (m+1)d + (n+1)$$

Now, $\lceil \frac{x}{p} \rceil = \lceil \frac{dw+r}{p} \rceil \leq \lceil \frac{d(m+1)p+(n+1)p}{p} \rceil = d(m+1) + (n+1) = C(w)$

Thus, $\lceil \frac{x}{p} \rceil$ is the minimum of $C(w)$.

We know from case 1 that the smallest w_0 that minimizes $C(w)$ satisfies $w_0 \leq p$, so $C(w_0) = \lceil \frac{x}{w_0} \rceil$. By definition, at the minimum, $\frac{x}{w} \leq \lceil \frac{x}{p} \rceil$, so w_0 is the smallest w for which $w \geq \frac{x}{\lceil \frac{x}{p} \rceil}$.

Hence, $w_0 = \left\lceil \frac{x}{\lceil \frac{x}{p} \rceil} \right\rceil$. □

Corollary : *The minimum value of*

$$C(w) = \lfloor \tfrac{z_l}{w} \rfloor \lceil \tfrac{w}{p} \rceil + \lfloor \tfrac{z_r}{w} \rfloor \lceil \tfrac{w}{p} \rceil + \lceil \tfrac{z_l (mod\ w)}{p} \rceil + \lceil \tfrac{z_r (mod\ w)}{p} \rceil$$

is $\lceil \frac{z_l}{p} \rceil + \lceil \frac{z_r}{p} \rceil$. *The smallest* w *for which* $C(w)$ *reaches minimum is* $\max\left(\left\lceil \frac{z_l}{\lceil \frac{z_l}{p} \rceil} \right\rceil, \left\lceil \frac{z_r}{\lceil \frac{z_r}{p} \rceil} \right\rceil \right)$.

If c is the communication cost per packet and e is the execution cost of one data item then the time a processor $P(i)$ spends in computing a wavefront strip of length p_h is

$$E = cC(w) + wp_h e \tag{6}$$

Corollary shows that the smallest w that minimizes $C(w)$ in (5) is less than or equal to p_l. Consequently, if w_0 minimizes expression (6) then $w_0 \leq p_l$. But for $w \leq p_l$

$$\frac{z_l}{w} + \frac{z_r}{w} \leq C(w) = \left\lceil \frac{z_l}{w} \right\rceil + \left\lceil \frac{z_r}{w} \right\rceil \leq \frac{z_l}{w} + \frac{z_r}{w} + 2$$

Hence,

$$\left(\frac{c}{w}\right)\left(\frac{z_l + z_r}{p_h}\right) + we \leq \frac{E}{p_h} \leq \left(\frac{c}{w}\right)\left(\frac{z_l + z_r}{p_h}\right) + we + \frac{2c}{w} \tag{7}$$

E/p_h is the execution cost (computation cost plus communication cost) per unit length of computation along the direction of computation. Expression (7) suggests that to find the optimum wavefront we should minimize $\frac{z_l+z_r}{p_h}$.

$P = min\left(\frac{z_l+z_r}{p_h}\right) =$

$$\min_{\substack{\theta \\ \beta < \theta < \alpha + \pi}} \left\lceil \frac{\max_i (x_i cos\theta + y_i sin\theta, 0) + \max_i (-x_i cos\theta - y_i sin\theta, 0)}{\min_i (y_i cos\theta - x_i sin\theta)} \right\rceil \tag{8}$$

At any angle θ of the wavefront at most three distance vectors are needed to determine P. As θ changes the needed vectors change, but they remain the same when θ stays within a range of angles. The angle at which the vectors change satisfies at least one of the following conditions

$$x_i cos\theta + y_i sin\theta = x_j cos\theta + y_j sin\theta$$
$$y_i cos\theta - x_i sin\theta = y_j cos\theta - x_j sin\theta, \quad \text{for some } 1 \le i, j \le n,\ i \ne j$$

Let $\{\gamma_1, \ldots, \gamma_m\}$ be a sorted list of all θ in $\beta < \theta < \alpha + \pi$ for which the above conditions are satisfied, i.e., $\{\gamma_1, \ldots \gamma_k\}$ is the sorted list of all $\theta_{ij} = arctan\left(\frac{x_j - x_i}{y_i - y_j}\right)$ and $\phi_{ij} = arctan\left(\frac{y_j - y_i}{x_j - x_i}\right)$ $1 \le i, j \le n$, $i \ne j$ such that $\beta < \theta_{ij}, \phi_{ij} < \alpha + \pi$. As previously, let $\gamma_0 = \beta + \delta$ and $\gamma_{m+1} = \alpha + \pi - \delta$, where δ depends on the resolution of the implementation. For each range of angles θ in (γ_j, γ_{j+1}), $j = 0, 1, \ldots, m$ we need to find the n distance vectors ($n \le 3$) which define P. In each of the ranges $\gamma_j \le \theta \le \gamma_{j+1}$, P can be written as

$$P = \frac{a cos\theta + b sin\theta}{c cos\theta - d sin\theta} \qquad c cos\theta \ne d sin\theta$$

for some constants a, b, c and d. Now,

$$\frac{\delta P}{\delta \theta} = \frac{ad + bc}{(c cos\theta - d sin\theta)^2}$$

If $ad + bc = 0$, $P = 1$, so for all $\theta, \gamma_j \le \theta \le \gamma_{j+1}$, P is minimum. Otherwise the minimum is at the boundaries of the range. So the global minimum of P can be obtained by finding $\theta \in \{\beta - \delta, \alpha + \pi - \delta\}$ which minimizes (8). Thus, the optimum direction of computation can be obtained in $O(n^2)$ time. Once θ is known, all the parameters other than w in (6) can be calculated. Often $max(\lceil z_l / \lceil \frac{z_l}{p} \rceil \rceil, \lceil z_r / \lceil \frac{z_r}{p} \rceil \rceil)$ is the smallest w that minimizes E/p_h, but sometimes [10] it maybe necessary to search a small range of values (in $w \le max(\lceil z_l / \lceil \frac{z_l}{p} \rceil \rceil, \lceil z_r / \lceil \frac{z_l}{p} \rceil \rceil)$) to find the best w.

In our analysis we have assumed a continuum of data elements in an array. In reality the arrays are discrete, so the analysis is approximate. When z_l and z_r are much larger than p_l, the algorithm gives a more accurate result.

The method can be applied to any set of uncoupled recurrence equations. First, a good data alignment should be determined using the methods described in section 5. Let us assume that the processor $P[I, J]$ needs to communicate with n distinct processors $\{P[I + x_i, J + y_i] : 1 \le i \le n\}$ to evaluate all the array elements assigned to it. Under this assumption, it is necessary to consider pairs $\{(x_i, y_i) : 1 \le i \le n\}$ as distance vectors defining the optimum direction of computation.

6 Conclusion

A straightforward translation of an EPL program oriented towards a CM-style SIMD machine may be performed based on the choice of some set of projections for the data structures, and on the substitution of data-parallel operations for sequential loops. This straightforward translation may be improved by alignment of data elements in the computation in such a way as to reduce the communication cost.

In the distributed memory environment alignment is even more important due to the high cost of communication. We have discussed the complexity of the alignment problem and presented two exact algorithms and one polynomial-time approximate algorithm for finding a good alignment for arrays defined by a set of uncoupled recurrence equations. For more general type of index references, a good alignment may require inverting the data element subscripts, e.g. for $A[I,J] = B[J,I]$ we can easily invert B to align with A. The complexity of the alignment problem without any restriction still remains an open question.

To reduce the total execution cost we also need to find a good wavefront of computation. Assuming a continuum of data elements in two-dimensional arrays computed on a linear array of processors, efficient algorithms have been presented to determine the optimum wavefront of computation and the optimum width of data elements that a processor should compute in order to minimize the total execution time. In reality, the arrays are discrete, and it is still to be seen how well the algorithms work in a real implementation. The research is ongoing on the implementation issues and on finding algorithms for an enumeration of points that belong to a wavefront region assigned to a single processor.

References

[1] W.B. Ackerman, *Data Flow Languages*, Computer, Vol. 15, No. 2, pp. 15-25, February 1982.

[2] G.S. Almasi and A. Gottlieb, *Highly parallel computing*, The Benjamin/Cummings PC, New York, NY, 1989.

[3] van Emde Boas, P. 1981. *Another NP-complete problem and the complexity of computing short vectors in a lattice*, Rep. 81-04, Math. Inst. Univ. Amsterdam

[4] C. Bron and J. Kerbosh, *Finding All Cliques of an Undirected Graph*, CACM, Vol. 16, No. 9, 1973, pp. 575-577.

[5] K.M. Chandy and J. Misra, *Parallel Program Design - A Foundation*, Addison-Wesley, New York, 1988, p. 179.

[6] M.J. Flynn, *Some Computer Organizations and Their Effectiveness*, IEEE Trans. on Comp. Vol. C-21, 1972, pp. 948-960.

[7] W.D. Hillis and G.L. Steele, Jr. *Data Parallel Algorithms*, Comm. of ACM, Vol. 29, 1986, pp. 1170-1183.

[8] Kannan, R. 1980. *Minkowski's convex body theorem and integer programming*, Math. Operations Res. Vol. 12, No. 3, August 1987, pp. 415-440

[9] Sinharoy, B., Szymanski, B. 1990. *Complexity issues of the alignment problem and the closest vectors in a lattice*, Technical Reports, Computer Science Department, Rensselaer Polytechnic Institute, September, 1990

[10] Sinharoy, B., Szymanski, B. 1990. *Finding optimum wavefront of computation*, Technical Reports, Computer Science Department, Rensselaer Polytechnic Institute, September, 1990

[11] B. Szymanski, *EPL - Parallel Programming with Recurrent Equations*, in Parallel Functional Programming, B. Szymanski, Edt., ACM Press, New York, NY, 1991, in press.

Languages, Compilers and Run-Time Environments
for Distributed Memory Machines
J. Saltz and P. Mehrotra (Editors)

Parallelizing Programs for Distributed-Memory Machines using the Crystal System

Marina Chen, Dong-Yuan Chen, Yu Hu,
Michel Jacquemin, Cheng-Yee Lin, and Jan-Jan Wu

Computer Science Department, Yale University, 2158 Yale Station, New Haven, CT 06520

Abstract This paper presents our position towards the issues raised by the program committee. It describes the Crystal language, its parallelizing compiler, and the performance of two benchmarks on four kinds of parallel machines. We show how a high level program specification can be efficiently compiled for different target machines and give reasonable performance.

1 Introduction

The grand challenge of high performance computing requires innovative software technologies as well as fundamental algorithmic solutions for realizing the full capability of the new generation of massively parallel computers. As stated in the goal of this workshop, distributed memory architectures are playing an increasingly important role in high performance computation as parallelism is exploited at larger scale. Like many researchers in this field, we now believe strongly that directly programming massively parallel machines by explicit communication or synchronization commands is not the way to go. It requires explicit control and microscopic management of parallel resources; it is also tedious, error-prone, and often unwieldy for producing and maintaining efficient application code.

We describe in this paper our position towards the issues put forward by the program committee of this workshop via our experience with constructing the Crystal parallelizing compiler. We believe that the task of programming massively parallel machines can be made practical without sacrificing the efficiency of the target code. We illustrate that the dual goals of programming ease and efficiency can be achieved by starting from a high-level problem specification that is architecture independent, through a sequence of optimizations tuned for particular parallel machines, leading to the generation of efficient target code with explicit communications. The target machines used to demonstrate our results include the Intel iPSC/2, Intel iPSC/860, nCUBE 6400, and the Connection Machine 2. The source language used is Crystal, a functional language. We also discuss how a parallelizing FORTRAN system for distributed-memory machines can be constructed via the Crystal system.

We first provide our view to the questions raised by the program committee in Section 2. Section 3 provides the Crystal parallel programming model, which we believe transcends the particular language and syntax given. We describe in Section 4 the structure of the Crystal system and compilation techniques developed. In Section 5, performance results of compiler-generated code are given. We then give a brief description of our on-going "Crystalizing FORTRAN" project in Section 6.

2 Summary of Our Position

Q: What additional information is required to efficiently map a sequential program onto a distributed memory machine?

A: First, if the sequential program is loosely synchronous in nature [15] and operates on some regular data structure such as arrays, automatic parallelization for distributed memory with high efficiency is entirely achievable, likely in the next few years when many new compilation techniques become available.

If the data structure is irregular (e.g. tree structure), we believe that the most crucial additional information required from the user is on the algorithmic contents of the sequential program: the sequential program must use an *incremental* algorithm to update and change the connectivity of the data structure. This incrementality will always be required if performance is of concern, no matter how sophisticated future compilers and run-time systems will be.

In the short term, practical systems will require information from the user for scheduling and partitioning data structures in order to minimize communication overhead and achieve load balancing. But we believe that with the incrementality assumption above, scheduling and partitioning information may not be necessary in the long run when sophisticated compile-time analyses are coupled with automated run-time scheduling and data partitioning techniques.

Q: What constructs need to be added to conventional languages to express the above information?

A: Incrementality requires re-thinking of the algorithm. An interim solution for user-directed scheduling and data distribution will require constructs such as domain morphisms in Crystal, to be described later. Data types can be used to specify the intensional aspect of the program and to direct the compiler. For example, Crystal uses types of index domain to indicate parallel schedules. Typing pointers can facilitate the dependence analysis of pointer data structures.

Q: What compiler techniques are required to transform a high-level specification for execution on nonshared memory machines?

A: Parallelization for distributed-memory machines requires, at the very minimum, all types of loop transformations, domain alignment, generating parameterized data layout, and generating explicit communication from program references. The Crystal compiler illustrates construction of such a basic compiler where additional analysis and optimization modules can be added.

Q: What are the run-time optimizations necessary for efficient implementation of the restructured code?

A: The run-time system must at the very least support high-level and aggregate communication routines efficiently coded for optimized performance, as opposed to merely supporting the "send" and "receive" primitives.

Hybrid compile-time and run-time support will be the way of the future. New compile-time analysis for pointers and indirect references will prove to be crucial in optimizing run-time system performance.

Q: Are minor modifications and annotations of conventional languages adequate or do we need new programming paradigms and styles?

A: Our experience with Crystal indicates that getting conventional languages to work by adding minor modifications and annotations will be easier than teaching old programmers new languages. However, new thinking is required for parallel and incremental algorithms to achieve high performance, even though you can program in the same old FORTRAN language.

Caveat The above position statement is speculative in nature, and some claims may require years to substantiate.

We now turn to something more concrete, the Crystal language and compiler.

3 The Crystal Model and its Language and Metalanguage Features

Crystal is a functional language with data parallel constructs. The goal of the Crystal language [14, 12, 13, 17, 16] is to provide programmers with high-level mathematical notations for expressing the algorithmic contents of a problem with as little low level implementation as possible.

Unique to Crystal as a functional language is the extension of this class of languages with first order functions defined over *index domains* to express composite data structures for which the notion of locality of data references can be explicitly defined. *Index domains* are abstractions of the "shapes" of composite data structures, which in most current programming languages are not first-class objects. *Data fields* generalize the notion of distributed data structures, unifying the conventional notions of arrays and functions. *Communication forms* defined over an index domain are means of specifying the data dependencies, and the inverse of a communication form provides useful directives for optimizing inter-processor communication. Finally, of central importance is the notion of *domain morphism*, which describes the reshaping of index domains aimed at optimizing data or control structures for efficiency reasons, as well as the necessary mapping from the logical structure of the problem to the physical domain of the machine and sequencing in time.

Data Fields A function f from domain A to codomain B is denoted $f : A \to B$. A *data field* f is a function defined over some index domain D (to be explained later) into some domain of values V, and is defined using function-abstraction:

f = df x:D { exp[x] }.

For example, the following data field defines the factorial function.

```
fac = df n : int { if n=0 then 1 || else n*fac(n) }
```

3.1 Index Domains

An *index domain* D consists of a set of elements (called indices), a set of functions from D to D (called communication operators), a set of predicates, and the communication cost associated with each communication operator.

In essence, an index domain is a data type with communication cost associated with each function or operator. The reason for making the distinction is that index domains will usually be finite and they are used in defining distributed data structures (as functions over some index domain), rather than their elements being used as values. For example, rectangular arrays can be considered to be functions over an index domain consisting of a set of ordered pairs on a rectangular grid. Also, the elements of an index domain can be interpreted as locations in a logical or real space and time over which the parallel computation is defined. We thus classify index domains into certain *kinds* (second order types) according to how they are to be interpreted (for example, as time or space coordinates).

Basic Index Domains Let e_1, e_2, ...,e_n be expressions denoting integer values. An *interval* index domain is constructed by interval(e_1,e_2), with e_1 being its *lower bound* and e_2 being its *upper bound.* It contains $e_2 - e_1 + 1$ points indexed from e_1 to e_2. If $e_2 < e_1$, then interval(e_1,e_2) is empty. An *enumerated* index domain is constructed by dom{e_1;e_2;...;e_n}. It contains n points indexed by the values of e_1,..., e_n. Having duplicate elements is permitted and data fields defined over them will have only one value for the same index.

Index Domain Constructors and Operators Let d_0, ...,d_n be index domain expressions. The product domain is denoted by the expressions prod_dom(d_0,...,d_n). Let x_0 be an expression denoting an element in d_0, and x_n an element of d_n; the tuple (x_0,...,x_n) is an element of prod_dom(d_0,...,d_n).

Let x be a formal, d a domain expression, e another domain expression with occurrences of x, and f a filter (i.e., a boolean expression) with occurrences of x. The expression dom[x:d|f] is a *domain restriction* denoting the restricted domain that contains only points of d that pass the filter.

Functions are provided for computing cardinality, lower and upper bounds of a domain, and testing membership.

Example Below are examples of domain expressions.

```
d1 = interval(1,3)
d2 = dom[(x,y):prod_dom(d1,d1)|(x <= y)]
```

The domain `d1` contains points indexed by the set { 1,2,3 }. The domain `d2` contains points indexed by the set { (1,1),(1,2),(1,3),(2,2),(2,3),(3,3) }.

3.2 Kinds of Index Domains

As discussed above, it is useful to indicate how an index domain is to be interpreted by "typing" index domains with "kinds" (second-order types). Analogous to the first-order typing, $D[\mathcal{K}]$ will mean that the index domain D is of kind $\mathcal{K}$. The following are the kinds we have found useful for compiler optimizations:

Universal ($\mathcal{U}$): the kind of any index domain as well as any other data type, such as the integers and the reals.

Temporal ($\mathcal{T}$): the kind of index domain representing time coordinates (subkind of $\mathcal{U}$).

Spatial ($\mathcal{S}$): the kind of index domain representing space coordinates (subkind of $\mathcal{U}$).

Processor ($\mathcal{P}$): the kind of index domain representing processor coordinates (subkind of $\mathcal{S}$).

Memory ($\mathcal{M}$): the kind of index domain representing memory locations within a processor (subkind of $\mathcal{S}$). Memory hierarchy can be introduced with other kinds $\mathcal{M}_i$ which are subkinds of $\mathcal{M}$, where i ranges over the levels of the memory hierarchy.

3.3 Index Domain Morphisms

Index domain morphisms formalize the notion of transforming one index domain into another, with the kinds of the domains indicating the change of interpretations.

Definition Let D and E be two index domains. An *index domain morphism* is a function g from D to E such that for all elements x and y in D, if there exists a composition τ of communication operators $\tau_1 \circ \tau_2 \circ \cdots \tau_k$ over D such that $y = \tau(x)$, then there is a composition τ' of communication operators $\tau'_1 \circ \tau'_2 \circ \cdots \tau'_{k'}$ over E such that $g(y) = \tau'(g(x))$.

The extra constraint ensures that if there is a path in the first domain from x to y, then there is a path from $g(x)$ to $g(y)$.

Reshape Morphisms For any index domain morphism $g : D \to E$, a *left inverse*, if it exists, is an index domain morphism $h : E \to D$ such that $h \circ g = 1_D$, the identity morphism over D. If g is also a left inverse of h (i.e., $g \circ h = 1_E$), then h is called the *inverse* of g and is denoted by g^{-1}. A morphism that has an inverse is commonly known as an isomorphism but here will be called a *reshape morphism* to emphasize the idea of "reshaping" one index domain into another.

To require the existence of the left inverse implies that a reshape morphism must be bijective. However, we can easily derive a reshape morphism from an injective domain morphism by restricting the codomain as follows: Given an injective domain morphism $g' : D \to E$, the image of D under g', denoted `image(`D`,`g'`)`, is an index domain whose elements are the image of the elements of D and whose communication operators are those of E. Clearly, $g : D \to$ `image(`D,g'`)`, derived from g', now has a well-defined left inverse.

Here are examples of some useful reshape morphisms:

1. An *affine morphism* is a reshape morphism which is an affine function from one product of intervals to another. Affine morphisms unify all types of loop transformations (interchange, permutation, skewing) [2, 3, 6, 28, 29], and those for deriving systolic algorithms [18, 26, 27, 10]. For example, if `d1 = interval(0,3)` and `d2 = interval(0,6)`, then `g = fn(i,j):prod_dom(d1,d2){(j,i):prod_dom(d2,d1)}` is an affine morphism which effectively performs a loop interchange.

Another example illustrates a slightly more interesting codomain `e` of the morphism `g1` by taking the image of a function `g1`.

```
d0  = interval(0,3)             d = prod_dom{d0,d0}
e   = image(d,g1) where g1 = df(i,j):d{(i-j,i+j)}
g   = df(i,j):d{(i-j,i+j):e}    ginv = df(i,j):e{((i+j)/2,(j-i)/2):d}
```

Whenever it is legal to apply this affine morphism to a 2-level nested loop structure— consistent with the data dependencies in the loop body [1, 2, 4, 5, 7, 28])— a similar structure, but "skewed" from the original, is generated. The most common case is when elements of the inner loop can be executed in parallel, but where only half of the elements are active in each iteration of the outer loop. In this example, the index domain `e` has holes, so guards in the loops must test whether `i+j` and `i-j` are even, since only these points correspond to the integral points in `d`. In the Crystal Metalanguage [30], such a transformed loop is derived algebraically. This particular reshape morphism happens to be one that can be automatically performed by all existing parallelizing compilers. However, the reshape morphism as defined in Crystal is quite general and it can be used to describe transformations that are hard to do automatically by compiler. Once such a morphism is given, the Crystal metalanguage performs as much algebraic simplification as possible to generate efficient transformed code.

2. A *uniform partition* of a domain D is a reshape morphism $g : D \to D_1 \times D_2$, with the property that the codomain has a greater number of component domains (i.e., is of higher dimensionality).

For example,if `d = interval(0,11)`, `d1 = interval(0,3)` and `d2 = interval(0,2)` then

`g = df i:d[`$\mathcal{S}$`]{(i/3,i mod 3):prod_dom(d1[`$\mathcal{P}$`],d2[`$\mathcal{M}$`])}`

is a uniform partition that distributes the elements of an index domain of the spatial kind as follows: the 12 elements are partitioned into 3 blocks of 4 elements each, each block is assigned to a processor, and each element in a block is assigned to some memory location.

There are numerous other forms of reshape morphisms ranging from "piece-wise affine" morphisms for more complex loop transformations [25], to those that are mutually recursive with the program (to be transformed) for dynamic data distribution. Reshaping morphisms provide programmers user directives for helping the compiler generate optimized code.

4 The Crystal Compiler

The Crystal compiler consists of three major stages: the front-end, middle-analysis, and back-end as shown in Figure 1. The frond-end builds the abstract syntax tree and other necessary data structures for an input Crystal program.

The middle-analysis consists of the traditional semantic and dependence analyses, the more novel reference pattern and domain analyses, and other source level transformations. At the heart of the compiler is a module for generating explicit communication from shared-memory program references [19, 21, 22]. Index domain alignment[20, 23] considers the problem of optimizing space allocation for arrays based on the cross-reference patterns between them.

The availability of massively parallel machines opens up opportunities for programs that have large scale parallelism to gain tremendously better performance than those that do not. We have recently obtained new results in program dependency analysis (more accurate dependency tests in the presence of conditional statements) [24] and developed new loop transformation techniques [25], both aimed at extracting more parallelism than existing techniques.

The back-end contains code generators and run-time systems. The code generation consists of two separate steps: the Crystal code generator produces procedure calls to the communication routines supported by the run-time system together with *Lisp code for the CM/2 or C code for the hypercube multiprocessors. The sequential code together with run-time library routines forms interface between the parallelizing compiler and the single processor (e.g. superscalar architecture) compiler, as shown in Figure 1.

The second step of code generation is to invoke a vendor-supported compiler to compile *Lisp or C into lower-level or machine code. In the case of Connection Machine 2, the *Lisp compiler generates PARIS instructions, which we found can be further optimized by a simple *expression compiler* that provides significant performance improvements as shown in the next section. Since then, Thinking Machines Corporation (TMC) has developed a new instruction set with the so-called *slice-wise* data representation that allows far better control of the underlying hardware and thus potentially offers much better performance. Unfortunately, TMC is not committed to supporting *Lisp targeted to the slice-wise instructions. Consequently, our current approach of *Lisp-Paris-Expression compiler will not be used in future development. A direct path to some kind of intermediate code will be taken instead.

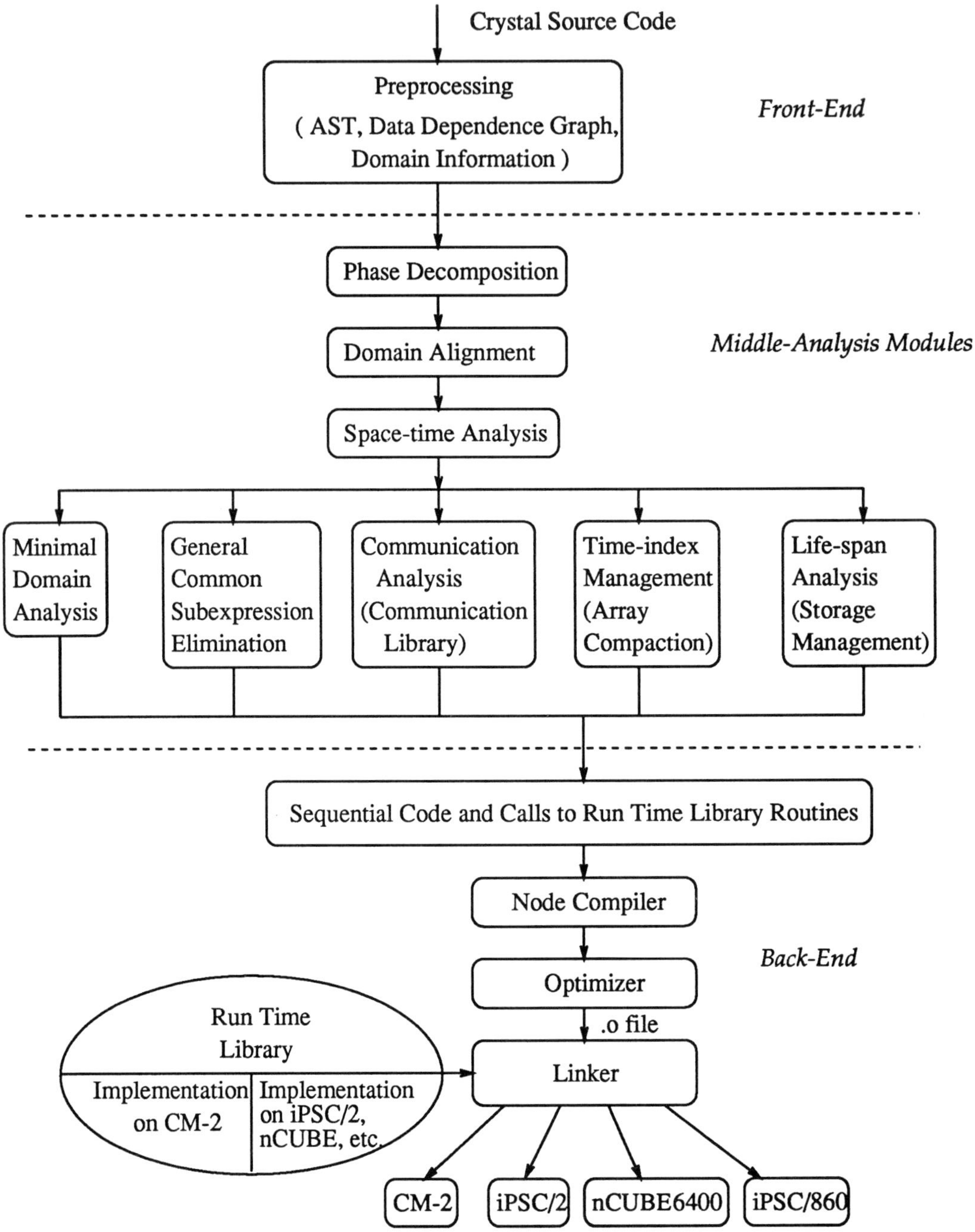

Figure 1: The Sturucture of Compiler

5 Performance Results

Two benchmark programs, one for weather forecasting and the other for semiconductor simulation, are used to examine the performance of the compiler-generated code on three MIMD hypercube multiprocessors, namely, Intel iPSC/2, iPSC/860, and nCUBE 6400, and the Connection Machine which is of SIMD architecture.

The performance results with the highest megaflop rates obtained for the compiler-generated code on these four machines are given in Table 2 and Table 3. As a reference, we also give the peak and nominal megaflop rates of each of the four machines in Table 1.

5.1 Machine Configuration and System Software Used

The Intel iPSC/2 located at Yale has 64 Intel 80386 processors, runs Unix V/386 3.2 as its host operating system, NX 3.2 for the nodes, and provides the Intel 3.2 C compiler.

The iPSC/860 machine (iPSC/2 with i860 node processors) located at Oak Ridge National Labs (ORNL) has 128 processors, but at most 64 processors are used for this experiment. This machine has the C compiler supplied by Portland Group.

The nCUBE 6400 located at Sandia National Labs has 1K processors although only 64 processors are used for our experiment. It runs Sun 4 as its front-end and provides the NCC 3.11 C compiler.

The timing results for the Connection Machine 2 are measured on an 8K processor CM-2 where each processor has 256K bits of memory and each group of 32 processors share a 64-bit Floating Point Units. CM software version 6.0 and *LISP compiler 6.0 are used. The *Lisp compiler generates PARIS instructions which are in the so-called *field-wise* data format.

An expression compiler developed at Yale generates optimized field-wise CMIS instructions whose memory accesses are greatly reduced. The performance results with and without the expression compiler are presented for the two applications. All results on the Connection Machine are extrapolated to a full CM-2 with 64K processors, i.e. 2K 64-bit floating-point units.

Table 1
Performance of parallel machines used

Machine	#Nodes	Peak Mflops/node	Nominal Mflops/node
iPSC/2 (Yale)	64	1.10	0.65
iPSC/860 (ORNL)	128	80.00	6.00 – 10.00
nCUBE 2 (Sandia)	1024	8.00	1.00
CM-2 (Seduto, TMC)	8096 (512 FPU)	7.00	-

5.2 Shallow Water Equation Solver

Shallow Water equations are used to model the global motions of atmospheric flows in weather forecasting. The algorithm is iterative, operating on two-dimensional grids with local computation at each grid point and data exchanges between neighboring grid points. The Crystal program for this Shallow Water equation solver is given in the appendix.

Table 2 presents the execution time and megaflop rates of this application for different machines. In this experiment, 64 processors are used for each of the three MIMD machines. The problem size used is 256K×120 (area × iteration). For the Connection Machine, a much larger problem size, 16M× 120, is used. Due to difficulty with the node compiler of the i860 chip, we aren't able to get much beyond 2 megaflops per processor. Given the same problem size, the computation on an iPSC/860 processor is 8 times faster than that of an iPSC/2 processor while its communication capability is about 4.5 times faster, thus resulting in a higher percentage of communication overhead for the iPSC/860. Quadrupling the problem size for iPSC/860 increases the total rate to about 180 megaflops, with the percentage of computation time slightly lower at 87% due to the superlinear effects of data caching.

For this application, CM-2 has more significant communication overhead, about 60% of which is due to local data copying and 40% actual interprocessor communication. One possible explanation for the higher percentage of communication overhead for the CM result is the following: Each processor on a hypercube machine computes a sub-grid, and the data exchange involves only the boundary grid points whereas the each CM processor iterates over the virtual processors, forcing the data movement of all grid points either by actual communication between processors or by local copying within processors.

Table 2
Performance of the Shallow Water Equation Solver

Machine	Total Time	Computation		Communication		Mflops
	Seconds	Seconds	%	Seconds	%	
iPSC/2	85.208	80.392	94.3	6.846	5.7	24.00
iPSC/860	11.805	10.371	87.9	1.552	12.1	173.21
nCUBE 2	31.269	29.479	94.3	2.377	5.7	65.39
CM-2 (*LISP)	67.862	43.530	64.1	24.332	35.9	1840.00
CM-2 (*LISP/CMIS)	47.472	23.152	48.8	24.320	51.2	2630.00

The speedup of execution time with an increasing number of processors on these machines are shown in Figures 2(a) and 2(b). The problem size used is 64K×120 for hypercube machines, and 4M×120 for CM-2. As a CM-2 cannot be configured into many different sizes, the 4K processor configuration is used as the basis. Some of the points in Figure 2(b) are extrapolated from the timings on one machine size with different number of virtual processors (vp-ratios). We can do this because vp-ratio is the predominant

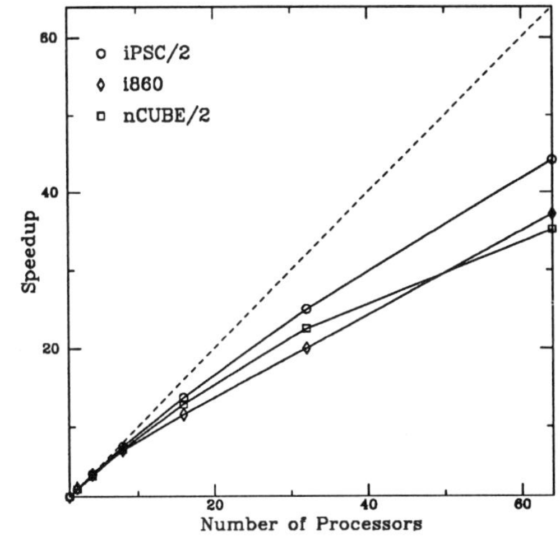

(a) Speedup of Shallow Water Code on Hypercube Machines

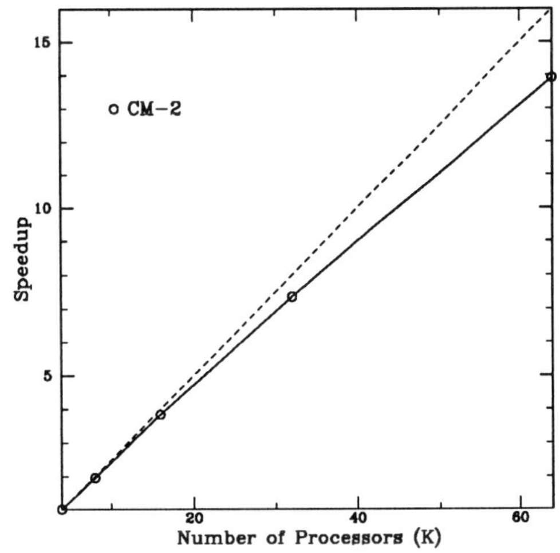

(b) Speedup of Shallow Water Code on CM-2

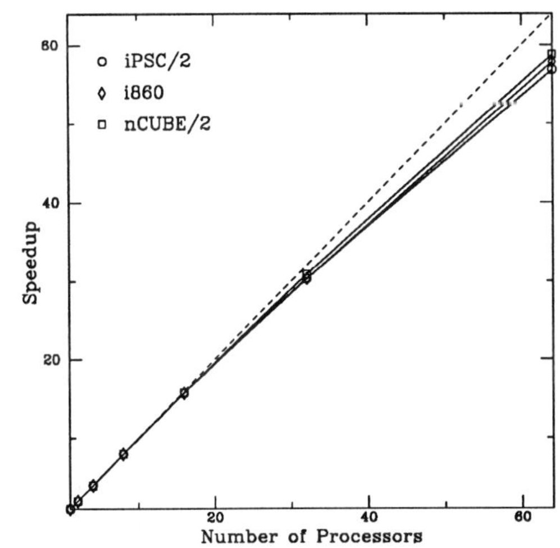

(c) Speedup of Bohr Code on Hypercube Machines

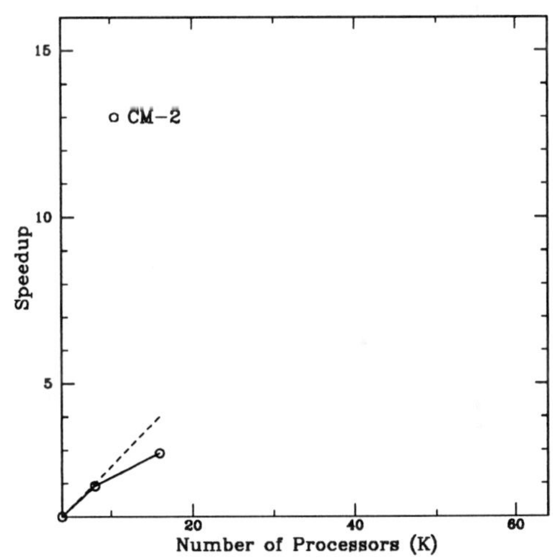

(d) Speedup of Bohr Code on CM-2

Figure 2: Speedups of Shallow Water and Bohr applications.

factor for determining the computation time and communication time between adjacent processors.

Bohr Code

Bohr code is an application using Monte Carlo methods for semiconductor simulations. It contains many independent trials (nmax is the local array size in each trial) which can be done concurrently on different processors, with a global reduction summarizing the result of all trials.

Table 3 presents the execution time and megaflop rates for this code. Similar to the above, 64 nodes are used for the three MIMD machines for this benchmark. The problem size used is 4K×4 (trials × nmax) for the MIMD machines and 256K× 64 for the CM.

Since the only communication needed for this application is a global reduction at the end of program execution, communication time is an almost a negligible portion of total execution time.

Table 3
Performance of Bohr code

Machine	Total Time	Computation		Communication		Mflops
	Seconds	Seconds	%	Seconds	%	
iPSC/2	12.413	12.331	99.3	0.081	0.7	26.40
iPSC/860	3.348	3.320	99.2	0.028	0.8	97.87
nCUBE 2	8.148	8.115	99.6	0.033	0.4	40.22
CM-2 (*LISP)	45.054	43.926	97.5	1.128	2.50	2370.00
CM-2 (*LISP/CMIS)	31.460	30.350	96.5	1.110	3.53	3400.00

The speedups of Bohr code on different machines are shown in Figures 2(c) and 2(d). The problem size used here is 4K×4 for the three MIMD machines, and 16K×10 for CM-2.

For obtaining speedup results on the CM-2, the same problem size must be used for all machine configurations. Due to the heavy use of memory in this application, the largest problem size which can fit on a 4K-processor configuration will run on a 16K-processor machine with one virtual processor per node. Consequently, a larger machine will be useful only for a larger problem. Hence the speedup results are only given for three configurations. Again, we extrapolate the speedup results based on a single physical machine size. According to the timing result, the small percentage of the reduction time indicates the accuracy of extrapolation although, in isolation, global reduction depends on the machine size as well as the problem size.

6 Crystalizing FORTRAN

The clean semantics and nice algebraic properties of a functional language such as Crystal have greatly facilitated the development of compilation techniques for distributed-memory machines. Our goal of making a functional language practical for parallel computing remains unchanged. The scientific-engineering community, however, still uses FORTRAN as its most common language (both for existing and new code).

There exists a large body of work on how to analyze and subsequently parallelize FORTRAN programs for vector and shared-memory machines. Thus we want to take advantage of the preprocessing and program analysis technologies of these FORTRAN compilers and combine them with those of the Crystal middle-analysis modules and back-ends to construct parallelizing compilers for distributed-memory machines.

As a joint effort with Ron Y. Pinter of IBM Scientific Center in Haifa, Israel and Shlomit S. Pinter of Dept. of Electrical Engineering, Technion, Israel [11], we have now made an initial investigation as to whether such systems can produce reasonably efficient code [9]. Figure 3 gives the top level view of a translator from FORTRAN to Crystal (FC-Translator) based on dependence information generated by Parascope [8] and/or Parafrase2. Text files are used to exchange information between these programs. The translation algorithm turns each loop nest into a Crystal data field where the dimensionality of its index domain is a function of the number of loop levels, the dimensionality of the array variables, and the dependence relation. The main source of inefficiency of the translated Crystal program lies in extraneous conditionals generated due to the control structures occuring in the FORTRAN program. FORTRAN programs that preallocate a large array and then use portions of that array piece-by-piece will be translated to a Crystal program containing many conditionals. Extensive symbolic simplification and partial evaluation are necessary for optimizing the translated Crystal code.

The FORTRAN-77 program for the Shallow Water equation solver we obtained from Sandia National Labs. is translated by the prototype translator described in [9]. The translated Crystal program is then parallelized using the Crystal compiler for the four parallel machines. The initial result is quite encouraging: only about 25% worse than the hand-crafted Crystal program in the compiler-generated-parallel-code performance on all machines.

References

[1] J. R. Allen. *Dependence Analysis for Subscript Variables and Its Application to Program Transformation.* PhD thesis, Rice University, April 1983.

[2] J. R. Allen and K. Kennedy. Automatic loop interchange. In *Proceedings of the SIGPLAN'84 Symposium on Compiler Construction*, pages 233–246. ACM, 1984.

[3] J.R. Allen and K. Kennedy. Automatic translation of FORTRAN programs to vector form. *ACM Transactions on Programming Languages and Systems*, 9(4):491–542, October 1987.

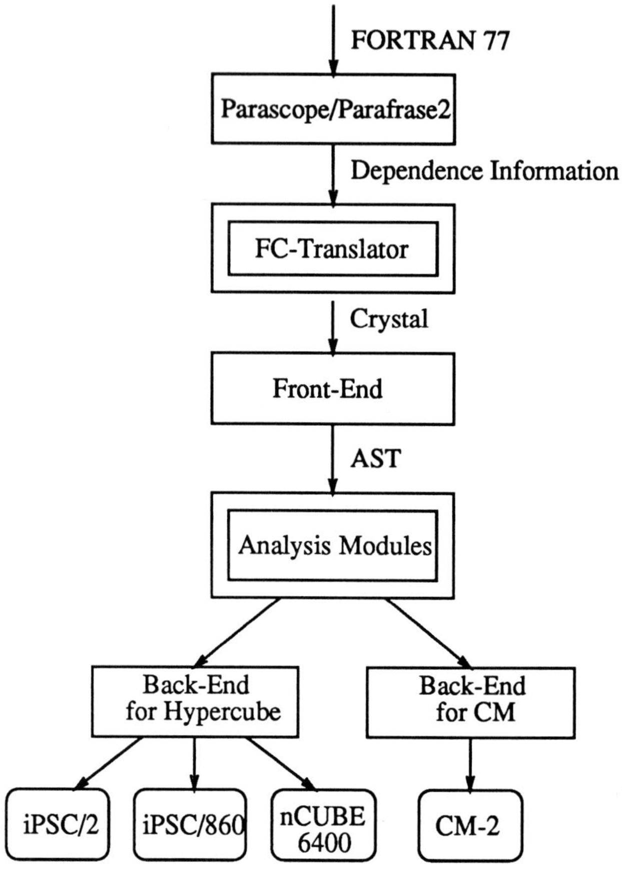

Figure 3: Top level view of FORTRAN to Crystal translator.

[4] U. Banerjee. Data dependence in ordinary programs. Master's thesis, University of Illinois at Urbana-Champaign, November 1976.

[5] U. Banerjee. *Speedup of Ordinary Programs.* PhD thesis, University of Illinois at Urbana-Champaign, October 1979.

[6] U. Banerjee. A theory of loop permutation. Technical report, Intel Corporation, 1989.

[7] M. Burke and R. Cytron. Interprocedural dependence analysis and parallelization. In *Proceedings of the SIGPLAN'86 Symposium on Compiler Construction*, pages 162–175. ACM, 1986.

[8] Alan Carle, Keith D. Cooper, Robert T. Hood, Ken Kennedy, Linda Torczon, and Scott K. Warren. A practical environment for scientific programming. *Computer*, pages 75–89, Nov. 1987.

[9] Dong-Yuan Chen and Marina Chen. Parallelizing FORTRAN programs for massively parallel machines via Crystal. Technical report, Yale University, 1991.

[10] M. Chen, Y. Choo, and J. Li. Compiling parallel programs by optimizing performance. *The Journal of Supercomputing*, 1(2):171–207, July 1988.

[11] M. Chen, R. Pinter, and S. Pinter. "Crystalizing" FORTRAN. Technical report, Yale University, 1990.

[12] Marina Chen, Young-il Choo, and Jingke Li. Compiling parallel programs by optimizing performance. *The Journal of Supercomputing*, 1(2):171–207, July 1988.

[13] Marina Chen, Young-il Choo, and Jingke Li. Theory and pragmatics of generating efficient parallel code. In *Parallel Functional Languages and Compilers*, chapter 7. ACM Press and Addison-Wesley, 1991.

[14] Marina C. Chen. A parallel language and its compilation to multiprocessor machines. In *The Proceedings of the 13th Annual Symposium on POPL*, January 1986.

[15] Geoffrey C. Fox, Mark A. Johnson, Gregory A. Lysenga, Steve W. Otto, John K. Salmon, and David W. Walker. *Solving Problems on Concurrent Processors.* Prentice Hall, 1988.

[16] Michael Henry. Crystal compiler primer, version 3.0. Technical report YALEU/DCS/TR849, Dept. of Computer Science, Yale University, March 1991.

[17] Michel Jacquemin and J. Allan Yang. Crystal reference manual, version 3.0. Technical report YALEU/DCS/TR840, Dept. of Computer Science, Yale University, March 1991.

[18] R. Karp, R. Miller, and S. Winograd. The organization of computations for uniform recurrence equations. *Journal of the ACM*, 14(3):563–590, July 1967.

[19] Jingke Li and Marina Chen. Generating explicit communications from shared-memory program references. In *Proceedings of Supercomputing'90*, 1990.

[20] Jingke Li and Marina Chen. Index domain alignment: Minimizing cost of cross-reference between distributed arrays. In *The Proceedings of the 3rd Symposium on the Frontiers of Massively Parallel Computation*, 1990.

[21] Jingke Li and Marina Chen. *Proceedings of the Workshop on Programming Languages and Compilers for Parallel Computing*, chapter Automating the Coordination of Interprocessor Communication. MIT Press, 1990.

[22] Jingke Li and Marina Chen. Compiling communication-efficient programs for massively parallel machines. *IEEE Transaction on Parallel and Distributed Systems*, 1991.

[23] Jingke Li and Marina Chen. The data alignment phase in compiling programs for distributed-memory machines. *Journal of Parallel and Distributed Computing*, 1991.

[24] Lee-chung Lu and Marina Chen. Subdomain dependency test for massively parallelism. In *Proceedings of Supercomputing'90*, 1990.

[25] Lee-chung Lu and Marina Chen. A unified framework for systematic applications of loop transformations. Technical report, Yale University, 90.

[26] D.I. Moldovan. On the analysis and synthesis of VLSI algorithms. *IEEE Trans. on Computers*, C-31(11):1121–1126, Nov. 1982.

[27] P. Quinton. Automatic synthesis of systolic arrays from uniform recurrent equations. In *Proceedings of 11th Annual Symposium on Computer Architecture*, pages 208–214, 1984.

[28] M.J. Wolfe. *Optimizing Supercompilers for Supercomputers.* PhD thesis, University of Illinois at Urbana-Champaign, 1982.

[29] M.J. Wolfe. *Optimizing Supercompilers for Supercomputers.* The MIT Press, 1989.

[30] J. Allan Yang and Young-il Choo. Parallel-program transformation using a meta-language. In *Proceedings of The Third ACM SIGPLAN Symposium on Principles and Practice of Parallel Programming, Williamsburg, Virginia*, pages 11–20, April 1991.

A Appendix

This appendix contains a Crystal program for the Shallow Water Equation Solver.

```
!!   This Crystal code is written based on a Fortran 77 program used
!!   by Sandia National Labs.  The theoretic part of this code is
!!   based on the paper "The dynamics of finite-difference models of
!!   the Shallow Water equations" by R. Sadourny, J. ATM SCI Vol 32 #4
!!   April 1975.

!! Index Domains
!! -------------

time = interval(0,itmax)
e = prod_dom(interval(0,m),interval(0,n))
space_e = prod_dom(interval(0,m-1),interval(0,n-1))
ee = interval(0,min(m,n)-1)
D = prod_dom(interval(0,m-1),interval(0,n-1),interval(0,itmax))

!! Constants
!! ---------

m = 32                          mp1 = m+1
n = 32                          np1 = n+1
itmax = 10                      pi = 4.*atan(1.)
a = 1000000.                    di = tpi/m
```

```
dt = 90.                          dj = tpi/n
time = 0.0                        tpi = pi+pi
dx = 100000.                      alpha = .001
dy = 100000.
fsdx = 4./dx
fsdy = 4./dy

!! Data Fields
!! -----------

tdt = df (k) : time { if k==0 then 90.0 || else 180.0 fi }

tdts8 = df (k) : time { tdt(k)/8.0 }
tdtsdx = df (k) : time { tdt(k)/dx }
tdtsdy = df (k) : time { tdt(k)/dy }

psi = df (i,j) : e { a*sin((i+.5)*di)*sin((j+0.5)*dj) }

u0 = df (i,j) : space_e {
        if i>0  then -(psi(i,j+1)-psi(i,j))/dy
        || i==0 then -(psi(m,j+1)-psi(m,j))/dy
        fi }

v0 = df (i,j) : space_e {
        if j>0  then (psi(i+1,j)-psi(i,j))/dx
        || j==0 then (psi(i+1,n)-psi(i,n))/dx
        fi }

u = df (i,j,k) : D { if k==0 then u0 || else unew(i,j,k-1) fi }
v = df (i,j,k) : D { if k==0 then v0 || else vnew(i,j,k-1) fi }
p = df (i,j,k) : D { if k==0 then 50000. || else pnew(i,j,k-1) fi }

cu = df (i,j,k) : D { .5*(p(i,  j,k)+p((i-1) mod m,  j,k))*u(i,j,k) }
cv = df (i,j,k) : D { .5*(p(i,j,k)+p(i,(j-1) mod n,k))*v(i,j,k) }

z = df (i,j,k) : D { (fsdx*(v(i,j,k)-v((i-1) mod m,j,k))
                     -fsdy*(u(i,j,k)-u(i,(j-1) mod n,k)))
                     /(z_p(i,j,k) + z_p(i,(j-1) mod n,k)) }

z_p = df (i,j,k) : D { p(i,j,k)+p((i-1) mod m,j,k) }

h = df (i,j,k) : D { p(i,j,k)+.25*(h_u(i,j,k) + h_u((i+1) mod m,j,k)
                            +h_v(i,j,k)+h_v(i,(j+1) mod n,k)) }

h_u = df (i,j,k) : D { u(i,j,k)*u(i,j,k) }
h_v = df (i,j,k) : D { v(i,j,k)*v(i,j,k) }

unew = df (i,j,k) : D { uold(i,j,k)+tdts8(k)*(z(i,(j+1) mod n,k)+z(i,j,k))
                             *(unew_cv(i,j,k)+unew_cv((i-1) mod m,j,k))
                             -tdtsdx(k)*(h(i,j,k)-h((i-1) mod m,j,k)) }

unew_cv = df (i,j,k) : D { cv(i,(j+1) mod n,k)+cv(i,j,k) }
```

```
vnew = df (i,j,k) : D { vold(i,j,k)-tdts8(k)*(z((i+1) mod m,j,k)+z(i,j,k))
                              *(vnew_cu(i,j,k)+vnew_cu(i,(j-1) mod n,k))
                              -tdtsdy(k)*(h(i,j,k)-h(i,(j-1) mod n,k))  }

vnew_cu = df (i,j,k) : D { cu((i+1) mod m,j,k)+cu(i,j,k) }

pnew = df (i,j,k) : D { pold(i,j,k)-tdtsdx(k)*(cu((i+1) mod m,j,k)-cu(i,j,k))
                                -tdtsdy(k)*(cv(i,(j+1) mod n,k)-cv(i,j,k)) }

uold = df (i,j,k) : D {
        if k==0 or k==1 then u0(i,j)
        || else u(i,j,k-1)+alpha*(unew(i,j,k-1)-2.*u(i,j,k-1)+uold(i,j,k-1))
        fi }

vold = df (i,j,k) : D {
        if k==0 or k==1 then v0(i,j)
        || else v(i,j,k-1)+alpha*(vnew(i,j,k-1)-2.*v(i,j,k-1)+vold(i,j,k-1))
        fi }

pold = df (i,j,k) : D {
        if k==0 then 50000.
        || k==1 then p(i,j,0)
        || else p(i,j,k-1)+alpha*(pnew(i,j,k-1)-2.*p(i,j,k-1)+pold(i,j,k-1))
        fi }

!! print initial values (only those on diagonals)
!! ---------------------------------------------------

iuold = df (i) : ee { uold(i,i,0) }
ivold = df (i) : ee { vold(i,i,0) }
ipold = df (i) : ee { pold(i,i,0) }

? "Print initial values:"
? iuold
? ivold
? ipold

!! print final values (only those on diagonals)
!! ---------------------------------------------------

funew = df (i) : ee { unew(i,i,itmax) }
fvnew = df (i) : ee { vnew(i,i,itmax) }
fpnew = df (i) : ee { pnew(i,i,itmax) }

? "Print Final values:"
? funew
? fvnew
? fpnew
```

Languages, Compilers and Run-Time Environments
for Distributed Memory Machines
J. Saltz and P. Mehrotra (Editors)

Iteration Space Tiling for Distributed Memory Machines

J. Ramanujam† and P. Sadayappan‡

†Department of Electrical and Computer Engineering, Louisiana State University, Baton Rouge, LA 70803-5901. Email: jxr@max.ee.lsu.edu

‡Department of Computer and Information Science, The Ohio State University, Columbus, OH 43210-1277. Email: saday@cis.ohio-state.edu

Abstract

This paper addresses the problem of compiling nested loops for distributed memory machines. The relatively high communication start-up costs in these machines renders frequent communication very expensive. Motivated by this, we present a method for aggregating a number of loop iterations into **tiles** where the tiles execute atomically. Since synchronization is not allowed during the execution of a tile, partitioning the iteration space into tiles must not result in deadlock. We present an approach to determine the shape, size, allocation and scheduling of tiles for efficient parallel execution of 2-level tightly nested loops on distributed memory machines with given execution and communication costs.

1 Introduction

Distributed memory machines (multicomputers) offer high levels of flexibility, scalability and performance but programming these machines remains a difficult task. The message-passing paradigm employed in these machines makes program development significantly different from that for conventional shared memory machines. It requires that processors keep track of of data distribution and that they communicate with each other by explicitly moving data around in messages. As a result, parallelizing compilers for these machines have received great attention recently [2,5-7,12-15,21-24,27,29-32]. In addition, with current technology, the communication overhead is still at least an order of magnitude larger than the corresponding computation. The relatively high communication start-up costs in these machines renders frequent communication very expensive. This in turn calls for careful partitioning of the problem and efficient scheduling of the computations as well the communication.

Motivated by this concern, we present ways of partitioning nested loops and scheduling them on distributed memory machines with a view to optimizing the granularity of the resultant partitions. Nested loops are common in a large number of scientific codes and most of the execution time is spent in loops. In addition, they often lend themselves to simpler analyses. We present a method for aggregating a number of loop iterations into **tiles** where the tiles execute atomically – a processor executing the iterations belonging to a tile receives all the data it needs before executing any one of the iterations in the tile, executes all the iterations in the tile and then sends the data needed by other processors. Since synchronizations are not allowed during the execution of a tile, partitioning the iterations into tiles must not lead to deadlock. Given a perfectly nested loop to be executed on a multicomputer with given execution and communication costs, the tile shape and size have to be chosen so as to optimize the performance; in addition, the tiles must be assigned to processors to minimize communication costs and reduce processor idle times. We present an approach to determine the shape, size, allocation and scheduling of tiles for 2-level nested loops on distributed memory machines.

There have been tremendous advances in recent years in the area of intelligent routing mechanisms and efficient hardware support for inter-processor communication in message passing distributed memory machines [8]. These techniques reduce the communication overhead incurred by processor nodes that are incident on a path between a pair of communicating processors – this in turn greatly simplifies the task of mapping the partitions onto the processors. Therefore, we do not address the mapping problem here.

Section 2 discusses dependence analysis and other background material and presents a discussion of related work. In section 3 of this paper, we discuss the issues involved in tiling. Section 4 relates the concept of **extreme vectors** to deadlock-free tiling leading to section 5 where an algorithm to compute the extreme vectors in 2-dimensional iteration spaces is presented. Section 6 presents a method to choose deadlock-free tiles. Section 7 discusses **tile space graphs (TSGs)** and the scheduling and allocation of two dimensional tiles. In section 8, we discuss the determination of tile size so as to optimize the execution of nested loops on multicomputers. Section 9 summarizes the work and concludes with a discussion of further work.

2 Background

Good and thorough parallelization of a program critically depends on how precisely a compiler can discover the data dependence information. These dependences imply precedence constraints among computations which have to be satisfied for a correct execution. Many algorithms exhibit regular data dependences, *i.e.* certain dependence patterns occur repeatedly over the duration of the computation.

2.1 Data Dependence

Consider a loop structure of the form:

Example 1:
for $I_1 = l_1$ to u_1 do
  ...
    for $I_d = l_d$ to u_d do
      $S_x(\vec{I})$
      ...
      $S_y(\vec{I})$

---

where l_j and u_j are integer valued linear expressions involving $I_1, \ldots, I_{j-1}$ and $\vec{I} = (I_1, \ldots, I_d)$. $S_x, \ldots, S_y$ are assignment statements of the form $X_o = E(X_1, \ldots, X_k)$ where X_o is an output variable produced by expression E evaluated using some input variables $X_1, X_2, \ldots, X_k$.

The input variables of a statement are produced by other statements, and sometimes by the same statement at an earlier execution. Each computation is denoted by an index vector $\vec{I} = (I_1, \ldots, I_d)$.

Consider two statements S_x and S_y surrounded by perfectly nested loops. Note that S_x and S_y need not be two distinct statements. Data dependences are defined in [1, 3, 16, 17, 20, 28, 29]. A **flow dependence** exists from statement S_x to statement S_y if S_x computes and writes a value that can be subsequently (in sequential execution) read by S_y. Note that not all nest levels need to contribute to the dependence. A flow dependence implies that instances of S_x and S_y must execute as if some of the nest levels have to be executed sequentially. An **anti-dependence** exists between S_x and S_y if S_x reads a value that is subsequently written to by S_y. An **output dependence** exists between S_x and S_y if S_x writes a value which is subsequently written to by S_y. When dealing with loops (where the unit of scheduling is an iteration), dependence relations are represented as precedence constraints among the iterations of the loop.

2.2 Iteration Space Graph

Dependence relations are often represented in *Iteration Space Graphs* (ISG's); for an d-nested loop with index set $(I_1, I_2, \ldots, I_d)$, the nodes of the ISG are points on on a d-dimensional discrete Cartesian space and a directed edge exists between the iteration defined by $\vec{I_1}$ and the iteration defined by $\vec{I_2}$ whenever a dependence exists between statements in the loop constituting the iterations $\vec{I_1}$ and $\vec{I_2}$.

Many dependences that occur in practice have a constant distance in each dimension of the iteration space. In such cases, the vector $\vec{d} = \vec{I_2} - \vec{I_1}$ is called the **distance vector.** An algorithm has a number of such dependence vectors; the dependence vectors of the algorithm are written collectively as a **dependence matrix** $D = [\vec{d_1}, \vec{d_2}, \ldots, \vec{d_n}]$. In addition to the three types of dependence mentioned above, there is one more type of dependence known as **control dependence.** A control dependence exists between a statement with a conditional jump and another statement if the conditional jump statement controls the execution of the other statement. Of these data dependences, only flow dependence is inherent to the computation. In our analysis, we consider distributed memory machines where considering flow dependences alone is sufficient. Methods to calculate data dependence vectors can be found in [1, 3, 28, 29].

2.3 Related work in tiling and other memory optimizations

Chen et al. [6, 7] describes how Crystal, a functional language, addresses the issue of programmability and performance of parallel supercomputers. Gallivan et al. [9] discuss problems associated with automatically restructuring data so that it can be moved to and from local memories in the case of shared memory machines with complex memory hierarchies. They present a series of theorems that enable one to describe the structure of disjoint sub-lattices accessed by different processors, and how to use this information to make "correct" copies of data in local memories, and how to write the data back to the shared address space when the modifications are complete. Gannon et al. [10] discuss program transformations for effective complex-memory management for a CEDAR-like architecture with a three-level memory. In the context of hierarchical shared memory systems, Irigoin and Triolet [11] present a method, which divides the iteration space into clusters referred to as *supernodes*, with the goals of vector computation within a node, data re-use within a partition and parallelism between partitions. The procedure works from a new data dependence abstraction called dependence cones. King and Ni [12] discuss the grouping of iterations for execution on multicomputers; they present a number of conditions for valid tile formation in the case of two-dimensional iteration spaces. Mace [18] proves that the problem of finding optimal data storage patterns for parallel processing (the "shapes" problem) is NP-complete, even when limited to one- and two-dimensional arrays; in addition, efficient algorithms are derived for the shapes problem for programs modeled by a directed acyclic graph (DAG) that is derived by series-parallel combinations of tree-like subgraphs. Wolfe [27, 30] discusses a technique referred to as *iteration space tiling* which divides the iteration space of loop computations into *tiles* (or blocks) of some size and shape so that traversing the tiles results in covering the whole space. Optimal tiling for a memory hierarchy will find tiles such that all data for a given tile will fit into the highest level of memory hierarchy and exhibit high data reuse, reducing total memory traffic. In addition, in the context of loop unrolling, partitioning of iteration space graphs is discussed by Nicolau [19] and Callahan *et al.* [4].

2.4 Related work on compiling programs for multicomputers

Balasundaram and others [2] at CalTech are working on interactive parallelization tools for multicomputers that provide the user with feedback on the interplay between data decomposition and task partitioning on the performance of programs. Koelbel et al. [13, 14] address the problem of automatic process partitioning of programs written in a functional language called BLAZE given a user-specified data partition. A group led by Kennedy at Rice University [5] is studying similar techniques for compiling a version of FORTRAN 77 for the Intel iPSC/2 that includes annotations for specifying data decomposition; they show how some existing transformations could be used to improve performance. Rogers and Pingali [21] present a method which, given a sequential program and its data partition, performs task partitions to enhance locality of references. Zima et al. [15, 32] discuss SUPERB, an interactive system for semi-automatic transformation of FORTRAN 77 programs into parallel programs for the SUPRENUM machine, a loosely-coupled hierarchical multiprocessor.

3 Issues in tiling of iteration spaces

As mentioned earlier, the relatively high communication start-up costs in distributed memory machines renders frequent communication very expensive. For example, the message start-up time for Intel iPSC/2 in 250 μs for a packet where as the transmission cost per packet between neighboring nodes is about 10 μs; and access to local memory takes negligible time. Hence, we focus on collecting iterations together into *tiles* where each tile executes atomically with no intervening synchronization or communication; as a result, we are able to amortize the high message startup cost over larger messages at the expense of processor idle time.

Each tile defines an atomic unit of computation comprising of a number of iterations. All necessary data must be available before the beginning of execution of the tile and all data that are needed by some other processors for the execution of other tiles is available when the execution of the tile is complete – thus no synchronization or communication must be necessary during the execution of the tile. This imposes a constraint that the partitioning of the iteration space into tiles does not result in deadlock. This means that there are no cycles among the tiles. Thus the division into tiles must be compatible with the dependences on the nodes of the ISG. To keep code generation simple, it is also necessary that all tiles are identical in shape and size except near the boundaries of the iteration space.

Given the conditions on tiling, the problem is to choose a tile shape and size that minimizes execution time on a distributed memory machines with specified communication set-up and transfer costs and instruction execution rate. The approach involves:

1. determining valid partitioning of the iteration space (shape)
2. scheduling tiles
3. allocating tiles to processors to minimize communication and to reduce processor idle time
4. determining the granularity of tiles.

4 Extreme vectors and deadlock free tiling

We focus on tiles which are 2 dimensional subsets of 2-D iteration spaces. Tiles in 2-D spaces are defined by two families of parallel lines. Each such line is defined by a normal to it. Hence, tiles in 2-D iteration spaces are defined by a set of *two* vectors which are normals to the tile boundaries. Tiles defined in such a manner are parallelograms (except for those near the boundary of the iteration space). The shape of the tiles is defined by the families of lines and the size of the tiles is defined by the distance of separation between adjacent pairs of lines in each of the two families.

For tiles in 2-D iteration spaces to be legal, dependence vectors crossing a boundary between any pair of tiles must all cross from a given tile to the other *i.e.* the source of all the dependence vectors that cross the boundary must be in the same tile and their sink in the other. Any two vectors H_1 and H_2 define legal tiles if

$$H_i \cdot \vec{d_j} \geq 0, \qquad i = 1,2 \tag{1}$$

for all d_j in the set of dependence vectors **or** if

$$H_i \cdot \vec{d_j} \leq 0, \qquad i = 1,2. \tag{2}$$

The tile boundaries are aligned along the families of parallel lines in the 2-D case i.e. the tile boundaries are aligned along the normal to the vectors H_1 and H_2. The condition given here is from [11].

Based on results in linear and integer programming [25], the set of solutions to the system of linear inequalities in (1) is equivalent to the set of vectors that are expressible as a non-negative linear combination of two **extreme vectors** *i.e.*, the set of points that lie in the positive hull of two extreme vectors. In the case of 2-dimensional iteration spaces, the extreme vectors are a subset of the dependence vectors themselves. Thus, given a set of n distinct dependence vectors ($n \geq 2$), $\vec{d_1}, \vec{d_2}, \ldots, \vec{d_n}$, one can always find two vectors say $\vec{d_1}$ and $\vec{d_2}$ (from among the $\vec{d_i}$) such that

$$c_i\vec{d_i} = a_i\vec{d_1} + b_i\vec{d_2} \tag{3}$$

where $i = 1, \ldots, n$, $a_i, b_i \geq 0$ and $c_i > 0$. The vectors $\vec{d_1}$ and $\vec{d_2}$ are the two **extreme vectors.** Without loss of generality, we assume $\vec{d_1}$ and $\vec{d_2}$ are linearly independent. If the dependence matrix has rank 2, *i.e.*, the iterations of the nested loop can not be executed in parallel without requiring proper synchronization (DOACROSS loop) [29], $\vec{d_1}$ and $\vec{d_2}$ will be linearly independent.

Condition (1) is only a sufficient condition for the following reason: it is always possible to choose tiles that are small enough - the extreme example being tiles consisting of exactly one iteration where there are dependences that have their source and sink in that iteration.

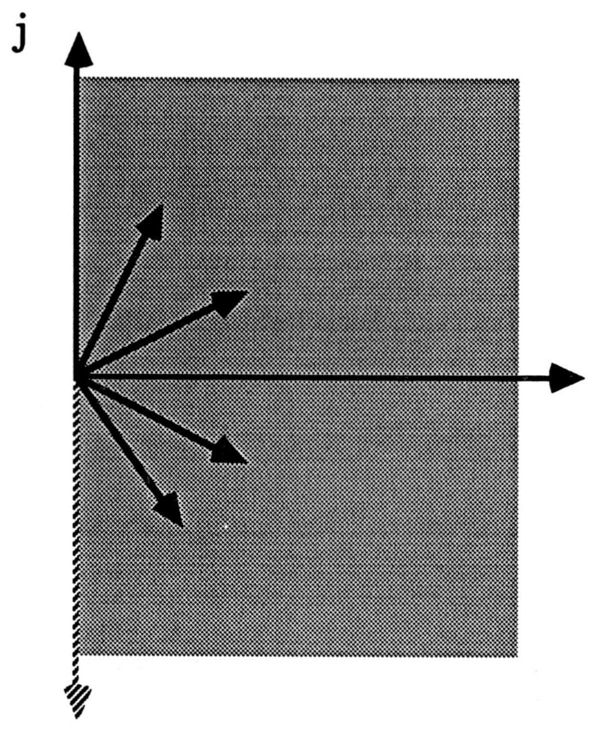

Figure 1: 2-dimensional iteration space and dependence vectors

5 Computing the extreme vectors

Here, we present an $O(n)$ algorithm for computing the extreme vectors, where n is the number of distance vectors and we assume that $n \geq 2$. It is based on the fact that in two dimensional iteration spaces, the first non-zero component in any distance vector must be non-negative and there are exactly two components to deal with. Therefore, distance vectors in 2-D iteration spaces are of one of the two following forms: $(0, \oplus)$ and $(+, *)$ where 0 stands for zero, $+$ represents positive integers, $*$ stands for all integers and $\oplus$ stands for non-negative integers. The distance vectors, therefore belong to the *first* and *fourth* quadrants (where the usual X-axis corresponds to the outer loop index variable i and the inner loop variable j is represented by the Y-axis). This is shown in Figure 1. The extreme vectors are the two vectors which have the maximum span from among all the dependence vectors *i.e.* every other dependence vector lies in the cone of the extreme vectors.

Let the components of each distance vector d_i be $(d_{i,1}, d_{i,2})$ where $d_{i,1}$ is the distance along the outer loop and $d_{i,2}$ is the distance along the inner loop. Find the ratio $r_i = \frac{d_{i,2}}{d_{i,1}}$ for all the dependence vectors (including the signs). The vectors with the highest and lowest values (one vector for each) are the extreme vectors. Note that if $d_{i,1} = 0$ for any d_i, then that vector is an extreme vector. If there is more than one vector with $d_{i,1} = 0$, we choose the vector with the smallest value of $d_{i,2}$ from among those. The largest and the smallest values among the r_i can be found in $O(n)$ time.

Consider the following loop:

Example 2:
for $i = 1$ to N
  for $j = 1$ to N
    $A[i,j] \leftarrow A[i,j-1] + A[i-1,j+2] + A[i-1,j] + A[i-1,j+1]$

The iteration space graph (ISG) is shown in Figure 2(a) and the distance vectors are shown in Figure 2(b). The loop has the following distance vectors $d_1 = (0,1)$, $d_2 = (1,-2)$, $d_3 = (1,0)$ and $d_4 = (1,-1)$; the ratios are $r_1 = \infty$, $r_2 = -2$, $r_3 = 0$ and $r_4 = -1$. r_1 has the highest ratio and and r_2 has the lowest ratio and therefore d_1 and d_2 are the extreme vectors. It is easy to verify that this is indeed the case.

However, in the case of higher dimensional iteration spaces, the extreme vectors need not be dependence vectors themselves [23, 24].

5.1 Transformational view of finding extreme vectors

The problem of finding extreme vectors in higher dimensions is discussed in [23] and in greater detail in the Ph.D. dissertation of the first author [24]. Here, we present the intuition behind the procedure in terms of 2-dimensional spaces. Intuitively, a transformation T is applied to the dependence matrix D such that every entry in the transformed dependence matrix is non-negative – in 2 dimensions, this is the minimum amount of "skewing" or "shearing" applied to the set of dependence vectors so that they "rotate" into the first quadrant. For the loop in example 2, the dependence matrix D is: (the columns are the dependence vectors):

$$D = \begin{pmatrix} 0 & 1 & 1 & 1 \\ 1 & 0 & -2 & -1 \end{pmatrix}$$

and transformation T is:

$$T = \begin{pmatrix} 1 & 0 \\ 2 & 1 \end{pmatrix}$$

and the transformed dependence matrix is:

$$D^+ = \begin{pmatrix} 0 & 1 & 1 & 1 \\ 1 & 2 & 0 & 1 \end{pmatrix}$$

6 Choosing deadlock-free tiles

The extreme vectors can always be used to form valid tiles. In addition, any non-negative linear combination of the extreme vectors can also be used as vectors (normals) defining the tile boundaries. Among the set of possible tilings, only the tiles defined by the extreme vectors lead to minimal communication. Choosing one of the tile boundaries aligned along an extremal vector results in communication only along the other tile boundary. Thus when we have n dependence vectors in two dimensional iteration spaces ($n \geq 2$), tile boundaries aligned along the extremal vectors $\vec{d_1}$ and $\vec{d_2}$ result in potential inter-processor communication across one of the tile boundaries alone for $\vec{d_1}$ and $\vec{d_2}$ and across both tile boundaries due to the rest of the dependence vectors (non-extremal vectors).

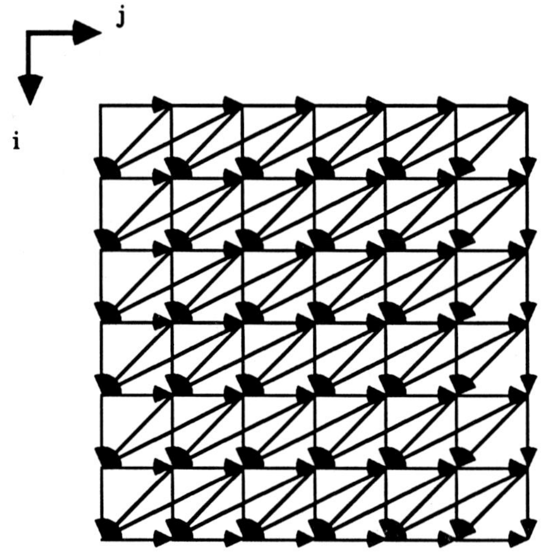

Figure 2(a): ISG of the loop in Example 2

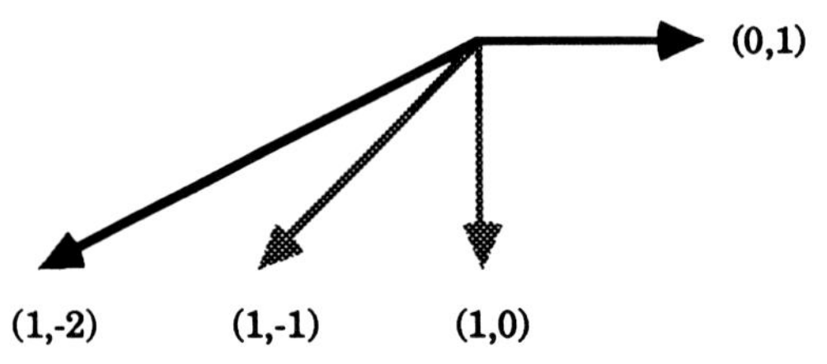

Figure 2(b): Distance vectors of Example 2
Note: The extreme vectors are shown darker

Figure 2: Iteration Space Graph and Distance Vectors for Example 2

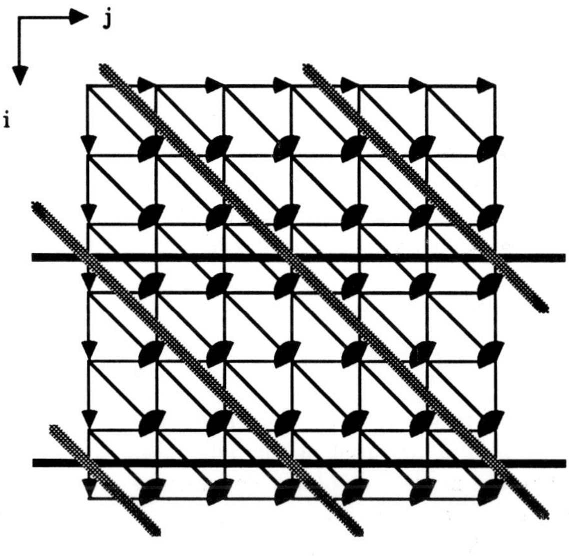

Figure 3: Tiles along $(0, 1)$ and $(1, 1)$ for example 3.
Note: Boundaries are shown in thicker lines. The slanted $(1, 1)$ boundary leads to deadlock.

With a view to reducing communication, one might consider aligning the tile boundaries along some of the non-extreme dependence vectors. Consider the following loop:

Example 3:
for $i = 1$ to N
  for $j = 1$ to N
    $A[i, j] \leftarrow A[i, j-1] + A[i-1, j] + A[i-1, j-1] + A[i-2, j-2]$

In tiling the above loop, if tile boundaries were along the vectors $(1, 1)$ and $(0, 1)$, number of synchronization points (data communicated across the boundaries) is less than the case where the boundaries are aligned along $(0, 1)$ and $(1, 0)$ but the former defines illegal tiles. Figure 3 illustrates this. In fact, we show the following result:

Theorem 1 *Tiles of arbitrary size aligned along any of the dependence vectors other than the extreme vectors are* **illegal** *tiles.*

Proof: Given a set of n distinct dependence vectors, $\vec{d_1}, \vec{d_2}, \ldots, \vec{d_n}$, where $\vec{d_1}$ and $\vec{d_2}$ are linearly independent extreme vectors i.e., any dependence vector $\vec{d_i}$ can be written as:

$$c_i\vec{d_i} = a_i\vec{d_1} + b_i\vec{d_2}$$

where $i = 1, \ldots, n$, $a_i, b_i \geq 0$ and $c_i > 0$. If a tile boundary is oriented along a non-extreme $\vec{d_i}$, then the vector defining the family of parallel lines is orthogonal to $\vec{d_i}$ i.e.,

$$H_i \cdot \vec{d_i} = 0$$

Therefore,

$$H_i \cdot \left(a_i\vec{d_1} + b_i\vec{d_2}\right) = 0$$

Thus $H_i \cdot \vec{d_1}$ and $H_i \cdot \vec{d_2}$ must have opposite signs, which violates the condition for legality, *i.e.* either $H_i \cdot \vec{d_j} \geq 0$ or $H_i \cdot \vec{d_j} \leq 0$ for all d_j in the set of dependence vectors. Hence the result.

□

Note that if the extremal vectors are not linearly independent, then all the dependence vectors have the same unit vector along them – in which case tiling along that direction is always valid. The condition is a sufficient condition for generation of free size tiles (FST). Given the dependences, one can always choose tiles of a fixed size which violate the condition but are still valid.

7 Tile Space Graph (TSG)

Given the dependence vectors in the ISG and the tile boundaries, the precedence relationships (dependences) among the tiles is captured in the Tile Space Graph (TSG). We assume here that tile size is larger than the magnitude of any dependence vector *i.e* the tile size along each dimension is larger than the largest of corresponding components of the dependence vectors. This assumption leads to the following situation:

- The source and sink of any dependence vector that crosses a tile boundary are neighboring tiles.
- There are no two distance vectors d_1 and d_2 that cross the boundary between two tiles T_i and T_j such that the source of d_1 and the sink of d_2 lie in T_i while the sink of d_1 and the source of d_2 lie in T_j i.e. tiling does not result in deadlock.

If the components of the dependence vectors are large in magnitude, it is possible to choose small tiles, which are valid tiles but do not satisfy the condition that dependence vectors crossing a given tile boundary all do so in the same direction. For example, when the dependence vectors are $(0,1)$, $(1,0)$ and $(5,-1)$, tiles defined by the vectors $(0,1)$ and $(1,0)$ are valid as long as the length of the tile along the first dimension is less than or equal to 5, even though $(1,0)$ is not an extreme vector.

7.1 Scheduling of tiles

We are interested in choosing the size of the tile in order to optimize the execution time; hence we are interested in free size tiles (FSTs). In 2-D space with a regular ISG, any free size tile (FST) can only depend on at most 3 neighbors which satisfy exactly one of the following 3 conditions:

1. The tile depends on three neighbors exactly; in this case, two of those neighbors both depend on the third neighbor.
2. The tile depends on only on one neighbor.
3. All tiles are independent (in which case, the ISG defines a fully parallel loop)

Cases 2 and 3 correspond to the condition when the rank of the dependence matrix is not 2 for the case of 2-nested loops. Case 1 corresponds to the case when the dependence matrix has rank 2 and we will discuss this case. Figure 4 shows a sample TSG for 2-D iteration spaces with all the possible TSG vectors namely, $(0,1)$, $(1,0)$ and $(1,1)$. Since tiles are executed

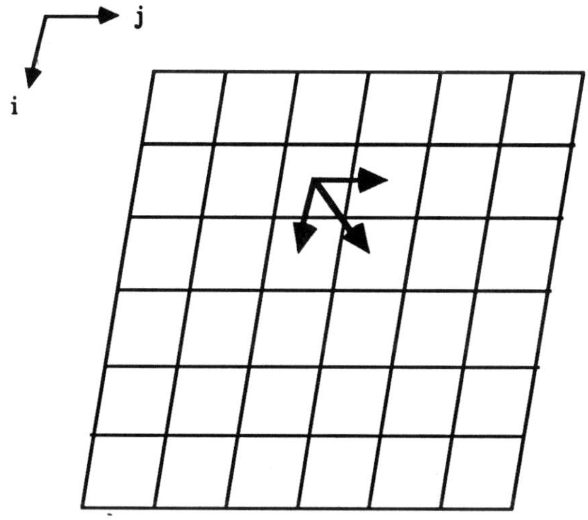

Figure 4: Tile Space Graph for 2-nested loops.
Note: The tile space vectors $(0,1),(1,0)$ and $(1,1)$ are also shown.

atomically, the $(1,1)$ is automatically covered by the other two. Therefore, the tiles in the Tile Space Graph (TSG) have uniform dependence vectors $(0,1)$ and $(1,0)$. For scheduling of tiles, the scheduling hyperplane must satisfy the conditions of Lamport's result on wavefront execution [17, 26]. The scheduling hyperplane given by $(1,1)$ which is a line at angle of 45 degrees satisfies the conditions for a valid schedule. Figure 5 shows the wavefront schedule for 2-D tile spaces. If both tile space vectors are present, $(1,1)$ defines the optimal scheduling of tiles. The computations within a tile can be executed in lexicographic order. If each processor in the multicomputer have vector capability, then one can define wavefronts for the computations within each tile.

7.2 Allocation of tiles to processors

In general we may have many more tiles than the number of processors. The tiles must be allocated so that inter processor communication is minimized while the computation is load-balanced through time. Since the tile space has $(1,0)$ and $(0,1)$, choosing allocations of tiles along either direction "internalizes" all communication in that direction. Because of the presence of presence of both tile dependences $(0,1)$ and $(1,0)$, no more than one tile can be active along either a row or column. Thus, allocating the tiles to processors by row or column results in minimal processor idle time. Idle time is experienced only in the beginning and near the end of execution of the iterations. The interplay between load balance and communication depends on tile size and this is discussed in the next section.

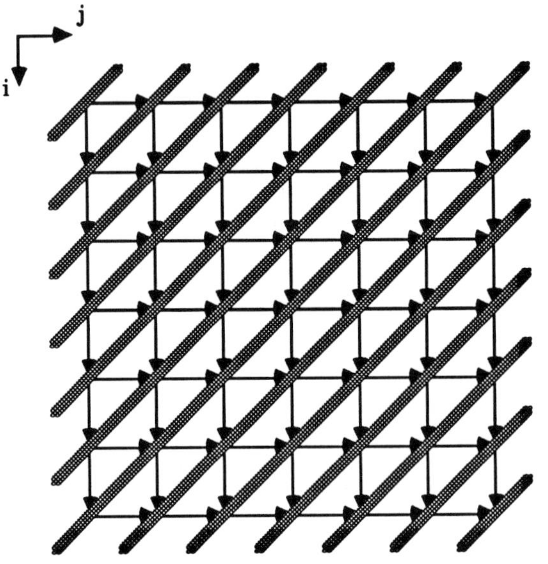

Figure 5: Wavefront scheduling of tiles in 2-D iteration spaces.
Note: The wavefronts are shown using thicker lines.

8 Optimizing tile size

Let the computation be defined by an ISG of dimension $n_i \times n_j$ i.e., the outer loop (say indexed by i) runs from 1 to n_i and the inner loop (say indexed by j) runs from 1 to n_j. We make this assumption that n_j and n_i are comparable. Let the tiles be defined by parallelograms whose sides are l_i along the i axis and l_j along the j axis and let $l_i = l_j = l$ for simplicity of the expressions. This results in rhombic tiles. We will assume for now that the number of processors is unlimited and later show the result for a limited number of processors. Also, we assume for now that $n_j = n_i = n$. Finally, we assume that all tiles in a column of the Tile Space Graph are allocated to the same processor. Let the setup cost for a packet be s; let the cost of data transmission be w. See Figure 6 for description of various terms. (All these costs are normalized with respect to the cost of executing a single iteration). Thus the communication cost model is:

$$t_{comm} = s + w \times \text{length}$$

Let $c_i * l$ be the number of data items that may have to be sent across the vertical boundary (along the i axis in the TSG) and $c_j * l$ be the number of data items that may have to be sent across the horizontal boundary (along the j axis in the TSG). Since, we assume a column allocation of tiles, data must be communicated only across the vertical boundary (the boundary along the i axis.) The cost of sending $c_i * l_i$ values to another processor is

$$s + wc_il_i$$

Since columns of tiles are allocated to processors in a wrap-around fashion, if the network connecting the processors has Hamiltonian cycle, the above cost is accurate. Given that $l_i \times l_j$

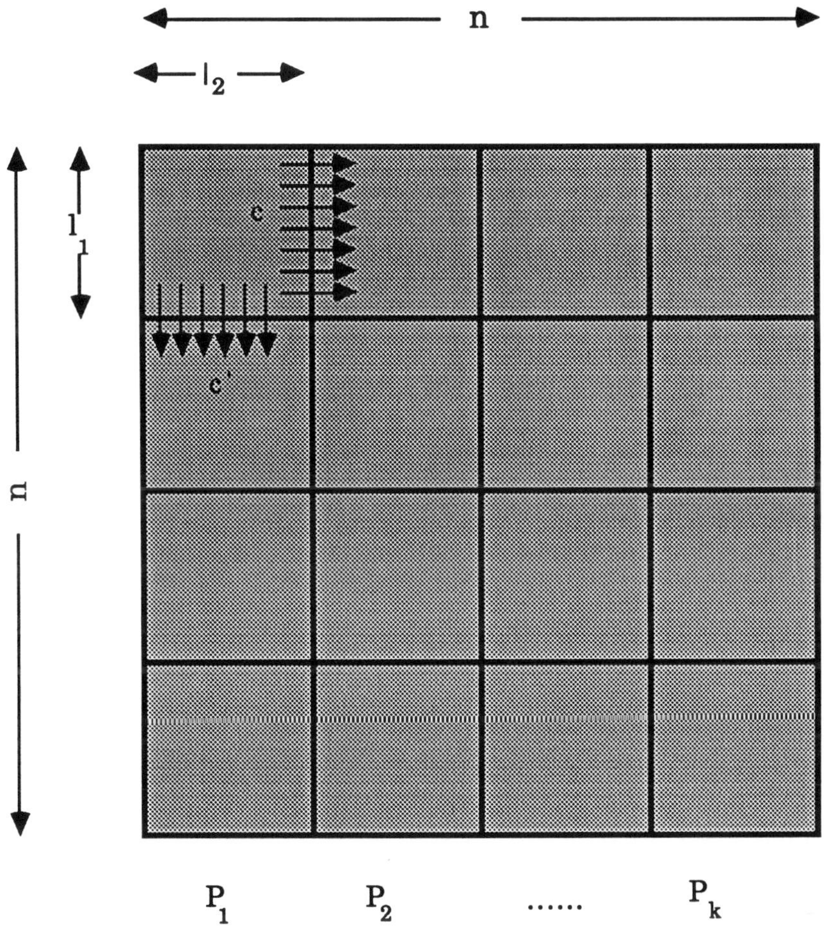

- Unbounded number of processors
- Column allocation
- $c < c'$

Figure 6: Tile size determination in 2-D iteration spaces

nodes have to be executed in a tile, the cost of execution of the tile is:

$$\frac{n}{l_i}[l_il_j + s + wc_il_i] + \left(\frac{n}{l_j} - 2\right)[l_il_j + s + wc_il_i] + l_il_j$$

The optimal tile size is one that minimizes this cost. In order to derive an expression for the optimal cost, (by solving for zeros of the derivative of the cost with respect to l) we assume that $l_i = l_j = l$ and that $\frac{n}{l} >> 1$. The time for execution (cost) is:

$$\text{Time,} \quad T = \frac{2n}{l}\left[l^2 + wcl + s\right]$$

Setting $dT/dl = 0$, we get

$$\frac{dT}{dl} = 0$$
$$\Longrightarrow \quad \frac{2n}{l}[2l + wc] - \frac{2n}{l^2}\left[l^2 + wcl + s\right] = 0$$

assuming $s \neq 0$. This leads to

$$l^2 = s \quad \text{or} \quad l_{opt} = \sqrt{s}$$

If $s = 0$, then

$$T = 2nl\,[l + wc]$$
$$\Longrightarrow \quad l_{opt} = 1$$

Similar results can derived for an overlapped communication model.

Thus, the tile boundaries induce a Tile Space Graph for which we have identified that the wavefront schedule $(1,1)$ is a valid scheduling hyperplane and in the case of dependence matrices whose rank is 2, this is also the optimal schedule when unlimited processors are available for loop execution.

9 Discussion

In this paper, we presented an approach to determine the shape and size of tiles for execution of nested loops on distributed memory machines; we presented sufficient conditions for legal tiles and a way to choose tile shapes for 2-D iteration spaces. In addition, we presented methods to allocate and schedule tiles on the processing nodes of a distributed memory machine and to determine the tile size that minimizes the execution time under our model. Given that $(1,1)$ is a valid scheduling wavefront in the Tile Space Graph, the amount of parallelism (the number of tiles that can potentially be executed in parallel) in the execution of tiles increases and then decreases; thus it is conceivable that increasing the tile size along each dimension uniformly and then decreasing the same might lead to more efficient execution. Further research needs to be done in estimating the effect of varying the tile size on the performance of parallel execution of tiles.

References

[1] R. Allen and K. Kennedy, "Automatic Translation of FORTRAN Programs to Vector Form," *ACM Trans. Programming Languages and Systems,* Vol. 9, No. 4, 1987, pp. 491-542.

[2] V. Balasundaram, G. Fox, K. Kennedy and U. Kremer. An interactive environment for data partitioning and distribution. *Proc. 5th Distributed Memory Computing Conference (DMCC5),* Charleston, S. Carolina, April 1990.

[3] U. Banerjee, *Dependence Analysis for Supercomputing,* Kluwer Academic Publishers, Boston, MA, 1988.

[4] D. Callahan, J. Cocke and K. Kennedy, "Estimating Interlock and Improving Balance for Pipelined Architectures," *Journal of Parallel and Distributed Computing,* Vol. 5, No. 4, Aug. 1988, pp. 334-358.

[5] D. Callahan and K. Kennedy, "Compiling Programs for Distributed-Memory Multiprocessors," *The Journal of Supercomputing,* Vol. 2, Oct. 1988, pp. 151-169.

[6] M. Chen, "A Design Methodology for Synthesizing Parallel Algorithms and Architectures," *Journal of Parallel and Distributed Computing,* Vol. 3, Dec. 1986, pp. 461-491.

[7] M. Chen, Y. Choo and J. Li, "Compiling Parallel Programs by Optimizing Performance," *The Journal of Supercomputing,* 2, 1988, pp. 171-207.

[8] W. Dally and C. Seitz, "Deadlock-free Message Routing in Multiprocessor Interconnection Networks," *IEEE Trans. Computers,* Vol. C-36, No. 5, pages 547–553, May 1987.

[9] K. Gallivan, W. Jalby and D. Gannon, "On the Problem of Optimizing Data Transfers for Complex Memory Systems," *Proc. 1988 ACM International Conference on Supercomputing,* St. Malo, France, pp. 238-253.

[10] D. Gannon, W. Jalby and K. Gallivan, "Strategies for Cache and Local Memory Management by Global Program Transformations," *Journal of Parallel and Distributed Computing,* Vol. 5, No. 5, October 1988, pp. 587-616.

[11] F. Irigoin and R. Triolet, "Supernode Partitioning," in *Proc. 15th Annual ACM Symp. Principles of Programming Languages,* San Diego, CA, Jan. 1988, 319-329.

[12] C. King and L. Ni, "Grouping in Nested Loops for Parallel Execution on Multicomputers," *Proc. International Conf. Parallel Processing,* 1989, Vol. 2, pp. II-31 to II-38.

[13] C. Koelbel, P. Mehrotra and J. van Rosendale, "Semi-automatic Process Partitioning for Parallel Computation," *International Journal of Parallel Programming,* Vol. 16, No. 5, 1987, pp. 365-382.

[14] C. Koelbel and P. Mehrotra, "Semi-automatic Process Decomposition for Non-shared Memory Machines," in *Proc. 1989 International Conference on Supercomputing,* May 1989.

[15] U. Kremer, H. Bast, H. Gerndt and H. Zima, "Advanced Tools and Techniques for Automatic Parallelization," *Parallel Computing,* Vol. 7, 1988, pp. 387-393.

[16] D. Kuck, R. Kuhn, B. Leasure, D. Padua and M. Wolfe, "Dependence Graphs and Compiler Optimizations," *Proc. ACM 8th Annual Symposium on Programming Languages,* Williamsburg, VA, Jan. 1981, pp. 207-218.

[17] L. Lamport, "The Parallel Execution of DO Loops," *Communications of the ACM,* Vol. 17, No. 2, Feb. 1974, pp. 83-93.

[18] M. Mace, "Memory Storage Patterns in Parallel Processing," Kluwer Academic Publishers, Boston, MA, 1987.

[19] A. Nicolau, "Loop Quantization: A Generalized Loop Unwinding Technique," *Journal of Parallel and Distributed Computing,* Vol. 5, No. 5, Oct. 1988, pp. 568-586.

[20] D. Padua and M. Wolfe, "Advanced Compiler Optimizations for Supercomputers," *Communications of the ACM,* Vol. 29, No. 12, Dec. 1986, pp. 1184-1201.

[21] A. Rogers and K. Pingali, "Process Decomposition Through Locality of Reference," *Proc. ACM SIGPLAN 89 Conference on Programming Language Design and Implementation,* Portland, OR, Jun. 1989, pp. 69-80.

[22] J. Ramanujam and P. Sadayappan, "A Methodology for Parallelizing Programs for Multicomputers and Complex Memory Multiprocessors," in *Proc. Supercomputing 89,* Reno NV, Nov. 13-17, 1989, pp. 637-646.

[23] J. Ramanujam and P. Sadayappan, "Tiling of Iteration Spaces for Multicomputers," *Proc. 1990 International Conference on Parallel Processing,* Vol 2, pages 179-186, August 1990.

[24] J. Ramanujam, "Compile-time Techniques for Parallel Execution of Loops on Distributed Memory Multiprocessors," Ph.D. Thesis, Dept. of Computer and Information Science, The Ohio State University, Columbus, OH, September 1990.

[25] A. Schrijver, *Theory of Linear and Integer Programming,* Wiley-Interscience series in Discrete Mathematics and Optimization, John Wiley and Sons, New York, 1986.

[26] M. Wolfe, "Loop Skewing: The Wavefront Method Revisited," *International Journal of Parallel Programming,* Vol. 15, No. 4, 1986, pp. 279-294.

[27] M. Wolfe, "Iteration Space Tiling for Memory Hierarchies," in *Parallel Processing for Scientific Computing,* G. Rodrigue (Ed.) SIAM, Philadelphia PA, 1987, pp. 357-361.

[28] M. Wolfe and U. Banerjee, "Data Dependence and Its Application to Parallel Processing," *International Journal of Parallel Programming,* Vol. 16, No. 2, 1987, pp. 137-178.

[29] M. Wolfe, *Optimizing Supercompilers for Supercomputers,* Pitman Publishing, London and MIT Press, 1989.

[30] M. Wolfe, "More Iteration Space Tiling," in *Proc. Supercomputing 89,* Reno NV, Nov. 13-17, 1989, pp. 655-664.

[31] M. Wolfe, "Loop Rotation," Technical Report CS/E 89-004, Oregon Graduate Center, May 1989. Also to appear in a monograph to be published by Springer-Verlag.

[32] H. Zima, H. Bast and H. Gerndt, "SUPERB: A Tool for Semi-automatic MIMD/SIMD Parallelization," *Parallel Computing,* Vol. 6, 1988, pp. 1-18.

Languages, Compilers and Run-Time Environments
for Distributed Memory Machines
J. Saltz and P. Mehrotra (Editors)

Systolic Loops

Michael Wolfe

Oregon Graduate Institute, Beaverton, OR 97006, USA

Abstract

Massively parallel machines are programmed large through data parallelism. This corresponds to partitioning the data (typically arrays) among the processors and partitioning the work (loop iterations) to align with the data. Often (if not always) there is communication required between the processors. Automatically detecting when communication is required and scheduling the communication is the subject of much recent research. In this presentation we will focus on a method of classifying loops into several categories. One obvious category is the case when each processor can pre-load all the data required for completion of its partition of work. In the general case, this may require an unbounded amount of memory at each node. With limited memory at each node, the amount of data loaded locally at one time must be fixed. We therefore distinguish another loop category, which we call systolic loops, which may be theoretically parallel, but in which we interleave the computation and communication to reduce memory requirements. Our work focusses on explicit program transformations to generate optimized object code from a parallel or sequential input program.

1. SUMMARY

In this paper we discuss some issues about how programs which are written with a shared memory computer model can be compiled for machines with distributed memory. We focus on parallel loops as the source of parallelism and user-directed storage distribution for laying out the data in the processor ensemble; the parallelism may have been specified by the user or discovered automatically. This work is related to and builds on the work of others [3, 6]. The reader is assumed to know the basics of data dependence relations and iteration spaces [2, 13]. We assume in general a multidimensional mesh or ring ensemble of processors.

We introduce several important types of loops which can be processed with this paradigm. A *local-data* loop comprises computations on data which is all stored on the processor computing that iteration. A *preload-data* loop comprises computations on data that can all be preloaded into the processor; this job is simplified if the addresses are reversible (the "owner" processor of the data knows its destination). Both these types of loops have *essential* loop nest equal to the dimensionality of the processor array. Some loops that are not fully parallel but have dependences with reversible addresses can be classified as *linear dependence* loops. Loops which use non-reversible addresses, whether parallel or not, are *random access* loops; these present special difficulties since the processor holding a section of data may not know what other processor or processors need to use this section. A *systolic* loop can occur when the essential loop nest is greater than the dimensionality of the processor array, and data must flow (systolically) across the ensemble. *Serial* loops can and should be executed in a distributed fashion, across the processor ensemble, to reduce the total amount of data traffic.

This paper really focuses on the systolic loop, so called because a similarity to systolic array execution. We summarize how systolic arrays are designed from Uniform Recurrence Equations, by finding mapping functions from the iteration space ($\bar{I}=I_1 \times I_2 \times \cdots \times I_d$) to a time dimension ($T(\bar{i})=\lambda\bar{i}$, where λ is a $1 \times d$ array) and a processor or spatial dimension ($S(\bar{i})=A\bar{i}$, where A is a $a \times d$ array such that $a \leq d-1$). We then show how finding this time function is essentially equivalent to *loop skewing,* which is a loop restructuring technique used to implement the wavefront method on nested loops. We show that loop skewing can be used to reshape the iteration space so that one dimension will correspond to the time function, and collapsing this dimension out of the iteration space will give the processor mapping; a feasible mapping will satisfy all data dependence constraints with the time function, and all data communication will be mapped onto the limited interprocessor network. We show how the constraints of a more general purpose distributed memory computer differ from those used in systolic architecture design.

2. TARGET PROCESSOR ARCHITECTURE

For this work the target processor design is a multidimensional mesh of processors (or multidimensional ring or torus; sometimes the end-around connections are useful). Each processor has some amount of local memory which can be directly addressed; the local memory of other processors is not directly addressable. To get data from one processor to another, the processors must communicate directly; that is, action is required by both the sender and receiver of the data. This is similar to the design of current hypercube computers.

We assume that the processor array is programmed in a high level language which is similar to Fortran with two extensions: parallel loops (either explicit or implicit) and explicit storage distribution. A parallel loop is syntactically similar to a DO loop with an assertion by the user (or by the compiler itself, if automatically discovered) that the iterations of the loop do not depend on each other, and can be executed in any order. Storage distribution is a method of laying out the user arrays in the program into the processor array, similar concepts have been proposed in the BLAZE language [6]. For instance, a matrix may be laid out across a ring of processors by rows or by columns; an more advanced layout scheme would be by diagonals or antidiagonals. A matrix might be layed out across a 2-dimensional processor array by square submatrices. The actual syntax or mechanics of whether parallel loops are automatically or manually identified or how the storage distribution functions are specified is beyond the scope of this paper; we note however that while great progress has been made in the automatic discovery of parallel loops, storage layout is a new and perhaps difficult problem.

3. EFFICIENT PARALLEL LOOPS

What kind of loops can be executed efficiently on the target architecture? We classify loops into several categories depending on how that loop index is used to access the distributed arrays. Notice that we ignore loops that do not index a distributed array dimension; for instance, if matrices are distributed by rows, then loops which only index the columns are ignored, since those loops will be executed serially on each processor. Also, if array data is distributed in multiple dimensions, then we consider the all the pertinent nested loops together. We make six important loop classifications (though these may not be comprehensive):

- Parallel loop which uses only "local" data, meaning that all the data needed for executing this loop is already stored on this processor.
- Parallel loop which can pre-load all its data requirements with "regular" array accesses.
- Parallel loop with linear dependences.
- Parallel loop with random fetch and stores.
- Parallel loop with systolic data accesses.
- Serial loop.

Each of these is discussed in slightly more detail below. The rest of the paper concentrates on the systolic loop.

3.1. Local Data Loop

We use storage distribution similar to that proposed for the Blaze language [6]; in particular, the distribution is specified in general terms (without knowledge of the number of processors). Thus, the only loops which access local data all the time are those where the distributed dimensions are accessed by the same function of the loop index, such as:

```
     DO I = 1, N
S1:    A(I) = B(I) + C(I)
S2:    D(I) = A(I) + 1
     ENDDO
```

These cases will be trivial to recognize and compile.

3.2. Preloaded Data Loop

This is the case on which the Blaze work concentrates [6]. In the distributed memory message passing paradigm used here, both the sender and the receiver of a message must be active in any communication. This means that only array accesses with invertible subscript functions can be simply pre-loaded. For instance, to execute the loop:

```
        DO I = 2, N-1
S1:       A(I) = B(I-1) + C(I+1)
S2:       D(I) = A(I) + 1
        ENDDO
```

the value of B(I-1) is needed at processor I; thus processor I-1 must know to send that value on to processor I. From the point of view of processor J=I-1, the destination of B(J) is processor J+1, for J=1:N-2. Similarly, the destination of C(K) is processor K-1, for K=3:N. If the subscript function is f(I) (where I is the parallel loop index), processor I must expect a message from processor f(I); also, processor J=f(I) must send a message to processor I=f^{-1}(J). Non-invertible subscript functions will put a loop into the "random access" category. The Blaze approach works equally well here, where prior to the execution of the loop, each processor will send the data which it "owns" that is needed by other processors and receives data that it needs but does not own. The loop is then executed with all local data. Storage for the additional data can be dynamically allocated, statically allocated in auxiliary locations, or in some cases statically allocated as "overlap" rows or columns in the local arrays. A trivial observation is that data anti-dependence relations between statements in different loop iterations can be satisfied by this pre-loading process and will therefore not affect the execution of the parallel loop at all (no other synchronization will be necessary).

3.3. Linear Dependence Loops

This category includes loops that have some data dependence relations between loop iterations, but as in the previous category, only allows invertible subscript functions. Communication between processors during the execution of the loop will slow down execution of the loop but still allow fully distributed execution. In the following example:

```
        DO I = 2, N-1
S1:       A(I) = A(I-1) + A(I+1)
S2:       D(I) = A(I) + 1
        ENDDO
```

the reference to A(I+1) can be pre-loaded into each processor. However the reference to A(I-1) will require that each processor wait for the previous processor to complete S_1. this will serialize execution of this statement. There is one interesting subcase: loops with only lexically forward dependences. In this case there is still data communication, but the statements of the loop are not necessarily serialized:

```
      DO I = 2, N-1
S1:     A(I) = B(I) + C(I)
S2:     D(I) = A(I-1) + 1
      ENDDO
```

Each processor can compute its local element of `A(I)`, send it on to processor `I+1`, receive its value from `I-1`, then compute its local element of `D(I)`. The explicit communication from S_1 to S_2 will cause (perhaps significant) overhead in the execution of the loop, but it is still perfectly parallel. Another observation: ***loop alignment*** [1,5,11], a program transformation used to remove just this sort of loop-carried data dependence relation, will not always be effective for distributed memory machines in our scenario. The aligned version of the loop would be:

```
      DO I = 1, N-1
S1:     if(I>=2) A(I) = B(I) + C(I)
S2:     if(I<=N-2) D(I+1) = A(I) + 1
      ENDDO
```

This removes the interprocessor communication due to `A`, but adds communication for `D`. Loop alignment may be occasionally useful; moreover, the mechanisms used in loop alignment (expansion of the loop index set and addition of if statements to control execution of some of the statements, such as data communication) will be needed here.

3.4. Random Access Loops

Loops which access data in a random fashion (with non-invertible subscript functions) will be difficult to execute in parallel on message-passing machines. Even with a simple loop such as:

```
      DO I = 1, N
S1:     A(I) = B(IP(I)) + C(I)
S2:     D(I) = A(I) + 1
      ENDDO
```

there is no data dependence relation preventing parallel execution. However, suppose that `N=5` and `IP=(5,4,3,5,2)`. Processor 1 will know that it needs `B(5)`; but to get `B(5)`, processor 5 will need to forward that value to processor 1. For processor 5 to know where `B(5)` is needed, it needs to invert the subscript function *f*`(I)=IP(I)`. If `IP` is used several times as an index function, it may be reasonable to take the time to build an auxiliary inverse index array, `IIP`, where `IIP(I,*)` hold the index of the elements `IP` that have a value of `I`. In this example, `IIP=((),(5),(3),(2),(1,4))`; one way to construct an inverse index array would take `N` steps, passing `IP` through each processor to test for its value and pick off the index. Another method to build the inverted index is by using an 'inspector' phase [7]. If random fetches and stores from remote memory are supported, then random access loops can be treated as preloaded-data loops.

3.5. Systolic Loops

In our work, these loops are related to Uniform Recurrence Equations, which are mapped onto systolic processor arrays. We call a loop *systolic* if a distributed array dimension is indexed by two nested loop variables, or if two aligned distributed array dimensions are indexed by different loop variables. By definition, the loop must be at least doubly nested. For example, a matrix multiply:

```
          DO I = 1, N
            DO J = 1, N
              DO K = 1, N
S1:             A(I,J) = A(I,J) + B(I,K)*C(K,J)
              ENDDO
            ENDDO
          ENDDO
```

will be a systolic loop. If the arrays A, B and C are distributed by rows (or columns), then the first dimension of A and C (second dimension of A and B) are indexed by different loop variables, I and K (J and K). The subject of the rest of the paper is our method to handle systolic loops.

3.6. Serial Loops

Any loop that cannot be classified as some type of parallel loop will be left serial, by default. Execution of serial loops can still be (and should be) distributed among the processors, to increase the use of data in local memories. We believe that more experience with the programming methodology described here will allow us to create new classifications of parallel loops which will then reduce the number of serial loops.

4. UNIFORM RECURRENCE EQUATIONS AND SYSTOLIC ARRAYS

Systolic loops as defined above are related to Uniform Recurrence Equations (UREs) and our method to compute them is related to the methods used to map UREs onto systolic processor arrays. A URE can be described as a nested loop where each statement is an assignment where the left hand side is an array that is simply indexed by each of the loop variables, as A(I,J,K). The right hand sides will usually include the same variables, with the subscripts differing from the corresponding left hand side subscripts by a constant in each array dimension. One way to write a matrix multiply as a URE is:

```
          DO I = 1, N
            DO J = 1, N
              DO K = 1, N
S1:             C(I,J,K) = C(I-1,J,K)
S2:             B(I,J,K) = B(I,J-1,J)
S3:             A(I,J,K) = A(I,J,K-1) + B(I,J,K)*C(I,J,K)
              ENDDO
            ENDDO
          ENDDO
```

Much work has been done in mapping "near"-UREs into UREs, to take advantage of the same compiling techniques [10].

Mapping a *d* dimensional URE onto a *d-1* dimensional systolic processor is done by projecting the *d* dimensional iteration space onto a time dimension and *d-1* spatial (processor) dimensions. The time projection is constrained by the data dependence relations in the URE, and the spatial projection is constrained by the feasibility of the interconnections in the processor array. A typical method maps the time dimension first, then searches for a spatial mapping that fits the connection constraints, ending with success or failure (though the spatial mapping can be done first). In the above URE, the data dependence relations that must be observed are:

$$S_1[i,j,k]\ \delta\ S_1[i+1,j,k]$$
$$S_2[i,j,k]\ \delta\ S_2[i,j+1,k]$$
$$S_3[i,j,k]\ \delta\ S_3[i,j,k+1]$$

A useful result is that if there is a time mapping that satisfies these constraints, then there is an *affine* time function; usually this is sufficient, so we would look for a time function:

$$T(I,J,K)=aI+bJ+cK+d$$

with the goal of minimizing the total time of the computation. The data dependence relations give rise to the relations:

$$T(i,j,k) < T(i+1,j,k) \quad \Longrightarrow \quad 0 < a$$
$$T(i,j,k) < T(i,j+1,k) \quad \Longrightarrow \quad 0 < b$$
$$T(i,j,k) < T(i,j,k+1) \quad \Longrightarrow \quad 0 < c$$

Choosing the smallest values of a, b and c that satisfy these conditions (though that does not necessarily always guarantee a feasible spatial mapping or even the smallest total execution time), and setting d=0 for simplicity, we get the timing function:

$$T(I,J,K)=I+J+K$$

Other recent work has attacked the problem of finding feasible timing functions when the data dependence constraints do not cancel out all the index variables [4].

Now we might search for a spatial mapping that would satisfy any interprocessor connection constraints. Usually we have a great deal of freedom here, since we are trying to design a custom systolic array processor for this algorithm; however, many people define a systolic array as one that is planar and tesselating, allowing only for nearest neighbor connections. This means that communication between processors in a single time step must be between neighboring processors, or that the "Manhattan distance" of the projection of two communicating iterations in the iteration space onto the processor space must be less than the time difference between those two iterations in the time dimension.

In general, the method tries to find a $1 \times d$ array λ (for the timing function) and a $d-1 \times d$ array A (for the spatial mapping function) such that

$$T(\bar{i}) = \lambda \bar{i}$$

$$S(\bar{i}) = A\bar{i}$$

5. SYSTOLIC ARRAYS, WAVEFRONTS AND LOOP SKEWING

It can easily be seen that the type of mapping done for systolic array processors is essentially equivalent to that used by the "wavefront" method of computing a loop [8, 9]. One way to implement the wavefront method is via *loop skewing* [12]. Loop skewing reshapes the iteration space of a nested loop from a rectangular to rhomboid shape. A simple loop:

```
DO I = 2, N-1
  DO J = 2, N-1
    A(I,J) = (A(I,J-1) + A(I-1,J)) / 2
  ENDDO
ENDDO
```

has a rectangular iteration space with the dependence relations as shown:

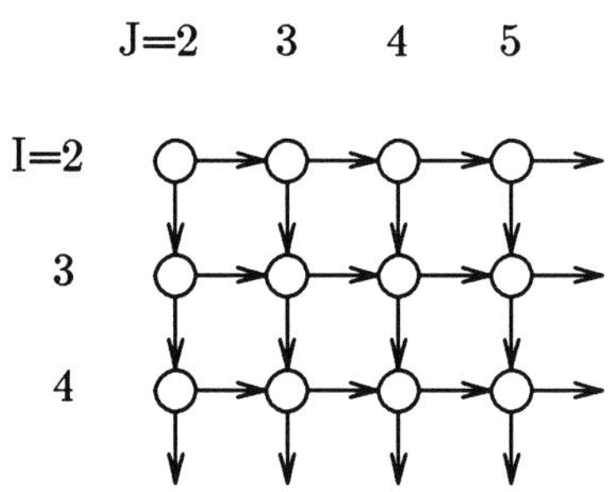

We can skew the J loop with respect to the I loop by changing the J loop limits (and adjusting the uses of J within the loop):

```
DO I = 2, N-1
  DO J = I+2, I+N-1
    A(I,J-I) = (A(I,J-I-1) + A(I-1,J-I)) / 2
  ENDDO
ENDDO
```

The skewed iteration space is now:

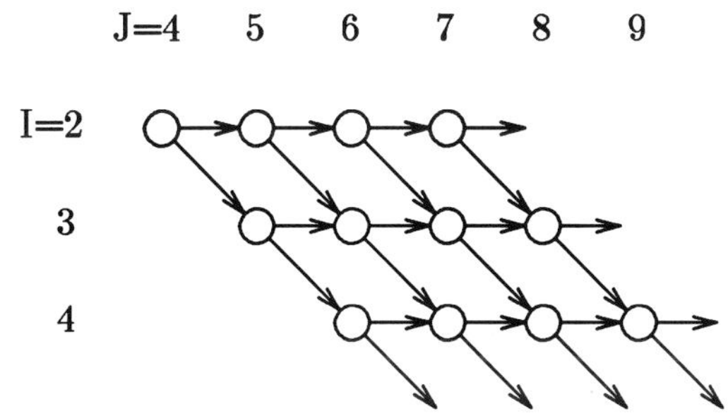

Loop skewing is always legal and has no effect on the numerical accuracy of the results. The goal when wavefronting is to skew the loops as little as possible to make all the dependence relations in the iteration space go "forward" in some dimension; if that is possible (as in the above example), then by interchanging that loop to the outermost level and executing it serially, all the dependence relations will be satisfied and the other loop or loops can be executed fully in parallel.

We can relate this directly to systolic array terms. Executing some loop serially corresponds to mapping that loop index onto the time dimension; the skewing process corresponds to finding the λ array. The only constraint is that the chosen skewed loop cannot correspond to an index that would have a zero element in λ; canonical loop skewing in fact would require that the corresponding λ value be one, but it is easily modified to account for other values. Mapping the spatial dimension(s) corresponds to collapsing the iteration space along the time dimension. Note that additional skewing of loop indices can occur to change the spatial mapping function. In the above example, the time function of the skewed iteration space corresponds to the `J` loop dimension, leaving the `I` dimension for the spatial dimension. This projection must satisfy the constraint that any data communication (whether or not caused by data dependence relations) must be projected onto the feasible interprocessor connection network. Here, the projection of the iteration space onto the `I` dimension would indeed show that only nearest neighbor connections are necessary. Additional skewing of loops or skewing by factors other than one may be performed to stretch the time dimension or otherwise change the shape of the iteration space, and thus the time or spatial mapping. As with canonical systolic array mapping, a search for a feasible and optimal skew is necessary, though we expect that in practice satisfactory performance will result after searching only a few potentially interesting cases.

6. SYSTOLIC LOOP PROCESSING

There are several important differences between compiling systolic loops onto distributed memory machines and compiling Uniform Recurrence Equations onto systolic arrays. First, when dealing with systolic arrays, we often have the freedom of rearranging the interconnection network to suit the problem; on the other hand, when dealing with distributed memory machines, we may be able to take advantage of a richer (non-planar) interconnection network, such as a hypercube network. Second, when dealing with systolic arrays, the data flows through all the processors and the outputs flow out the back or bottom, and there is some freedom in arranging the order in which the inputs are presented; on a distributed memory computer, the data starts out residing in some processor's local memory, and any results must end up in that same memory.

To map a systolic loop on a processor, we will skew and rearrange the iteration space such that one dimension of the modified iteration space will correspond to the time dimension and the other dimensions will be projected onto the distributed memory processor network. Following the work of systolic arrays, we use a trial and error heuristic, with the assurance that if a solution is not found after a very finite search, we will declare failure and revert to serial execution of the loop (or return to the user with a diagnostic that this loop should be manually restructured). The constraints are essentially the same as for systolic arrays: the data dependence relations must be satisfied (as with loop skewing to implement the wavefront method), and all data communication in the rearranged iteration space must project onto feasible interprocessor communication links. This last constraint must hold not only for steady-state communication, but also for any initial communication needed to start the computation.

We show this by example. Taking the matrix multiply program, let us assume that the arrays are stored by rows on a linear array or ring of processors (in this work we assume that the distribution of data to processor memory is done by the user; future work may produce heuristics to handle common cases, but it may be computationally infeasible to try to find the best data distribution automatically). The column accesses are then of no consequence, and the algorithm reduces to:

```
DO I = 1, N
  DO K = 1, N
    A(I,...) = A(I,...) + B(I,...)*C(K,...)
  ENDDO
ENDDO
```

The dependence relations in the iteration space suggest that using the K loop for timing function would be sufficient:

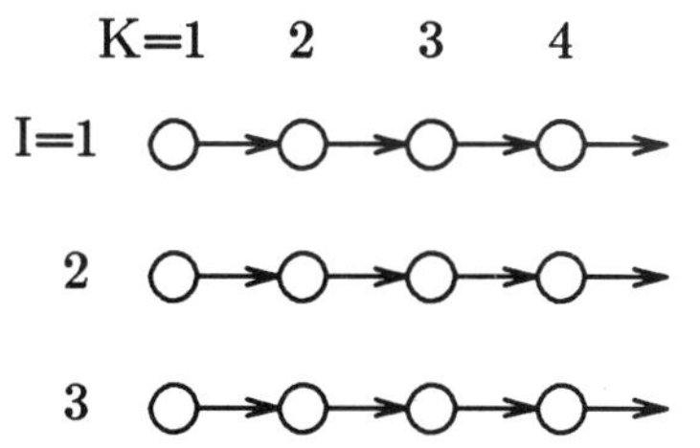

There are no data dependence relations in this subalgorithm that prevent simultaneous execution of all iterations of the `I` loop. However, the communication required by references to the `C` array gives rise to the communication structure:

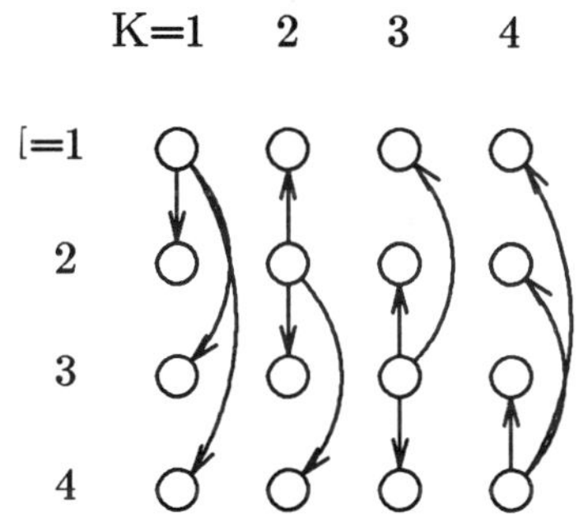

If the `K` loop corresponds to time steps, then the communication pattern will not map onto the interprocessor nearest neighbor network.

However, we can treat the communications similar to dependence constraints, with the additional flexibility that they can be reordered. In particular, skewing the `I` loop with respect to the `K` loop would give the iteration space:

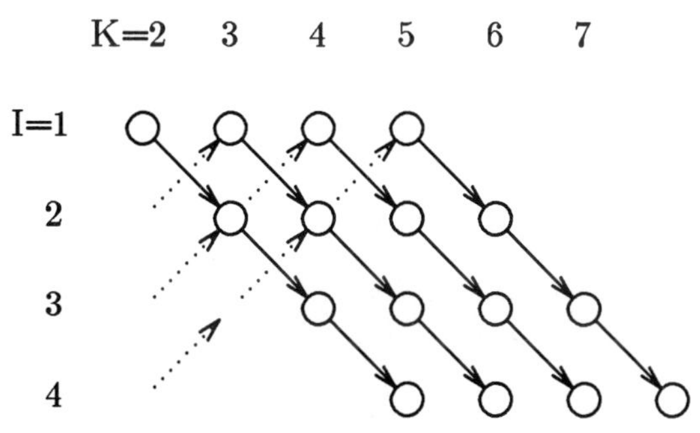

The dotted lines in the graph correspond to passing data along without using it in any local computation. Notice that even processors which are not yet active in any computation must participate in the communication process.

A similar method works for a mesh or torus of processors when the arrays are distributed by square submatrices (or in the limit, by elements). Limited space prevents presentation of such an example. We hope to implement and experiment with a program restructuring tool that will attempt to discover loops that can be automatically mapped onto distributed memory computers, once the user has distributed the data storage across the ensemble.

7. OTHER WORK

This work builds on two sources. Prior work done in advanced program restructuring techniques, such as data dependence computation [2,13], automatic parallelism detection and loop skewing [12], are the basis for the restructuring approach taken here. Other work done in mapping Recurrence Equations onto systolic arrays [10] has also been useful.

There has been a great deal of work in automatic discovery of parallelism, but less work in mapping parallel algorithms to specific architectures. The BLAZE approach [6] of letting a user specify the data distribution and optimizing the communication between processors seems promising.

We believe that other approaches for programming distributed memory machines, such as those that require distinct cooperating programs for each address space, will prove unacceptable to the user community. Functional or single-assignment languages may be fruitful, and we believe our techniques will also apply in that domain.

References

1. R. Allen, D. Callahan and K. Kennedy, Automatic Decomposition of Scientific Programs for Parallel Execution, in *Conf. Record of the 14th Annual ACM Symp. on Principles of Programming Languages*, ACM Press, New York, 1987, 63-76.
2. J. R. Allen and K. Kennedy, Automatic Translation of Fortran Programs to Vector Form, *ACM Transactions on Programming Languages and Systems 9*, 4 (October 1987), 491-542.
3. D. Callahan and K. Kennedy, Compiling Programs for Distributed-Memory Multiprocessors, *J. Supercomputing 2*, 2 (October 1988), 151-169, Kluwer Academic Publishers.
4. M. B. Gokhale and T. C. Torgerson, The Symbolic Hyperplane Transformation for Recursively Defined Arrays, in *Proc. of Supercomputing 88*, IEEE Computer Society Press, Los Angeles, 1988, 207-214. Orlando, FL, November 14-18, 1988.
5. D. A. P. Haiek, in *Multiprocessors: Discussion of Some Theoretical and Practical Problems*, Ph.D. Thesis, Univ. of Illinois UIUCDCS-79-990, Urbana, IL, November 1979.
6. C. Koelbel, P. Mehrotra and J. Van Rosendale, Semi-automatic Process Partitioning for Parallel Computation, *Intl J. Parallel Programming 16*, 5 (October 1987), 365-382.

7. C. Koelbel, P. Mehrotra and J. Van Rosendale, Support Shared Data Structures on Distributed Memory Architectures, in *Proc. of the 2nd ACM SIGPLAN Symposium on Principles and Practices of Parallel Programming (PPOPP)*, 1990, 177-186. March 14-16, 1990.
8. L. Lamport, The Parallel Execution of DO Loops, *Communications of the ACM 17*, 2 (February 1974), 83-93, ACM.
9. Y. Muraoka, , Parallelism Exposure and Exploitation in Programs, Univ. of Illinois at Urbana, Dept. of Comp. Sci. Rpt. 71-424, February 1971.
10. S. V. Rajopadhye, in *Synthesis, Verification and Optimization of Systolic Architectures*, PhD Thesis, University of Utah, December 1986. (UMI 87-02411).
11. K. Smith and B. Appelbe, Replication and Alignment: A Unified Theory, GIT-ICS 88/36, Georgia Institute of Technology, October 1988.
12. M. Wolfe, Loop Skewing: The Wavefront Method Revisited, *Intl J. Parallel Programming 15*, 4 (August 1986), 279-294.
13. M. Wolfe and U. Banerjee, Data Dependence and Its Application to Parallel Processing, *Intl Journal of Parallel Programming 16*, 2 (April 1987), 137-178.

This work was supported by NSF Grant CCR-8906909 and DARPA Grant MDA972-88-J-1004.

Languages, Compilers and Run-Time Environments
for Distributed Memory Machines
J. Saltz and P. Mehrotra (Editors)

An Optimizing C* Compiler for a Hypercube Multicomputer

Lutz H. Hamel[a], Philip J. Hatcher[a], and Michael J. Quinn[b]

[a]Department of Computer Science, University of New Hampshire, Durham, NH 03824 U.S.A.

[b]Department of Computer Science, Oregon State University, Corvallis, OR 97331 U.S.A.

Abstract

C* is the synchronous, data parallel, C superset designed by Thinking Machines for the Connection Machine processor array. We discuss an implementation of C* targeted to the NCUBE 3200 hypercube multicomputer, an asynchronous machine. In the multicomputer environment, the major obstacle to high efficiency is the relatively slow interprocessor communication. We describe our C* optimizer that concentrates on reducing the cost of a C* program's message passing. We present the results of evaluating our system using three benchmark programs.

1 Introduction

Many applications are characterized by a large amount of inherent parallelism that can be exploited by modern parallel computers. However, implementing these applications using programming languages augmented by low-level parallel constructs can be painfully difficult. One remedy is to focus on the data parallelism in the application; that is, the parallelism achievable through the simultaneous execution of the same operations across large sets of data [Hillis and Steele 1986]. Many languages which might be classified as data parallel have been proposed, including Blaze [5], Booster [7], C* [12], Coherent Parallel C [2], Dino [13], The Force [3], Kali [4], the paralation model [14], Parallel Pascal [10], and Seymour [6]. Because data parallel languages are based on a more abstract model of parallel computation than conventional parallel programming languages, there is good reason to believe that programs written in data parallel languages will be more portable across a variety of parallel computer architectures.

We believe a data parallel programming language should have the following features: fully synchronous execution semantics; a global name space, which obviates the need for explicit message passing between processing elements; parallel objects, rather than merely parallel scalars; and the ability to make the number of processing elements a function of the problem size, rather than a function of the target machine. The C* language satisfies these requirements.

Our work is closely related to recent efforts that translate to multicomputers sequential programs augmented with data distribution information [1, 11]. We feel that if the language is to contain data mapping constructs, then the language should be explicitly parallel. The C* programming model maintains the benefits of using a sequential language (deterministic results, no race conditions, ability to debug on a von Neumann architecture) while allowing the natural expression of inherently parallel operations (such as data reductions). We will demonstrate that just as sequential programs can be mapped to asynchronous parallel programs with the same behavior, C* programs can be mapped to equivalent asynchronous implementations.

Earlier we presented the design of a C*-to-C compiler based upon a general control flow model [9]. Our current work builds upon a new compiler design based upon a less general control flow model, i.e., one that does not support the `goto` statement [8]. The new compiler generates programs with significantly higher efficiency, programs that can rival the speed of hand-coded C programs on a hypercube multicomputer. This paper concentrates on describing the communication optimization phase of the new compiler. Since communication is so expensive on a hypercube, a good optimizer is a necessary condition for high efficiency.

Section 2 presents a brief description of C*. In Section 3 we summarize how our compiler addresses the goals of minimizing the number of interprocessor synchronizations and allowing for the efficient emulation of virtual processing elements. The details of our optimizing C*-to-C translator appear in Section 4. Section 5 describes how data flow analysis supports the optimizer. Experimental results are given in Section 6.

2 The C* Programming Language

C* is a high-level parallel programming language. It supports a shared memory model of parallel computation. A programmer can assume that all processors share a common address space. C* supports virtual processors. This allows a programmer the convenience of ignoring the actual number of physical processors available. All C* virtual processors execute synchronously. A synchronous execution model eliminates all timing problems, makes programs deterministic, and greatly reduces the complexity of program comprehension and the difficulty of program debugging.

The conceptual model presented to the C* programmer consists of a front-end uniprocessor attached to an adaptable back-end parallel processor. The sequential portion of the C* program (consisting of conventional C code) is executed on the front end. The parallel portion of the C* program (delimited by C* constructs not found in C) is executed on the back end.

The back end is adaptable in that the programmer selects the number of processors to be activated. This number is independent of the number of physical processors that may be available on the hardware executing the C* program. For this reason the C* program

```
domain cell {
    double r_coord;
    double z_coord;
    double r_velocity;
    double z_velocity
    double area;
    double energy;
    double pressure;
    double viscosity;
    double density;
    double temperature;
    double mass;
    double delta_volume;
};
```

Figure 1: Declaring a domain.

```
#define KDIM 54
#define LDIM 54

domain cell mesh[KDIM][LDIM];
```

Figure 2: Declaring virtual processors.

is said to activate *virtual* processors when a parallel construct is entered.

Virtual processors are allocated in groups. Each virtual processor in the group has an identical memory layout. The C* programmer specifies a virtual processor's memory layout using syntax similar to the C `struct`. A new keyword `domain` is used to indicate that this is a parallel data declaration. Figure 1 contains a domain declaration for the mesh points of a hydrodynamics simulation. As in C structures, the names declared within the domain are referred to as *members*.

Instances of a domain are declared using the C array constructor. Each domain instance becomes the memory for one virtual processor. The array dimension therefore indicates the size of the virtual back-end parallel processor that is to be allocated. Figure 2 contains a domain array declaration. Note that domain arrays can be multidimensional. The number of virtual processors allocated is the product of the array dimensions.

Data located in C*'s front-end processor is termed *mono* data. Data located in a back-end processor is termed *poly* data.

Figure 3 illustrates the C* *domain select* statement. The body of the domain select is executed by every virtual processor allocated for the particular domain type selected. The virtual processors execute the body synchronously. The domain members are included

```
[domain cell].{
    double temp1;
    temp1 = calculate_temperature(energy, density);
    temperature = (temp1 > TFLR ? temp1 : TFLR);
    pressure = calculate_pressure(temperature, density);
}
```

Figure 3: Activating virtual processors.

within the scope of the body of the domain select. These names refer to the values local to a particular virtual processor.

The code executing in a virtual processor of a C* program can reference a variable in the front-end processor by referring to the variable by name. A variable that is visible in the immediately enclosing block of a domain select statement is visible within the domain select. The C* compiler is responsible for making mono variables accessible at run time to the virtual processors.

Similarly, the members of a domain instance are accessible everywhere in a program. The members of one domain can be read and written from within a domain select statement for a different domain. Poly data can also be read and written from the sequential portion of the program. The syntax employed is to provide a full domain array reference followed by a member reference.

C*, like C++, has a keyword `this`. In C* `this` is a pointer to the domain instance currently being operated on by a virtual processor. Pointer arithmetic on `this` can be performed to access other virtual processors' members.

C* provides a set of *reduction* operators. These operators accumulate poly values into a mono location. All C assignment operators are overloaded for this purpose.

The sequential portion of a C* program is just C code and executes following the normal C semantics. Conceptually, the parallel sections of a C* program execute synchronously under the control of a *master program counter* (MPC). A virtual processor's local program counter is either active, executing in step with the MPC, or inactive, waiting for the MPC to reach it.

For example, the MPC steps through an `if-then-else` statement by first evaluating the control expression, then executing the `then` clause, and finally executing the `else` clause. A local program counter would also proceed first to the control expression. However, if the expression evaluated to zero (*false* in C), then the local program counter would proceed to the `else` clause and wait for the MPC to reach it. If the expression evaluated to non-zero (*true* in C), then the local program counter would wait at the `then` clause for the MPC.

The `while` loop is handled in a similar manner. The master program counter repeatedly visits the control expression and the body of a `while` loop until all virtual processors that entered the loop have exited. As virtual processors evaluate the control expression to zero (or execute a `break` statement), they go to the point immediately following the loop and wait for the MPC.

As well as being synchronous at the statement level, C* is also synchronous at the expression level. No operator executes within a virtual processor unless all active virtual processors have evaluated their operands for the operator. Once the operands have been evaluated, the operator is executed as if in some serial order by all active virtual processors. This seemingly odd use of a serial ordering to define parallel execution is required to make sense of concurrent writes to the same memory location.

Our implementation of C* allows additional information to be provided by the programmer in order to aid the compiler in the mapping of virtual processors to physical processors. The array dimension of the domain array establishes a *virtual topology*. A one-dimensional domain array is considered to be a ring of virtual processors. A two-dimensional domain array is considered to be a two-dimensional mesh of virtual processors. In general, an n-dimensional domain array is considered to be an n-dimensional mesh of virtual processors with wrap-around connections.

These virtual topologies establish a convention of *locality*. Virtual processors that are adjacent in a virtual topology should be mapped by a compiler to physical processors that are "near" each other. On some architectures this information will be of little value and can be ignored by the compiler. On other architectures this can lead to large efficiency gains if the programmer exploits the feature and the compiler effectively implements it.

For the common topologies (low dimension domain arrays), the compiler recognizes macros that provide convenient access to adjacent elements in the virtual topology. The macros take a domain element address and return the address of the appropriate adjacent domain element. In the one dimensional case macros called "successor" and "predecessor" are provided. In the two dimensional case the macros "north," "south," "east" and "west" are provided.

3 Design of the C* Compiler

3.1 Overview

Our design must address three important issues. The first two issues—minimizing the number of interprocessor synchronizations and efficiently emulating virtual processors—have been addressed in an earlier publication [8]. In this paper, we only present a brief summary of how our compiler design tackles these issues. The third issue—optimizing communication—is discussed in sections 4 and 5.

3.2 Minimizing the Number of Processor Synchronizations

In C* expressions can refer to values stored in arbitrary processing elements. All variable declarations state, implicitly or explicitly, which processing element holds the variable being declared. Therefore, the location of potential communication points can be reduced to a *type checking* problem. A sufficient set of synchronization points are the locations at which we identify message passing is potentially needed. We incorporate synchronization into the message-passing routines.

The C* construct:

```
while (condition) {
  statement_list1;
  communication;
  statement_list2;
}
```

is translated into the following C code:

```
temp = TRUE;
do {
  if (temp) {
    temp = condition;
  }
  if (temp) {
    statement_list1;
  }
  communication;
  gtemp = global_or (temp);
  if (temp) {
    statement_list2;
  }
} while (gtemp);
```

Figure 4: Translation of a C* `while` statement.

Parallel looping constructs may require additional synchronization. If the parallel loop body incorporates virtual processor interaction, the processors must be synchronized every iteration prior to the message-passing step. Of course, a virtual processor does not actually execute the body of the loop after its local loop control value has gone to *false*. Rather, the physical processor on which it resides participates in the message passing and the computation of the value indicating whether any virtual processors are still active. This means that our C* compiler must rewrite the control structure of input programs. Figure 4 illustrates how `while` loops are rewritten.

Since we have incorporated synchronization into communication, all physical processors must actively participate in any message-passing operation. This forces our compiler to rewrite all control statements that have inner statements requiring message passing. Figure 5 illustrates how an `if` statement is handled.

Communication steps buried inside nested control structures are pulled out of each enclosing structure until they reach the outermost level.

The technique just described will not handle arbitrary control flow graphs. For this reason we have not implemented the `goto` statement. We can, however, handle the `break` and `continue` statements.

3.3 Efficiently Emulating Virtual Processors

Once the message-passing routines have been brought to the outermost level of the program, emulation of virtual processors is straightforward. The compiler puts `for` loops

The C* construct:

```
if (condition) {
  statement_list1;
  communication;
  statement_list2;
}
```

is translated into the following C code:

```
temp = condition;
if (temp) {
  statement_list1;
}
communication;
if (temp) {
  statement_list2;
}
```

Figure 5: Translation of a C* `if` statement.

around the blocks of code that have been delimited by message-passing/synchronization steps. Since within the delimited blocks there is no message passing, there is no interaction between virtual processors. Therefore, it makes no difference in which order the virtual processors located on a particular physical processor execute.

4 The Optimizer

In the multicomputer environment, communication operations are very expensive relative to computation steps. On the NCUBE 3200 the communication cost can be further categorized: the overhead of starting a message is much more significant than the expense incurred while shipping each byte of the message. Therefore, the primary goal of the optimizer is to eliminate or combine message passing operations whenever possible.

One class of messages is eliminated by keeping copies of the sequential code and data on each physical processor. Every physical processor executes the sequential code. Note that this adds nothing to the execution time of the program. Because every physical processor has copies of the sequential variables, it can access sequential data by doing a local memory fetch. In other words, assigning the value of a `mono` variable to a `poly` variable can be done without any message passing. However, when a virtual processor stores to a `mono` variable, the value may have to be broadcast to update all physical processors' copy of the `mono`.

In order to combine communications, the optimizer attempts to move read operations backward through the program (toward the beginning) and attempts to move write operations forward through the program (toward the end). We define a read operation to be the creation of a local copy of a non-local piece of data. A write operation involves writing a value to a particular non-local variable or address. Data can be read earlier if it is known that no statements altering the data will execute on the source processor prior to the reader using the copied data. Write operations can be delayed until the data is actually needed.

We are willing to move read operations out of control structures. As described in an earlier section, a node of the hypercube must always execute a communication primitive. Even though the corresponding communication operation may be nested within a conditional statement that has evaluated to false on all virtual processors of the particular node, the condition may have evaluated to true elsewhere in the hypercube. The communication primitive relies on the active participation of all nodes in order to synchronize the processors (and to avoid any possibility of buffer deadlock). Therefore, we are willing to make a conditional read unconditional, since (1) the message primitive must be executed, (2) the incremental cost of sending longer messages is marginal, and (3) it does not alter the semantics of a program to read a value that is not subsequently used.

Moving write operations out of control structures is a bit trickier, because it is incorrect to unconditionally execute a write operation if the controlling condition evaluated to false. Write operations can still be moved if the condition value is carried along. However, our intuition is that this is less useful—there usually seems to be less distance between a write operation and a statement that uses the result. Currently, we only try to move write operations out of simple loops to allow the writing of blocks of data.

Our technique of moving communication operations provides us with an implementation of several standard optimizations (with respect to message passing): common subexpression detection, vectorization, and the movement of invariant code out of loops. If the same distant, unchanging, value is being requested in several places in a block of code, our technique will move the data requests all to the head of the block and combine them into one message. If a block of data is being read a piece at a time by a loop that executes a constant number of times, our technique will combine these read operations into one block read operation. If the same, unchanging, piece of distant data is being read repeatedly within a loop, our technique will move the read out of the loop. These last two cases are distinguished by whether the value being read is dependent only on a simple loop control variable or whether the value being read is not dependent upon the loop in any way.

In addition, this technique, when it does combine communication operations, also reduces the synchronization requirements of the program, because in our implementation the synchronization points of a program are exactly those places where a message must be transmitted. By decreasing the number of communication points, we have decreased the number of synchronization points.

The optimizer also attempts to eliminate a communication when processing an assignment of a value to a `mono` variable. Since the assignment to a `mono` is in general the reduction of a set of parallel values to one value, a broadcast of the produced `mono` value may be necessary to keep all nodes' copy of the `mono` up to date. However, if it is known that all virtual processors will contribute the same value to the reduction, then no broadcast is required—all nodes can determine the result of the assignment. This requires that the compiler determine that all the virtual processors will execute the assignment and that the right hand side of the assignment will evaluate to the same value on all processors.

The elimination of a broadcast in the implementation of an assignment to a `mono` is an example of a more general optimization that we refer to as *sequentialization*. The goal is to locate pieces of code that need not be executed by all virtual processors—rather it is adequate to execute the code once per physical processor. One such case is an assignment to a mono variable of a expression that is known to evaluate, without local side effects, to the same value within all virtual processors. This can be implemented by just doing the assignment once per physical processor. The virtual processor emulation loop is terminated prior to the assignment and a new emulation loop is begun immediately after the assignment.

The sequentialization of control structures is also performed by our optimizer. If the control expression is known to evaluate to the same value on all virtual processors, then it need only be executed once per physical processor. The current virtual processor emulation loop is terminated prior to the control structure, an emulation loop is placed around the inner body of the control structure, and another emulation loop is begun immediately following the control structure.

This optimization saves on the overhead of executing the control structure, but it also can eliminate the need to broadcast a "global-or" value (as described in an earlier section) in the case that the control structure is a loop that contains a communication operation. This is important if the communication operation within the loop is not powerful enough to perform the "global-or" calculation as a side effect of its execution.

5 Supporting Program Analysis

To ensure the correctness of moving a communication operation, the optimizer performs a data-flow analysis that tracks which operands may be read and which operands may be modified by particular statements. A read operation may not be moved through a statement that potentially modifies a value being read. A write operation may not be moved through a statement that potentially either accesses or modifies a value being written.

At this point it is important to remember that all nodes are executing the same program. We do not move a read of a distant domain member x through a statement modifying the local x, because the same code might execute on the distant node and change the value of x that we are trying to read! Therefore our program analysis treats domain members as if they were simple variables.

To support the sequentialization optimization, the optimizer must perform an analysis of the control flow of the program. The question being answered is whether an expression or statement is guaranteed to be performed by all the virtual processors. This can also be formulated as a data-flow algorithm that propagates into each statement whether it is known for sure that the statement will be executed by all virtual processors. The algorithm proceeds by analyzing the expressions controlling iteration and selection statements. If it is known that all virtual processors will evaluate the expression to the same value, then all virtual processors will follow the same path through the particular control structure.

Our optimizer takes the approach that an expression is known to evaluate to the same value on all virtual processors if the operands of the expression consist of only mono

image size	hand C	current C*	future C*
512×512	14075	20656	14734

Table 1: Comparison of a hand-written C program to a C* program for the Mandelbrot set computation of a 512×512 image running on a 64 node NCUBE 3200. The units are NCUBE 3200 clock ticks—on our system there are 7812.5 ticks per second.

variables and constants. As described above, mono variables are replicated onto each physical processor, but the implementation guarantees that copies maintain coherency.

To vectorize communication operations, we require further analysis of loop control expressions. We require that the loop be known at compile time to execute a constant number of times. Currently, we look only for loop control variables that are being updated by constant amounts within the loop and are being tested against constants in the loop control expression.

6 Evaluating the Optimizer

We have evaluated our optimizer, which is still in prototype form, on several C* programs. We are interested in determining what efficiency, if any, is conceded by a programmer who decides to use the higher-level parallel programming model provided by C*. To this end we compare our compiled C* programs to hand-coded NCUBE C programs for the same algorithms. The hand-coded C programs are characterized by direct calls to the low-level communication primitives.

To measure the overhead of virtual processor emulation, we have chosen an algorithm—Mandelbrot set computation—that has no communication between virtual processors. Table 1 contains the raw data for a comparison of a hand-written C program to a C* program for the Mandelbrot set computation of a 512×512 image running on a 64 node NCUBE 3200. In the C* program each virtual processor contains one pixel. Therefore each physical processor is emulating 4096 virtual processors. The C program has a speedup of 56. The speedup is limited by a nonuniform image, which causes some processors to finish earlier than others.

The output of our current C* compiler executes at 68% of the speed of the hand-written C program. The difference is due primarily to the fact that the C programmer has made a space optimization by realizing that one set of variables is adequate to hold intermediate results on each physical node. These variables can be reused when computing multiple image points on one physical node. The C* program allocates a set of variables (as domain members) to each virtual processor. The domain members become arrays dimensioned by the number of virtual processors on a physical node. The compiler could eliminate some of these arrays by analyzing the domain members to see which ones are "dead" (hold values that will not subsequently be used) at the end of the virtual processor emulation loops. If a particular member is dead at the end of all emulation loops, then that member can be represented by a scalar that is shared between virtual processors on a particular physical processor. We do not currently perform this optimization, which we

```
#define N 100
domain mm { int a_row[N]; int b_col[N]; int c_row[N}; } m[N];
void main()
{
    [domain mm].{
        int i,j;
        int temp;
        for (i = 0; i < N; i++)
        {
            temp = 0;
            for (j = 0; j < N; j++)
            {
                temp += a_row[j] * b_col[j];
                successor(this)->b_col[j] = b_col[j];
            }
            c_row[(this-m-i+N)%N] = temp;
        }
    }
}
```

Figure 6: Matrix multiplication in C*.

call *scalarization*.

This optimization is made more important by the fact our C* compiler uses our own port of the GNU C compiler as a back end (the hand-written programs are compiled with GNU C too). GNU C aggressively assigns scalar local variables to registers, and the NCUBE 3200 has sixteen general purpose registers available. When the Mandelbrot program's temporaries are scalars and thus placed in registers, a large improvement in the running time of the program results.

In Table 1, the column labeled "C* future" shows the running time of the C* program assuming the compiler implements the scalarization optimization. The C* program would run at 96% of the speed of the hand-written program. This optimization will be implemented in our next version of the C* compiler.

We have also exercised our compiler on a row-oriented matrix multiplication program. The algorithm multiplies two $N \times N$ matrices using N elements of parallelism: each virtual processor holds a row of one factor matrix, a column of the other factor matrix, and a row of the product matrix (see Figure 6).

Table 2 contains the raw data for a comparison of a hand-written C program to a C* program for the matrix multiplication of various size matrices. A column is included in the table for a naive, unoptimized, translation of the C* program. The horrendous performance reported in this column indicates the paramount importance of optimizing communication operations!

matrix size	hand C	unoptimized C*	current C*	future C*
64 × 64	887	163,785	1556	1255
128 × 128	3972	698,590	8595	6444
256 × 256	26,740	3,185,689	57,477	40,392
512 × 512	201,602	15,970,744	423,370	286,997

Table 2: Comparison of a hand-written C program to a C* program for matrix multiplication running on a 64 node NCUBE 3200. The units are NCUBE 3200 clock ticks.

problem size	hand C	current C*	future C*
65536	922	3018	977
1,600,000	6724	18047	6842
4,800,000	16299	41118	16346
8,000,000	25431	62141	25363

Table 3: Comparison of a hand-written C program to a C* program for the prime number sieve running on a 64 node NCUBE 3200. The units are NCUBE 3200 clock ticks. The problem size is the range of numbers for which primes were computed.

For 512 × 512 matrices, the optimized C* program runs at 48% efficiency when compared to the hand-written C program.

A portion (40%) of the difference in the execution times is due to the fact that the optimized C* program does a communication for every virtual processor (512) and the hand-crafted C program does a communication for every physical processor (64, by grouping the columns in blocks of eight).

The rest of the difference in the execution time is due to various shortcomings of our current compiler. First, the scalarization optimization described above needs to be applied to the temporary variable being used to compute the dot products. Second, our current C* compiler unnecessarily captures the loop control expressions of "sequentialized" loops (see above) into temporary variables. This disrupts GNU C's opportunities to optimize the loop. Finally, our C* compiler currently implements an unnecessary extra level of buffering at the communication point that transmits the columns of B. Our next version of the compiler will eliminate these inefficiencies and should produce a program that will run at 70% efficiency when multiplying 512 × 512 matrices. The column in Table 2 labeled "future C*" projects the raw data for this version of the compiler.

We have also benchmarked our compiler using a program that computes prime numbers using the Sieve of Eratosthenes. This program has a virtual processor to physical processor ratio of one—the natural level of parallelism in the algorithm is to assign each processor a block of numbers to be checked for primality. Table 3 contains the raw data for a comparison of the C* program to a hand-written C program.

Both the C program and the C* program assume that the next prime will be found on the processor that holds the block of numbers containing the smallest values. In the C program this value is broadcast at each iteration to all other processors. In the C* program an assignment to a `mono` is performed. The primary cause of the inefficiency in the C* program is due to the fact that the compiler currently implements this assignment as a reduction of all right hand side values followed by a broadcast of the "winning" value. However, there is only one active virtual processor at the point of the assignment and just a broadcast of the one right hand side value would suffice. Since the grain size of this algorithm is small, the extra reduction operation dramatically affects performance.

We believe that a conditional statement that masks all but one processor is a common enough idiom that it should be recognized by the compiler. The next version of the compiler will do so and will remove the unneccesary reduction operation. The projected performance of the next version of the compiler on the prime sieve program is contained in Table 3 in the column labeled "future C*." The sieve program output by this version of the C* compiler will be very similar to the hand-written program.

7 Summary

We have discussed a compiler that translates C* programs into loosely-synchronous C programs. We have focused on the description of the communication optimizer, whose performance is a critical factor for our target architecture, a hypercube multicomputer. We have presented the results of applying this optimizer to three benchmarks and remain convinced that high performance is an achievable goal.

Acknowledgements This work was supported by National Science Foundation grants DCR-8514493, CCR-8814662, and CCR-8906622.

References

[1] D. Callahan and K. Kennedy. Compiling programs for distributed-memory multiprocessors. *The Journal of Supercomputing*, 2:151–169, 1988.

[2] E. Felten and S. Otto. Coherent parallel C. In *Third Conference on Hypercube Concurrent Computers and Applications*, pages 440–450, ACM Press, 1988.

[3] H. Jordan. The Force. In L. Jamieson, D. Gannon, and R. Douglass, editors, *The Characteristics of Parallel Algorithms*, pages 395–436, The MIT Press, 1987.

[4] C. Koelbel, P. Mehrotra, and J. Van Rosendale. Supporting shared data structures on distributed memory architectures. In *Second ACM SIGPLAN Symposium on Principles and Practice of Parallel Programming*, pages 177–186, March 1990.

[5] P. Mehrotra and J. Van Rosendale. The BLAZE language: A parallel language for scientific programming. *Parallel Computing*, 5:339–361, 1987.

[6] R. Miller and Q. Stout. An introduction to the portable parallel programming language Seymour. In *Thirteenth Annual International Computer Software and Applications Conference*, IEEE Computer Society, 1989.

[7] E. Paalvast. *The Booster Language*. Technical Report PL 89–ITI–B–18, Instituut voor Toegepaste Informatica TNO, Delft, The Netherlands, 1989.

[8] M. Quinn and P. Hatcher. Data parallel programming on multicomputers. *IEEE Software*, 7(5):69–76, September 1990.

[9] M. Quinn, P. Hatcher, and K. Jourdenais. Compiling C* programs for a hypercube multicomputer. In *SIGPLAN PPEALS 1988, Parallel Programming: Experience with Applications, Languages, and Systems*, pages 57–65, July 1987.

[10] A. Reeves. Parallel Pascal: An extended Pascal for parallel computers. *Journal of Parallel and Distributed Computing*, 1:64–80, 1984.

[11] A. Rogers and K. Pingali. Process decomposition through locality of reference. In *SIGPLAN '89 Conference on Programming Language Design and Implementation*, pages 69–80, June 1989.

[12] J. Rose and G. Steele. *C*: An Extended C Language for Data Parallel Programming*. Technical Report PL 87–5, Thinking Machines Corporation, Cambridge, MA, 1987.

[13] M. Rosing, R. Schnabel, and R. Weaver. Dino: Summary and examples. In *Third Conference on Hypercube Concurrent Computers and Applications*, pages 472–481, ACM Press, 1988.

[14] G. Sabot. *The Paralation Model*. The MIT Press, 1988.

Languages, Compilers and Run-Time Environments
for Distributed Memory Machines
J. Saltz and P. Mehrotra (Editors)

The Paragon Programming Paradigm and Distributed Memory Multicomputers

A. P. Reeves and C. M. Chase

School of Electrical Engineering, Cornell University, Ithaca, NY 14853

Abstract

Paragon is a programming environment for parallel computer systems. The main components of this environment are the Paragon programming primitives and a supporting run-time system. The Paragon environment is designed to be suitable for the realization of scientific programs on a wide range of multicomputer systems. These systems may contain a large number of independent processors; furthermore, they may be heterogeneous in that they involve different types of parallel processing resources. An essential new aspect to efficiently programming such systems is task management. Paragon is designed to allow the programmer to specify problem-based task management parameters without needing to know the details of the currently available system resources. This paper discusses the main characteristics of the Paragon environment.

1 Introduction

Multicomputer systems are emerging as viable computing vehicles for a wide range of computationally intensive scientific and signal processing applications. While a number of hardware multicomputer systems are at a mature stage, appropriate programming environments are lacking. Paragon is an experimental programming environment that is intended for the convenient and efficient programming of such resources.

The Paragon environment consists of a parallel programming language, a translator (i.e. compiler) and a collection of run-time support routines. The Paragon language is designed to permit the convenient expression of algorithms which naturally exhibit data parallelism. The translator and run-time environment provide for the execution of the algorithm while retaining as much of the parallelism as possible.

Paragon is designed to be an efficient programming environment for a wide range of parallel computer systems, especially multicomputer systems. Task management for these systems is the responsibility of the Paragon run-time environment. However, the Paragon language also attempts to provide semantic constructs that permit the programmer to specify task management information at a high level. The key new features of the Paragon paradigm are:

1. Clear language semantics that do not require the overspecification that is typical of conventional serial languages.

2. Facilities for the programmer to specify task-management information at the problem level without explicit references to hardware features.

3. A sophisticated run-time environment that may embody concepts of task management, dynamic load balancing, fault tolerance, and possibly some automatic algorithm selection.

The goals of Paragon are considered in more detail in [3]. An initial implementation has been developed for Paragon that currently runs on serial processors, the Intel iPSC/2 hypercube and on transputer networks. The first Paragon language is based on the SIMD model of computation and is implemented, for convenience, by a collection of C++ classes. The Paragon classes provide for the parallel evaluation of expressions, handle the data distribution requirements of the parallel program, and provide a convenient interface for interprocessor communication. While the current language syntax is based on the C programming language (to take advantage of the high-level development tools) there is no reason why the Paragon primitives could not be included in other programming languages such as Fortran.

1.1 Parallel Program Specification

There are several different ways of expressing parallelism that are appropriate in different situations. A number of desirable programming constructs that would be useful for a Paragon environment are given in Table 1. The constructs in this table are ranked in increasing grain size.

Table 1: Parallel Programming Constructs

Capability	**Application**
SIMD Constructs	efficient array arithmetic
(a) parallel expressions	and SIMD algorithms
(b) permutation operations	
(c) reduction operations	
(d) replication operations	
(e) selective execution	
(f) subarray selection	
Arbitrary data mapping	data-dependent transforms
(a) communication structures	and arbitrary permutations
(b) data locking	
Data Partitioning	independent region processing
(a) selective execution	
Data Streaming	function decompostion
(a) stream data types	

The *SIMD constructs* are well understood and are usually efficient on a range of parallel architectures. Many low-level image processing functions, such as convolution, can be effectively expressed with SIMD primitives. The problem with these constructs is that they cannot utilize all the independent capabilities of multicomputer systems. Parallel data manipulation is specified by a restricted set of permutation, reduction and replication functions.

Arbitrary data mappings provide greater flexibility for manipulating program data. Two techniques for expressing arbitrary data mappings are being considered for Paragon. *Communication structures* allow for the direct specification of the mappings by adopting a storage intensive approach. *Data locking* adopts an approach where the programmer can specify arbitrary access patterns through a sequence of elemental operations. Program determinacy is maintained by *locking* the distributed objects as either read only or write only.

Data partitioning is a high-level construct for specifying independent concurrent program threads. This structure is useful in situations where different algorithms are to be performed on different areas of an array. Data partitioning is being considered as a mechanism for the efficient implementation of conditional execution in Paragon.

Data streaming is a mechanism for achieving high-level function decomposition. This is useful for pipelined image processing applications such as the the processing of a sequence of image frames for real-time control. For effective resource distribution, it is important to specify this operation in the user's program rather than as a separate set of commands to the operating system. The initial high-level data streaming program construct that is being considered for Paragon is a *stream* data type. A stream would be defined to consist of objects of a given data type. Any instance of a stream data type in the program body would cause that program section to be executed as a separate concurrent process. Such a process would be terminated by a assigning a null data object to the stream.

The last two capability classes, data partitioning and data streaming, are currently still in the conceptual stage for Paragon. The initial implementation of Paragon embodies in its run-time system the ability to perform data (task) migration. The language development has included the SIMD constructs and a data mapping strategy. Mechanisms for data partitioning and data streams are currently being investigated. Further details of the current Paragon implementation are given in [1].

2 Programming in Paragon

The novel features of the current version of Paragon that permit the transparent utilization of parallel resources are illustrated by several image processing program examples. The current Paragon language is based on the C program syntax since it is implemented by a C++ package.

2.1 Array Data Specification

Parallelism in Paragon is specified through the use of explicitly parallel expressions involving distributed arrays. More complex data structures (e.g. lists, trees) are under consideration for Paragon. However, at present, the array data structure is the main conceptual entity used in Paragon. Distributed arrays in Paragon are specified with respect to a *shape* declaration.

At the programming language level, the Paragon shape is similar in concept to an array type with the difference that the former does not specify a base type. The shape declaration specifies how the array data is distributed and how the array can be indexed (i.e. the size of each of its dimensions). Any number of array objects may be derived from a single shape. Each derived array will have the same data distribution. If, at run time, a shape is redistributed then all arrays derived from that shape must also be redistributed; although, in some cases, a lazy redistribution policy may be possible.

When a distributed array, called a *parray*, is declared, it must be identified with both a shape and a base type. For example, a 10×10 distributed array A of integers could be specified as follows:

> **shape** ashape(10, 10);
> **parray** A(ashape, INT);

If no distribution is specified in the shape declaration, the Paragon environment will select an appropriate data distribution. An intelligent compiler can infer a great deal about the appropriate distribution for array data [2]. The Paragon environment also recognizes several distribution directives which can be included in the shape declaration. These directives can be used if the programmer wishes to force Paragon to choose a particular distribution.

Explicit distribution of shapes can be used to specify data transfers between resources. For example, if the shape of one parray is specified to be located on a file device and the shape of a second parray specifies a distribution on a set of processors, then an assignment between these two parrays will have the effect of moving the data between the file device and the processors. This mechanism can be used for both file I/O and for explicitly moving data between different processing resources.

The shape construct provides the programmer with a convenient abstraction for data distribution and redistribution. This abstraction is important in parallel computation since arrays with similar distributions can be processed more efficiently than arrays with different distributions. In Paragon, the programmer is explicitly made aware of when arrays have dissimilar distributions without being required to know the architecture-specific details of the data layout.

2.2 Data Parallel Program Constructs

The SIMD foundations of the Paragon language include total array expressions, and primitive permutation, reduction and broadcast functions. These facilities are suitable for efficiently implementing most low-level shift-invariant image processing operations. The use of these features is illustrated with a convolution example.

The convolution of a 2-dimensional array X by a $k_1 \times k_2$ kernel K is given by

$$Y_{\alpha,\beta} = \sum_{m=0}^{k_1} \sum_{n=0}^{k_2} K_{m,n} X_{\alpha+m,\beta+n} \tag{1}$$

In a typical application, Y and X are the same size and have large dimensions while K has much smaller dimensions. A possible C program for implementing this convolution is shown in Figure 1. To simplify the examples in this section, the value of elements close to the edge of the image are ignored. This program involves four loops: the two outer loops consider each pixel in turn and the two inner loops process all elements of the convolution kernel. Most of the parallelism is available in the two outer loops.

```
#define ksize 5;
#define isize 512;

int kernel[ksize][ksize];
int image[isize][isize];
int result[isize][isize];
int i1, i2, k1, k2, tsize;

. . .
tisize = isize - ksize + 1;
for(i1 = 0; i1 < tisize; i1++)
  for(i2 = 0; i2 < tisize; i2++) {
    result[i1][i2] = 0;
    for(k1 = 0; k1 < ksize; k1++)
      for(k2 = 0; k2 < ksize; k2++)
        result[i1][i2] += image[i1 + k1][i2 + k2] * kernel[k1][k2];
  }
```

Figure 1: Convolution in C

One problem with the conventional serial program style is the overspecification of program loops. The sequence in which the computations are to be performed is explicitly stated by the *for* loops. For the convolution algorithm, order is not important and a suitable program construct could simply indicate to do the operation for all elements of the image matrix and for all elements of the kernel. Overspecification of this type is undesirable for both the programmer and the compiler. The underlying algorithm can be obscured with overspecified code, and overspecified program loops require more complex compilation techniques to extract the parallelism.

A Paragon program which can distribute the image arrays across parallel resources is shown in Figure 2. In this program, the two outer program loops are replaced by parallel expressions that process all elements of the image at the same time. The two inner loops from the original C program are still present in this algorithm. These loops iterate through each element of the kernel. At each iteration, the contribution from one kernel element is computed for all pixels in the result. The convolution algorithm requires that the input image be skewed relative to the result. The Paragon code which accomplishes this skewing uses the *shift* function. Shift is a built-in Paragon permutation function that shifts all elements of its first parray argument by the amounts specified in the remaining arguments.

An alternate parallel programming style is illustrated in Figure 3 where increased parallelism is specified at the expense of data replication. If the kernel is declared to be a parray then the convolution can be computed by extending both the kernel and the image to an

```
int kernel[ksize][ksize];
shape imshape (isize, isize);
parray image(imshape, INT);
parray result(imshape, INT);
int k1, k2;

. . .
result = 0;
for(k1 = 0; k1 < ksize; k1++)
   for(k2 = 0; k2 < ksize; k2++)
      result += shift(image, k1, k2) * kernel[k1][k2];
```

Figure 2: Convolution in Paragon

appropriate four-dimensional shape, multiplying the two together, and then sum-reducing the product to yield a two-dimensional result. Once again, the image must be skewed in order to accurately produce the interactions between neighboring pixels. The Paragon program in Figure 3 demonstrates the method for computing a convolution using this style of programming. The *rep* function replicates a parray along one or more new dimensions. The first argument indicates the parray to be replicated, and the remaining arguments indicate which new dimensions are to be created, and the sizes for the dimensions. In Figure 3, the image is replicated along dimensions 3 and 4 to produce a parray of size $isize \times isize \times ksize \times ksize$ and the kernel matrix is replicated along dimensions 1 and 2 to produce a parray of the same size. The *skew* function is used to skew the hyperplanes of a multidimensional shape. The first argument indicates along which dimension the parray data is to be skewed, and the second indicates which hyperplane is affected. After the two calls to skew in the example, the following condition holds for the parray *bigimage*:

$$\text{bigimage}_{i,j,k,l} = \text{image}_{i+k,j+l} : 0 \leq i, j < \text{isize}, \; 0 \leq k, l < \text{ksize} \qquad (2)$$

The convolution is performed by multiplying the two replicated parrays together (element by element) and then sum-reducing the parrays over the dimensions of the kernel (corresponding to the inner two program loops of the C program).

This second formulation illustrates a programming style that specifies the maximum degree of parallelism by explicitly enlarging the data structures. We call this approach *extended* parallelism since it involves the creation of intermediate data structures larger than the program inputs. The intermediate data structures are usually created by data replication. On a given parallel implementation, the cost of actually replicating the data may be very high; however, an *intelligent* compiler may be able to generate code that avoids any actual replication.

A compromise to these two extremes in programming style is to use a concise loop programming construct that does not imply any specific sequence of operations. In Paragon this construct is called *forall*. The arguments to forall are a specification of an index set to be executed and a set of index variables. If an array specifies the index set then the

```
shape  kshape(ksize, ksize);
parray kern(kshape, INT);
shape  imshape (isize, isize);
parray image(imshape, INT);
parray result(imshape, INT);
shape bigshape(isize, isize, ksize, ksize);
parray bigimage(bigshape, INT);
parray bigkern(bigshape, INT);
. . .
bigimage = rep(image, 3[ksize], 4[ksize]);
bigkern = rep(kern, 1[isize], 2[isize]);
bigimage = skew(bigimage, 1, 3);
bigimage = skew(bigimage, 2, 4);
result = sum(bigimage * bigkern, 3, 4);
```

Figure 3: Convolution in Paragon With Extended Parallelism

following program block is executed once for every possible array index tuple for that array. For example, the convolution program shown in Figure 2 can be expressed as follows by using the forall construct:

```
forall (kernel, k1, k2)
    result += shift(image, k1, k2) * kernel[k1][k2];
```

One potential problem with the forall construct is that if dependencies do exist within the enclosed statements then nondeterministic behavior may result. A dependency analysis could be performed at compile time to identify loop-carried dependencies. However, there are no known techniques for identifying data dependencies in arbitrary expressions. Furthermore, it is not clear that all dependencies should be considered illegal since some do not cause problems.

Which level of parallelism is the best to use for program expression is still an open question. In Paragon, all three programming styles are currently supported. Many believe that the serial programming style is the most appropriate for all occasions. Paragon does not parallelize any serial program code; however, limited parallelization of serial code could be achieved, if desired, with a program restructuring preprocessor.

2.3 Communication Structures

The built-in permutation functions are highly efficient for many SIMD algorithms. They are matched to the concept of locality of adjacent elements of a parray which is currently a cornerstone of the parray data distribution strategy. However, there are many instances where the capability of specifying arbitrary mappings between data structures is important.

Arbitrary data mappings in Paragon are specified by *communication structures.* The programmer has two views of a communication structure: for the specification of a mapping it has the appearance of a data structure, while for the execution of a map function it is used like a parallel array function (i.e. in a similar way to the built-in permutation functions).

There are two types of communication structures in Paragon: the *maparray* and the *maplist.* The maparray can specify any one-to-one or many-to-one mapping between the elements of two shapes and is manipulated by the user in a similar way to a parray. The maplist can also specify one-to-many mappings; however, it is more difficult to manipulate, in general, than a maparray.

If a destination parray element in a mapping operation does not have any source parray element mapped to it, then its value is set to zero. When more than one source element is mapped to a destination element then the final value of the destination element is the sum of all associated source elements.

An important application of the communication structures is to transfer data between parrays that have different shapes. For example, consider that we wish to move data between a vector shape *vec* and and a matrix shape *mat* that are specified as follows:

```
shape vec(8);
shape mat(2,4);
```

(Currently we do not support a Fortran *equivalence* statement that would link two shapes to a common relative distribution). Recall that the user does not know the detailed distribution of the array data (which could possibly be changed at run time for a given shape). A maparray, vec2mat that converts between these shapes is declared by

```
maparray vec2mat(vec, mat);
```

The specification of the maparray is achieved with the *mapof* function that combines a number of index arrays. Consider the following specification:

```
vec2mat = mapof(indx(vec,1) % 2, indx(vec, 1) / 2);
```

Indx is a built-in Paragon index generator. That is:

indx(vec, 1) =

0	1	2	3	4	5	6	7

The maparray may be viewed as a parray which has the same shape as its source shape with each entry being an index into the destination shape; i.e.

vec2mat =

0,0	1,0	0,1	1,1	0,2	1,2	0,3	1,3

The inverse mapping can conveniently be specified once the forward mapping is known by using the *mapinverse* function:

```
maparray mat2vec (mat, vec);
. . .
mat2vec = mapinverse(vec2mat);
```

This specifies

mat2vec =	0	2	4	6
	1	3	5	7

The mapping from a vector to a matrix is now achieved by using the maparray as a function:

```
shape x(vec, INT);
shape y(mat, INT);
. . .
y = vec2mat(x)
```

For example if

x =	a	b	c	d	e	f	g	h

The result of applying vec2mat would be:

y =	a	c	e	g
	b	d	f	h

An efficient program to compute a histogram using the *maparray* programming construct is shown in Figure 4. The image directly defines a many-to-one mapping to the histogram

```
shape imshape (isize, isize);
shape hshape (g);

maparray histm (imshape, hshape);

parray image (imshape, INT);
parray hist (hshape, INT);

. . .
histm = mapof( hshape, image);
hist = histm(1);
```

Figure 4: Efficient Histogram Generation in Paragon

vector. The scalar argument of 1 in the last statement implies a parray of shape *imshape*; i.e., each element makes 1 vote to the histogram vector, the location of the vote is specified by the maparray *histm*.

The final example, is a program to compute an image rotation, and is shown in Figure 5. To perform the rotation, the rotated element locations are backprojected to their closest elements in the initial matrix grid and the nearest data element is copied to the rotated

```
shape imshape (isize, isize);

maplist rmap(imshape, imshape);

parray image(imshape, INT);
parray result(imshape, INT);
parray im1(imshape, INT);
parray im2(imshape, INT);
float theta;

. . .
im1 = indx(imshape, 1) * cos(theta) +
              indx(imshape, 2) * sin(theta);
im2 = indx(imshape, 2) * cos(theta) -
              indx(imshape, 1) * sin(theta);

rmap = mapinverse( mapof (imshape, im1, im2));

result = rmap(image);
```

Figure 5: Image Rotation in Paragon

matrix location. For a rotation by an angle of θ the result matrix R is specified with respect to the input matrix A by:

$$R_{i,j} = A_{\lfloor i\cos(\theta)+j\sin(\theta)\rfloor,\lfloor j\cos(\theta)-i\sin(\theta)\rfloor} \quad (3)$$

Some rotated elements fall outside the input matrix space and are set to zero. In a SIMD environment with only shift-like permutation functions, this mapping is difficult to implement; complex SIMD algorithms have been implemented and analyzed [4].

In Figure 5, the locations of the backprojected elements are specified by the parrays *im1* and *im2* The "nearest" neighbor is specified by rounding down to the nearest integer location. The correct mapping for the forward projection is simply specified by the *mapinverse* function. However, it is possible for one input element to map to more than one rotated matrix location; therefore, the forward mapping is one-to-many and must be assigned to a maplist rather than a maparray.

3 Paragon Primitive Implementation

The implementation of Paragon primitives on a distributed memory multicomputer is considered in this section. The main consideration for programming distributed memory systems is that there is a primary memory hierarchy of at least two levels. Each processor has a local portion of the main memory; access to this memory by its associated processor is fast.

However, access to the memory of a different processor usually involves an interprocessor communication through an interconnection network. This is often achieved by a message passing mechanism by which system calls are made to send and receive "messages". In some systems the time to access data in a distant processor (in which the message may have to traverse several interprocessor links) may take much more time than accessing data from an adjacent processor. Due to the significant interprocessor network latency and the message passing overhead, messages are usually made as long as possible.

3.1 Data Partitioning

The efficiency of programs on a distributed memory system is frequently highly dependent upon the strategies used for the decomposition of distributed data into segments and the placement of these segments onto the distributed processors. A goal of the Paragon placement policy is to maintain the concept of "locality" such that the time to access adjacent elements in an array is minimized while the time to access more distant elements may require more time. In practice, this means that two adjacent array elements are either stored in the same processor or, in the worst case, two adjacent processors. The programmer may supply additional information for array distribution by program directives that are associated with a shape declaration.

A key feature of the Paragon environment is that the distribution of the data is usually the responsibility of the system rather than the programmer. The first multicomputer implementations of Paragon are built upon a foundation that permits the run-time redistribution of data amongst the parallel resources. This Paragon environment has been tested on a 32-node Intel iPSC/2 Hypercube multicomputer and on a 16-node Transtech transputer system. Strategies for array distribution may be specified by the programmer. For example, it is possible to indicate that an array should be distributed by rows or maintained on a single processor. The distribution of the array data is determined at run time. A distribution map can be supplied for each shape when a program is loaded to specify an initial data distribution.

3.2 Dynamic Load Balancing

Many problems exhibit irregular computation patterns that result in processors being idle while waiting for others to complete. One solution to this is to reassign data elements to processors to minimize the idle time. The most appropriate redistribution strategy for any given case is highly application dependent. A standard static redistribution technique is to "hash" the locations of the data elements by some simple algorithm. For example, the array "wrapping" technique assigns adjacent data elements to adjacent processors which, while effective for some algorithms, contradicts the data locality principle.

The approach taken in Paragon is to permit dynamic redistribution of data while maintaining locality. This is a more flexible strategy that can adapt to data-dependent computation patterns if there is some temporal constancy in computation load. The evaluation of this strategy is one of the Paragon research goals. Currently, nonlocal distribution strategies, such as wrapping, are not directly supported by the Paragon primitives, but they can be implemented by user-defined libraries that are based on the Paragon primitives.

3.3 Distributed Memory Mechanisms

The current multicomputer implementations of Paragon are organized as follows:

1. All serial code is replicated and executed on each processor.

2. Each processor is allocated a rectangular section of the first two dimensions of a *shape*.

3. Each processor has a complete map of the distribution of each shape.

4. An inspector/executor mechanism is planned for maplists and maparrays.

Since the SIMD model of computation is enforced, there is no loss in speed for replicating the serial computations on each processor. In fact, in many cases, it would be less efficient to execute the serial operations on one processor and then broadcast the results to all other processors. This may be modified in the future when concurrent programming constructs such as data partition locking are implemented.

3.4 Rectangular Block Partitioning

For distributed data, the goal has been to maintain locality while permitting dynamic data migration for load balancing. The rectangular block strategy affects the first two dimensions of a parray. Only these dimensions are distributed. Each processor is assigned a rectangular partition of the parray data. The rectangular shape simplifies the maintenance of spatial locality and, where appropriate, the use of vector processor libraries. The usual distribution policy is to assign equal sized data partitions to all processors. Rectangular block partitioning is suitable for dynamic redistribution of data since the blocks assigned to a processor do not have to be the same size; however, all blocks together must cover the whole array. The problem with this strategy is that it is more difficult to find the processor on which a given array data element resides.

3.5 Computation Mechanisms

The basic arithmetic operators are extended to the parray data type. Execution of these operators treats each parray element as an independent computation, and no interprocessor communication is required since the two parrays must be the same shape.

There are a number of primitives in Paragon for dense array operations which treat the whole array as an entity. Interprocessor communication will generally be required during the execution of these primitives. Processors first generate the messages to send to other processors (all messages involve rectangular segments of the parray) and then each processor determines which messages it must receive. The implementation for these primitives is asynchronous on message-passing systems; i.e., no barrier synchronization is needed to detect completion, and is well matched to the block distribution strategy. These primitives are as follows:

Permutation Functions Three permutation functions are defined in Paragon: *shift, rotate* and *transpose*. The shift permutation is well matched to the data distribution strategy. Shifts of small distances usually require only a small amount of data to be moved between adjacent processors due to the locality property. The rotate permutation is similar to shift except that elements shifted out of an array edge are fed back in at the opposite edge.

Reduction Functions The basic reduction operators (sum, product, maximum and minimum) may be applied to any subset of the dimensions of a parray. These are implemented as follows: first, any within-processor dimensions are reduced, then any distributed dimension are reduced. The shape of the result is the most convenient shape derived from the shape of the reduced parray. The resulting parray must then be redistributed to match the shape of the destination parray.

Data Broadcast The explicit broadcast function is called *rep*. It replicates a parray along a given dimension to match the shape of another parray. An implicit broadcast occurs whenever a single element of a parray is accessed. This single element is a scalar which must be replicated on every processor.

Subarray Selection The subarray selection mechanism allows a subsection of an array to be extracted such that one index of some dimensions and all elements of remaining dimensions are selected; this is used, for example, to select a row or column of a matrix.

Assignments Between Compatible Shapes Two shapes are *compatible* if they have the same number of dimensions and each dimension is the same size; however, the distribution of two compatible shapes may be different. The assignment operator is capable of redistributing the data of a parray to match the destination shape distribution.

3.6 Arbitrary Data Mapping

The communication structures *maparray* and *maplist* are currently being implemented on the the distributed-memory Paragon implementations. The maparray will be stored as a parray having the shape of the source shape in which each element will contain an index tuple into the destination shape. With this organization, a number of parray operations can easily be extended to maparrays. The maplist requires a list of destination index tuples to be associated with each source array element. Each processor contains the portion of the tuple list that is associated with the local array elements of its source shape.

A naive implementation of these mappings may be somewhat costly. For each mapping, it is necessary for each processor to scan its source array and determine for each index tuple the processor and location within that processor that it corresponds to. Then messages must be constructed for sending data to other processors. Finally, once all messages have been sent, a barrier synchronization must occur so that processors can know that all messages for a mapping have been received.

There are two efficiency improvements that we intend to implement. First, a hashing function will be associated with shapes so that the destination processors for index tuples can be more rapidly determined. For regular data distributions, the hashing function can be a linear operation on the first two indices.

Second, we intend to implement the inspector-executor mechanism discussed by Joel Saltz et al. [5]. When a mapping is performed for the first time (or at compile time for static mappings), an *inspector* determines how to build the messages for the specified mapping and records this information. An *executor* then performs the mapping as specified by the inspector. Also, on this first mapping, each processor records the number of messages it must receive. When this mapping is used a second time, the inspector information is still available and the executor may be used directly. Furthermore, a barrier synchronization is not necessary since each processor knows how many messages it must receive. Therefore, the mapping will be very efficient if it is used a large number of times; there is no saving if it is only used once. If the mapping is changed, or if the distribution of one of the shapes is changed then the inspector information will be out-of-date and the inspector will have to be run again when the map is used next.

The map functions are very powerful and may be used for a wide range of applications. They can be designed to do all the mappings defined in the previous section including reduction operations. In addition, they can be used to copy data between different shaped data structures and to perform classical scatter and gather operations. However, there are two significant costs for this generality. First, a significant amount of memory is needed to store each communication structure (an index tuple is required for each source parray element for the maparray). Second, there is an additional computation cost if all parameters of the mapping are not known at compile time due to the need to run the inspector.

The storage needed for the communication structures can be avoided if the mapping is specified by a symbolic expression. In some programming languages, symbolic mappings are expressed by program loops. However, efficient processing of such loops requires a restructuring compiler. We are seeking methods for symbolic expression of data mappings that do not require restructuring.

3.7 Selective Execution

The selective execution for the SIMD model of programming is realized in Paragon with the *where* programming construct. The where construct is a parallel *if* statement that is controlled by a boolean-valued parray expression. The evaluation semantics for this construct are conditional assignment; that is, computations are performed on all elements of controlled parrays, but only array elements selected by the controlling boolean parray are stored. Both the semantics and implementation of this mechanism are very simple. Only the visible assignment operators in the controlled section of the *where* statement are affected; whereas, expressions, including any function calls, are not affected.

If only a small number of the parray elements are to be processed then the where construct is inefficient. What is needed is a conditional evaluation mechanism that only performs computations on the selected elements. The way we intend to implement this capability is with a sparse array data structure. We envision that a sparse data structure will consist of a list of sparse elements; each sparse element consisting of a data value and its indices in the defining shape. Paragon primitives will be extended to operate on the *sparse* parray data types. The semantics for these primitives on sparse parrays will be the same as for dense parrays.

There are two problems with implementing these operations on sparse arrays. First, a sparse data array has storage requirements and computation requirements that are data dependent, which complicates the partitioning and distribution of the parray. Furthermore, these requirements may change in time. Second, when primitives operate on two sparse parrays it will be necessary for them to be stored with their indices sorted into some canonical order so that associated element pairs can be efficiently associated with each other (zero valued elements are generated when no match for an element is found). We note that simple permutation primitives, such as *shift* and *rotate* will cause a change in the structure of the sparse array and will require an indices sorting operation on each processor.

The communication structures are well matched to the manipulation of sparse data structures; the maplist is already a sparse data structure itself. Furthermore, it is very simple to mask a communication structure so that only a small subset of the array elements are mapped. Finally, the inspector/executor mechanism can be extended so that the reordering permutation of data in each processor is recorded on the first mapping. Then the executor can very efficiently implement mappings on a sequence of sparse data structures that have the same sparse distribution.

In summary, it seems that two types of mechanisms are needed for array data structures and processing primitives: dense and sparse. Dense data structures are most efficiently manipulated with the SIMD Paragon primitives and are appropriate when most of the elements of an array are to be processed. The where program construct is used for selective evaluation. Sparse data structures are more appropriate when only a small fraction of the array data elements are to be processed. Communication structures are more appropriate for sparse data structures, in general, than the built-in (SIMD) primitives. The choice of which data structure is necessary may be highly problem dependent; in fact, some applications may require both data types. For example, consider a PDE problem with a close to rectangular boundary. The boundary is only a small fraction of the array elements and may be best represented by a sparse data structure while the interior elements may involve most of the array elements and be better represented by a dense structure.

Program primitives will be made available for the users to specify both dense and sparse data structures and to convert data between the two. However, since the semantics of operations on both data types is identical, it is quite possible that a parray data structure could be declared to be *generic*, then the system could determine, at runtime, the most appropriate representation based on the sparsity of the array and other system parameters.

3.8 What Is Missing From Paragon?

Paragon is being incrementally developed to provide a programming environment for a wide range of scientific applications. The current implementation supports the SIMD model of computation and the concepts of communication structures and sparse data structures are being explored.

The next capabilities for the environment that will be considered for implementation are concurrent program sequences and the processing of data streams as outlined in Section 1.1 It is expected that the concurrent program sequences will take advantage of the sparse data mechanisms.

A major issue with the writers of restructuring compilers is how to deal with data dependencies within serial loop program constructs. Paragon primitives do not currently support parallelization of such loops. Two mechanisms that will be considered for future implementation are a "wavefront" processing mechanism and a primitive for parallel prefix computations. The ability of these constructs to represent serial Fortran loops with loop-carried dependencies will be explored. Finally, the incorporation of dynamic load balancing strategies that we have developed for irregular problems will be considered [6].

4 Conclusion

A programming paradigm for multicomputers that is based on high-level primitives and addresses the issues of task management has been presented. This paradigm has been implemented on several distributed memory multicomputers by means of a set of programming primitives. Mechanisms for implementing these primitives in a distributed memory environment have been considered. Initial examples from image processing applications have been used to demonstrate the language features.

The current multicomputer implementation is built on the foundation that array data may be migrated between processors at run time. We feel that this will be crucial to the effective implementation of dynamic load balancing. However, the implementation of array data migration has raised a new set of implementation issues.

The programming environment is being developed in an incremental manner. The expectation is that convenient high-level programming primitives can be developed that have efficient implementation mechanisms. The current features include SIMD language constructs plus a mechanism for arbitrary data mappings. For the future, primitives for sparse data structures, concurrent data partitions, data streams and wavefront processing will be considered.

References

[1] A. L. Cheung and A. P. Reeves. The paragon multicomputer environment: A first implementation. Technical Report EE-CEG-89-9, Cornell University, July 1989.

[2] Jingke Li and Marina C. Chen. Index domain alignment: Minimizing cost of cross-referencing between distributed arrays. Technical Report YALEU/DCS/TR-725, Yale University, Department of Computer Science, November 1989.

[3] A. P. Reeves. Paragon: a parallel programming paradigm for multicomputer systems. Technical Report EE-CEG-89-3, Cornell University, January 1989.

[4] A. P. Reeves and C. H. Moura. Data mapping and rotation functions for the massively parallel processor. *Proceedings of Computer Architecture for Pattern Analysis and Image Database Management*, pages 412–419, November 1985.

[5] J. Saltz, K. Crowley, R. Mirchandaney, and H. Berryman. Run-time scheduling and execution of loops on message passing machines. *Journal of Parallel and Distributed Computing*, 8:303–312, 1990.

[6] M. Willebeek-LeMair and A. P. Reeves. Dynamic load balancing strategies for highly parallel multicomputer systems. Technical Report EE-CEG-89-14, Cornell University, December 1989.